Acknowledgements

To my parents, Homer and Betty Berger: Thank you for teaching me about Jesus from the very beginning of my life.
To my beautiful wife, Carrie: Thank you for loving Him above all things, and for loving us so very well.
To my children, Kayleigh and Will: Thank you for your constant support, and for filling my days with laughter. Kayleigh, thank you for designing the magnificent cover for this book.
To the people of First Baptist, Conroe: Thank you for walking along with me as we follow Him. I love this journey we're on!
Him we proclaim, warning everyone and teaching everyone with all wisdom, that we may present everyone mature in Christ. For this I toil, struggling with all his energy that he powerfully works within me. –Colossians 1:28-29. O Lord, please use this work to bring us all one step closer to that goal of being mature in Christ.

Also by this author: *Hark the Herald Angels Sing: A Christmas Devotional*

Zack,
God bless you as you seek Him!
[signature]

Lieutenant Dan Taylor: "Have you found Jesus yet, Gump?"
Forrest Gump: "I didn't know I was supposed to be looking for Him, sir."

Why should you read this book? I believe that Jesus of Nazareth is different from other great men and women of history. Studying the lives of figures like Winston Churchill, Martin Luther King, or Mother Theresa can be inspiring. But when people strive to know Jesus, it changes their lives for the better. The very act of seeking Him improves the seeker; I can't think of anyone else, alive or dead, like that. If you are already a follower of Jesus, I hope this book can help you know Him more fully. What I think the Church needs today more than anything else is to dig beneath all the petty social issues and political struggles we find ourselves consumed with and simply get to know Jesus as He truly is: Who was He? Why did He come? Why did He do the things He did? What does it mean to follow Him today? I am hoping this book will enable you to see aspects of His character you've never considered before. If you choose, this book can be read as a year-long daily devotional guide. Within the twelve chapters are three hundred sixty-five readings, each containing a Scripture reference and a paragraph or two of commentary. The readings are undated, so you can start any time of year. You can also read this a chapter at a time, like any other book; it's completely up to you. As you read, pray for God to help you know Jesus better than you ever have before. Keep a journal of any new insights you gain. And consider passing the book along to a friend who needs to know Jesus, too…or even reading it along with them.

I wrote this book with non-Christians in mind, as well. In the movie *Forrest Gump*, Lieutenant Dan, having lost both legs in combat, has no use for a God who seems either unaware of his problems, or impotent to help. He especially resents the pat answers and manipulative language of religion, with its promises that He can "walk with Jesus in the Kingdom of Heaven." (Of course, Lieutenant Dan later makes peace with God…and he does walk again.) Perhaps you've experienced the same frustration with religion. Maybe your experience with Christians can be summed up by words like "Hateful," "Self-righteous," "Overly political," "Homophobic," "Anti-Science." The goal of this book isn't to make you any of those things. In fact, if you get to know Jesus, you'll find that He wasn't any of those things, either. Could it be that the impressions you have of Jesus are based on false assumptions? Wouldn't you like to know what He was really like?

Or perhaps looking for Jesus has never really occurred to you. You're not particularly religious, and you can't think of any good reason to change that. Somehow this book has landed in your hands (Maybe one of your pushy religious friends gave it to you). Do me a favor: Read the first chapter, and see why I believe Jesus is the most important and influential person in human history, whether you believe the Church's claims about Him or not. Then consider the fact that this man-- a man so influential history is literally divided into everything that happened before Him, and everything that has happened since--this man didn't claim to know truth, He said He WAS Truth. He didn't come to teach us new facts about God; He said He WAS God. Either this was the most successful con artist ever…or the key to life as we know it. Shouldn't you make an informed decision about such a person, just in case? Wouldn't that be the most responsible thing to do?

One thing to note: I believe we can't truly know Jesus without studying the Bible; In other words, I assume that the Jesus of Scripture is the Jesus of history. There have been many books written about Jesus over the years, all claiming to reveal the "true" story. But I believe the true story of Jesus was completed 2000 years ago. This book is simply my attempt to guide you through that story. Please don't skip the Scriptures I reference; take time to read them carefully.

So come along on a journey with me. No matter who you are, I pray you'll find Him. I'm confident you will. After all, He said it Himself: *Everyone who seeks, finds* (Matthew 7:8).

Chapter 1: Who Was He?
The Impact of Jesus on Today's World

John 8:12

Who is the most powerful, influential person on the planet today? We could name our President; as leader of the lone global superpower, the Executive does indeed wield tremendous power. But that power is subject to Congressional overrides and term limits. We could name Steve Jobs, who before his untimely death pioneered so much of the technology that has changed the way we live. But there will be new and greater innovations in the years to come, and we'll look back on the name of Steve Jobs someday like we today look at the name of Marconi, the inventor of the radio.

Now consider this: There was a man who lived over 2000 years ago whose life directly impacts this planet in too many ways to list. Even people who are not believers in His divinity are astonished at the range of His influence. For just one example, here's a quote from HG Wells: "A historian like myself, who doesn't even call himself a Christian, finds the picture centering irresistibly around the life and character of this most significant man…the historian's test of an individual's greatness is 'What did he leave to grow?' Did he start men to thinking along fresh lines with a vigor that persisted after him? By this test Jesus stands first." Based on the Scripture we just read, Jesus Himself wouldn't have shied away from such an evaluation.

Yes, I believe Jesus is not only the most influential person in the history of the world; I believe He still influences more lives today than anyone else on the planet. In this first section, we'll look at His continuing influence. When Jesus walked the Earth two millennia ago, people often asked, "Who is this man?" I believe there is no more important question. As we begin this journey together, I pray that you'll come to know Him…for the first time, or better than you've ever known Him before. (By the way, if you'd like to learn more about Jesus' impact on our world, I highly recommend *Who Is This Man?* by John Ortberg)

The Birth of Compassion

Mark 6:30-34

One of the most remarkable things about Jesus was how He responded to people in need. Jesus often said and did things that offended people; He was not a bland "nice guy" by any means. But He never turned His back on people who were needy. On this day, for instance, Jesus and His disciples were trying to get away for some rest. They were exhausted after weeks on the road. A crowd of needy people followed them to their intended place of solitude. Instead of being annoyed (as I surely would be), Jesus saw the crowd and had compassion on them, for they were like sheep without a shepherd. Then He went to work, meeting their needs. That's how He lived. He would later tell His disciples that when we feed the hungry, clothe the naked, visit the sick or the imprisoned, He accepts that as a gift straight to Him. That's how much He identifies with the needy. In fact, He said, "Whatever you do for the least of my children, you've done it for me (see Matthew 25:31-46)."

That idea that the "least of these" are the most important people in God's eyes was utterly revolutionary. It changed the world, literally. When Jesus spoke those words, the known world was under the power of Rome, and Jesus Himself had a mere handful of poorly-resourced followers. Yet within 300 years, Christianity had conquered Rome. Sociologist Rodney Stark, who was not a Christian, wanted to know why this happened. After all, Christianity didn't spread the way other religions expanded--by military conquest or by being the belief system of a particular cultural or language group. He determined that Christianity spread because of compassion. He found stories in the ancient world of plagues which devastated cities. People would abandon their sick loved ones and flee the cities to avoid getting ill. But the Christians would stay, nursing the sick and the dying. Some of them died themselves, but they were looking forward to heaven, so it was a chance they were willing to take. The Roman Emperor Julian the Apostate—an enemy of Christianity—complained that the "impious Galileans" took care of their own poor and the poor pagans as well, making the pagan priests look bad. Christianity overcame the Roman empire not through violence or political intrigue, but through helping people who couldn't help themselves.

Jesus and the Leper

Matthew 8:1-4

Here's an example of Jesus' compassion. If you know anything about the life of Jesus, you may be wondering what's so remarkable about this particular tale. After all, He must have healed hundreds—if not thousands—of people. But there is something different about this healing. Notice that it says, *Jesus reached out His hand and touched the man.* We know that Jesus didn't have to touch Him in order to heal him. In fact, Jesus more than once healed someone when they weren't even in His physical presence (Luke 7:1-10 is one example). So why did Jesus touch this man? Luke tells us he had leprosy, which was a catch-all term in the ancient world for infectious skin diseases. These were the most feared diseases of all in the ancient world. Jewish law stipulated that a victim of leprosy was required to live outside the city limits, to wear ragged clothing, and whenever they saw another human being, they were to yell out, "Unclean!" It sounds cruel, but the point of these laws was to prevent the spread of disease. For the victims, it meant they lived lives of utter solitude.

So imagine what it would be like if tomorrow you discover a rash on your arm. You go to a doctor, and he confirms your worst fears: You've contracted leprosy. He immediately calls the police, who escort you out of town and drop you off. That's it. You don't see your friends or family again, unless they choose to travel to the outlying areas where lepers like you live...if you call such an existence life. Even then, they surely stand at a distance. Perhaps occasionally you sneak into town to watch your kids play, or just to be around other people. But when you do, you hide in the shadows, terrified of being caught, for that would mean immediate execution by stoning. Weeks, months, years go by without ever feeling the touch of another human being. You never thought of yourself as an affectionate person, but now you'd give anything for a simple handshake. I think Jesus touched this man because He understood all that. He knew this man didn't just need to be healed; He needed to feel human again. Today, we admire people who empathize with those who are suffering. Jesus is the one who taught us that value.

Compassion Spreads

Acts 4:32-36

Our Scripture refers to the way Jesus' followers lived in the years immediately after He was gone. They had a compassion for one another so radical, they virtually wiped out poverty in their community. Over the years, that generosity faded a bit, but it never really went away. Enough of the compassion of Christ remained in His people to make the world a very different place. In 325, at the Council of Nicea, Christian leaders ruled that from then on, whenever a cathedral was built, there had to also be a building for the care of the sick. These were the first hospitals, the very first voluntary charitable institutions. To this day, many hospitals carry a religious name. Later, a Swiss Christian named Jean Henri Dunant formed an organization to help wounded soldiers, and a Methodist preacher named William Booth started an organization to help the desperately poor of London, and that is how the Red Cross and the Salvation Army got their start. A morally wasted slave ship captain named John Newton met Jesus Christ, and became a pastor, hymnwriter, and passionate anti-slavery activist; He also wrote "Amazing Grace." Newton influenced a devout young member of Parliament named William Wilberforce, who then devoted his life to ending slavery in England. Emancipation was complete just a few days before Wilberforce's death. Across the pond in our own country, the people who fought against slavery for decades—Harriet Tubman, William Lloyd Garrison, Frederick Douglass, Harriet Beecher Stowe—were almost exclusively committed Christians. There are too many such stories to tell. That doesn't mean that Christians are the only people who have ever been compassionate. It doesn't even mean all Christians are compassionate. But Jesus simply changed the way we think about human need. He taught us to take responsibility for other people. Philosopher Mark Nelson put it this way: "Wherever you have an institution of self-giving for the lonely, schools, hospitals, hospices, orphanages for those who will never be able to repay, this probably has its roots in the movement of Jesus."

It still goes on today. In 2014, I was watching the news after the tornadoes that devastated Oklahoma. I heard an NBC news reporter say the following words to the anchor, Brian Williams, "We expect FEMA to be here to help out in a week or two, but the Baptist Men will be here tomorrow." A report some years ago found that if the average church billed its community for the social services it provides, the total bill would be $184,000. (Ram A. Cnaan, *The Invisible Caring Hand: American Congregations and the Provision of Welfare*. Two things to note: That was in 2002. I can only assume the number would be larger if the study were done today. Also, the average church size is 75 people, so many of the churches you pass on your way to work make an even larger contribution to society than that.) Quietly, through His people, Jesus continues to change the world for good.

Why do God's People Help Others?

Ephesians 2:8-9

Irreligious people sometimes get defensive about stories of Christian compassion. They realize there aren't any atheist hospitals or secular humanist orphanages. They will say things like, "Of course you Christians do good deeds. You think you have to buy your way into heaven." But that betrays a fundamental misunderstanding of the teachings of Christ. The Gospel doesn't say that we earn salvation by helping the needy. In fact, there is nothing we can do to earn salvation. It is a free gift, based on what He has done for us, not the other way around. But when we finally experience that love and grace, it's like nothing we've ever known. It changes our lives, and we want to do something to thank Him. Just going to church and singing songs doesn't seem like enough, so we follow His commands. We reach out to the least of His children as a way of loving Him.

People will only fully understand the Gospel when they experience the touch of Christ. And if you are a Christian, your job is to be His hands and feet. That's an incredible responsibility. It means much more than saying a quick prayer for hurting people you hear about in the news, or making an occasional contribution to charity. I read a report recently from the US Coast Guard. It said that, contrary to what you see in movies, people who are drowning don't signal for help. They don't wave their arms or cry out; they are too busy just trying to stay above the surface of the water, and usually, they sink within a minute or less. That means that we can't expect needy people to come to us, or even to cry out for help. We must be on the lookout for those who are drowning. We must pray and ask God to show us the people in our lives who are struggling just to survive, who need the touch of Christ to rescue them and set them free. Who will you touch this week? Will you pray that God will give you eyes to see them?

With All Your Mind

Matthew 13:53-58

I often read articles that say young adults are fleeing the Church in droves. Many of them say they feel like Christianity is intellectually confining and narrow-minded. They learn new things in their studies or in conversations with people who aren't Christians, things which they haven't heard in church. When they ask questions to try to reconcile this new information with Scripture, too often they are made to feel ashamed, as if asking questions is a bad thing (One young man asked a question in Sunday School which his teacher couldn't answer. The teacher told him his question was from Satan. The teacher wasn't joking.). They hear from their non-Christian friends and professors that faith and reason are two irreconcilable ways to view life; they increasingly begin to feel that remaining on the path of faith will mean turning off their brains, and they simply cannot do that.

To these young people--and others who find faith intellectually stifling--I would like to say the following: First, Jesus understands how you feel. As our story shows, when He tried to teach in His hometown congregation, the people rejected Him. Not because they could prove Him wrong; they were offended that He had challenged their assumptions. Second, Jesus never made anyone choose between their brain and their faith. Never. Anyone who does so isn't representing Jesus, no matter what title their church has given them. It is possible to follow Jesus faithfully while never stifling the intellectual curiosity you feel…in fact, I would say that chasing after knowledge, wherever it happens to lead, is a non-negotiable part of truly following Him.

Jesus the Teacher

Matthew 22:34-40

Jesus was raised as a Jew, which meant He grew up in an environment that treasured learning. He was a blue-collar worker from a poor family, but we can be sure He was rigorously educated in the Torah. Out of all the verses Jesus learned, none was more important than Deuteronomy 6:4, known by Jews as the "Shema." *Hear, O Israel, the Lord your God is one Lord.* This verse surely would have been on the doorpost of Jesus' childhood house in Nazareth. He very likely wore it on a leather strap around His wrist as well. Every Jew would have known by heart the words that come immediately after the Shema: *Love the Lord your God with all your heart, with all your soul, and with all your strength.* When Jesus grew up and began His teaching ministry, He said that this was the greatest of all commandments. But He added something to it: *Love the Lord with all your mind.* Jesus valued the mind. It's why He became the greatest teacher the world has ever seen. Imagine a teacher so compelling, people would walk for miles to stand all day and hear Him speak, sometimes without food. More than once, the Gospels say the crowds were "delighted" to listen to Him. One time, Jesus' enemies sent soldiers to arrest Him. They showed up in the middle of a sermon. They came back empty handed, saying, "We've never heard anyone speak like that." One of the signs of Jesus' genius is that His teaching was so deep, the most eminent scholars learned things from Him that they'd never known, while it was simultaneously so simple and memorable, small children could understand and repeat it.

Why was Jesus' teaching so powerful? I think there were a number of reasons. He used parables, as we'll see later in this study. These "stories with a message" were much more memorable than dry homilies. Also, people noticed that Jesus taught with authority. He didn't guess or speculate; He seemed to know what He was talking about. But mostly, I think Jesus' teaching was powerful because it changed people. It revealed things about themselves they'd never known, or were trying to conceal. It revealed truths about God no one had ever heard. Jesus once said, *then you will know the truth, and the truth will set you free.* Pray and ask God to tell you the truth you need to know most right now.

Jesus' Followers Valued the Mind

Acts 6:1-7

One of Jesus' last commands to His disciples was *Go therefore into all the world, making disciples of all nations, baptizing them in the name of the Father, the Son and the Holy Spirit, **teaching them**.* The disciples took Him at His word. Acts 5:42 says *Day after day in the temple courts and from house to house, **they never stopped teaching**.* Today's Scripture tells of a controversy in that early church, and the priorities that led to its solution. A big logistical/administrative issue had come up, one serious enough to split the early multi-ethnic church along racial lines. You might expect the apostles, as leaders of the church, to securely grab the reigns and steer the group toward a solution. Instead, the apostles essentially said, "We don't have time for this. We're supposed to be teaching. You need to elect a separate group of leaders to deal with these kinds of issues so we can fulfill our calling." They did; the seven men chosen to tackle the problem are today acknowledged as the church's first deacons. Again, those who knew Jesus the best said, "Our job is to teach. We can't do anything to compromise that high calling." Apparently, it was the right decision. Many more people became believers, including many Jewish priests. These were men of learning; they would never have come to believe Jesus was the Messiah if the church had not valued the ministry of teaching.

All People Have the Right to Learn

Acts 18:24-28

One of the hallmarks of early Christians was that they taught both men and women. This was highly unusual at that time. Jewish rabbis as well as Greek sages had only male disciples. But the apostles remembered that Jesus had many female followers. They probably also remembered the day when Jesus was at the house of Mary and Martha, and while Martha was doing the typical woman's work, serving the guests, Mary was sitting at Jesus' feet, learning. When Martha criticized her sister, Jesus said that Mary was the one using her time wisely. Essentially, He was saying, "Education isn't just for men in my Kingdom, but for all who want to learn." The early church continued this practice, although some of the New Testament letters reveal that there was some controversy in the male-dominated culture of the ancient Middle East. When a bright young preacher named Apollos first believed in Jesus, a Christian couple, Priscilla and Aquila, took him aside to teach him the core truths of the faith. Interestingly, whenever this couple is mentioned in Acts, the wife, Priscilla, is mentioned first, indicating that she took the leading role. This was highly unusual in that world, but one more sign that the teaching of the Gospel was changing things.

These days, we sometimes hear people say that Christianity is an enemy to women's rights. It is true that men within the Church have at times used their leadership positions to promote or uphold sexually repressive ideas. But that certainly wasn't the case with Jesus. And in spite of the flawed men in the Church's history, the impact of Christianity on women has been overwhelmingly positive. For instance, think of the nations today where women have the best standard of living, the most social, economic and educational equality. All of them are nations whose culture was birthed from a Christian tradition. On the other hand, the nations where women are most likely to be abused, oppressed, and mistreated are nations where the Gospel has little social influence. Jesus is the best friend women ever had...even for women who don't believe in Him.

How Jesus Inspired the Modern Educational System

1 Peter 2:5-9

The first generation of Christ-followers passed away. Decades rolled on. Barbarians sacked Rome, and the Dark Ages began. One of my high school classmates once asked our world history teacher if there was something wrong with the sun during the Dark Ages. She was serious. As you probably know, the term "Dark Ages" refers to the fact that what once had been considered civilization (The Roman Empire) was now mostly illiterate. Yet monks carefully preserved the ancient writings of the classical authors. The only reason we still have access to the works of Herodotus and Homer, Virgil and Cicero, is that monks diligently hand-copied their books and bravely guarded them from barbarian looters. Keep in mind, these were the works of pagan authors. Why would men of God risk their lives to protect such literature? Because as St. Augustine said, "All truth is God's truth." That means that there is something holy about all learning: history, philosophy, science, engineering, auto mechanics…even (it's hard for me to admit this) math.

Monasteries eventually gave birth to the first universities, including Oxford and Cambridge. When our forefathers came to this country, one of the first things they did was establish universities as well, including Harvard, Yale, Princeton, Brown, and William and Mary. Of the first 138 colleges and universities in this country, 92% were begun specifically to help people know and serve Christ better. Christian missionaries took learning with them. Many nations and people groups today owe their alphabet to Christian missionaries, who pioneered written languages. Cyrillic, for instance, was named for St. Cyril, who took the Gospel to the Slavic people and taught them to read it in their own language. Meanwhile, Christian reformers were on a mission of literacy at home. They wanted every person to be able to read the Bible for themselves so that they could know and serve God personally, not through a mediator. Where did they get this idea? They remembered the words of Jesus' close friend Peter, that every believer in Christ is a priest. The priests in Israel stood between the people and God. They offered sacrifices on behalf of the people, and taught the people God's truth. But Peter said all believers, young and old, male and female, of every ethnicity, are priests before God. We can each study His Word, hear His voice, communicate with Him in prayer. In a very real sense, it was the drive to help people fulfill their role in God's plan that first led to public schools as we know them today.

How Jesus Created Science

Psalm 19:1-6

Many people today believe that science and faith are naturally opposed to one another. I suspect that we Christians have at least as much to do with this idea as anyone outside the faith. From the Scopes Monkey Trial of the 1920s to ignorant public statements by believers on social media today, we've often positioned ourselves--unintentionally, perhaps--as having closed minds. Therefore, it would surprise most believers and unbelievers alike to learn that modern science was virtually birthed by Christianity. As our text today says, God created a beautiful universe. Therefore Christians of the Middle Ages and Renaissance, unlike Platonists, believed that matter was essentially good and should be studied. Many of the early pioneers of science, men like Kepler, Galileo, Copernicus, Pascal, Priestley, Pasteur, and Newton were devout Christians who studied science because learning about God's creation brought them closer to Him (The fact that the Church sometimes opposed these men does not diminish their very real faith). The notion of an inherent conflict between science and faith is a fairly recent idea, and one not corroborated by facts. A recent study by Rice University (*Religious Understandings of Science*) said that 36% of professional scientists believe in God. 18% attend church weekly, and 19% pray regularly. Those numbers aren't huge, but they show that one can be a person of science AND a person of faith.

A word here to high school and college students: There are all kinds of people in churches, educated and uneducated. Grace means you don't have to ace the SAT or even be intellectually curious to be accepted into God's family. Hallelujah! But don't let anyone tell you that your faith will be a hindrance to exploring the academic field you feel drawn toward. A Christian who feels drawn to biology, cosmology, physics, astronomy or any other field of science should be the best he or she can be, and should not fear that studying these subjects will hurt his/her faith. On the contrary, chase knowledge wherever it will lead you. If God created all things, and all truth is His truth, then learning will draw you closer to Him, not further away. As just one example, Dr. Francis Collins, eminent geneticist and head of the National Institutes of Health, wrote *The Language of God* as a memoir of how science led him to faith. Everything God made, from the vastness of outer space to the intricacy of a microscopic organism, speaks of His power, His artistry, His attention to detail. Learn as much as you can...and praise the one who made it all.

Fighting Ignorance

Romans 12:1-2

Modern Christians are followers of the greatest teacher who ever lived. We walk in a legacy of men and women who championed learning. We must continue to stamp out ignorance wherever it can be found. That begins, of course, in us. Jesus called us to love the Lord with all our *minds*. What are you doing to expand your mind? The pressures of our jobs often lead us to spend our free time consuming escapist entertainment of the most mind-numbing sort: reality television, first-person-shooter video games. At best, these are like corn syrup for the brain; a little bit is okay, but a heavy dose is deadly to our mental, emotional and intellectual health. Find a subject that interests you, and research it. Visit museums and national parks. Take continuing education courses. Spend time around smart people.

But loving God with our minds is more than mere intellectual stimulation. Romans 12:2 says, *Do not be conformed to this world, but be transformed by the renewing of your mind.* I like the way the New Living Translation puts that verse: "Let God transform you into a new person by changing the way you think." When was the last time you learned something new about God, or about how He wants to change you? That should be an ongoing experience for each of us. As a pastor, here are three things I wish every member of my church would do: 1) Read the Word daily. 2) Research difficult questions whenever you come across them and follow the truth wherever it leads. 3) Be involved regularly in a small group of people who together interpret the Word and apply it to life. For hundreds of years the Bible was off-limits to common people, chained to church pulpits, kept in a language only the most highly educated could read. Today, we live in the Golden Age of information. You can study the Word in print, audio, online, or on your smart phone. There are churches on every corner and Bible studies in homes, churches and online. If you can't think of the last time God changed your mind, pray now and invite Him to do so today. Then get ready.

Fighting Ignorance, Part II

1 Peter 3:13-17

Anyone who wants to follow the example of Jesus and His early followers will care about more than just their own intellectual life; they will want others to know the Truth as well. This begins with our support for educating our communities. Too many Christians, in my opinion, care only about securing a good education for our own children. But what about the kids our children share a world with? Several years ago, the church I pastored began sponsoring a local elementary school. It was a very rewarding partnership for both the church and the school. Find out how you can volunteer at a local school. Mentor a student. Encourage teachers you know. They are doing God's work. But we must go further, still…

1 Peter 3:15 says, *Always be prepared to give an answer to those who ask you the reason for the hope that you have.* That word "answer" literally means "defense." It's our job to defend our faith. Can I be absolutely blunt? It's bad enough that many people today have a skewed idea of what the Bible teaches. To make matters worse, there are far too many ignorant people who are speaking in the name of Christ. Because our 24-hour-news cycle needs ratings to survive, networks would rather feature an empty-headed, loud-mouthed preacher on a talk show than a thoughtful, eloquent spokesman of the faith; and because the internet gives a virtual megaphone to every hateful, racist, alarmist fool who ever opened a Bible, it is very hard to convince non-Christians these days that we're not all like that. It's going to take one hundred authentic Christians to counteract every one of them. All we can do is change people's hearts, one at a time. When someone is talking about religion or spirituality, jump into the conversation. I am not telling you get involved in arguments or debates. Those are rarely fruitful. Show them that thoughtful people believe in Jesus, and that they are loved. Yes, Jesus said harsh things, but those were always directed at the religious folks—because they should have known better—while the irreligious people loved Him. When you're in one of these conversations, remember: We can insult them or we can persuade them, but we can't do both. No one was ever converted because someone made them feel like an idiot. I'll tell you a way to know if you're making progress: If someone says to you, "I wish more Christians were like you," you're on the right track. Keep praying for them and talking with them. Ask God to give you some opportunities to change minds this very week.

Downward Mobility

1 Peter 5:5-7

Every year, I watch the Academy Awards on TV (yes, I'm that guy). Every year, I try and (usually) fail to predict who will win. But one prediction comes true every time: Most of the people who do win will take most of their speech time to thank their fellow cast members, directors, writers, producers, makeup artists, and if they are wise, their spouses. They will say something like, "This award really belongs to you. I'm nothing without you." They will mention their fellow nominees and say, "I am honored just to be mentioned in the company of such amazing artists." In fact, if someone flips the script and acts in a way that smacks of arrogance and self-promotion, it will be headline news the next day. Imagine someone says, "It's about time you pathetic fools recognize my greatness. I shall now pause to allow you to bask in my radiance. You're welcome." We'll be talking about it for weeks to come, in very negative terms. But the question is why? Why do we insist that people who win—in entertainment, athletics, or any other field—behave in a humble and gracious manner? That certainly hasn't always been the case (we'll discuss that more in the next reading).

One way Jesus changed our world was by turning humility from an insult into a virtue. He changed the way we view greatness. In our passage today, we see instructions from Peter, a leader in the early church, to young men. He tells them to willingly put themselves under the authority of older men. If you are a younger person--or can remember when you were--you know how hard that instruction is to follow. When we're young, we tend to think we know better than those who are older than us. Peter says, "Actually all of you should behave humbly toward one another." Then he quotes from Proverbs 3:34, which says God is on the side of those who are humble, and stands opposed to those who are proud. Peter learned this idea from Jesus. As we will soon see, it wasn't an idea he and the other disciples took to easily. In fact, Jesus had to repeat it many times. We're not so different, are we?

The Race for Honors

Philippians 2:1-11

In the society where Jesus lived, people occupied certain classes. The point of life was to try to rise out of your class and advance to the next. One didn't rise by putting others first; you had to be a ruthless self-promoter. Humility was not seen as a virtue. Humility was something that was forced upon you because you were a loser at life. At the bottom of society in the ancient world were slaves. Some slaves lived well, while others lived miserably, but no one aspired to be a slave. Ironically, there were more people in the slave class than any other. At the next level were freedmen; they had very low status, but at least they had won their freedom. Next up the list were citizens of the Empire. They had rights that most people didn't. Sometimes, in order to show their status, citizens would wear a toga. It was not a comfortable garment. It was too drafty in the winter and too bulky in summer; one hand was virtually useless, but at least it showed people how important you were. Can you imagine anyone wearing clothes just to impress others? Next up the ladder were the top 2 percent. Some of these people were called equestrians. They were the nobility. Their name originally came from the fact that they were wealthy enough to own a horse. Can you imagine social status being based on a mode of transportation? Above the equestrians were the senators, about six hundred or so. And on top of the pyramid was Caesar himself, who was thought to be a god. It wasn't enough just to be king, however. Kings in the ancient world, Roman and otherwise, wrote books about themselves with titles like, *The Achievements of the Divine Augustus*, in which they listed all their incredible accomplishments. They took titles like Herod the Great. Wouldn't it be fun if politicians did that today? Imagine if tomorrow you had campaign literature in your mailbox from "Hillary Clinton the Magnificent" and "Ted Cruz the Awesome." It would be worth it just for the fun late-night comedians would have with it. But back then, such displays of ostentation were deadly serious. It was all about advancing. They even had a name for this pursuit: The *cursus honorum*, or "the race for honors." Everyone was in that race.

Everyone except one, that is. Our text today is a classic Scripture. Paul is trying to persuade his friends in a church in Philippi to treat one another well by intentionally putting other people's needs first. Where did he get such an idea? From Jesus, as he goes on to say. Verses 5-11 are written in verse form; most Bible scholars believe they were originally an early Christian hymn. Imagine that; the followers of Jesus made up songs about Him that bragged about His decision to intentionally come in last. They boasted about how their hero put others first. If you actually meditate on this Scripture and put it into practice, it can change your life completely.

Dropping Out of the Race

Mark 10:35-45

In our text, we see two of Jesus' disciples asking to be given the seats of honor in His coming Kingdom. These men believed that Jesus was the Messiah God had promised the Jews for centuries. To them, that meant He would be a political-military hero who would destroy Israel's enemies and make Israel a dominant world power. They had read stories of the days of Solomon, the last time Israel was strong and prosperous, and how King Solomon had lived in luxury and glory. They were hoping to be second and third in command. When it says the other ten disciples were angry with James and John for asking this, we can be sure that their anger was because they wanted the same thing, and resented the fact that James and John might be getting ahead in the race. Actually, the Gospels tell us that several times, the disciples argued which of them was the greatest. That sounds silly to us, but it seemed very natural to them. Jesus taught differently.

First of all, He pointed out that among the Gentiles, the way to greatness was through asserting one's greatness over others. Self-promotion. The race for honors. He then said, *Not so with you.* The way to be truly great is to move downward. We must become the slaves of all. Remember, the lowest class of all were slaves. Jesus was telling us that to follow Him is to intentionally lose the race for honors, to put ourselves on the very bottom. This was such a mind-boggling truth, Jesus had to repeat it to His disciples over and over again, using different terms each time. Once (Matthew 18:3), He made the point by saying that we can only enter the Kingdom of God by becoming like a little child. We hear that and think, "Oh, we need a childlike, dependent faith." But in the world the disciples lived in, children weren't even seen as fully human. They had no rights. The word for child in both Greek and Latin means "not speaking." So for Him to say, "Become like a little child" was another way of saying, "Drop out of the race for honors. Let someone else get the attention. Put others before yourself."

A New Way to be Great

Isaiah 53:2-3

Jesus didn't just teach that stuff; He lived it. Jesus was born in poverty. His parents were from Nazareth, a place so backward, even their fellow Jews had a saying, "Can anything good come from Nazareth?" They were also unmarried. Every culture has a term for people who are born illegitimately. In Jesus' culture, the word was *mamzer.* It wasn't any more a compliment than the term we use today. In the ancient world, a great man would never do manual labor; He could afford to have others work for him. But Jesus spent most of His life working with His hands as a carpenter, building things for people who were higher up the social ladder than Him. Powerful men of that time liked to promote themselves as being strong and handsome. They would commission idealized statues of themselves. Does anyone really believe that Julius Caesar had abs like that in the days before supplements and weight training? That's the way Caesar wanted us to imagine him, not the way he actually looked. The people who knew Jesus didn't leave us statues or pictures of Him, but there is this description from the prophet Isaiah: *He had no beauty or majesty to attract us to Him, nothing in His appearance that we should desire Him.* I don't know how you picture Jesus in your mind, but that mental picture is probably much more handsome than He actually was.

Why does this matter? Because Scripture continually reminds us that Jesus was God in human flesh. He chose the circumstances of His birth. He chose His parents, His appearance. And as such, He chose to be lowly. On the night we now call Maundy Thursday, during the celebration we call the Last Supper, He took off his shirt, put a towel around His waist, and washed His disciples' feet. Footwashing was a necessity, but it was such demeaning work, even most slaves wouldn't do it. Imagine you were in a hospital and the President of the United States showed up to empty your bedpan: That gives you a faint idea of how shocking it was for Jesus to wash His disciples' feet. Jesus' behavior was often shocking, but nothing more so than this: He took all of His culture's ideas of what made a man great, and stood them on their head. He completely redefined what it meant to be a great person. Whose definition of greatness are you attempting to live up to?

Death of a Fool

1 Corinthians 1:18-25

And then He died on a cross. Crucifixion was the most painful, humiliating means of execution ever devised by tthe dark heart of man. Even the most graphic depictions of crucifixion today don't capture the true horror. Even in *The Passion of the Christ*, they showed Jesus partially clothed. That's not the way it truly was. For this reason, a Roman citizen could not be crucified, no matter how awful their crime. It was a punishment for slaves, meant to remind them of their lowly status and warn anyone who tried to change the status quo. Jesus lived like a slave and died like a slave. He chose this also; as He said in our Mark 10:45, He came to give His life as our ransom. Then something remarkable happened. People who believed in Jesus bought into His message. We see this in the writings of Paul. In most of his letters, Paul addresses himself not as apostle or bishop or author of half the New Testament. He calls himself "the slave of Christ." The early church began to embrace the cross, too. 1 Corinthians 1:18 says, *The message of the cross is foolishness to those who are perishing; but to us who are being saved it is the power of God.* Remember, the cross was the tool the earthly powers had used to show Jesus He wasn't worthy of advancement. It seemed like the ultimate repudiation of Christianity. But His followers said, "No, that's where the true power lies." They knew that Jesus had taught them that if they wanted to follow Him, they had to take up their cross. They had to be willing to die. They had to intentionally lose the race for honors. This is why Christians wear the cross, sing songs about it; How absurd it would seem to first-century people if they knew how we venerated an object of execution! This is how profoundly Jesus changed the way we think.

Years ago, Michael Card wrote a song about Jesus called "God's Own Fool." The lyrics are rather subversive, but completely accurate:

> Seems I've imagined Him all of my life
> As the wisest of all of mankind.
> But if God's holy wisdom is foolish to man,
> He must have seemed out of His mind.
> For even His family said He was mad
> And the priests said a demon's to blame.
> God in the form of this angry young man

Could not have seemed perfectly sane.
So come lose your life for a carpenter's son,
For a madman who died for a dream.
And you'll have the faith His first followers had
And you'll feel the weight of the beam.
So surrender the hunger to say you must know
And the courage to say I believe
For the power of paradox opens your eyes
And blinds those who say they can see.
When we in our foolishness thought we were wise
He played the fool and He opened our eyes
When we in our weakness believed we were strong
He became helpless to show we were wrong.
And so we follow God's own fool
For only the foolish can tell.
Believe the unbelievable; come be a fool as well.

It's Hard to be Humble

Colossians 3:12

Jesus lived in a world dominated by the race for honors, and He turned that system upside down. However, there are still cultures in our world that are ruled by honor. In those cultures, if a woman does something to make her family ashamed, she will often be publically killed by her own father, brothers or husband. It's called an *honor killing*. Notice that doesn't happen in cultures that have been shaped by the movement of Jesus. Yet, even in our society, the race for honor is alive and well. I read recently about a dating website exclusively for the physically attractive. In order to get into the mix, you have to submit photographs, and the members have to vote you as attractive enough. Recently, the site made news for expelling 5,000 members who had gained weight over the holidays. The company spokesman said, "Is it elitist? Yes, because that's what our members want it to be." We all have an inherent desire to put some distance between ourselves and the people we hope we're better than. The challenge of being a Christ-follower is that we must reject all of that. That doesn't mean it's wrong to try to be the best you can be. It means that the point of your life must be to serve God through serving others. It means that instead of trying to call attention to ourselves, we try to get out of the way so that Christ can be seen clearly.

How do we measure this? I'm pretty sure that if you think you're humble, you're not. So here are three questions to measure yourself by. See how you do. You might even ask someone else to observe you on these: 1) How do I treat people who are "lower" in status than me? That includes your employees if you're in a management position, but also waiters, retail clerks, bus drivers, or anyone who serves you. Would these people say that you treat them in a way that makes them feel valued and appreciated? 2) How often do I serve someone else? The Jesus movement started a revolution in marriage by saying that a husband should love his wife the way Christ loved the church (Ephesians 5:25-31), laying down His life for her. Wives then were seen as the property of their husbands, but Christian men were to serve their wives. That should be true in all our relationships. How often this week will you find yourself doing something for someone else without any thought of being repaid or recognized? 3) How do I react when someone disagrees with me? A person of humility is able to learn from his opponent. He doesn't have to "win" the argument, because he's more concerned about representing Christ well and persuading people than he is about personal vindication. Is that true of you? See what happens this week when anyone challenges you.

Hypocrisy Detector

Luke 6:41-42

Years ago, I attended a meeting for pastors about reaching our neighborhoods. The leader did something unusual. She took us to a mall and dropped us off. She said we should approach 10 random people and ask them if they went to church, and if not, why not. This was in a town where there are churches on virtually every corner, so I expected to meet at least someone who went to church. I didn't. People said, "Churches just want your money. I believe in God, but I don't need those people to tell me about Him. Churches are full of hypocrites." That's a word that gets used a lot in reference to Christians these days. In a book called *Unchristian,* by Dave Kinnaman, we learn that 85% of young adults outside the church think that most Christians are hypocrites. 47% of young adults inside the church think the same thing. I wonder how many of the people who use that word know where it came from.

Hypocrite is a Greek word. It originally referred to actors in a play, who would wear masks so that people in the huge theaters could see the emotion they were trying to convey. Jesus began using that word to describe religious people. One way Jesus changed the world was in the way we think about religion. Before Jesus, it was assumed that religion was purely external. Just do certain good deeds, avoid certain vices, perform certain rituals, and you would be good with God. After Jesus, most people believe that there needs to be some internal transformation, or else those external rituals are meaningless. Interestingly, the primary idea many people use to criticize Jesus' followers today wouldn't exist if not for Jesus. (That doesn't mean our critics are wrong, by the way).

A New Idea of God

Deuteronomy 12:29-32

Another way Jesus changed religion is in the way we view God. The world Jesus was born into was dominated by polytheism, particularly the Greek pantheon of gods. Most of us remember the stories of Greek mythology we learned in school. The interesting thing about those gods: They were powerful, but they weren't good. Imagine taking a bunch of drunk teenagers at Spring Break, giving them absolute power and immortality, and you'd have the Greek pantheon. Other cultures were also polytheistic. Their gods weren't particularly virtuous, either. Some of them were downright terrifying. Only the Jews believed that there was one God, and He was good. The Greeks didn't believe religion could make you good; if you wanted to become moral, you spoke to the philosophers, not the priests. You spoke to the priests if you wanted good luck. Jesus taught that knowing God was the only way to truly become good. Today, ethical monotheism, or the belief that there is one God, that He is good, and that those who know Him best should behave morally, is the dominant belief system of our culture. That came from Jesus. It came first from the Jews, who for centuries were a tiny island of ethical monotheism in the midst of a swirling vortex of barbaric, sex-obsessed, violent pagan religions. In fact, much of the Old Testament is comprised of God telling the Israelites, over and over again, "I have given you the Promised Land; you defeated all these nations against huge odds, because I was with you. But if you start mixing their religious practices with the ones I taught you, it will be worse for you than if you'd been defeated militarily." The Israelites failed in this often. But they held onto God effectively enough that ethical monotheism, specifically the worship of Yahweh and following His Law, was the sole religion of the Jews in Jesus' day. Jesus and His followers brought the worship of Yahweh to the entire world. This made ethical monotheism the dominant thought pattern of all humanity. Therefore, when people reject Christianity because, for instance, "I don't believe a good God would allow so much evil," I want to ask them, "Where did you get the idea that God is good?" Ironically, it came from the very Person they are rejecting.

Jesus vs. Religion

Matthew 23:1-3

A few years ago, a young man named Jefferson Bethke posted a spoken-word video on Youtube entitled, "Why I hate religion but love Jesus." It quickly went viral. As of this writing, it has been viewed nearly thirty million times. When Bethke's video first came out, many religious leaders took great offense. They wrote op-eds and appeared on television news programs talking about all the good that organized religion does in society. Personally, I think the kid was spot on. It was Jesus' opposition to the religious leaders of His day that got Him killed. His courageous, insightful teaching on what religion should truly be forever changed our idea of how people should serve God. We've already looked at two ways Jesus changed religion. But perhaps most significantly, He changed the way we view those who are outsiders to our faith. Over the next three readings, I'll list three ways Jesus differed from the religious leaders of His day...and from much of organized religion (even many manifestations of Christianity) today.

Religion uses words to label; Jesus used words to heal. The religious leaders in Jesus' culture had certain labels they fixed on people: They called Gentiles "uncircumcised dogs." People who earned a living in disreputable ways were called by the name of their dishonorable vocation, to remind them of why they weren't good enough: "Tax collector;" "Prostitute." And then there were people who had committed sins that—in the eyes of the leaders—disqualified them from participation in the life of the synagogue. These people they simply called "sinners." If you were the child or grandchild of one of these people, the leaders called you a sinner, too. And if you had a terrible, crippling illness, they said, "She or her parents must have done something awful in the past, or else God wouldn't have let something so awful happen to her." The words they used didn't help these people; they just let them know where they stood, which was far outside the love of God. But Jesus used words differently: *Woman, you are set free,* He said to a disabled woman, as He healed her. I am willing to bet that those simple words were more powerful and meaningful to this woman than all the thousands of words her religious leaders had said to her over the years. To a tax collector and known crook, He said, *Salvation has come to this household, for this man too is a son of Abraham.* To worried people living on the margin between life and starvation, He reminded them that God pays attention to every tiny bird, and that you are much more valuable to God than birds. To people who have so much on their plate they don't think they can stand it any longer, He said, *Come to me, all who are weary and heavy burdened, and I will give you rest.* And to a dying thief who made a last-minute conversion, He said, *Today, you will be with me in paradise.*

Outsiders Became Insiders

Luke 13:10-17

Religion drives outsiders away; Jesus drew them in.
Religion in Jesus' day was all about drawing lines, determining who was in and who was out (sadly, it still often is). This is one of the things that made Jesus so furious about the religious leaders; they chose to emphasize the rules they were good at keeping, and ignore the ones that were inconvenient for them. The example we see in today's text is about the Sabbath. God created the Sabbath day as an act of mercy for people. We need time off, or we will burn out; the Sabbath was God's way of giving us a break. But the religious leaders had turned it into a burden for the people, not a gift. They had invented all sorts of rules for the Sabbath. One was that no one could seek medical attention on that day. That command isn't anywhere in Scripture; it was just another way for the religious leaders to draw an artificial line that would exclude some people, to make the club of "who's in" smaller. But the Law did say that a person could care for his animals on that day. Jesus' point was that this woman was more valuable than an animal. He pointed out that the religious leaders themselves had fed and watered their livestock that very morning, but they were angry that their fellow human was healed. He stabbed their hypocrisy with the dagger of the truth, and it hurt them.

Jesus was different. The religious leaders noticed that the main people attracted to Jesus were the very people they hated most. They began calling Him, "A friend of sinners, tax collectors, and prostitutes." To them, that was the ultimate insult, the ultimate sign that Jesus couldn't be Messiah, or even a good man. But to Jesus, that was a compliment. That is what He came to do. In my own Christian background, a person could be considered a good Christian even if they were a racist, a gossip, had a quick temper or held grudges. But if they drank alcohol, slept around, or used foul language, they couldn't possibly be a child of God. What kinds of double standards do you have? If you're a Christian, does your life draw people closer to the salvation found in Jesus, or does it drive them away? To put it more bluntly, what do you do on a regular basis that draws outsiders closer to Him?

True Righteousness

2 Corinthians 5:16-21

Religion breeds self-righteousness; Jesus makes others righteous. Why did the religious leaders label people and make up rules that made it impossible for outsiders to get to God? Because we all like to feel superior to others. We make fun of someone who we feel is unattractive, unintelligent, or socially awkward because doing so makes us feel beautiful, smart, and sophisticated by comparison. To the religious leaders, nothing was more important than feeling righteous. So they marginalized as many people as possible so that they could feel super-righteous by comparison. But the God they claimed to be worshipping came to live among them, and told them they weren't righteous at all. What He valued was not the religious guy who said, "Thank God I'm not a sinner." What He valued was the self-identified failure who wept and said, "Lord I can't do it on my own; please save me." That's the problem with mere religion. It gives us rules to follow and rituals to accomplish, and when we've done those things, we feel good about ourselves. We have a reason to look down on others, who weren't as diligent as we were. A sure sign that you are following religion and not Jesus is that you feel a sense of satisfaction and superiority when you look at people on the outside. A follower of Jesus isn't better than anyone else; He's just more aware of, and broken by, the sin in his own life.

Think about this: If Jesus had wanted to, He could have walked around comparing Himself favorably to every human alive. On the day of His arrest and trial, He could have accused His accusers by saying, "Have you guys ever sinned? I haven't. I should be judging you, not the other way around." And He would have been telling the truth! He was the only person who has ever lived who was truly SELF-righteous. But He didn't do that. Instead, He did the opposite. Instead of emphasizing His own righteousness, He took on our sin. He paid the price for what we had done In words that blow my mind, 2 Corinthians 5:21 tells us *God made Him who had no sin to become sin for us, that we might become the righteousness of God in Him.* Jesus didn't just identify Himself as a sinner. He BECAME sin itself. That way, we could become righteousness itself. So which are you more like? Do you feel satisfaction when you look at others? Or do you feel a strong desire to help them discover the righteousness that you yourself have been given?

The Birds and the Bees

Luke 7:36-50

It's time to talk about sex. And when it comes to that particular subject, we contemporary Americans have a rather peculiar attitude. If a person from some other civilization time-traveled to our day and spent a short time here, he would notice our obsession with sex. It's the subject of most of our humor, our advertising, our movies, music and television. If you've ever read the Bible all the way through, you know that the Bible has a lot to say about sex. Its language is very frank. There are lots of passages that preachers like me find it difficult to preach on; we have to do verbal gymnastics to avoid embarrassing the prudish side of our congregation and titillating to distraction the immature side. The result is that many preachers and churches avoid the subject altogether, while others seem obsessed with it. So here's an ironic fact: Even though Jesus was a lifelong celibate single person, He changed the way we think about sex and marriage more than any other person who has ever lived. Today, even though we live in an increasingly irreligious culture, most people still choose to get married in a church; they take vows in the name of Jesus, a man who never married. Why is that? And how does Jesus' sexual ethic still challenge us, whether we are religious or not?

Although Luke doesn't say this specifically, we can easily infer that this woman's "sinful life" means that she had sinned in some sexual way. Perhaps she was a prostitute. Or maybe she was simply a woman who had been involved in an affair or had been married more than once. There's nothing unusual about her crashing this dinner party. It was part of Israelite hospitality that the poor could come into a banquet like this. But notice how Simon the Pharisee reacts to the way Jesus treats her. His attitude was consistent with that of most religious people of His day. Sexual sin was seen as different from other sins. It made people dirty. It carried a special kind of shame. Religious people haven't changed that much, have they? Look at vv. 44-50. Notice two things Jesus didn't say: First, He didn't say, "There's nothing wrong with her lifestyle." Instead, He acknowledged her sin, as did she. He said, *her **many** sins have been forgiven.* He also didn't say, "Because she showed me love through this extravagant act of anointing my feet with perfume, she has earned forgiveness." Instead, she loved Him **because** she was forgiven. What does that word "forgiven" mean, exactly? Does it mean that Jesus ignored her past failings completely? Does it mean she was now considered as righteous in God's sight as the most chaste person alive? Absolutely. How we react to that truth says a lot about how Christ-like we are.

Did Jesus Talk About Sex?

Matthew 5:27-28

Most of Jesus' interactions were with His fellow Jews, but the larger Gentile culture viewed sex quite differently. For the Greeks and Romans, sexual ethics were much less restrictive…as long as you were a man. A woman in that culture could be punished for adultery, but not a man…unless he slept with another man's wife, and then it was seen as a property crime; he had wronged his fellow man. A writer of that time period said, "We have mistresses for our enjoyment, concubines for our daily needs, and wives to bear us legitimate children." Since we tend to think of the Romans as being enlightened, it may surprise some of you to learn that pedophilia in Roman society was not condemned. In fact, it was taken for granted that powerful men would have sexual relationships with boys as young as 12. A writer from that time named Tatian said the Romans liked to "round up herds of boys like herds of grazing mares." The anything-goes sexual ethic mirrored the stories of the Greek gods. Their myths are full of stories of illicit affairs between gods and goddesses, and dalliances with human women that produce unwanted children. It's hard to know sometimes whether you're reading about Zeus or the Rolling Stones. Our popular culture today views sex more like the Romans than the Jews. The sexual revolution started in this country over 50 years ago; we were told that if we threw off the old standards of sexuality—which were called "repression"—and embraced a new freedom, it would be good for us. Has it? Are there more happy marriages today? Are there fewer unwanted children? Do people, in general, have healthier, more unselfish relationships with the opposite sex than fifty years ago? You tell me. Or to put it another way, consider this story: The pastor Andy Stanley was talking to a woman who had visited his church. She said that the Christian ideas about who should have sex and who shouldn't were unrealistic. In response, Stanley asked her, "Has sex outside marriage made your life better or just more complicated?"

People sometimes say, "Jesus never talked about pre-marital sex or homosexuality." He didn't have to. It wasn't an issue in First-Century Israel. No one came up to Jesus and asked, "Is it alright for me to have sex with my girlfriend?" They knew what the Word of God said about it. After Jesus was gone, and the apostles took the Gospel into a wider, non-Jewish world, they had to confront the Greek and Roman attitude toward sex, and so we see them talking about it specifically in the letters of the New Testament. Throughout the Bible, the Word is clear and consistent: Sex is meant for a man and a woman, within marriage, period. It's worth noting that when Scripture talks about sex, it uses a word that means "to know." Scripture shows far more respect for sex than our popular culture does. Biblically, sex is not a commodity or a recreational activity; it's an act of intimacy between two people who have committed their lives to one another. Jesus didn't just endorse the sexual ethic of Scripture to that point. He went further: In our Scripture today, He wasn't saying that it's a sin to find someone attractive. He was telling men, "Women are not for your sexual gratification. They are people, just like you. Treat them with respect." Notice also that Jesus didn't put the onus of responsibility on women. He didn't say they should cover themselves lest men be distracted by their beauty. We as men are responsible for how we look at women. Jesus wasn't hung up on sex like His fellow Jews (and too many of His contemporary followers). But He also didn't buy into the cheap, anything-goes ethic of the broader world.

Counter-Cultural Sexuality

Hebrews 13:4

After Jesus was gone, His followers changed the world in part by living out His teachings on sex and marriage. In a world that made our contemporary hook-up culture look Puritan by comparison, they had the audacity to live according to biblical sexual ethics like the Scripture we just read. They celebrated loving marriages and taught that children were a gift far more important than treasure. They had a special esteem for men and women who chose to be single and celibate for a lifetime. The rest of the world didn't know what to make of this. As Tim Keller puts it, the ancients were generous with their bodies but stingy with their money, while Christians were generous with their money and stingy with their bodies. Because of them, a new idea developed about what constituted the ideal family. Roman men were expected to keep lovers, both young women and young men. That was not seen as scandalous until Christianity took hold. Today, in spite of all the ways our current culture has changed its views on sexuality, it's still taken for granted that the ideal family includes a mother and father who love one another and are faithful to one another for a lifetime. That idea is sometimes mocked, not because it doesn't work, but because some say it's unrealistic. But I could name dozens of couples who prove that it's very realistic indeed.

Jesus had changed things so much, after He was gone one of His primary biographers, His disciple Matthew, recorded Jesus' genealogy. In it, he included the names of five women, which was very unusual. In a genealogy in those times, women were only listed if they were especially prominent, like a daughter of a king. Matthew wanted to highlight these five women for a very important purpose. Their names are Tamar, Rahab, Ruth, Bathsheba, and Mary. The only thing they have in common is a hint of sexual scandal, in some cases deserved, in others (Ruth and Mary) not so much. In fact, Bathsheba isn't actually named; she is called, "The wife of Uriah," to remind us that she and King David committed adultery. Why did Matthew write the genealogy this way? Short answer: Because God's Holy Spirit inspired Him to do so. Why would He do that? Because He wanted us all to know that sexual sin, just like any other sin, is what Jesus came to redeem us from. People who have stumbled in this way are no less forgiven, and God is no less proud of His children who He redeemed from a life of sexual sin. The great news is that God has a better way than the one our culture preaches. And even for people who have failed to keep God's standards, there is redemption.

Call Him Father

Matthew 6:9

As the story goes, a Scottish Presbyterian Church had a new pastor who had spent most of his life in the ivory towers of academia, teaching theology to young seminary students. He loved to pray lofty public prayers, using obscure theological terms. One day, his head was bowed as he held forth. Suddenly, there was a tug at the coat of his vestments. He looked down to see a little Scottish woman in a choir robe standing there. She said, "Just call 'im Father and ask 'im for somethin'." We all nod our heads in approval at that story. But where did we get this idea that we could come to God just as we are, without one plea? Most other religious traditions have very strict rules about who can get close to their god; even if you're one of the favored few, there's usually an elaborate set of rituals that one must go through before you speak to God. Yet most Christians think nothing of praying to God in the shower, in the car, lying in bed in the middle of the night, or anywhere else, anytime we have a need, a question, or a fear. Is it just presumption that makes us think that we deserve that kind of access to an infinitely holy, awesomely powerful God? For that matter, what makes us think we can call Him Father?

Jesus changed the way we relate to God. Jesus taught us to call God "Father." We see it here at the beginning of the Lord's Prayer. Now, there are some references in the Old Testament to God as the Father of Israel. But no Israelite before Jesus would have referred to Yahweh as "Abba." That word in Jesus' native tongue, Aramaic, means "Father." Except linguists will tell you it's not a formal word like our English word "Father." It is a word of intimacy. It's probably the first word most Jewish babies would have learned; something like "Papa." It's interesting to look at every time Jesus uses that term, and notice the pronouns He uses. For instance, when He talks about forgiveness, He says, "Your Father," which excludes Himself, for He never sinned. When He talks about His sonship and mission in life, He says "My Father," which excludes the rest of us. But here, He teaches us to pray, "Our Father." Christians are a diverse people, but all adopted sons and daughters of a King who loves them.

A God of Love

John 3:16

This idea of a God of love was revolutionary. In John Ortberg's book *Who Is This Man?* He puts it this way: "In the ancient world, the spiritual realm was understood to be real but not morally transcendent. Aristotle said, 'It would be eccentric to claim to love Zeus.' No one wrote songs that said, 'Zeus loves me, this I know, for the *Iliad* tells me so.' Adherents of Eastern religions generally did not believe in a personal god at all. Whenever someone says, 'I believe in a God of love,' We hear the echo of the Nazarene." In our Scripture, which is perhaps Jesus' most famous statement, He defined the love of God as a love that is willing to pay the highest price for our sakes. It is literally true: God would rather die for you than live without you!

We tend to be skeptical when powerful people say they care about people who are lower on the socio-economic ladder. A CEO might say he loves his employees; but if a cleaning lady in his company showed up at his mansion for supper uninvited, he would call the police instead of inviting her in. Could it be that Jesus was simply saying what poor, hurting people wanted to hear, just to increase the size of His following and make Himself look magnanimous? Well, think about how Jesus treated people. When parents brought their children to Jesus so that He could bless them, His disciples were horrified. What a breach of protocol! They tried to run the little urchins off, but Jesus rebuked His disciples. He said, *Let the children come to me, for the Kingdom of Heaven belongs to such as these.* In that time, children weren't seen as having rights and worth…except by Jesus. Or think of a rich young man who came to Jesus seeking answers. Jesus told this man the thing keeping him from the Kingdom was his great wealth; that he should sell all he had and give it to the poor. The young man went away sad, unwilling to part with his treasure. But Mark 10:21 says, *Jesus looked at him and loved him.* Jesus' heart went out to this man who would ultimately reject Him! There are many other such stories, and we'll see them as we move on through Jesus' life. What they tell us is that Jesus liked people. He wasn't some aloof genius who emerged occasionally for a performance. He wanted to be with the crowds. The historian Paul Johnson, writing of Jesus, said: "His life was a series of public meetings punctuated by casual encounters that turned into significant events. Jesus not only encouraged these encounters, but treasured them…There is nothing like them in the entire literature of the ancient world, sacred or secular." We don't read these kinds of stories about Socrates or Aristotle, or any of the Caesars, or for that matter, Buddha or Mohammed. Jesus loved people.

The Torn Curtain

Galatians 3:28

The Gospels tell us that at the moment of Jesus' death, the curtain in the Temple was torn in two. This was no mere piece of fabric. It was the barrier between the Holy of Holies, where God dwelt, and the rest of the Temple. No one crossed that barrier, except the High Priest, and he only did so once a year, on Yom Kippur (The Day of Atonement). It separated the worshippers from the presence of God Himself. To this day, Orthodox Jews believe the presence of God is still on the Temple Mount in Jerusalem. When I visited Israel, we went to the Temple Mount. The Temple is long gone, but there are signs sponsored by Orthodox Jews, warning tourists and others not to visit the site; we might unknowingly step into the presence of God and be struck dead by His wrath. On the day Jesus died, that curtain was torn without being touched by a human hand. Jesus' followers believed that was God's way of saying, "Because of Jesus' death, there is no more separation. Anyone who wants to know me can know me." Later a follower of Jesus named Paul would write the passage we just read. The world had never seen such an egalitarian statement. It was scandalous, in fact. Yet as the movement of Jesus Christ spread, so did this idea that all human beings have an inherent dignity and worth. Missionaries today are often seen as tools of imperialism, who defiled native cultures, but Christian missionaries who believed Galatians 3:28 actually did more to advance human equality than anyone. They saw a world full of people who were separated by language, color and culture, but who were one in the eyes of God. When Thomas Jefferson wrote the famous words, "We hold these truths to be self-evident, that all men are created equal," he wasn't expressing a personal devotion to Jesus--Jefferson was not an orthodox Christian. But he was echoing the life and ideas of this man from Galilee. I submit that without Jesus, there would never have been a Declaration of Independence, or heroes like Martin Luther King, who helped us realize the full ramifications of its meaning. In His life and His death, Jesus opened a door to God that wouldn't be open without Him. And in doing so, He changed the world, even for millions who will never believe in Him.

Loving People isn't Easy

John 13:34-35

A few years ago, Fred Phelps, the founder of Westboro Baptist Church, died. Phelps and his church of about forty people—mostly family members—in Topeka, Kansas, specialized in publicity stunts. They protested at the funerals of fallen American service people, holding up signs that named the people they believed God hates. Even the name of their website is hateful: Godhatesfags.com (please don't visit it). I read that when he died, Phelps had been excommunicated from the church he founded. I find that so ironic, and yet so fitting. This man founded a church based on hate, and ended up being chewed up and spit out by the same hateful machinery that he himself constructed.

It's easy for me to judge someone like Fred Phelps. Truth is, the world doesn't think of the love of Christ when they think of us, either. We have no excuse. A large portion of American evangelical Christianity has somehow decided that feeling anger and disgust over the sins of other people is the same thing as righteousness, and that denouncing unbelievers is the same thing as being a bold witness. Let's be clear about something: The Bible never commands us to tell anyone that God hates them. We are not commanded to point out the sins of people who aren't believers. We never see Jesus in the Gospels railing on the sinfulness of pagans, or Paul standing outside Greek theaters or bathhouses, telling them how foolish their choices are. Sometimes I see my Christian friends getting into intense arguments over morality with unbelievers. I find that baffling. Why are we getting angry when people who don't believe the Bible act like people who don't believe the Bible? Would we rather they pretend to share our values, even though they don't know our Savior? What we ARE commanded to do, over and over again, is make disciples of Jesus Christ.

How do we do that? The same way Jesus did: By getting out of our pews and off our high-horses and investing ourselves in the lives of the people around us who don't know Him. I read recently that here in America, 1 in 5 non-Christians doesn't even know a single Christian. That ought to make us weep. So this week, write an encouraging note to someone. Invite someone to lunch. Ask someone if you can pray for them. And here's a tip: Just because you assume that someone doesn't need friends doesn't make it so. In my experience in ministry, I have learned that some of the loneliest people are those who look like they have everything life can offer.

The Ragtag Armada

Acts 1:4-8

It's 1940, and the Nazis look unstoppable. They've easily conquered France, who at the time had the largest army in Europe. The Dutch and the Belgians have already surrendered. The United States isn't interested in getting into another foreign war, and isn't ready to fight in the first place. All that is left between Germany and total domination of the hemisphere is Great Britain. And right now, the British army is one step from total annihilation. A quarter million British troops, plus 100,000 allies, are trapped on a beach in a place called Dunkirk. The German army is on one side, and the waters of the English Channel are on the other. The Royal Navy has only enough ships to save around 17,000. Churchill has already told the House of Commons to prepare for "hard and heavy tidings." Suddenly, a strange sight appears in the Channel. Fishing boats, tugboats, sailboats, yachts and ferries, all driven by civilians, have come to the rescue. Before German commanders can move in for what once looked like an easy victory, 338,000 soldiers are rescued by this ragtag armada. Quite simply put, when the forces of evil were about to win, ordinary people stepped up and saved the day...and the war.

Now let me tell you another story; one I like even more than that one. Jesus Christ is nearing the end of His time on Earth. He has come to die for the sins of mankind, to defeat sin and death and Hell with one self-sacrificing act of heroic love and unimaginable power. But dying on the Cross and rising again the third day aren't the end of His work. He knows that someone will need to take the message of His love to the world. Someone will have to show people how to receive this amazing gift, and teach them to follow Him into eternal and abundant life. To put it in terms of our previous story, humanity was on the verge of annihilation. We were trapped between the forces of evil and the bondage of our own sin. Jesus chose a small group of true believers to be the spark that started a movement that would save the world. As we close out this chapter on how Jesus changed the world, we need to consider the church. Yes, the local church, for all its flaws, is still God's ragtag armada, the hope of the world.

The Beginning of a Movement

Matthew 16:13-19

This is a famous passage. Some scholars have called v. 18 the most controversial verse in the entire New Testament. I want to unpack four important terms, so that we all understand what Jesus is saying here. First, there's *Upon this rock*. The name Peter, which Jesus has given to Simon, means "rock." So it's obvious He's talking about Peter himself. Next, there's the word *church*. At the point Jesus said this, there was no such thing as a church. The term Matthew uses in Greek is *ecclesia,* which means "community" or "assembly." So Jesus is saying, "Peter is going to be the starting point for the group of people I am building." The disciples thought the Messiah was going to lead Israel; it must have surprised them to hear that Jesus was building a new group of people separate from the political nation of Israel. By the way, let's address the elephant in the room. Some Christians point to this verse as proof that Jesus named Peter as the first pope; the infallible, unquestioned leader of the Christian movement. But if that's true, the early church certainly didn't see him that way. In Acts 8, we see the Church sending Peter and John on an assignment. Get that? The Church told Peter what to do, not the other way around. In Acts 11, people in the church question a decision Peter made. In Galatians 2, Paul publicly rebukes Peter. That doesn't sound like an unquestioned leader to me. So I believe what Jesus is saying is, "I am starting a new kind of people. Peter is going to be the first one in the group. I can build on this guy."

Next, He says *the gates of Hades will not prevail against it.* I always believed Jesus was saying, "Hell itself won't be able to stand up against my church." In saying that, I thought He was referring to Hell as the domain of Satan, the headquarters of evil, the way we used to talk about Moscow. But then I realized two things: first, Hell is not the Devil's headquarters. It is his final destination. Satan doesn't live there; but he will someday, very much against his will. Second, Jesus didn't use the term *Gehenna,* which we translate "Hell." He used the term "Hades," which is another way of referring to death. So what He's actually saying is, "Death won't be able to stop my Church. My Church will last forever." Finally, let's look at that term, *keys to the Kingdom*. Based on everything else Jesus told His disciples between this time and the day He ascended into Heaven, it's obvious that He's talking about the Gospel. He's saying, "By the time I'm done here, you'll have a story to tell, and it will be the greatest story ever told. When you tell this story, people will get set free. Chains will fall off. Lives will be transformed. The people you rescue down here on Earth will be truly rescued because of the power of Heaven itself." Jesus had just brought us all in on His rescue movement with this one man, Peter.

Against All Odds

Matthew 16:21-23

You would expect that Peter would be a new man after that day. You would think that he would go out and prove Jesus right for trusting him this way. You would be wrong. The very next story we read is about Jesus telling His disciples He's going to be arrested and killed by the religious authorities. Peter rebukes Jesus, and Jesus says to Peter, "Get behind me, Satan." Considering who it is who is saying these words, that's the worst thing Jesus could possibly have called anyone. If you had been there that day, you might have asked Jesus if He was changing His mind about the whole "upon this rock" thing. Things didn't get much better after that. The night Jesus was going to be arrested, He asked His three best friends, James, John and Peter, to pray for Him. They fell asleep instead. Then when He was arrested, Peter totally disavowed Jesus, said, "I don't even know the man," and ran away in fear. Imagine you had been alive right then and didn't have foreknowledge, and someone had asked you, "Which will last longer, the Roman Empire or the movement started by Jesus Christ?" You would have taken Rome in a heartbeat. They were the most powerful nation the world had ever seen, with money, military might, sophisticated leadership, intellectual superiority, roads, technology, and an empire's worth of natural resources. Christ's followers looked like a handful of uneducated, cowardly Galileans. Yet today, Rome is a memory, and the Christian Church is the largest, most influential organization in the history of the planet. As John Ortberg has pointed out, the term "Christians" meant "little Christs." It was meant as an insult, originally, a term of derision conferred on Jesus' followers by people who thought their beliefs were a joke. But today, "Little Christs" are the largest, most influential movement in the world, while "Little Caesars" is a pizza joint. Maybe Jesus knew what He was doing, after all.

God's Fallible People

Romans 15:17-21

Let's be honest: These days, the Church isn't seen in such a good light. People bring up our historical mistakes: The Crusades, the Inquisition, the support of many Christians in the South for slavery and then segregation, anti-semitism, homophobia, oppression of women, coddling sexually abusive priests, the list goes on.

Besides that, every non-Christian I've ever met can tell me stories about Christians they know who are hateful, judgmental, hypocritical jerks. But I respond to that with two statements. First, everything I just mentioned is true because at times Christ's followers fail to live up to His teachings. In other words, the problem isn't Jesus, it's that His followers don't practice what He preached. So what the world needs is not less of Jesus, it's more. Second, if you judge Christianity in a fair and unbiased way, you would see that the good Christianity has done far outweighs the bad. For just one example, a sociologist named Robert Woodberry has studied nations in the developing world that have more stable, democratic governments, better health care, education and infrastructure than other nations with similar factors. What they all have in common is that in the 1800s, they had significant ministry from Protestant missionaries who were out to spread Christianity. Woodberry, in fact, said that if you wanted to build a healthy nation, the number one most effective thing you could do is to go back in time and invite thousands of Protestant missionaries to your country (Robert Woodberry, *The Missionary Roots of Liberal Democracy*). And he wasn't simply talking about do-gooders on humanitarian missions. His research specifically indicated that missions which were evangelistic in nature produced the change. Yes, those same missionaries also worked to eradicate disease, built schools, advocated for the advancement of women's rights, and so on. But it was the spread of the Gospel that made the nation healthy. If Woodberry is right, no organization, philosophy or movement in history has done as much to make the world a better place than Christianity.

Why the Church?

1 Corinthians 3:9-17

There's a question I haven't answered. I have compared Christ's movement called the Church to the ragtag armada that rescued Alllied soldiers at Dunkirk. But there's a problem with that analogy. Britain had limited resources. God doesn't. Why would God use a ragtag armada? He could have recruited the very best people. Why does He use those who are average at best? Because it's not about the people; it's about God. If the Church were like most businesses, social organizations, athletic teams, movie studios and political parties--if we only chose the best and the brightest--then any success we achieved, any positive difference we made would be chalked up to our high admission standards. The message would be, "Those people really know how to put together an organization." But in reality, the Church is the place for everyone, especially those who fall short. We can't ever claim to be successful on our own. Truth is, we're nothing without Him. So if we succeed, it makes Him look good, not us. If we turn to Him, rely on Him, we have the keys of the Kingdom, and people get transformed. And since we're clearly not composed of the best and the brightest, the only explanation available is, "The God they believe in must be real. And He must be amazing." This is exactly what Jesus had in mind, as He explained in Matthew 5:14-16, *You are the light of the world. A city situated on a hill cannot be hidden. No one lights a lamp and puts it under a basket, but rather on a lampstand, and it gives light for all who are in the house. In the same way, let your light shine before men, so that they may see your good works and give glory to your Father in heaven.*

The Apostle Paul would go on to tell us more about God's purpose for the Church than anyone. In today's Scripture, He compares the Church to a field God is planting, a building He is constructing, and a sanctuary He protects. In other passages, the Church is known as the Bride of Christ. So the Church, in spite of all her many flaws, is the pride and joy of the Lord. It is His life's work. Be careful how you speak of the Church; it is His wife, after all. You may grow disillusioned with the Church, but don't give up on it...He never will.

.

Chapter 2: The Expectation of a Messiah

Daniel 7:13-14

We've seen how Jesus, a common laborer-turned-preacher from a backward outpost of the Roman near East, who was executed as a criminal after being rejected by His own people, somehow became the most influential person of all time. But now, let's step back. Let's forget about the Jesus of icons, stained-glass windows, and big-budget movies. For the rest of this book, let's trace the life of Jesus as if we're hearing about it for very first time; as if we've never even heard the name Jesus.

In order to do that, we must begin centuries before He was born. God's chosen people Israel began to believe that a deliverer, a champion, a hero was coming. They called their hero *HaMashiach,* Hebrew for "The Anointed One." We know the term better as the Messiah, or its Greek version, the Christ. The expectation of a Messiah began in the days of Israel's decline, when people retold the old stories of God's miraculous interventions on their behalf and wondered, "Where is God now?" As they went back through the Torah (the first five books of our Old Testament), they saw hints of what God was planning. They saw them also in the life of David, Israel's greatest king. Then the prophets, especially Isaiah, came along and refined the vision of who this Messiah was and what He would do. Daniel described Him as one who would look like any other person--"like a son of man"--but who would clearly be something more. He would rule over every nation forever. Imagine being a part of an oppressed group of people like the Jews. Imagine your forefathers, as far back as anyone could remember, had lived on a knife's edge, constantly in danger of extermination from famine, disease, or military invasion. Now imagine you hear that God will someday send a person anointed by Him, filled with His power, His righteousness, His justice…to make things right, once and for all. Think of the hope that would fill you upon gaining such knowledge. In this chapter, we'll look at a few of the more than 300 prophecies the Israelites clung to. We will see how, when Jesus was born, the expectations of a Messiah had reached a fever pitch. We'll also see why Jesus lived the way He lived…and died the way He died.

Stomping the Snake
Genesis 3:14-15

"If this world was created by an all-powerful, benevolent God, why do so many terrible things happen?" This is a common question in our age; it has led a great many people to reject faith in the God of the Bible, or any god at all. But there is no indication that the ancients wrestled with this idea. The Jews certainly didn't. They knew why the world was full of evil, and it wasn't God's fault. The creation story in Genesis 1 tells us God did make a perfect world, a world He could look upon and pronounce "very good" (Genesis 1:31). In Genesis 2, the creation story is retold in a different form, with a special emphasis on the creation of humanity. In God's original creation, man and woman commune with Him and with each other in harmony and peace. But then in chapter 3, everything changes. Humanity chooses to abandon God's plan; they decide they can be gods themselves, rejecting their relationship with their Creator in favor of the ability to follow their own appetites. God then must confront the man and woman, and tell them the awful consequences of their rebellion. When sin came into the world, it brought sickness, violence, conflict, hatred, hardship of all kinds, and death. Most of all, it brought separation between humans and God. After delivering this devastating news, God turns His attention to a third party: a talking snake who managed to convince the man and woman that turning away from God was a good idea. Today's Scripture shows what God said to this serpent.

As Israel developed in their understanding of God, they became aware of a figure known as "the devil" or "Satan" (the word literally means "the enemy"). He isn't an equal counterpoint to God, but he is still very troublesome in his ability to deceive and discourage God's people. Jewish teachers began to understand that the serpent of Genesis 3 wasn't simply a talking snake; it was Satan himself. They began to see v. 15, therefore as a promise from God. Yes, the enemy would always be around, a constant curse, bringing ongoing hardship to our lives, like the copperhead snakes we used to find and kill around my house in the summertime (and one which bit my father, sending him to the hospital). But someday, a Human would have the power to destroy the Devil entirely. Whereas Satan would nip at his heel, this Great One would crush the Devil's head. Clearly, this wouldn't be an ordinary man. This was a job for the Messiah Himself. When he arrived, He would vanquish the ancient enemy forever. How exactly would He accomplish this? The teachers didn't know. But they knew the outcome of the battle was predetermined, and all who were on the side of the Messiah were destined to be winners.

Birth of a Nation

Genesis 12:1-8

Have you ever wondered why the Jews are sometimes called "the chosen people?" Well, here you go. This is how God chose to make Himself known to a world that was fatally, terminally alienated from Him. He would create a new race of people who would live in a covenant with Him. He would bless them, guide them, protect them, and make them strong in the midst of larger, hostile nations all around them. They would follow His commands and experience life as it was meant to be lived; and through their blessing, all nations of the world would be drawn to God. It all started with a childless seventy-five year old who suddenly was confronted by a deity he had never met, and commanded to leave Ur, a huge city full of opportunities, for some distant place that would be revealed to him later, all on the vague promise that his obedience would ultimately benefit all of humanity. The story of Abram (whose name God later changed to Abraham) and Sarai (later Sarah) is one of the greatest examples of faith the world has ever seen. The story of his descendants, the Jewish people, is even more impressive. Think of the trials these people have been through: persecutions, inquisitions, pogroms, a Holocaust, a two-millennia dispersion, and they are still a people, with a distinct ethnic and religious identity. We cannot say that of any other people group. By all odds, the Jews should have vanished centuries ago, to become a mere footnote in history like the Hittites or the Sumerians. Their continued existence on the world stage strongly indicates that there really is a God who has chosen them for a greater purpose.

In v. 3, God promises Abram, *all peoples on earth will be blessed through you.* What did God mean by that? How on earth would a new race of people manage to make life better for all races, all nations? Was this simply hyperbole on God's part? Or did God have much more in mind than He was telling Abram at the time?

The Test

Genesis 22:1-18

I have to admit, I have a hard time with this story. As a father, it's painful to read; even more painful to put myself in Abraham's shoes. Twenty-five years passed from the time God first spoke to Abraham about making him a great nation. When his wife Sarah finally gave birth, she named their son Isaac. Interestingly, the name means "laughter." It's an appropriate name, because when the man and his wife, who were 100 and 90 respectively, first heard that this baby would be a reality, they laughed at the idea of it. You have to admit that the idea of a family that brings Pampers AND Depends home from the grocery store is funny. It's humorous to think of parents and child all sharing strained peas because none of them have any teeth. Imagine how happy they were!

Then, a few years later, old Abraham finds himself carrying a knife up a hillside, his little boy tottering behind him with a stack of wood, completely oblivious. Why would God ask such a thing of his faithful follower? Abraham lived in a time and place where it was common to believe that if you really wanted to succeed in life, you have to sacrifice one of your children. We think of that as barbaric, and it is, but we're not so different. We have sayings like, "Got to spend money to make money," "You have to break some eggs to make an omelet" and "no pain, no gain." These are all true in their own way, but as a society we make idols of these concepts. We willfully sacrifice our families, our integrity, our health just to get what the world calls the good life. We gain the world, and lose our souls. God put Abraham through this awful experience not simply to test the old man's faith, but to show him that Yahweh was different from the man-made gods of that day. He didn't require a human sacrifice; in fact, He hated that kind of religion (Deuteronomy 18:10, Leviticus 18:21, Jeremiah 7:31). To Abraham and us, He says, "It's not about the size of the sacrifice you can offer me. It's about what I can provide for you. It's not about how you can impress me with your devotion. It's about how I can amaze you with my grace." God provided a lamb for the sacrifice, just like Abraham had predicted (v. 8). Then in v. 18, He reiterated His promise: *And all the nations of the earth will be blessed by your offspring because you have obeyed My command.* What did Abraham's obedience have to do with the blessing of the world? Could it be that Abraham's statement "God will provide a lamb" meant more than he knew at the time? Could it be that someday God would sacrifice His only Son, as Abraham did not? We see these things now, with the benefit of thousands of years of redemptive history. But Abraham simply had to trust and obey.

A Family Thing

Genesis 49:8-10

Gather with me by the bedside of a dying man. Jacob, son of Isaac and grandson of Abraham, is nearing the end of his days, and he has one last responsibility to fulfill before his strength is gone. Jacob has lived an amazing life: He has fled from a homicidal brother, encountered angels, fallen in love with a beautiful woman, wrestled with God (!), reconciled with his brother, and received from the Lord a new name: Israel. He has also raised twelve sons, who will go on to be the patriarchs of the Israelite people; for generations to come, all Jews will identify themselves as members of one of these twelve tribes. Now, he gets ready to bless his sons. This is customary for Middle-Eastern fathers, and it serves as a final word of advice mixed with hope for his children and future generations. But for Jacob, it's more than that. As a servant of God, his blessing is also a prophecy, a divinely inspired view of what history holds for the descendants of these twelve boys.

To the surprise of everyone in the huge throng gathered around Jacob's deathbed, he pronounces Judah the future ruler of nations. Everyone knows Joseph was Jacob's favorite son. But now he calls Judah a lion and predicts, *The scepter will not depart from Judah, nor the ruler's staff from between his feet until he comes to whom it belongs, and the obedience of nations is his.* Who is this person to whom the scepter belongs, who will receive the obedience of nations? Some translators believe that "he to whom it belongs" should be translated "Shiloh," a word that means "peace-bringer," and was later the name of a town in Israel where the Jews worshipped for a time. The rabbis looked back at this prophecy of their forefather and knew they had one more piece of the Messianic puzzle. Whoever their hero would be, they knew He would come from the tribe of Judah.

Truth Bombs

Deuteronomy 18:15-19

Centuries pass. The children of Israel move to Egypt (that's another long--but fascinating--story). They become prosperous and numerous. The Egyptians become suspicious of these "Hebrews," thinking soon they will take over everything (sound familiar?). So they enslave them. For four hundred years, the chosen people toil away, brutally subjugated. Then God chooses a most unlikely hero: Eighty-year-old Moses, a fugitive murderer. Through a series of spectacular events that Jews still celebrate today, they gain their freedom and begin the long march home to Canaan, the land God originally promised to Abraham (another long, fascinating story--the Bible is full of them). By now, Moses is nearing his own end. Like Jacob hundreds of years before, he has words he needs to share with the next generation. But these words are for an entire nation, not just an extended family. Those "last words" of Moses make up the book of Deuteronomy. Here in the 18th chapter, Moses promises that God will raise up "a prophet like me." Over the years, Israel came to understand that this wasn't referring to Joshua, Moses' immediate successor, or to any of the men or women who led Israel in years to come. It was another reference to the Blessed One Abraham was told of, the Lamb God would provide, the Lion of Judah who Jacob foresaw. Now we know something else about this promised deliverer: He will be a prophet.

What does that mean? Many people think "prophet" means "one who sees the future," as if God is promising a psychic friend who will tell us all how to avoid problems and succeed in life (Incidentally, do you ever wonder why people consult psychics? If they are psychic, shouldn't they call you instead? And when you call them, why do you have to tell them who you are? Shouldn't they already know? Anyone? Okay). Actually, a prophet is someone who delivers a message from God to the people. It's usually a word of warning. In other words, prophets tell you what you don't want to hear. Do you need someone like that in your life? When you are on the cusp of having a massive coronary, do you want your cardiologist to tell you everything's hunky-dory, or drag you forcibly into the surgical suite? When your best friend knows that your teenager feels alienated and is considering running away, should he tell you the truth, or keep it quiet to avoid rocking the boat? We need the truth. The anointed One God was sending would be a teller of uncomfortable truths. Thank God, He loves us enough to tell us what we don't want to hear. Whether or not we listen and heed His life-saving words is on us.

The Covenant

2 Samuel 7:1-17

God's original plan for Israel was that they would have no king or standing army. They would simply obey the Law God had given to them through Moses, and He would protect and provide for them. They would be the most blessed people on Earth, and when people observed this, they would say, "Surely there is a God in Israel!" But the people didn't like the plan. They wanted to be like other nations, with a king and an army they could see, instead of a God they couldn't. So they chose a king…and he was a disaster. In the midst of the reign of mad King Saul, God dispatched the prophet Samuel to the little village of Bethlehem to anoint a new king, a "man after God's own heart." That was David, the flawed warrior-poet who turned out to be Israel's greatest king, author of the Psalms and builder of a mighty nation. When he had finally become king over all Israel, David wanted to do something to thank God for His faithfulness in taking a lowly shepherd boy so obscure his own father forgot about him, and making him ruler over the people of God. He wanted to build a temple, a place to house the Ark of the Covenant, the gold box that carried the stone tablets of the Ten Commandments and reminded Israel of God's presence. Since the days of Moses, the Ark had been kept in a tent (The Tabernacle). Now that David had a house for himself, he wanted to build a house for God.

God had a better idea. Instead of David making a house for God, God would make a covenant for David. Most people today don't really understand this idea of covenant. We are used to contracts, in which both parties have obligations, and the contract is void if one party fails to live up to the terms. For example, if your employer stops paying you, you'll probably stop coming to work. But a covenant is different. In God's covenants, he says, "I will do my part no matter what you do. I know you will fail. I know you will disappoint me. But I will not fail to do what I have promised." God's love is unconditional. He is like a perfect parent, who doesn't always approve of His children's actions, who certainly doesn't endorse or subsidize their poor decisions, and who even disciplines them when necessary, but never, ever stops being their Dad. The covenant God made with David said that his dynasty would reign forever. If you read the rest of Israel's history, you know that some of David's descendants were good, just men, and others were the worst kind of scoundrels, unfit to lead a gang of thugs, much less the people of God. Yet the people understood that God's promise to David wasn't just for himself and his family; it was for the nation. The Promised One would be a son of David. That term "Son of David" became very important as a title for the Messiah. It led many to believe that He would be a sort of "super-David," who would do all the things David did (produce military victories, especially), only magnified. But God had something far, far better in mind. That seems to be the pattern with Him.

Anointed One

Psalm 2

Music can be a powerful thing. I have heard thousands of sermons in my life, and I've long forgotten most of them (including ones I preached). But I still remember the lyrics to songs I heard when I was a kid. Music has a particular magic; if you hear a song from your past, it can take you back to the moment in time when that song was important: riding in the passenger seat of your best friend's car on a summer day, impatiently counting the hours until the end of school, awkwardly slow-dancing with the cute girl from Algebra class. You can tell a lot about people from the songs they sing. When my daughter became a teenager, she would play her music for me in the car. Sometimes, I would play the songs I had listened to in my teens. Frequently, I was embarrassed to find out the songs I listened to back then weren't as good as I remembered them. Sometimes, I realized a song I loved in those days had lyrics that were, well, less innocent than I recalled.

The songs of the Jews were called Psalms. They were meant to be used in worship. Our worship songs today tend to be catchy, happy little tunes. But the Psalms were all over the map; some were incredibly long (Psalm 119 is the longest), while others were just a few lines. Many praised God, but others cried out to Him for justice. The Psalms were honest songs from a people whose relationship with God could be raw at times. David himself, an accomplished musician, is believed to have written many of the Psalms, including this one. There are two things I want you to notice about this Psalm: One, it marks the first time the term "Anointed One" is used. It could simply refer to the King of Israel in the face of hostile nations. But the people of God came to believe it meant the Leader who God had promised, and they took that term, Anointed One, *Mashiach* (Messiah) in Hebrew, and began to pray for Him to arrive. The other thing to notice is that the Anointed One is referred to as the Son of God in verses 7 and 12, the first time that term is used in Scripture. Now we know something else about this promised deliverer. And in closing, ask yourself: What do the songs I listen to say about me?

God of the Runt

Micah 5:1-5

Pierre Salinger was press secretary for John F Kennedy. One day, they were traveling in Air Force One and hit some turbulence. Salinger was understandably shaken and said, "I wonder what the newspapers would say if this plane went down." The President quipped, "Well, your name would be on the front page of every newspaper in the world, Pierre…in very small type." In today's reading, Micah foresees the coming of the Anointed One. Verse 4 refers to Him as a shepherd, a motif often found in Scripture (Jacob, Moses, David and many other notable biblical figures were shepherds). In contrast to the others, this shepherd will tend a human flock. And verse 5 says "this one will be our peace." As we will soon see, Isaiah would call the Messiah "The Prince of Peace." But what sort of peace would He bring? Most significantly, Micah's prophecy tells us the actual place the Messiah would be born: Bethlehem. Micah calls Bethlehem "Ephrathah," which was its ancient name, and refers to it as "too little to be among the clans of Judah." Only he doesn't use the normal Hebrew word for "little,' which would only be a reference to size. No, he uses the uncommon word *tsair,* which specifically means "insignificant." This tells us that in those days, when people were discussing the regions of Israel, they didn't even mention Bethlehem. Jerusalem? Now that was a city. And if you wanted to talk outside Israel, there was Rome, Athens, and dozens of other picture-postcard cities filled with beauty, culture, money and power. Those were the places for a world Savior to be born, not an insignificant speck like Bethlehem. If you mentioned Bethlehem at all, it was in very small type.

What was God up to, in choosing to bring the long-awaited hero into the world in such a humble place? I believe it fits a consistent pattern: God is a God of grace. That means Yahweh is, was and always shall be the God of the runt, spiritually speaking. He favors those who are well aware of their own failures. Notice how God, throughout history, steered big events into this tiny town, one his own prophet Micah called "insignificant." Bethlehem was the place where Rachel died, and her tomb was a destination for pilgrims. It was also the hometown of David, Israel's greatest king. Now his Messiah would be born there, guaranteeing that village's place in history. Throughout Scripture, God chooses the runt of the litter to be His champions: He chose Moses, an old man with a murder rap, to deliver His people. He chose Gideon, an admitted coward, to lead the greatest military upset in history. Samson had self-control issues and bad taste in women. Jacob was known to be a con man. Joseph came from a dysfunctional family. Deborah? Well who's going to let a woman lead them into battle? Josiah was too young. Abraham was too old. Elijah was too doggone hairy. Because He is a God of grace, insignificance is actually a strength in His eyes.

A God Who Redeems our Mistakes

Isaiah 9:1

The early part of the book of Isaiah, including chapter 9, was written when a man named Ahaz was king of Judah. Ahaz was a godless man, even though his father and grandfather had been faithful followers of Yahweh. But now, he was in trouble. He was desperate enough to have an audience with Isaiah, the prophet who had advised his father and grandfather. His problem was that two nations had formed a coalition and were threatening to invade Judah, a tiny nation with very little military strength or political power. Isaiah told him, "Don't worry about this. God is on your side. He will rescue you from these armies. They will not defeat you." Ahaz had a problem. God Almighty told him how to handle it. All Ahaz had to do was trust in God like his forefathers had. But Ahaz wouldn't do it. Instead, he gathered all the gold he could scrape up in his kingdom and paid the empire of Assyria to fight on his side. Assyria was the dominant power in the Middle East at the time. They were ruthless and barbaric. Hiring the Assyrians to fight in a small, regional war like this was like setting a live cougar loose in your house to deal with an infestation of mice. Yes, it will probably get rid of the mice, but then you'll have an even bigger problem on your hands. In the end, the spiritual fallout from Ahaz's decision was devastating to him personally and to the people of God.

Like Ahaz, we've all had times when we knew the right thing to do, and have chosen not to do it. And we've paid the price. For all of us who have failed, Isaiah 9 is a message of hope. Isaiah writes this during a time of national disgrace, and he's saying, "God isn't through with us. He still has a plan. We'll have another chance to do the right thing." Chapter 9 points to a time centuries in the future when God's Messiah would come. Their problems would have a solution. Isaiah was writing to prepare them for this, so that, when the Messiah arrived, God's people would make a better decision than the one they'd made in his generation. When God first established Israel, it was divided into twelve sections, according to the twelve tribes of Israel. Zebulun and Naphtali, mentioned in v. 1, had the northernmost territories. So when Assyria invaded, they were the first to be conquered. People of that time figured they must have deserved it. Later on, that was known as the region of Galilee, since it was right on the coast of the Sea of Galilee. Even long after the invaders were gone, Israelites looked down on people from Galilee. They chose to live way up there in the North, instead of close to Jerusalem where the temple was, so they must not be as righteous. They were seen as a little bit backward, too--the rednecks of Israel. Galilee was the last place anyone expected a Messiah to come from. Yet God had a plan for redeeming this region, and through them, His people. When He's in charge, our mistakes never have the last word in our lives.

The Joy-Bringer

Isaiah 9:2-3

Notice two things about these verses: First, they are in the past tense, even though they're talking about something that will happen in the future. That's how certain God was that this would happen. Notice also the two metaphors in v. 3. When the Messiah comes, it will be like harvest time. In an agricultural society, harvest is the best time of year. The work is done, now it's time to rest and enjoy the rewards! Often, there would be celebrations at harvest, and rightly so. The other metaphor says Messiah's coming will be like when we've won a battle. Everyone is full of relief (that we survived) and exhilaration (at having won). You congratulate each other and start dividing up the spoils. The Messiah will bring that kind of joy. In these prophecies, the Anointed One is often spoken of in nationalistic or religious terms; He will put Israel back on the map, and He will bring glory to God. But here, Isaiah shows us a way this Promised Hero will affect each of us personally: He will bring us joy.

Let's admit that joy isn't a characteristic we often associate with the devoutly religious. I once had a friend describe evangelical Christians this way: "People who always seem angry, mostly because they think someone, somewhere might be having fun." Yet if God created the world, that means He also created happiness, joy, and pleasure. He chose to make delicious food, laughter, and that feeling you get in the pit of your stomach when you jump from a high place into a pool of water…and let's not forget about sex. God made that, too, and according to Scripture, expects us to enjoy it with our spouse. Yet joy means more than just taking advantage of good circumstances. Recently, I had lunch with a young man who is planning to enter full-time ministry. This past year, he contracted a disease that attacks nerves in his face. Every day, there's a better than average chance he'll have soul-crushing pain; there is no cure. Yet he is one of the most joy-filled people I've ever met. God's Messiah came, in part, to bring that kind of joy to all people...a joy that transcends our circumstances. If you don't have that kind of joy, perhaps it would be wise to ask Him to show you why.

The Liberating Hero

Isaiah 9:4-5

When Isaiah mentions "the day of Midian's defeat," he's talking about a famous story in Israel's history: the day Gideon and 300 men armed only with torches and trumpets defeated the Midianites, an army so large it couldn't be counted (Judges 6-8). Until that day, God's people had been under the brutal occupation of Midian. They were so oppressed, they couldn't even plant and harvest. Whenever they did, the enemy would swoop in and steal it all. Suddenly, unbelievably, Midian was defeated. Suddenly, a family could escape the cave they'd been living in and make a real living for themselves. Imagine the people joyfully making bonfires of the clothes the enemy soldiers had left behind, laughing as they broke the enemy spears over their knees, rejoicing and singing songs at their new-found freedom. That's what God promises it will be like when the Messiah comes.

But think about what that would cost. When God chose to intervene in Israel's problems (which were very much of Israel's own making), they became His problems. In most similar situations, we choose not to get involved. Here's a scenario. You have a friend who you suspect is being abused by her husband or boyfriend. One day, she comes to you, bruised, bleeding and with fear in her eyes. She says, "This time, if I go back home, I'm afraid he might actually kill me. But I don't have any place to go." You have a choice. You can say, "I can't intervene. You brought this upon yourself; you need to find a solution." After all, if you take her into your home, if you call the police, you have instantly put yourself in danger. What if he comes looking for her? What if he gets there before the police do? Even if that doesn't happen, what about when he gets out of jail? Won't he come after you? But if you do nothing, you're not a true friend. You can't say you love your friend and stay uninvolved. This was the dilemma faced by a God who claimed to love His people: How could He see them in their sin and suffering, their lostness and slavery, and not get involved? He couldn't; and He wouldn't. Thank God.

What's in a Name?

Isaiah 9:6

This verse is familiar to many today; when we read it, we picture holly-and-ivy-bedecked Christmas cards and hear strains of Handel's *Messiah.* Of course, Isaiah had very different thoughts when he wrote this prophecy down. He was looking forward to the birth of a child who would change the world forever, the Messiah his people--and all people--needed. In verse six, he dwells on the names this baby will be called. In our culture, we name children after relatives, after celebrities, and after fictional characters. Some names are chosen because we like the way they sound. And some names seem to be formed from a losing hand of Scrabble. But in biblical times, names always meant something. They revealed character. A parent would name a child based on his hopes for that child, or what he was feeling when they were born. If the child's character turned out to be different from his name, they would change the name to fit his character. For instance, there was a man in 1 Samuel named Nabal, which means "fool." I doubt his parents gave him that name. Given all that, when God calls Himself by a particular name in Scripture, we know it's meaningful. He is trying to tell us something specific and important about Himself. So we will stay on this verse for the next four readings.

Wonderful Counselor: The word wonderful means something that is so extraordinary that it inspires awe in the hearts of all who encounter it (Literally "full of wonder"). The word counselor refers to a person who has more understanding, wisdom and insight than you do and who helps you make the right decisions. People these days pay tremendous amounts of money to people to give them counsel, to make their lives better. We pay accountants, lawyers, personal trainers, consultants. There are plenty of counselors out there, but God was promising a Wonderful Counselor; One whose counsel is never self-serving, who is always right, and who is always free of charge. A friend who will show us how to be the people we were created to be, to live in a way that is eternally significant.

If you have ever been to a football game, you have learned that there is one incontrovertible fact of life: Most men believe they are smarter than the man who coaches their favorite football team (I realize women are into football as well, but I haven't seen this delusion manifest itself in the female gender…yet). I once played on a team in which our quarterback's dad was convinced he knew more than the coach of our team. During games, he would often call his son over to the stands so that he could give him instructions. Problem was, these instructions were often in competition with, or even contrary to, the instructions our coach was giving him. In one of our games, during a key moment, there was a timeout. The team huddled together on the sideline around our coach, who was running through the strategy. Meanwhile, the quarterback's dad was yelling to him from the stands. I saw our coach literally grab the quarterback by the facemask and pull his face toward his own and hold it there until their eyes met. It was as if he was saying, "Listen, kid. If we are going to win, there can only be one head coach on this team." There are all sorts of counselors out there. We can listen to our friends, to popular culture, even our own common sense. But when we say, "God has given me a Wonderful Counselor. From now on, He's the one I listen to," that's when abundant life begins.

Mighty God

Isaiah 9:6

Isaiah was the first to comprehend a revolutionary truth: the Messiah would be more than a man. He would be God in human flesh. When Isaiah calls Him "Mighty God", he is talking about His power to do mighty things. He created everything that exists with a few spoken words. He created a nation from the offspring of a 100-year old man. He led that nation--Israel--out of bondage in Egypt, in the process overthrowing the greatest military power in the world and producing awe-inspiring plagues and miracles. He empowered heroes like Gideon, Deborah, and Samson to accomplish things that made them the subjects of campfire tales. He drafted a forgotten boy from the shepherd field, enabled him to slay a giant, and made him a King. He made His people a light to the world and refused to let them die, even though they were smaller and weaker than most nations; even though they were often faithless and turned their backs on Him. We are talking here about a mighty God, a God who can indeed do the impossible. And now He would live among us, walk in our shoes, suffer alongside us…and save us all.

Someone might say, "That's all well and good, but I've never seen God do anything like that in my life." Some might say God doesn't do miracles like that anymore. But God hasn't changed; we have. I say there are two likely reasons why we don't often see God as mighty today. One is because we don't do anything that requires faith. We never step out where it's dangerous; we never take any risks for the sake of righteousness and justice, and so we don't need to trust Him. The other reason I believe we don't see miracles anymore is that we don't believe in the power of prayer. If we did, then we'd pray more. We would set aside time each day to seek His face. We would gather in greater numbers in our churches, not to be seen or to be entertained or uplifted, but to storm the gates of Heaven, asking for help. We would come together in individual homes and over lunch at restaurants and just spend time before the Mighty God. We would realize that's the only way to save marriages, to rescue families, to see the sick healed and the lost saved and our communities transformed…to see His Kingdom come, His will be done on Earth as it is in Heaven. Is He your Mighty God? Then pray.

Everlasting Father

Isaiah 9:6

Have you ever wondered why some people don't believe in God? Professor Paul Vitz of New York University did. Atheism is such an unusual thing in humanity; all but a tiny minority of people across generations and cultures believe in some concept of a god. As a psychologist, Dr. Vitz wanted to know what led a person to reject what nearly the whole world believes to be true: that we are not alone in the universe, that someone created us and cares for us. So he studied the most notable atheists over the last four centuries. He studied scientists, politicians, soldiers, authors, philosophers, and found that they had one thing in common: A defective relationship with their fathers. Either their fathers were absent from their lives, or their fathers had been a negative force. He put this in his book *Faith of the Fatherless; the Psychology of Atheism.* In a presentation at Colombia University, Dr. Vitz cited the following examples.

Sigmund Freud wrote that his father was a sexual pervert. Thomas Hobbes's father was an Anglican clergyman who got into a fight with another man in the churchyard and, subsequently, abandoned his family. Ludwig Feuerbach, at age 13, was abandoned by his father, who openly took up living with another woman in a different town. Voltaire fought constantly with his father, causing him later to reject his surname. Schopenhauer's father committed suicide when he was 16. Both Bertrand Russell and Nietzsche lost their fathers at the age of four. Sartre's father died before Sartre was born, and Camus was a year old when he lost his father. Hume also lost his father in early childhood. Hitler's father was a violent man who unmercifully beat Adolf, his mother, and even the family dog; he died when Adolf was 14. Stalin's father also administered brutal beatings to his son. That certainly doesn't mean all atheists have daddy issues. But it may indicate the spiritual and emotional crisis that can occur when a father is missing from the home, or when he fails to live up to his responsibilities. God was promising through Isaiah to be Father to the fatherless. The Jews thought of God as Father to their nation, but never saw Him as a Father to individual people in any personal way. But that, apparently, is exactly what God had in mind through His Messiah.

Prince of Peace

Isaiah 9:6

The Messiah would bring peace. But think about what that really means. It doesn't mean an absence of conflict and pain. Nowhere does God promise us a problem-free life this side of Heaven, no matter what popular preachers may be selling. But peace means security, stability, a sense of confidence and refusal to give in to fear in all circumstances. That is what God would bring into the world through His Messiah. He wants to bring peace to your relationships, so you can have harmony with your spouse, your kids, your co-workers, even those who are now your enemies. He wants to bring peace to your trials, to show you how to overcome even the worst circumstances. He wants to bring peace to your life, so that you can sleep easy and experience joy no matter what is going on. But first, He wants you to get right with Him. Your relationship with God is the key. That is where the peace begins. If you want peace in your life, first you must have peace with God.

A professor I had once said that former students occasionally write to him, confessing some awful thing they had done when they were taking his class. "I cheated on my final exam." "I plagiarized on a research paper." "I lied about a book I said I had read." One or two have been so plagued with guilt, they have even sent back their diplomas. To each one, the professor writes a letter, saying, "Ask God's forgiveness, not mine." There can be no peace in life until there is peace with God. His Messiah came to give us that peace. Search your heart today. Is there unconfessed sin in your life? Is there something you are holding back from Him? Give it over today to the Prince of Peace, and experience His forgiveness.

Unleashing Heaven

Isaiah 9:7

Verse 7 is less well-known than verse 6, but it's just as exciting. Isaiah pictures a new kind of King. He wouldn't claim power in a flash; instead, His government would gradually increase. And as it did, everywhere His reign spread, peace, justice and righteousness would follow. "Peace" is *shalom* in Hebrew, a word that means something like "the way things ought to be." As we've just seen, the Messiah would enable people to set things right with God, with their neighbors, and even with their inner selves. We hear the term "justice" and think of people who commit crimes being punished. But most of the time when that term is used by Biblical writers, they are talking about fairness for those who are weak and oppressed. In the Mosaic Law that was intended to serve as Israel's constitution, God made numerous provisions for the socially marginalized. For instance, harvesters were instructed to leave behind some crops so that the poor could "glean" food for themselves. Land that was taken in foreclosure was supposed to be returned to the original family and all debts cancelled in the Year of Jubilee, to be held twice every century. And God sternly warned His people that if they were not compassionate to the poor, the alien, the widow and the orphan, He would exact vengeance on their behalf. "Righteousness" means being conformed to the character of God, following His commands and living in a way that is pleasing to Him. When the Messiah came, He would somehow enable God's stumbling, bumbling people to lead lives of moral excellence. Following Him, they would stand blameless in the spectacular presence of a holy God, shining as lights to the world. It's striking how much Isaiah 9:7 sounds like a political campaign speech. God is saying, "Let me rule, and here's how your lives will change." But this was more than a politician promising an improved economy. This is the Creator and Ruler of the Universe saying, "Someday, Heaven is coming down to Earth. And nothing will ever be the same again." Has Heaven come down to your life?

The Power of Hope

Isaiah 9:7

Today, we often use the term "hope" to mean the same thing as "wish." As in, "I hope my girlfriend doesn't dump me," "I hope I don't lose my job in this round of layoffs," "I hope my team wins the championship." We don't have assurance; we just hope for a good outcome. In contrast, the Biblical concept of hope means certainty of something good that's coming. Hope is a kid marking the days until summer vacation. It's an older couple getting the guest room ready for a visit from their grandkids. It's the French Resistance surreptitiously spreading the word that the Allies are coming. When Isaiah said things like, *there will be no end...from that time on and forever...the zeal of the Lord Almighty will accomplish this,* he was spreading hope. The same God who created the Universe with spoken words will not be stopped. The Messiah will come.

Think about the most popular fairy tales and fantasy stories of our time: Star Wars, The Lord of the Rings, and Harry Potter. In all three, good triumphs over evil because there's a hero who sacrifices everything to face the forces of wickedness. In all three, life triumphs over death…there is even a note of resurrection. In all three, love never really dies. Harry can enjoy talking with his parents and Dumbledore, even though they've passed on. Luke Skywalker can do the same with Obi-Wan and Yoda. And Frodo sails off to the undying lands after he's destroyed the ring of power. Those aren't new themes; they have been in existence for as long as people have been telling stories. Two Oxford literature professors were talking one day about why fairy tales and fantasy literature are so popular. One was a devout Catholic, and the other was an atheist. They both agreed that such stories are popular because they tap into our most profound hopes for life. So the atheist professor said something like, "It's a shame none of those things is true." But the Christian professor, JRR Tolkien, who would one day write The Lord of the Rings, pointed out that he believed they *were* true. They had actually happened. God's Messiah was the hero who courageously faced evil. He died and rose again, and so death was swallowed up by life. He opened the way so that we could live forever, and see our loved ones again, so love never dies. And eventually, that other professor did become a believer too. It occurred to him that the reason we long for these things is that we were made to long for them. That hunger has a solution; we long for them because they are real. That professor's name was CS Lewis.

The In-Your-Face God

Isaiah 40:1-5

A few years ago, a major city built a new facility for homeless alcoholics. But this wasn't a treatment facility. The residents of the home could drink all they want, as long as they paid their rent and didn't do anything violent. The director of the program said he was saving taxpayers millions of dollars a year in treatment costs by keeping 75 formerly homeless drunks off the streets. But think about what he was saying: "These people can't really change. And intervention is hard; it costs too much money and takes too long. Let's just keep them away from the rest of us." That's what God could've said about you and me. We may not all be alcoholics, but we're all sinners, nonetheless. And a voice inside us says, "That's okay. Just accept that about yourself. In fact, learn to celebrate your own choices!" But one thing God will never do is let us be happy in our brokenness. Rather than give us a safe place to live any way we choose, God will continually invade our lives, constantly intervening to steer us back in the right direction. The choice of whether to repent or not is up to us, but God doesn't give up the fight.

God's intervention is the reason for the book of Isaiah, in fact. The Israelites were captives in the land of Babylon because God refused to let them be happy in their sin. Now, He inspires Isaiah to write, *Comfort, my people...her hard service is completed, and her sins are paid for.* But they don't get off scot-free, to be released into the same situation. No, that would be like taking a homeless alcoholic off the streets for a night and then sending him right back out in the morning, without any help for permanent change. No, God says *the glory of the Lord will be revealed.* He's talking about the coming of the Messiah. Israel will return to their homeland, then someday in the future, they would have God among them in a new way. When God's people read these words, their imaginations ran wild. Some pictured a return of the time of Moses, with spectacular judgments upon Israel's enemies. Others imagined it would be like the days of Solomon, when wealth was so prevalent in the land, chunks of silver were as common as gravel stones. No one seemed to think the coming of God's Messiah would demand any sacrifice from them. It is in our nature to be resistant to God's intervention. We want Him to keep a safe distance from us. Just deposit a check into my account twice a month, Lord, and heal me when I'm sick. Don't call me...I'll call you. But He doesn't operate that way. He wants to live alongside us, share life with us, show us the way. Are you living life with Him...or holding Him at arm's length?

Remember the Plan

Isaiah 49:1-7

I read this recently: "At my age, 'getting lucky' means walking into a room and remembering what I came there for." I was disappointed to read that; not because I found it inappropriate in some way, but because it hit home. I want to believe I'm too young to find that funny! But I did, nevertheless. All of us, old and young, get distracted from the main thing. God's people certainly do.

Isaiah is an interesting book. It is thought by most Bible scholars to be two books in one. The first book (Isaiah 1-39) was written just before a huge calamity occurred: God's people would be conquered by the empire of Babylon; their capital city, Jerusalem, would be sacked, the temple would be burned, and many of the people themselves would spend the rest of their lives in exile in a foreign land. Isaiah 1-39 predicted this and prepared the people for it. Chapters 40-66 seem to have been written during and after this exile, detailing God's plans for His people in the future; reassuring them that, even though they had lost their homes and nation, He wasn't done with them yet. Why did God allow such a catastrophe to happen to His chosen people? Because they lost sight of their purpose. Remember the promise God gave to Abraham when He formed the Jewish race: *I will bless those who bless you, and will curse those who treat you with contempt, and all peoples on earth will be blessed through you* (Genesis 12:3). God's plan was for His people to be different, to worship one God and live according to His will. As they did this, He would bless them with incredible joy and security, and all nations would see and be drawn to Him. But rather than be distinct, God's people yearned to be like other nations (1 Samuel 8:20, Ezekiel 20:32). They emulated the religious, moral and sexual practices of the nations around them. They saw their chosen status as an entitlement, not as the responsibility that it was. They believed that they were superior to other peoples, not indebted to them.

In this second half of Isaiah, the prophet often talks about The Servant. In verse six, it seems that He is using this term to refer to Israel. He's reminding them of their purpose. "Remember why I brought you here? It wasn't for your own sake. It was to be a light to other nations. That plan hasn't changed, even though you've lost your nation and temple. You're still part of my plan." It was only much, much later that the people of God came to realize that The Servant in Isaiah wasn't just referring to them, but also to His Messiah, who would come from His people. Much, much later, they would see that this Messiah wasn't just meant to save them; He was meant to save the world. What is your purpose in life? Why did God create you? How do you fit into His plan to redeem the world? We can easily get distracted from His plan, for the same reasons Israel did: A self-absorbed mentality, envying what others have. The good news is that our failures are not fatal. He still wants to include you in His eternity-changing plans. Today is as good a day as any to tell Him you're ready for a course correction.

Wait…what?

Isaiah 52:13-53:3

When Isaiah wrote about the Servant of God, most readers assumed he was referring to Israel. But if so, what did the Lord mean by these words? They expected painful consequences when they diverted from God's plan, but these words seem to indicate the Lord's Servant was destined for suffering. What could Isaiah be talking about? This Servant would be born unremarkable and unattractive. He would live a life of sorrow and suffering, feeling the rejection and hatred of the world. He would even apparently be beaten beyond recognition (verse 14). Yet somehow, through His suffering, the Servant would change the world (verse 15). The same scholars who were confused at these words must have also been perplexed by a much older writing--Psalm 22. Take a moment to read that Psalm. The narrator describes himself as "a worm, not a man," hated by everyone. He is rejected by God, and executed by men. His hands and feet are pierced, and his tormentors gamble for his clothing as he hangs, dying in humiliation and pain. Note that these words were written centuries before the dark heart of man invented crucifixion. One has to wonder what those original readers of these two texts thought they were about. It would be a long, long time before they found out.

Many presentations of Christianity these days present a shallow pop-therapy designed to help us fulfill our dreams, with the assumption that God only wants His children to be blissfully happy. Scripture tells us another story. Sometimes, God's plans for His children include pain. Circumstances that seem irredeemably negative can, in fact, be redemptive in themselves. But we cannot see our circumstances that way if we think of God as a cosmic wish-fulfiller, the Fairy Godmother who exists to "bibbety-bobbety-boo" us into the life we've always wanted. Someone once told me, "American Christians usually pray for God to lift the burden of suffering from their shoulders. Third-world Christians pray for stronger shoulders to bear the burden of suffering." Which is more like you?

Sacrifice

Isaiah 53:4-6

In 1981, the movie *Chariots of Fire*, about two Olympic Athletes in 1924, won the Academy Award for Best Picture. One of those athletes, Eric Liddell, was depicted in the film having to choose between his track career and his calling as a missionary. In real life, Liddell went on to serve as a missionary in China after winning the gold medal. He stayed even after the Japanese invaded China in the late 1930s. He would die in a Japanese prison camp in 1943. In 2008, just before the Beijing Olympics, Chinese officials revealed that Liddell had been offered freedom as part of a prisoner exchange, but he allowed a pregnant woman to go in his place. At the same time Liddell was imprisoned, Father Maximillian Kolbe, a Polish Franciscan, was making his own sacrifice. He had been sent to Auschwitz in 1941. In July of that year, three prisoners escaped, and the Nazi guards declared that ten prisoners would die by starvation as a result. One of the men who was chosen to starve cried out, "My wife! My children!" Kolbe offered to take his place. According to the camp janitor, every day Kolbe led the other nine people chosen to starve in prayer. He was the last of them to die.

We love hearing stories of that kind of courage, whether it's a soldier diving on a grenade to protect the other men in his foxhole, a firefighter rushing into a building on the verge of collapse, or a teacher who steps between a crazed shooter and her students. Science struggles to explain this willingness to die for others. Shouldn't our evolutionary instinct be to preserve our own lives at all cost? Or are we hard-wired to protect the lives of others, in order to perpetuate our species? If so, why are such sacrifices so rare that they are remarkable? If this is our instinct, why are most of us selfish and cowardly, while these rare humans perform heroic acts of self-sacrifice for others, even strangers? In the verses we read today, we learn that the Servant of God's suffering will not simply result in greater character for Himself. Instead, His pain will benefit everyone else, somehow. His wounds will bring us healing. His punishment will result in our forgiveness. He will do no wrong and be destroyed; we will do no right, and be exonerated…because of His death. Maybe we love stories of self-sacrifice because they remind us of the God who made us.

A Different Kind of Hero

Isaiah 53:7-9

By the time Isaiah was writing these words, the people of God were hungry for a hero. They had seen the collapse of their nation and the failure of their political and religious leaders. Yet somehow, against all the odds, they were still intact as an ethnic group, still speaking Hebrew, still worshipping Yahweh, when other, larger nations had vanished from the world scene. They knew someday a great Champion would arise and rescue them. They knew He would be a King, the Son of David, their greatest leader. They must have struggled to reconcile those images of a triumphant warrior with Isaiah's words about The Servant. This man would die like a sacrificial lamb at Passover, not even fighting back against His enemies. Other details, like His being buried with a rich man, seem obvious to us thousands of years after their fulfillment (see Matthew 27:57-60), but would have been impossible for those first readers to understand. If we can fault God's people for anything, it is that they were so confident that they knew how to interpret the prophecies of Isaiah and others…and in the end, they were so very wrong in what they expected the Messiah to be.

Sadly, we don't often see humility in God's people today, either. Preachers tell their congregations, "The Lord told me what our church should do. Either you agree with me, or you're standing in His way." Politicians, trying to curry the evangelical vote, claim that God Himself commanded them to run for office. Believers baptize their own social and political views, and argue for them with the inflammatory passion of medieval priests exposing heresy…even when the Scriptures don't address the issues they're so sure of. I'm not saying we should lack the courage of our convictions. There is plenty in the Bible that is clearly and unambiguously stated, and as God's people, we should stand by those truths with our very lives. But we must be people of humility: Not claiming certainty where the Bible doesn't offer it. We should be willing to listen to people of opposing viewpoints, and respect them even when we disagree. And when it comes to the Bible's vision of the future, we should be honest enough to say, "Here's what I think God's word means. We'll see in the end."

The Scapegoat

Isaiah 53:10-12

In times of great stress, innocent people are sometimes blamed for the ills of a larger group. After a crushing loss, sports fans will often blame their defeat on the referee who blew a call, the outfielder who dropped an easy pop fly, or the kicker who shanked a chip-shot field goal. Rock fans for decades have blamed Yoko Ono for the breakup of the Beatles, even after Paul McCartney dismissed that idea in a 2010 interview. Much more darkly, Germans in the 1930s, economically and emotionally devastated after their loss in World War I, gravitated toward a leader who told them their troubles were the fault of the Jews. We call this process "scapegoating." Interestingly, the idea--and the term--come from the Bible. In Leviticus 16, God tells the Israelites to observe an annual Day of Atonement (Yom Kippur), in which the entire community would fast, and the High Priest would symbolically place the sins of the people on the head of a goat, who then would be driven from the camp to wander in the desert until dead. This unfortunate animal was called *azazel* in Hebrew, a term the first English translators rendered as "scapegoat."

That is exactly what The Servant is. He is our scapegoat. Only we aren't the ones depicted as ostracizing Him in Isaiah 53; God Himself is. This makes God seem monstrous, until you read these last three verses. Not only will the Servant's pain and death result in salvation for many, but He Himself will experience vindication. *He will see His offspring; He will prolong His days…*does verse 10 mean that He will live after His atoning death? Verse 12 even speaks of Him achieving something like a military victory; not through battle, but through His own self-sacrifice. While we humans are quick to find people to blame for our problems, The Servant of God would take the guilt of humanity upon Himself.

Champion of the Underdog

Isaiah 61

In this chapter, we've briefly touched on a few of the prophetic texts that foretold the coming of God's Messiah. There are so many others we could have considered. But we'll end with this one. If you go back to the establishment of Israel, it is obvious God wanted this to be a unique nation. Not only would they have no King or standing army, they would have no generational poverty, either (see Deuteronomy 15:4). In the Law handed down to Moses, God commanded His people to care for the orphan, the widow and the immigrant. One example was in Leviticus 25: Every 50 years, the people were to celebrate a Year of Jubilee. In that special year, all debts would be cancelled. Slaves would be set free. People who had sold their lands to pay off debts would get them back, free of charge. It was like an automatic "reset" for the society. What a wonderful idea! But here's the problem: As far as we can tell, Israel never even tried it. There is no historical record of the nation ever celebrating a Jubilee. Isaiah 61 says that when the Messiah comes, He will make up for this oversight. His very life will be a Jubilee. Because of Him, the folks on the bottom will finally catch a break. Our world has its golden rule: He who has the gold makes the rules. And those rules insure that, no matter what happens in the markets, the halls of government or the court of public opinion, those with money, power and popularity can turn things to their advantage. The rich always get richer. The powerful always come out on top. The beautiful always win first place. But look who Isaiah 61 says the Messiah will be associated with: The poor, the brokenhearted, the captive, the prisoner.

One day, centuries after this was written, a young rabbi and purported miracle-worker, only just beginning to gain notoriety, visited His hometown congregation on the Sabbath day. They quickly invited Him to be their guest speaker. He took the scroll of the prophet Isaiah and chose this chapter as His text. After He read aloud these words of God's justice flipping the scales of society, He audaciously told the people who had known Him for His entire life, "These words were written about me. I am the fulfillment of this prophecy" (my paraphrase of Luke 4:16-30). The home folks weren't fond of this interpretation. In fact, they tried to kill Him. But it didn't stop Him…

Chapter 3: His Early life

Matthew 1:1

I love biographies. I enjoy studying the lives of men and women who changed the world. But when we get to the life of Jesus, who I believe is the greatest, most influential person in human history, there is no standard biography. Four early authors wrote down their versions of His life's story, and those accounts form the first four books of our New Testament. But they lack much of the information we tend to look for in a biography. We know very little about His parents, even less about His childhood, and absolutely nothing about His teens and twenties. The very first of these accounts begins with, of all things, a dry recitation of Jesus' male ancestors. I can only imagine what a modern-day editor would have told Matthew about starting a book that way. But Matthew, Mark, Luke and John weren't trying to write a bestseller. They weren't even trying to tell the life story of a great man. They were writing Gospels. The word means "good news." Imagine you live in an ancient city that is under attack from an invading army. You enfold yourself around your children, huddled in your home, praying for God to spare your lives as the awful sounds of war rage just beyond your walls. At last, there is quiet. Then you hear the voice of a herald, calling everyone to the city gates. You leave your home, trembling. Will we all be captured or enslaved? You arrive in the midst of the gathering throng, and see that the herald is one of your own city's soldiers. He shouts, "Victory! We have turned back the invaders! By God's grace, we are free!" That, my friends, is good news. And that is what these books are meant to be. Everything that is written in the first four books of the New Testament was intended not to give us historical information about Jesus of Nazareth, but to tell us why He is the best thing that ever happened.

So, it must be asked, why begin such a story with a genealogy, as Matthew does? To many who read this in the first century, this was extremely pertinent information. Matthew wanted to prove that the Jesus He knew was the promised Messiah. In order to do that, He had to show that Jesus was descended from Abraham, Isaac and Jacob (v. 2), from the tribe of Judah (v. 3) and a son of David (v. 6). But he also included some unexpected names on the list: Four women who most of us would have preferred to keep secret. In those days, women weren't often listed in genealogies; in a patriarchal society, no one really cared who your mother was. Women were only mentioned if they had some status that made you look good; the daughter of a king or high priest, for instance. These four women were quite the opposite; they were more like the skeletons in Jesus' closet. Why did Matthew mention them? We'll look at their stories next.

Notes From a Scandal

Matthew 1:3, Genesis 38

Tamar is the first of the four women mentioned. Her story is the kind of tale many people are surprised to find in the Bible. We need to understand certain things in order for this story to have its full impact: 1) The historical texts of the Bible (like Genesis) describe what happened--often in gritty, earthy detail. But that description does not mean an endorsement of the activities presented. 2) A custom known as Levirate marriage is in view here. When a woman was widowed without a son, the next closest male relative was to marry her and provide her with a son, so that her deceased husband's line would not disappear, and so that she could be provided for in her old age. God endorsed this practice; in the Law of Israel, any man who was unwilling to perform his duty as next of kin was to be publicly shamed. This custom is at the heart of the story of Ruth, which we'll consider next. 3) The writer does not endorse Tamar's actions, but in a society where an unmarried woman had no ability to provide for herself, we can understand why desperation would drive her to this. Judah, on the other hand, comes off as a mean-spirited hypocrite.

The climax of the story occurs when Tamar produces Judah's seal, cord and staff—the equivalent of having his credit card, social security card, and driver's license. It's like one of those movies where the villain is someone prominent, like a governor or a CEO. And just when it seems he'll get away with his crimes, the hero produces a recording of the villain admitting to his evil plans. We know what usually happens in those movies. The villain is enraged, and tries to eliminate the hero and the incriminating evidence. There is every reason to expect that Judah will respond that way, too. He could have killed Tamar with his own two hands. In that culture, who would have stood up for the rights of a twice-widowed, unwed mother accused of prostitution? At the very least, he could have said, "She tricked me! I'm the victim here!" As a prominent man, the culture would have been more forgiving to him than to her. But instead, an amazing thing happens. Judah's heart is changed. He confesses his sin. Not just the sin of soliciting a prostitute, but more importantly, the sin of not taking care of his daughter-in-law. Not only that, he absolves Tamar. He says, "She was right, and I was wrong."

There is absolutely no human explanation for why a man so coldhearted he would condemn his own daughter-in-law to be burned alive would suddenly vindicate her and confess his own sin. The only explanation is this: There is a God in the world whose full-time occupation is the transformation of human beings. And the only possible reason Matthew would include a reference to a scandal in the life of Jesus' patriarch is that he wanted us to know that Jesus came for the forgotten, condemned Tamars of this world, as well as for the self-righteous, respectable Judahs. Both are equally broken; both need a God who can save.

The Not-so-Pretty Woman

Joshua 2

Rahab is an even more unlikely woman to appear in the genealogy of the Messiah (Matthew 1:5). First, she was a pagan foreigner. To a people as obsessed with racial purity as the First Century Jews, that fact alone should have disqualified her. She was also a prostitute. We need to discard our Hollywood notions of the world's oldest profession. It was and is a terrible life, and most women who find themselves there do so because they have no alternative. Speaking of Hollywood, lest we picture Rahab as Julia Roberts in biblical garb, her name means, essentially, "Big Mama." This story precedes a tale familiar to every kid who ever sat in a Sunday School class: The fall of the walls of Jericho. But before those walls fell, two Israelite spies found themselves trapped inside. Think of the opportunity Rahab had when they showed up inside her brothel. If she turned these two in, she'd be a hero. Maybe she'd receive a big reward from the king that would set her up for life, and could say goodbye to all those loathsome clients of hers and live a comfortable life. But instead, she did a totally unexpected thing. She risked her life to save theirs. With that one act of kindness for two strangers, Rahab not only gave up her chance to be a national hero, she made herself a traitor to her own people. Why would she do such a thing? As she explained in verses 8-13, Rahab decided to place her life in the hands of the God of Israel. "Your God IS God," she said. This is a genuine conversion story. Rahab went on to marry a Jewish man, and along with being listed in Matthew 1, she also is mentioned in Hebrews 11 and James 2 as an example of great faith, alongside heroes like Abraham and Moses. God didn't just turn Rahab's life around; He took her from a miserable, cursed existence to being one of the greatest heroes in biblical history. Guess what? He's still the same God today; the God of the (very) extreme makeover.

Ruth's Redeemer

Ruth 1

A long, long time ago, the town fathers of the Italian city of Florence decided that a city as great as theirs needed a great work of art in front of the City Hall. Someone suggested a massive statue of a biblical character; something to convey strength and majesty. So they commissioned the great artist Agostino di Duccio for the project. Duccio ordered a 19 foot slab of white marble for his statue. The workers at the quarry dutifully cut out the rock. But somewhere in the process of moving the slab from the quarry to Duccio's studio, the slab was dropped, and a long, deep crack formed on one side. The artist was indignant. He demanded a new piece of rock. The town fathers refused; the expense was simply too great. Neither side would budge. And so the cracked slab of white marble lay there on its side in Florence for 38 years, an expensive pile of junk and a constant source of embarrassment to the town. Many of us can identify with that rock. We started out life with great plans and dreams. Somewhere along the way, those dreams shattered. Now what are we left with? A life that doesn't seem to amount to much. A feeling of general uselessness. And no one seems to care. Like Naomi in this story, we went out full and came back empty.

Ruth is the third woman listed in Jesus' genealogy (Matthew 1:5). Her presence there is a surprise because of her race; Moabites like Ruth were banned from worshipping in the assembly of Israel. Yet here is this young Moabite woman, yearning to be true to her mother-in-law and the God of Israel. Two widowed women had very little way of making a living in that culture, so Ruth decided to "glean" barley. Essentially, she would follow the reapers in a barley field and pick up whatever they happened to drop. It was hard, unrewarding work. But the owner of the field, a man named Boaz, saw her hard work and was smitten. One of my favorite love stories of all time then ensues (You can read the story in a few minutes; I encourage you to do so). Here's the key point: Boaz happened to be a distant relative of Naomi's deceased husband. That brought Levirate marriage (remember the story of Tamar) into play. In fulfilling this responsibility and rescuing Ruth and Naomi from starvation, Boaz is called a "kinsman-redeemer." The kicker to the story is that Boaz and Ruth eventually have a son, grandsons, and great-grandsons, among whom is David, the King.

Remember that hunk of white marble in Florence? After nearly four decades, the town fathers decided to give another artist a shot. They approached the son of a local official. He was only 26, but what he lacked in experience, he made up for in zeal and ambition. He took that cracked marble and worked on it for three years, non-stop. When the work was completed, the results were far greater than anyone had dared hope. People from all over Europe came to Florence to see this 14-foot marble statue of David relaxing after having defeated Goliath. And to this day, Michelangelo's "David" is one of the most beloved art works in the world. The Messiah descended from Ruth and David would be a master at redeeming lost causes.

The Other Woman

2 Samuel 11

Notice how Matthew lists the fourth woman in Jesus' genealogy in Matthew 1:6. He doesn't call her by name, but instead "the wife of Uriah." Her name was Bathsheba. Not only was she the wife of another man, that man was one of David's thirty "mighty men," his most loyal and fierce soldiers. As was her father, Eliam (also called Ammiel). Her grandfather, Ahithopel, was one of David's most trusted advisors. Today, her name is synonymous with the word "seductress." She is known to many as the woman who brought down a kingdom. But when I read 2 Samuel 11, I see a king making the biggest mistake of his life; surrounded by sycophants, none of whom confronted him when he was about to commit an unspeakable crime against one of his best men, against his own family, and against God Himself. If you read on to chapter 12, you see that God--through his prophet Nathan--has harsh words for David, but none for Bathsheba. I wonder how much choice she had in the matter. David was king; could a woman tell him no and expect to live? Even if she was a willing participant in this tryst, shouldn't we follow the lead of Scripture and hold David (the one who initiated the affair) more responsible?

Whether Bathsheba was just another victim of this tawdry incident, or the femme fatale we've made her out to be, here is the undeniable truth: David had many sons. But God chose the son of Bathsheba and David over his more legitimate half-brothers to be Israel's next king. Not only did He jump the line of succession, He made this boy the wisest man who ever lived, and the king who presided over Israel's golden age. Centuries later, the Messiah descended from Bathsheba would often encounter women of poor reputation. He was different from the lust-fueled men who used them, or the self-righteous men who judged them. He reflected instead the feelings of the God who had sent Him.

Let it Be

Luke 1:26-38

There is a fifth woman in the genealogy of Jesus: His mother, Mary of Nazareth. One can make the argument that Mary is the most famous woman in human history. Today, her image graces cathedrals around the world. Desperate believers cry out to her for relief. Some claim to have been visited by her. The Beatles even sang about her. But let's get beyond the iconic Mary of religion, and look at the true woman as presented by Scripture, a humble village girl engaged to a carpenter. None of the Gospel writers ever imply that she was anything more than that; certainly not sinless, perpetually virginal (Mark 6 and Matthew 16 both mention that Jesus had younger brothers and sisters), or someone God intended for us to pray to. But this one story tells us quite a bit about her character.

Most scholars assume that Mary was very young at this point, since Jewish girls in this time were married in their early teens. If you know any Middle-School girls, it makes Mary's composure and courage even more remarkable. Picture such a child, engaged in morning chores--milking, weaving, preparing bread--when at once the room is filled with blinding light, and she is stunned speechless by the sight of a creature beyond her imaginings. Up to this point, hers has been a small life: learning from her mother how to be a good wife to her intended; wondering what it will be like on her wedding night; dreaming of raising children of her own; praying they would grow up to obey God and bring honor to the family. It turns out God's plans for her are much larger…and more disturbing. She will be the mother of the Messiah. But this will only happen after an unintended, extramarital pregnancy which she'll never be able to adequately explain. In typical fashion, God does not give her details or make promises. He simply tells her His plans. When He did this with mighty Moses, the great deliverer tried to negotiate his way out of the job. When He did this with Gideon, the poor man insisted God had the wrong guy. In contrast to these great heroes of her people, Mary says words that have inspired millions: *I am the Lord's servant; let it be unto me according to your word.* Mary was never meant to be an icon; but she is a reminder that the one irreplaceable factor in a life of significance is simple obedience to God.

Joseph's Dilemma

Matthew 1:18-25

If we know little about Mary, we know even less about Joseph. We know that he was a carpenter from Nazareth, the son of Jacob of the tribe of Judah, and we know He bore no blood relationship to Jesus. Wouldn't you love to know more? What was Mary and Joseph's relationship before this? Were they in love, or just two people dutifully prepared to obey their parents in this arranged marriage? How did Mary tell Joseph about her pregnancy? What was his initial reaction? These are all mysteries to us, the subject of fanciful narratives by novelists and preachers who wish they were novelists. But what we do see of Joseph here shows us that his character was the equal of his intended bride's. God chose a good man to be the stepfather of His Son.

He was recognized in his hometown as a righteous man, which was a technical term (I am indebted to a sermon by John Ortberg entitled "Recognizing Divine Interruptions" for this insight). It meant that Joseph was conspicuous in obeying the Torah. He didn't work on the Sabbath, kept the Kosher diet, attended synagogue and all the festivals and fasts, and was above-board in all of his business dealings. To be a righteous man, or a *tsaddiq* in Hebrew, was a highly desired status. Israelite parents would have wished this for their sons, like American parents hope their children will attend an Ivy League School, or earn a football scholarship, or sing on Broadway. For Joseph, this meant he was held in high esteem by his community. People were glad to do business with him, because he was a tsaddiq. In the future, he could look forward to being one of the elders who sat at the town gates, respected for his wisdom and integrity, helping lead the town. But all that was in jeopardy with Mary's announcement. Under Jewish law, he had the right to publicly expose her, even to have her stoned by the village for her sin. The fact that he didn't do this says something about Joseph's character. He simply wanted a legal break of the engagement--a necessity in that culture--to preserve his status as a *tsaddiq*. Even after the visit from the angel, Joseph still had a dilemma: To obey God meant losing his status. In many ways, he had even more to lose than Mary. Everyone would assume he had gotten her pregnant out of wedlock. No one would ever look at him the same again. His business, his prospects for the future, would be altered forever if he followed God's plan and stuck by his fiancé. I imagine his thoughts: "When she told me she'd been visited by an angel, I thought she was crazy. Now I'm wondering if I am."

Joseph obeyed God. That doesn't seem terribly romantic to us; there is no indication of Joseph's personal feelings about this. But (and again, thanks to Ortberg for this idea) years later, after Joseph was long dead, his firstborn Son would tell a crowd that in order to be truly righteous, one must be even more righteous than the religious leaders of Israel. Jesus meant that our righteousness must be more than simply following rules; we have to change our plans to fit God's plans for us, even when it's hard. He might have thought to Himself, "Because one man had that kind of righteousness, I had a father."

Offspring of a Virgin's Womb

Matthew 1:21-23

The virgin birth of Jesus is a controversial subject. Skeptics laugh at its physical implausibility. However, if a Being exists who could create all living matter from scratch, creating a baby without sexual intercourse wouldn't be a difficult undertaking. Many believers accept the virgin birth's veracity, but have no idea why it is important. In our text, Matthew references the original prophecy, delivered by Isaiah the prophet to Ahaz, the weak-willed, faithless king of Judah. It was a time of national crisis, but Isaiah brought good news: "Just trust in God, Ahaz. Turn over a new leaf. Watch how I can vanquish your enemies." In Isaiah 7, the prophet foretold a sign: The virgin would conceive and give birth to a child named Immanuel, (God with us). Yet when the angel spoke to Joseph, he commanded him to name the child Jesus. This is a Greek name (*Iesus*) corresponding to the Hebrew name *Yeshua* (Joshua). It was an old, heroic Hebrew name, meaning "God's salvation." Immanuel, which the prophet had mentioned, was apparently meant to be the child's true identity, not His proper name.

So what does this virgin birth mean to us? It is the first indication that <u>this child would be no ordinary baby</u>. True, He was born of a woman just like the rest of us. He had a body that had physical limitations. We can be sure that He caught the flu, He got hungry, He experienced exhaustion—just like us. He had emotions like ours, and felt things like anger, frustration, discouragement and temptation. But at the same time, the virgin birth says He was more than a man. No earthly man was His father. He was conceived by the Holy Spirit. God Himself formed that child inside Mary's womb, and that makes Him unique. It is also a reminder that <u>God can do anything</u>. Back in Isaiah 7, Ahaz ignored the prophet's encouragement. He refused to change His ways, even with the promise of God's deliverance from Israel's enemies. But centuries later, two obscure young Israelites, Mary and Joseph, would choose to believe in the impossible. And whereas the wishy-washy King is known only to Bible scholars and trivia buffs, Mary and Joseph went on to be the most significant parents in history.

The Firebrand

Luke 1:5-25, 57-66

Once again, God chooses an old, childless couple. Zechariah the priest is in the Holy of Holies, offering the incense. Because of the number of Israel's priests, this is almost certainly the only time in his life he will have this honor. Picture an old man holding the flame in trembling hands. What a time for God to startle him! Once Zechariah recovers from his shock, doubts begin to form. This man has served God faithfully for a lifetime; He is one of Israel's spiritual leaders. Yet young, untrained Mary has far more faith than he. So he spends his wife's entire pregnancy mute. When his speech returns, upon the birth of his son, his first words are a spontaneous, majestic hymn of praise to God. And what about Elizabeth? Imagine the joy she must have felt for those forty weeks!

And what sort of child was this? We know him today as John the Baptist. His life's purpose was to prepare the people for the Messiah (v. 16). The prophets had foretold his coming (Isaiah 40:3, Malachi 3:1). But no one was prepared for the kind of ministry he would have. The adult John shocked the Israelite establishment, dressing in camel skins and living alone in the desert. His preaching was confrontational; he called his audiences "brood of vipers" and told them they were all deserving of God's wrath. He even persuaded them to be baptized. Baptism had traditionally been a ceremony for Gentiles seeking to convert to Judaism. Essentially, being baptized was a repudiation of one's past life, and a promise to live differently. In telling Jews to be baptized, John was implying that their Jewishness wasn't enough. They needed something else. Yet his inflammatory rhetoric took Israel by storm. People by the thousands flocked to the desert to hear him, and to be baptized. He eventually was beheaded for publicly pointing out King Herod's personal infidelity. Jesus called him the greatest of men (Matthew 11:11). John followed a long tradition of men and women whose devotion to God made them seem weird and even dangerous to a world that thinks alienation from its Creator is normal. He serves as a reminder: God loves us absolutely, but sometimes before we can experience that love, we have to face uncomfortable truths about ourselves. God loves us enough to tell us that truth. Hallelujah.

Battle Cry of the Virgin

Luke 1:39-56

It doesn't take much imagination to guess why Mary made this hasty trip to the Judean hill country to visit her cousin, Elizabeth. Mary's unplanned pregnancy had thrown her world into turmoil. Who could she talk to? Surely Elizabeth, wife of a priest and herself the recipient of an unexpected pregnancy, would understand and could offer some words of wisdom. But as it turns out, it was Mary who blessed Elizabeth, not the other way around. The Spirit of God revealed to Elizabeth that she was looking not merely at her young cousin, but at the mother of the Messiah. He revealed the same thing, apparently, to the unborn John the Baptist, who did a prenatal backflip in celebration. And then Mary broke out in song. Was this a song she had been working on since the day Gabriel told her about this child? That's my guess. It bears some similarity to a song sung by Hannah, yet another childless woman whose womb was miraculously opened (1 Samuel 1-2). Perhaps Mary took Hannah's song and put her own spin on the words. The Church has traditionally called Mary's song The Magnificat, for the Latin word for "magnify." It is almost certainly the first Christian hymn ever composed.

For a song written by a meek peasant girl, The Magnificat is surprisingly militant. It speaks of God as one who is consistently on the side of the marginalized, the bullied, the forgotten. He humiliates the proud, dethrones dictators, and snatches away the ill-gotten gains of the one-percenters. These are dangerous words, words that would mean death if spoken in the earshot of the powerful. Little wonder that The Magnificat is memorized and treasured by Christians in poor nations, and often ignored by American believers. We prefer to believe in a God who approves of our priorities, blesses our efforts at personal fulfillment, and hates all the same people we do. But the Virgin was right: When God shows up, He declares war on our complacent self-centeredness. It is as just a war as has ever been waged.

A Less-than-Ideal Birth

Luke 2:1-7

We've romanticized the birth of Jesus to a ridiculous extent. When we think of it, most of us picture a children's play at church; Joseph is wearing his dad's bathrobe. Mary is holding a baby doll. Or we picture Christmas cards or front yard Nativity sets, with cartoon animals staring peacefully at a perfect, sleeping baby. The whole thing is sanitized, serene, adorable. I am certain that's not how it was. I imagine a Joseph who was equal parts enraged ("Why a census? Why now? And how can there be no room in any inn in town?") and terrified (After all, he had never been intimate with Mary. Now he would be assisting her in giving birth). I think Mary must have regretted accompanying Joseph with every bump on the nearly 80 mile journey from Nazareth to Bethlehem. I would be willing to bet she wished her mother was there, especially when the contractions began. I have witnessed childbirth, twice. It is neither quiet nor clean. I'm sure Mary experienced pain like nothing she had ever imagined. I am sure the process took much longer than she thought it would. I am sure Joseph saw and heard things that he was in no way prepared for. The emergence of that baby, slick with amniotic fluid and blood, face deformed by the treacherous journey through the birth canal, screaming his head off, must have struck both mother and father with more relief than joy.

There are many misconceptions about the birth of Jesus. We picture it in a stable; the word is never in the story. It says she laid Him in a manger. An animal feed trough was as likely to have been found in a cave or an open field as a stable. Luke doesn't mention animals, either. If they were there, it would introduce not pastoral beauty, but a range of awful sounds and smells to the scene. When my wife and I were expecting our first child, we toured local hospitals, choosing the one we thought offered the most comfortable rooms. We interviewed obstetricians, selecting the one who filled us with the most confidence. When the big day came, our bags were packed with everything we would need. Both sets of parents were there. Several friends dropped in as well. The doctor and nurses were professionally smooth. At my insistence, my wife received an epidural injection when the pain became acute. Within hours after our daughter's birth, she was being examined by a skilled pediatrician. God has infinitely more resources than I. Yet when His only Son was being born into the world, He chose squalid conditions, an inexperienced birthing coach, and no reception or medical care. What a strange way to welcome history's most important baby into the world!

Why Shepherds?

Luke 2:8-20

Luke gives us no description of these men, but he didn't need to. The word "shepherd" was enough for the people of Luke's day to know what kind of men these were. Shepherding was a despised profession. Shepherding was what you did when you couldn't get work of any other kind. It wasn't the kind of job you went home from at night; shepherds lived with the sheep. In most cases, it was far better to be a slave than a shepherd. So we can imagine what kind of men these shepherds were. Picture them around the fire that night. Imagine the roughest, most desperate and anti-social men you have ever known, and you're likely to be close. A few probably had criminal records. Perhaps some had skin diseases or other physical afflictions that made them ritually unclean in Jewish society. Others could have been the product of mixed-race unions, which was considered a sin in those times. Still others (we can assume) had made bad lifestyle choices that resulted in their families and hometowns disowning them. In other words, these men had nothing in the world except the sheep and each other. We can picture them sitting around the fire, a very rough and motley crew, swapping dirty jokes, complaining about their lot in life, or simply sleeping.

And suddenly there was a flash of unapproachable light like nothing they knew was possible. The shepherds were terrified out of their wits. And then the news…the Savior is born. Even men as rough and unreligious as these knew that the God of the Jews had promised a Messiah. Whether they believed or not before, they were believers now.

I imagine that they were surprised when they found the child. Not just surprised at the humble surroundings of the manger, or the youthfulness and poverty of his parents, or even at the fact that the Son of God looked like a normal newborn. I believe they were surprised to find that they were the only ones there. Because think of what that means: God could have told anyone that night about the birth of His Son. He could have told everyone. Instead, He told only them. The last people on earth you would expect to find on God's speed dial got the one and only call from heaven to witness the most important birth in human history. Why? Of all the details of the Christmas story, this is perhaps the most puzzling. The answer is simple, and I believe it was clear to the shepherds that night. The child would be the Messiah of the forgotten man, the rejected woman, the neglected child. He loves everyone and can save anyone, but He is particularly interested in the poor, the blind, the lame, and most of all, the "sinner." Ironically, the very people who are least likely today to be found in a church dedicated to the name of Jesus were the only people invited by His Father to the birth.

With Angelic Host Proclaim

Luke 2:13-14

Can you imagine what this must have been like? Perhaps you picture be-winged Rubenesque naked infants, like we see in certain old-fashioned Christmas cards. Maybe you see chiseled physiques soaring effortlessly, like something out of a superhero movie. But a quick survey of scriptural encounters between humans and angels reveals that, well, we probably CAN'T imagine what it was like:

- An angel appears to Manoah and his wife, foretelling the birth of Samson (Judges 13).
- Isaiah sees the Lord and His angels in the temple (Isaiah 6).
- Ezekiel comes face to face with the glory of God (Ezekiel 1).
- An angel reveals to Daniel the things to come (Daniel 10).
- Gabriel visits Zechariah and Mary before the births of John the Baptist and Jesus (Luke 1).

If you take the time to read these stories, you will see a couple of things they tell us about angelic encounters. First, **when people encounter angels, it is a terrifying experience**. In these stories, courageous, devout prophets tremble in fear and faint dead away when they come into contact with these supernatural beings. They have spent their lives telling people about the God no one can see; when they first encounter His messengers, they are so filled with a sense of their sinfulness, they can't even stand, much less speak. When ordinary people see angels, their response is similar. Manoah is sure he will die. The angels have to tell Zechariah, Mary and the shepherds "don't be afraid." Second, **when people encounter angels, they struggle afterwards to describe what they saw.** Daniel saw a man made of lightning, flame and red-hot metal. Ezekiel saw creatures that defied any earthly analogy. Isaiah called them seraphim, without really telling us what such beings looked like (aside from their six wings). Samson's mother simply called the angel "awesome," in the truest non-Keanu-Reeves form of that word. And Zechariah was struck mute by his brush with the supernatural. Angels can also take on a non-threatening, human form (Genesis 18, Hebrews 13:2). But based on the fact that the angel had to say "Don't be afraid," I'm guessing these angels were in their "defying human description" manifestation.

And why were they there? The Greek word for angel simply means "messenger." They had come to make sure someone knew who this child was, and what He came to do. "Peace on earth and goodwill to men" is the way their message reads in the old King James Version, which sounds as bland and non-specific as a political slogan. But in the Greek, the actual meaning is more like "peace and goodwill to those who accept Him." Some would accept this child; many, perhaps most, would not.

Simeon's Joy

Luke 2:21-35

For centuries, God's people looked for their Deliverer, the Messiah. Godly men and women followed the Lord, prayed diligently, but died having never seen the fulfillment of their prayers. That makes the story of Simeon all the more poignant. Simeon understood--in a way no one else at the time did--who this baby was and why He had come. In v. 30, Simeon says, *For my eyes have seen your salvation, which you have prepared in the sight of all nations; a light for revelation to the Gentiles, and the glory of your people Israel.* In Simeon's words were truths that no one had really grasped yet. He said that Jesus was born to be salvation to "all nations," not just the Jews. "The nations" or *goyim* in Hebrew, was how the Jews referred to non-Jews. It was often used as a slur. What Simeon was saying was in essence, "It doesn't matter anymore who your parents were, or what color your skin is, or what kind of life you have lived until now. Now that the Messiah is here, you can be saved!" In v. 34, Simeon begins to prophesy to Mary and Joseph. *This child is destined to cause the falling and rising of many in Israel, and to be a sign that will be spoken against.* The word rise is a Greek term (*anastasis*) that actually means "resurrection." Jesus came to bring new life to many. The term fall is a Greek word (*ptosin*) that means more than just a setback. It means destruction. In other words, this child would bring new life to some, and destruction to others. Isaiah 8:14 calls Jesus the stone of stumbling. Jesus Himself would go on to say in Matthew 10:34, *I did not come to bring peace on earth, but a sword. For I came to set a man against his father, and a daughter against her mother, and a daughter in law against her mother in law. And a man's enemies will be the members of his own household.*

Simeon's prophesy ends with a stunning prediction for Mary. I picture him fixing the young mother with a terrifying gaze as he says, *And a sword will pierce your own soul, too.* We, looking back through the eyes of history, know that he is prophesying the death of Jesus on the cross, which Mary would one day witness personally. At that moment Simeon must have been the only person on earth who understood just what it was that the Messiah came to do. He wasn't born to be a general, a politician or a philosopher. He was born to die a sacrificial, atoning death. Only Simeon understood that, and that means only Simeon grasped the fullness of God's love for us. He doesn't just tolerate us; He yearns for us. He doesn't just accept us; He pursues us. His love is great enough that He was willing to pay the ultimate sacrifice to reconcile us to Himself. I believe that's why Simeon said to God, "Now I can die in peace." Now that He grasped the depths of God's love, the old man needed nothing more out of life.

Wise Men and Herod

Matthew 2:1-8

There are so many fascinating details about this story. Let's look at the main characters, starting with the wise men. Their technical name, *magi,* indicated that they practiced an ancient art somewhat similar to astrology, guiding kings and other powerful men with the wisdom they acquired through their diligent study of the stars and other fields of knowledge. In today's terms, they were professional scholars (By the way, there is nothing in Scripture to indicate that there were three of them, or that they were kings, despite what the popular Christmas song says). These magi came to King Herod's court looking for a King whose birth was announced in the stars.

King Herod was brutal, paranoid, and the consummate political survivor. He had originally backed Mark Antony to rule Rome after the death of Julius Caesar, but when Antony was defeated by Octavian (who became Caesar Augustus), he somehow convinced the new emperor he was on his side all along. Given the Kingship of all Israel by Rome, he was hated by most Jews, but mitigated their criticism by funding a massive renovation of the Temple. Herod "the Great" (as he so humbly dubbed himself) was a monstrously egotistical ruler, so his first thought was to use the magi as unwitting spies to help him locate this potential usurper. The people of Jerusalem were disturbed, we presume, because any shakeup in the status quo was trouble they didn't need. If their king was upset, it meant heads were going to roll (often literally, in Herod's case). It didn't matter if the arrival of these magi indicated the fulfillment of prophecy; if it meant short-term trouble for the people, they didn't like it either.

And what of the religious leaders in Jerusalem? When Herod asked them where the Messiah was to be born, they quickly and accurately quoted Micah's prophecy that predicted Bethlehem as the birthplace. But why didn't they follow that knowledge to Bethlehem? That may be one of the biggest mysteries of this story. Like the magi, the scribes and teachers were eminent scholars. It seems that, unlike the magi, their knowledge of spiritual things was confined to their heads…it hadn't penetrated their hearts. And so the most important event in human history--the entry of God's Son into the world--occurred, and those charged with leading people to God stayed away, while foreigners with no previous connection to God came great distances to be there. It would be much the same when the child grew up.

Overjoyed

Matthew 2:9-12

As we've already seen, there are plenty of misconceptions regarding the wise men. They weren't kings; there probably weren't three of them. There is an ancient text that says they were trying to smoke a rubber cigar, but scholars disagree on its veracity (that was a joke, by the way). Here's another misconception: Nothing in the text indicates that this happened on the night Jesus was born. Forget the Nativity scenes and children's Christmas programs that show shepherds, wise men and adorable animals crowded into a stable; v. 11 says they found the Christ child in a house. There is reason to believe He may have been as old as two by this time. The ultimate irony of this story is that the Messiah who God's people had sought for years was finally here, and none of them came to visit. A group of pagan scholars, however, did. Many have attempted to find significance in the gifts of the magi: The gold represents Christ's kingship, incense represents His willingness to be sacrificed, myrrh (a spice sometimes mixed with wine to form a bitter, stupefying drink) represents His coming death. But these are all simply speculations on our part. I suspect the wise men themselves simply wanted to bring the best products of their nation, as a tribute to one they believed was sent from God. I also suspect that these gifts came in quite handy for a poor couple far from home, who would soon need to get out of the country quickly (more on that next).

Here is what I want to focus on: Verse 10 says that when they found the place where Jesus was, they were overjoyed. The Greek term Matthew used here is somewhat redundant. It literally says, "they rejoiced with exceeding great joy." Picture a kid on Christmas morning, a young couple deeply in love, a football player lifting the Super Bowl trophy...none of these compare to the joy these scholars felt when they found the Son of God. Honestly, religion doesn't tend to bring joy or laughter to most people. But this child Jesus certainly did. Later He would say that His teachings were *so that my joy may be in you and your joy may be complete* (John 15:11). You may associate Christianity with disapproving, scowling old women and red-faced, ranting preachers. But the originator of the faith was a man who brought joy with Him wherever He went...even as an infant. And the wise men would only be the first of multitudes of Gentiles who would find their ultimate joy in the Jewish Messiah.

The Flight to Egypt

Matthew 2:13-15, 19-23

Not only was Jesus born in dubious circumstances, His early life was anything but stable. According to Luke, eight days after His birth, Joseph and Mary took their son to Jerusalem to be dedicated at the temple, where they met old Simeon. They then took their Son home to Nazareth. Matthew says that by the time the wise men arrived, the family was back in Bethlehem. Why had they left Mary's hometown to live in Joseph's ancestral village? We don't know (Perhaps the busybodies of Nazareth chased them and their "illegitimate child" away). When the vision from God came to Joseph, it was urgent enough that the young family left in the middle of the night. They might have sold the magi's gold to finance their journey. It was 75 miles from Bethlehem to the border with Egypt, no easy trip by camel, especially with a young child. And now, Joseph and Mary had their third home in their son's brief life. The Son of God, who had been born homeless, was now a refugee in Africa.

Scholars believe the family didn't stay there long; in fact, Jesus probably was too young even to remember the trip (although Coptic Christians in Egypt believe the family stayed in several different places in their country; they consider these to be holy sites). It's likely that His earliest memories were of growing up in Nazareth, a town so obscure, it wasn't even mentioned in the Old Testament. Jews of Jesus' day didn't see it as prime real estate, either (John 1:46). The "prophet" Matthew mentions in verse 15 is Hosea, who was actually talking about Israel. Just as God took Israel from out of Egypt in the time of the Exodus, Jesus and His family would come back to their home country. I wonder if any of this biblical symbolism occurred to Joseph and Mary. I suspect it didn't. I imagine this young couple instead was simply surprised that, rather than bringing them blessings and prosperity, saying yes to raising God's Son had brought them troubles aplenty. I imagine them wishing at times the angel had never visited, that God had placed this burden on someone else. It's important to remember that the Bible never promises a blissful existence to those who obey God; in fact, the opposite is often true, at least in the short term. Jesus understood this well. Later, He would tell prospective followers to consider the cost before they said yes to His invitation (Luke 14:28-33).

Slaughter of the Innocents

Matthew 2:16-18

Here's a part of the Christmas story you won't hear about in carols, or see depicted in Christmas cards or pageants. I've never heard a sermon on this passage of Scripture. Some doubt its veracity; they note that Josephus, the eminent Jewish historian of this era, did not mention this atrocity. But that's not surprising. Herod was notorious for killing anyone who might be a threat to his power, including three of his own sons (which prompted one contemporary wag to note, "It's better to be Herod's pig than his son." At least, as a Jew, he wouldn't have killed the pig). Bethlehem was a village of only a few hundred at that time. The number of infants killed during this awful event surely numbered less than a dozen; merely another in a long, bloody list of tragedies for a murderous, paranoid old tyrant.

The real question here is why? If God is all-knowing and all-powerful, couldn't He have intervened as soldiers ripped infants away from their screaming mothers? In 2012, when twenty small children and six teachers were shot to death at Sandy Hook Elementary in Connecticut just before Christmas, many people struggled with the same question. Couldn't he have prevented a mentally disturbed young man from coldly destroying so much innocent life? Logic dictates the answer: Absolutely. Skeptics, therefore, say that means one of two awful truths: Either God isn't as powerful and wise as we think He is, or He is powerful and wise…but simply doesn't care. Yet the very existence of the Christ child tells me that this is false thinking. If God didn't care about human suffering, He wouldn't have sent His Son on a mission of redemption. As difficult as it may be for us to accept this, God has a plan for solving the world's suffering that we cannot fully comprehend. If He is a transcendent God, we would not expect to completely understand His ways, any more than a five-year old understands why his mother makes him get a flu shot every Fall. Far from being uncaring or impotent, God has a plan to address suffering and evil that will bring all of creation to its knees in awe. And it begins with this child.

What Was He Like as a Child?

Luke 2:41-50

After the infancy narratives of Matthew and Luke, we know almost nothing about the childhood of Jesus. In the second century, an unknown author tried to fill that gap with a book called *The Infancy Gospel of Thomas* (scholars agree that the book was written at least a hundred years too late for it to have been penned by the disciple Thomas). In it, the young Jesus seems more like Damian from *The Omen* than a budding Savior. He crafts sparrows out of clay, then when Joseph reprimands him for doing so on the Sabbath day, brings them to life. When a child in Nazareth runs into him, he strikes the child dead; when the child's parents complain, he afflicts them with blindness. The early church rejected this account, with good reason. In all of Scripture, the text you just read is the only story of Jesus between His infancy and the start of His ministry. While it's certainly not as sensational as those fictitious stories in *Thomas,* it is a revealing account nonetheless. The fact that Mary and Joseph took the pilgrimage from their home in Nazareth to Jerusalem every year at Passover shows that they were observant Jews. By the most direct route, it was a 75-mile journey, which would have taken at least three days. Some scholars believe Luke 2 records the first time Jesus would have gone on this journey, in preparation for His Bar Mitzvah the next year.

Any parent can imagine the panic Mary and Joseph must have felt at losing their oldest child in a huge city like Jerusalem. The fact that He was missing three days must have heightened their terror and their sense of guilt. I can't blame them for asking young Jesus, "Why have you treated us like this?" Their question reveals something else, besides their confusion. Apparently, Jesus had never done anything like this before. Apparently, up to this point, Jesus had been like every other little boy. Which leads to my big question: When did Jesus realize He was NOT like every other boy? When did He come to understand His true identity and destiny? Scripture doesn't tell us, but maybe it was that week during Passover. Seeing the Holy City (perhaps for the first time), quizzing the ancient teachers and supplying the answers they couldn't (wouldn't you give anything to have been there?), maybe it dawned on Him who His true Father was, and what He had sent Jesus to do. If so, that had to be a terrifying realization for a twelve-year-old boy. Here is what we know for certain: That boy would visit the temple again during a Passover two decades later…and the teachers that day would treat Him very differently.

His Ordinary Life

Luke 2:51-52

Jesus began His ministry when He was about thirty (Luke 3:23). We have absolutely no stories of His life between the ages of twelve and thirty; some call these the "lost years" of Jesus. What was He doing during this time? He apparently worked as a carpenter (Mark 6:3), perhaps in an apprenticeship to His father (Matthew 13:55). The large, growing city of Sepphoris was nearby; Joseph and Jesus may have worked on new building projects there instead of in the sleepy village of Nazareth. We also know, from Luke 2:51, that Jesus lived in obedience to His parents. This must have been difficult at times; if ever there was a teenager who actually WAS smarter than His parents, it was Jesus! But in submitting to them, He was fulfilling the fifth commandment (Exodus 20:12). Verse 52 says He *grew in wisdom and stature, and in favor with God and men.* This tells us that Jesus developed, emotionally, intellectually and spiritually, as His body grew physically…just like other children. His moment in the temple at age twelve notwithstanding, He wasn't the ultimate child prodigy, an old sage in a kid's body. He must have seemed, in many ways, completely normal to His parents and neighbors.

The big question is why Jesus waited until age thirty to begin preaching, performing miracles, and preparing disciples for the work of God's Kingdom? There are two good theories. One speculates that Joseph died when Jesus was a young teenager, since he is not mentioned again after the episode in the temple (in Mark 6, Jesus' brothers, sisters and mother are mentioned, but not Joseph). Accordingly, Jesus would have had to stay home, providing for His mother and siblings until one of His brothers was old enough to take over the family business. The other theory notes that a Jewish priest was not allowed to perform His duties until age thirty, and speculates that Jesus knew He would not be received as a teacher before that age. Either way, the New Testament scholar William Barclay makes an excellent point: *If Jesus was to help men, he had to know how men lived. And because he spent these thirty years in Nazareth, he knew the problems of making a living, the haunting insecurity of the life of the working man, the ill-natured customer, the man who would not pay his debts. It is the glory of the incarnation that we face no problem of life and living which Jesus did not also face.*

An Unconventional Life

Mark 3:20-35

We jump ahead in the narrative, just for a brief moment, to see something heartbreaking: Jesus was (at least for a time) estranged from His own family. Think about it from the perspective of Jesus' brothers. A Jewish man of those times was supposed to get married, have children, and work a trade. The oldest son was supposed to take care of His widowed mother. Yet Jesus at thirty was unmarried, unemployed, and traveling the countryside with a group of vagabonds, angering the respectable civic and religious leaders and damaging the family name. Perhaps they had always slightly resented this strange oldest brother, who never seemed to do anything wrong. Certainly they didn't believe His claims about Himself (John 7:1-5). Now they heard the Nazarene gossips talking about how Joseph's son had lost his mind, or was perhaps possessed by a demon. "Poor Mary," they must have said. "I don't know what I'd do if some boy of mine acted that way." "I'm just glad his father didn't live to see this, rest his soul." Together, they convinced Mary, who must have had her own concerns ("Is this really what the Lord had in mind? The angel didn't say anything about our own leaders opposing Him. Maybe He just needs to come home.").

Now think about how it must have made Jesus feel. I am sure, like most men, He would have loved having a wife, children, and a stable, secure existence. Now, because He had answered the call of God, He felt that He no longer had a family at all. Later, He would say, *Do not suppose that I have come to bring peace to the earth. I did not come to bring peace, but a sword. For I have come to turn a man against his father, a daughter against her mother, a daughter-in-law against her mother-in-law— a man's enemies will be the members of his own household.* Jesus wasn't advocating the destruction of the nuclear family; that would contradict the very Scriptures He consistently affirmed. But He was saying that sometimes following the call of God is too radical for our loved ones to understand. Sometimes the cost of answering that call is more difficult than we can imagine. Certainly it was in His case.

The Unlikely Superstar

Matthew 3:1-12

We've talked already about the ministry of Zechariah and Elizabeth's son, who we know as John the Baptist. The most surprising thing about this cousin of Jesus (aside from his unusual attire and brash attitude toward religious leaders) was that a ministry based on telling the Jews--so proud of their chosen status before God--that they had to repent of their prior lives and essentially become new people in order to be acceptable to the Lord was so incredibly successful. Why would a self-consciously moral people receive such harsh teaching this way? Did they think He was the Messiah? True, this was a time of great Messianic expectation, but John made it explicitly clear that he was not the chosen One. He was there to prepare the way for Him. Why would people walk for miles into an arid wasteland to stand and listen to an opening act, particularly one who made them feel badly about themselves?

Seven and a half centuries before, the prophet Amos had predicted there would one day be "a famine for hearing the words of the Lord" in Israel (Amos 8:11-12). The very structure of our Bibles speaks to his prophetic accuracy. The period between the writing of Malachi (the last book of the Old Testament) and the birth of Jesus was around four hundred years. During that time, the rabbis were carefully preserving the Torah and writing voluminous commentaries that would become the modern-day Talmud. But there was no new revelation from God. When John showed up, people recognized in Him the true voice of the Lord. That is what they were hungry for, without even knowing it. As it happens, we're all like them. We don't realize we're starving until we taste what we were made to feast upon.

Celebrity Syndrome
John 3:22-30

If our long-dead ancestors were to time-travel to 21st century America, they would notice how obsessed we seem with celebrities. The term refers to people we celebrate; people we pay special attention to, talk about, listen to. There's even a documented psychological disorder called Celebrity Worship Syndrome. One published psychologist speculated that 1/3 of the population might be afflicted with this disorder. On the lower levels, it's pretty harmless. At the extreme level, you track the celebrity's movements. You truly believe there's a connection between you and him or her. You may even think your favorite celebrity is communicating with you through some sort of code; perhaps hidden messages in his movies or songs. In 1981, long before anyone coined the diagnosis Celebrity Worship Syndrome, John Hinkley Jr tried to kill President Reagan because he thought his favorite movie star, Jodie Foster, would be impressed by his actions. I think we can all see the evil in that. I would argue that every one of us has a problem with a very different form of celebrity worship. The person we most worship, are most obsessed with, love thinking and talking about, is ourselves.

John was different. Put yourself in John's position. You are the hottest topic on the lips of every Israelite. Everyone who is anyone wants to hear you preach; and they are so inspired by your preaching, they get baptized by the thousands in the river Jordan as a way of symbolizing the life change they desire. But now, most of the people who used to drink in your teachings everyday are leaving you. They are going to that new rabbi, Jesus. John's response to this is amazing. Notice that he makes a wedding analogy. Imagine a best man at a wedding who is determined to draw attention to himself. Instead of wearing the tuxedo the bride and groom picked out, he rents one that is loud and bright and distinct from the rest of the wedding party. During the ceremony, he makes loud comments and witty asides that he finds entertaining. And at the reception, he grabs the microphone and insists on singing a special song to the bride and groom. Would you say that's a good "best man?" No, the job of a wedding attendant is to make a big deal about the bride and groom. I was in a wedding once, when a groomsman pulled a practical joke on the groom at the wedding. He had the keys to the car that the bride and groom would use to drive to the airport, and he filled it to the top with hot-air popcorn. I'm sure he thought it would be hilarious, but when the groom found out—in front of everyone—he didn't find it funny at all. In fact, he was furious. It was one of the most awkward things I have ever witnessed. Now, when I do a wedding, I try to tell the groomsmen: "Today isn't about you. I know you are old friends, and you want to laugh and have a good time. There will be time for that later. Right now, your job is to make the bride and groom look good, and to make sure nothing happens that will mess up their special day." In other words, we are celebrating them.

John's point is that his job is to celebrate the bridegroom, who is Jesus. That is true humility. Frederica Matthews-Green said, "Every day, ego builds a cardboard fortress that humility has to tear down." John shows us the way.

Jesus is Baptized

Matthew 3:13-17

We jumped ahead in the story of Jesus' life. Now let's settle back into the timeline: Jesus, at thirty years of age (per Luke 3:23) left His home in Nazareth to begin His true life's work. He began with two very unorthodox decisions: He wandered into the Judean desert for a forty day fast, where Satan himself was waiting. But first, he visited his cousin John at the Jordan River, to be baptized by him. John's reaction was understandable. His baptism was a sign of repentance; those baptized were making a public statement of their own unworthiness and need of personal transformation. But John had known Jesus His entire life. He had recently called Him *the lamb of God, who takes away the sin of the world* (John 1:29), and said it so persuasively, one of his own followers left him to follow Jesus. Of all the people in all the world, John thought, Jesus of Nazareth is the last one who needs to reject His former life and become someone new. Jesus' response was enigmatic: *It is proper for us to do this to fulfill all righteousness.* What did He mean? Some believe that, since He came to identify with sinners, He had to be baptized as they were. At the very least, it meant, "This is what God wants me to do, even if it doesn't make sense from a human point of view."

As He came out of the water, a dove landed on Him, and a voice from Heaven said, *This is my Son whom I love; with Him I am well-pleased.* Matthew doesn't tell us how eyewitnesses reacted to seeing and hearing this; we can imagine how awe-inspiring it must have been. But no one understood what it all meant. Even John, later rotting in Herod's prison for the simple crime of calling out that despot's personal sins, eventually began to question Jesus (Matthew 11…see Jesus' surprising response to John's doubts). But to Jesus, this moment must have been incredibly meaningful. As far as we know, this was the first time God the Father had made personal, audible contact with Him in His earthly body. According to Scripture, the Father, Son and Holy Spirit had enjoyed blissful union for eternity, only to be interrupted for thirty years by the Son's incarnation. This could well have been the first time in thirty years Jesus had heard His Father's voice. It must have seemed as exhilarating as skydiving into a tornado, yet as comfortably familiar as a phone call from an old friend. He would need both that inspiration and that assurance for what was coming next.

Tempted

Luke 4:1-4

After thirty years of obscurity in Nazareth, Jesus was beginning His life's work. He started by being baptized at the Jordan, a spectacular event that included an audible endorsement from God the Father. Jesus then chose to retreat to the Judean wilderness for forty days of fasting. An enemy was waiting for Him there. According to Matthew's account, this was no accident: *Then Jesus was led by the Spirit into the desert to be tempted by the devil* (Matthew 4:1). The Spirit of God sent Jesus there for this express purpose. Perhaps this was a sort of "boot camp" to prepare Jesus spiritually and emotionally for the next three years of His life, when He would bear the weight of the world on His shoulders as no one ever had, or ever will. Some scholars see in this time an echo of the Old Testament story of Israel in that same wilderness, on their way to the Promised Land. They spent forty years in that desert, and ultimately failed. Jesus, in spending forty days there, would show that He could succeed where His people had fallen short. I have visited the area around the Dead Sea. It is desolate country, a place that would drive a lonely wanderer to desperate madness…if he managed to survive. Jesus was stuck there for over a month, with no food, and with no companionship save that of the most deceptive, hateful being in the universe. For Satan's part, this must have seemed like a plum opportunity. My friend Joe McKeever once wrote that Satan may not have known who Jesus was until that voice from Heaven announced Him as God's Son. Now that he knew, now that his ancient divine antagonist had encased Himself in frail human flesh, the devil would throw everything in his nefarious arsenal at Him.

The Gospels only list three specific temptations Jesus faced during that time, although we can assume there were hundreds of separate temptations over the course of forty days and nights. We will look at each of the three, starting with the temptation to turn stones into bread. Verse 2 seems like an almost-comical understatement: *He ate nothing in those days, and at the end of them, He was hungry.* Jesus answered each of the three temptations with a quote from Deuteronomy, Moses' last words to the people of Israel in the desert. This one was from Deuteronomy 8:3. What would have been so wrong with Him having something to eat? The temptation, I believe, was not simply to break His fast. It was to use His miraculous powers in a self-serving way. It's a common conversation starter: "If you could choose one superpower, what would it be?" It's fun to think about what life might be like with super strength, invisibility, foreknowledge, or the ability to fly. People worldwide would admire you; your enemies would cower before you; no one could stop you from taking whatever you wanted. Yet the Gospels tell of a man more powerful than any who has ever lived…and who never once used those powers to benefit Himself.

Rejecting the Easy Way

Luke 4:5-8

Christians sometimes say to me, "I know the Bible says Jesus was tempted. But that doesn't mean He *wanted* to sin, does it?" I tell them it means *precisely* that. Jesus was fully human. He had the same desires that you and I have. If He had not felt the desire to do something wrong, it wouldn't have been a temptation. Think of the first temptation: Don't you imagine a man who had been without food for forty days at least entertained the thought of producing bread for Himself? Of course He did. But this second temptation must have been far harder to resist.

Satan proposed a simple transaction: You worship me, and I give you the world. Jesus quoted Deuteronomy 6:13, a restating of the First Commandment, in rejecting the offer. There is no biblical indication Satan had the authority to offer Jesus--or anyone else--world power. But Jesus certainly could have claimed it by force. At the very least, the devil's offer planted that seed in His mind. He must have thought to Himself, "If I became King of the world, I could punish evil, abolish poverty, eradicate disease, and make this world a paradise...and trade in my impoverished existence for the comfort and adulation all men crave." Besides, Jesus knew the long, arduous road that lay ahead of Him, and the hellish way it would all end. This was an opportunity to skip all of that. Jesus would hear this same temptation again and again in the years to come, from His enemies (*Save yourself, if you're God's Son*) and His friends (*Never, Lord! This shall never happen to you*--speaking of the Cross). He had come to do more than rule humans; He had come to redeem them, and there was no shortcut, no easy way to accomplish that.

Testing God

Luke 4:9-12

Satan tried a new tactic: He quoted Scripture himself. In the words of AW Tozer, "The devil is a better theologian than any of us, and is a devil still." Picture the two of them standing at the top of the temple in Jerusalem, which sat at the highest point of the city, towering over the Kidron Valley. Satan leans over and whispers, "Psalm 91 says God will rescue you from harm. Why not make Him prove it?" Jesus' answer was from Deuteronomy 6:16. In that verse, Moses was reminding the Israelites of a dark day in their history, when they complained against God because of the lack of water in their journey across the desert. Their request was, in essence, "If God loves us so much, let Him prove it. Produce water right here in the desert." God did so, but their impertinence was costly to their relationship with Him. Imagine having a spouse, a child, or a best friend who constantly demanded, "Prove that you love me." Would you feel manipulated? Of course. Moses was warning the people not to do the same to God; a warning they ignored, with tragic consequences.

For Jesus, this must have been truly tempting. Perhaps He thought to Himself, "Father, you said at the Jordan that I was your Son, and that you loved me. Why not do this one thing, just to shut the devil up? It would make me feel so good…" We all think like those Israelites from time to time. "God, if you give me this job, I will go to church every Sunday from now on." "Lord, after all I've done for you, how could you let me get cancer?" "Father, I love her. If you want me to be happy, don't let her break up with me." Jesus stood strong. He walked out of the desert weary, emaciated, sun-scorched…and victorious. He was ready for the marathon ahead.

Until an Opportune Time

Luke 4:13

Satan doesn't appear as an active participant in any other story in the Gospels. It would be easy to assume that, having failed in his duel with Jesus in the desert, the devil simply slunk away in shame…if not for this verse, and Hebrews 4:15. Hebrews 4 shows Jesus as our ultimate High Priest. The High Priest in Israel was the man who, more than any other, helped God's people stay in a good relationship with Him. Jesus, the author of Hebrews says, is the High Priest we all need. His life and death have given us the opportunity to be right with God. But there's more. He is a High Priest who understands what it's like to be us. *For we do not have a high priest who is unable to sympathize with our weaknesses, but we have one who has been tempted in every way, just as we are—yet was without sin* (Hebrews 4:15). How literally should we take that phrase, "tempted in every way?" I believe we can take it very literally. Our verse today says that Satan left Jesus "until an opportune time." Put yourself in Jesus' place for a moment. If you had such a monumental mission to carry out, with few comforts, resources, or encouragements, and had an enemy who was determined to make you stumble, how often do you think that enemy would find an opportune time? I am certain Jesus faced temptation constantly, every day of His life. When His enemies spread lies about Him, He felt the temptation to vaporize them instantly. When He saw an attractive woman, He felt the temptation to see her as an object, not a fellow human being. When He was hungry, tired and surrounded by needy people, He felt tempted to use His power to take by force the status and prosperity He deserved. When His own family rejected Him, His own disciples misunderstood Him, and His crowds dwindled, He felt the temptation to abandon this crazy redemption project and leave this world to its own well-deserved end. But ultimately, He did none of those things. Hebrews tells us He was without sin. Why is this so important? Why did Satan work so hard to convince Him to slip up? Because God's Messiah was destined to fulfill the role of the sacrificial lamb, and a sacrifice had to be flawless. If Jesus had sinned even once, His death would have been the just punishment for His own transgressions. In order to save the world, He had to be a sinless Savior.

Chapter 4: Jesus the Teacher--His Parables

John 7:31-32, 45-46

In action movies, we all know what will happen when a mob of thugs is dispatched to capture or kill the hero. He single-handedly defeats them with a combination of strength, speed, skill and deception. Or, as in the case of young Kevin McCallister in *Home Alone,* with paint cans, Christmas ornaments, a blowtorch and a tarantula. In this real-life story, Jesus overcomes the posse sent to arrest Him simply by the power of His words. "No one ever spoke like this man," they say, glassy-eyed, upon their return. People said that quite often when they first heard Jesus. They came from miles around to listen to Him. They stood in the hot sun for hours, not even stopping for meals. He must have been the most compelling speaker who ever lived. But it wasn't just that His speech was engaging; His words opened up a new reality to those who heard them, and to the millions who have read them since. As Mark Hopkins writes, "Certainly, no revolution that has ever taken place in society can be compared to that which has been produced by the words of Jesus Christ."

His teaching technique was surprising. Aside from The Sermon on the Mount and some pronouncements about the End (we'll consider all of those later), He seems to have done most of His teaching through stories, metaphors, and images. When I was a small child, the worst part of a typical week was the Sunday sermon. It wasn't easy to sit still and silent as the preacher talked on and on about matters I had neither the capacity nor the desire to comprehend (That wasn't the fault of my pastors, by the way). But once in a while, our church would have a guest preacher who told stories. Those were the sermons I paid attention to. We all love a good story. Jesus was a master storyteller. In this section, we'll take a look at His stories, and how they changed the world.

Why Parables?

Matthew 13:10-17

Jesus was not the first teacher in history to use parables (extended analogies intended to make a point). But as far as we know, no one in history ever used them as consistently and effectively as He. His disciples wondered why He taught this way. His answer, in Matthew 13:10-17, is surprising. At first glance, it sounds as though Jesus is saying He uses the parables to hide spiritual truth from people, instead of revealing it. But if Jesus was trying to embed lessons in a complex code accessible only to the initiated, He wasn't very good at it. Most of His parables are easily understandable, even to children. So what did He mean?

In this text, Jesus is speaking to His disciples. Jesus didn't recruit His followers from rabbinical schools; they were blue-collar workers. They were not the sort of people who were seen as knowledgeable. In vv. 14-15, Jesus quotes from Isaiah 6, a prophecy that said God's people would miss the obvious truth about Him. In vv. 16-17, He tells these rough, uneducated followers that they are now privileged to know things about God that sages and teachers longed to apprehend. Jesus is saying that parables are designed to tell the truth in a memorable way to anyone who really wants to know the truth. To those people, these stories will present life-changing revelation in a way they can handle, apply to their lives, and remember forever. But to those who think they--and they only--have a corner on the market of theology, these stories will seem like trifles. They won't take the time to ponder their meaning, and they will dismiss them as foolishness, along with the God who inspired them. Jesus was right: These stories really are a treasure. Let's enjoy them together.

The Greatest Story Ever Told

Luke 15:1-10

(Please note: I am deeply indebted to Timothy Keller's excellent book *The Prodigal God* for many of my ideas on Luke 15) Of all Jesus' parables, the story of the Prodigal Son is easily the most famous. So that's where we'll begin; but first, consider this observation: All of us, by personality, fall along a spectrum between rule-keeper and rebel. The rule-keeper is a guy who does what is expected of him. As a kid, he makes his parents proud. In school, he turns in his homework on time and gets perfect scores in conduct. He chooses a respectable career and lives in a good part of town. He goes to church on Sundays, pays his taxes, follows the deed restrictions, drives the speed limit, and replaces all his divots. Then there's the rebel. He's the black sheep of his family. All his life, he feels like everyone--his parents, his school, his church—is trying to force him into a mold that doesn't fit, to make him into someone he's not. Whereas the rule-keeper's highest goal is to be seen as good and respectable by society, the rebel's highest goal is to find happiness on his own terms, no matter what anyone else thinks about it. Rule-keepers look at his odd clothes, his weird life choices and his brushes with the law as a cry for attention, or immature rebellion, but he's just trying to be true to himself, unlike all those "sell-outs."

You could say that the great culture war of our era is just a battle between the rule-keepers and rebels. The rule-keepers say there are certain standards of right and wrong, and the root cause of the downfall of our culture is that as a society, we've ignored and rebelled against those standards. The rebels say that rule-keepers are just bigots who want to force their version of morality on everyone else. If they would just accept people for who they are instead of trying to force them into some narrow box, then the world would be a happier and more peaceful place. Which side is Jesus on? The somewhat surprising answer we get from Luke 15 is that He is on neither side. He spent much of His time with rebels (v. 1); but He told this story to a group of classic rule-keepers (v. 2), hoping both would come into God's family.

The first thing Jesus does--before He gets to the famous story--is tell two shorter ones. In the first story, a shepherd who has one hundred sheep loses one. Instead of saying, "No big deal; I have 99 more," he searches tirelessly until he finds it, then brings it home ready to celebrate. In the second, a woman loses one of 10 valuable coins. She turns her house upside down looking for it. When she finally finds it, she calls her neighbors over. They have a big party to celebrate the finding of that coin. Who would think to compare God to a giddy housewife? Who in that era would dare suggest that God is more excited about the people who are disreputable coming into His family than He is about the rule-keepers who are already in the family? Yet that's exactly what Jesus taught. Most of all, both stories told the people something they didn't know about God. Religion had always told them that you had to work hard and search tirelessly to find God and get to Him. But Jesus said that God comes looking for us, and when He finds us, the joy He feels is far out of proportion to what we think we're worth.

Prodigal Son or Prodigal God?

Luke 15:11-24

Notice that Jesus never uses the term, "the prodigal son." That's a term that we've invented. By the way, do you know what the word "prodigal" means? It's not "wild" or "rebellious." It literally means a reckless spender, someone who spends until he has no more. Hold onto that...we'll come back to it. Truthfully, this parable would more appropriately be called "The story of the two lost sons." (We'll read about the older son next) The father, obviously, represents God. The sons represent the two ways of life we just spoke of: The rebel and the rule-keeper. Jesus includes some striking details. When the younger boy says, "Give me my share of the estate," two things are happening here. First, it is a supreme sign of disrespect for his father. The estate was to be given out upon the father's death. At that point, the older son was entitled to 2/3 of the estate, the younger was to get 1/3. But what this boy says is essentially, "Drop dead, dad." Second, the father couldn't simply write his son a check. In those times, most of a person's wealth was made up of land, not liquid cash. So in order for him to honor the son's request, the father had to sell off 1/3 of his holdings. In that culture, land was a part of one's security and identity. Imagine today a man built a company from scratch, then the son said, "Sell that company and give me a third of the proceeds. I want out." The focus is not on some wild, immoral things the son did. It's on how he has wounded his father and ruptured the relationship.

If anyone in that age would have been telling this story other than Jesus, it would have ended after v. 13. The moral would be, "You disrespect your father, indulge in wild living, and the fun won't last for long. Sooner or later, the money will run out, and you'll be left with nothing." No one would have even considered the question, "How can the younger boy come home?" The question would have been irrelevant. After what he had done, the way he had disgraced the family, he was as good as dead to them. But Jesus goes on to tell about the boy coming up with a plan to make things right: I'll apply to be one of my father's hired hands. It seems this boy was thinking, "My father has always treated his employees fairly. I will work for my dad until I can save up the money to pay back what I took from him. Then maybe things can be like they were. But if not, at least I'll be trying." That's what most people think Christianity is: It's our way of paying off our debt to God. We do good deeds, attend church, give offerings and pray, and we're earning points that offset the bad stuff we've done. Rule-keepers tend to be good at that game, and tend to end up proud and self-righteous. Rebels often decide they've got no chance to play the game, so the best way to live is chase happiness now in whatever form they can find it. But notice that when the son gets home, his father doesn't even listen to his plan. He cuts him off and says, "Let's have a party. My son is home!" The party here is extravagant. If the story were told today, the dad would rent out the top floor of the Four Seasons, bring in lobster and caviar, and hire the kid's favorite rock star to provide the entertainment. This is Jesus' way of saying that the rebel son coming home was the father's dream come true, the answer to his prayers. So the true prodigal in this story is the Father, who is generous in a way that would have seemed foolish in that time. This story must have shocked everyone who heard it. Could God really be like this?

The Big Brother Syndrome

Luke 15:25-32

Humanity is made up of rebels and rule-keepers. Jesus told this most famous of His stories to a group of rule-keepers, in order to correct their attitudes about the sinful people who were coming to Jesus for salvation (vv. 1-2). So in light of that, the older brother is really the main character of the story. Notice that he says to his father, "I have never disobeyed you," and the father doesn't contradict him. This young man was a rule-keeper extraordinaire. He was hard-working, dependable, and consistent in doing everything his dad expected of him. But he was just as lost as the rebellious younger son. In fact, the real surprise of the story is not that the Father takes the younger son back. The biggest surprise is that at the story's end, the rebel is back in the family, and the rule-keeping older son is still outside. Jesus is showing us that you can be a diligently moral, devoutly religious person and still be lost.

There are several things here that show that, although the older son was a rule-keeper, he didn't really love his father. The first thing is that the boy refuses to go into the party, making his father come out to meet him. Then, his first word to his father is "Look!" In most families, if a son—even a grown man like this one—had treated his father like this, he probably would have slapped his son across the cheek, then headed back to the party saying something like, "Come back when you know your proper place in this family." And the man's neighbors would have been on his side. Then he refers to the younger son as "This son of yours." He won't even claim him as his brother.

Next, there's the boy's statement, "You've never even given me a young goat so I could celebrate with my friends." What he's really saying is, "When are all my good deeds going to pay off?" And his line about his brother squandering his money with prostitutes…Where did that come from? He has no idea what his brother has done. Obviously, he's just been stewing in his own resentment, imaging all the wicked pleasures his brother must be indulging in…just like a self-righteous religious person. Essentially, he tells his father, "I don't care that my brother is home. I don't care that you're throwing the party of a lifetime and you want me there. All I care about is that my idiot brother gets rewarded for shaming us, and my good behavior has brought me nothing." In other words, he has the exact same problem as the younger son had at the beginning of the story: He doesn't love his father. He just wants his father's money. The younger son tried to get what he wanted by breaking the rules, by taking the money before his father passed away. The older boy went about it in a much more respectable way: By keeping all the rules and making his father proud, but the motive was the same…he didn't serve his father because he loved him; he served him because he thought it would pay in the end.

And yet, the father shows the older boy the same grace he showed his little brother. "Come back in. You know that I love you. And we have something to truly celebrate!" But that's where it ends. Why would Jesus leave the ending open? I believe it's because He was making an appeal to the rule-keepers who were His audience. He was saying, "Stop being so angry about prostitutes and tax collectors being accepted into God's loving arms. We should be excited about that! Now come on into your Father's love. There's room for you, too!" It's poignant to picture Jesus literally pleading with these men who hate Him… "I love you like this Father loved his boy. Won't you please come home?" The ironic truth is that Jesus, in His earthly life, primarily appealed to rebels, while churches today tend to be full of rule-keepers. We religious folks have a disturbing tendency to be like this older brother. Could it be that the Church which calls itself by Jesus' name actually behaves more like Jesus' enemies?

God's Fuzzy Math

Matthew 18:21-35

This is one of many parables Jesus told about grace, or unmerited favor from God. Grace is, in my opinion, the single most distinct idea that Jesus brought into the world. In this story, the King represents God, and the unforgiving servant represents you and me. Notice that the words of the second servant in v. 29 are almost identical to the words of the first servant in v. 26. Only the amounts are different…very different. The first servant has a debt before the king of 10,000 talents. Bible scholars debate about the exchange rate of talents to modern-day dollars, but a conservative estimate says that a typical wage-earner would have had to work for 164,000 years to come up with 10,000 talents. On the other hand, the second servant owed the first servant the equivalent of a few dollars. The application is obvious: The sin debt God is willing to forgive us is so massive that any grudge we may have against anyone else is tiny in comparison. None of us has any excuse for being unforgiving. But here's where the story gets uncomfortable for all of us: The King is so furious at the first servant for his unforgiving attitude that he throws him in prison to be tortured until he can repay the debt. In other words, he will be tortured for the rest of his life, since it's impossible to repay. As with all parables, it's not wise to press the details. The Bible is clear that God isn't cruel and vengeful like this King. But Jesus gives His one-sentence explanation in a way that hardly lets us off the hook: If we don't forgive, we won't be forgiven.

What does Jesus mean? In order to understand that, let's take a look at the question that prompted this story. Peter asked, "Lord, how many times should I forgive the jerk who keeps pushing my buttons? Is seven times enough?" Peter must have felt very magnanimous. The rabbis of that time were quite clear that someone should be forgiven three times at most, but not four. Peter was offering more than double the going rate! And Jesus must have shaken His head, as He did so many times…as He still must do when He watches you and me. Then He told this parable about how it's not our job to bring vengeance upon those who anger or hurt or offend us. After all, we've been forgiven by God of far worse. If we are really God's children, we should embrace the same fuzzy math that God used when He looked at our massive sin debt and said, "Let's call it even." In fact, the clearest sign of a true believer is that he or she consistently shows grace to others. That's what Jesus wants His people to be known for.

The Equalizer

Matthew 20:1-16

This is one of many of Jesus' parables that talks about the Kingdom of God. It was actually His favorite subject. Theologians will tell you it means "the sovereignty, reign, and rule of God." Think about it this way: God made this world exactly the way He wanted it. Scripture tells us that it was then warped and perverted by human sin. But God didn't settle for that. He broke into this world on a mission of rescue, reconciliation, and redemption. So when Jesus talks about the Kingdom of God, He's talking about returning this world and the people who live in it to the way God originally intended. He's saying, "Come and join my Kingdom, and help me make this the world it was supposed to be." Everywhere that Christ is truly Lord, that's the Kingdom of God. And in the Kingdom, a very different set of rules, priorities and truths apply. The Kingdom of God is something you might miss, if you're not careful.

Peter had just gotten through asking Jesus, "Lord, we've given up everything to follow you. What will there be for us?" Jesus assured Peter that whatever we give up for God on Earth will be repaid hundredfold. But then He tells this parable, I believe, to say, "But you can't look at it in purely mathematical or economic terms. If you want to fully experience my Kingdom, you have to follow Kingdom rules. You have to start seeing through Kingdom eyes." Please note: This isn't a story about who is saved and who is lost. Everyone in the story gets paid. But Jesus knew that His disciples had been raised in a system of legalistic religion, where it was assumed that God's favor came on the merit system. Jesus operated instead on the grace system: He favored those who were most aware of their sinfulness and need of God, not those who had worked the hardest at being righteous. He knew this would be a hard concept for His disciples to accept...as it is for most of us today. Verse 15 is rather interesting. In the original Greek, it says, "Do you have an evil eye because I'm good?" Jesus had previously said in the Sermon on the Mount (Mt. 6:22-23), *The eye is the lamp of the body. If your eyes are good, your whole body will be full of light. But if your eyes are bad, your whole body will be full of darkness. If then the light within you is darkness, how great is that darkness!* Life in the Kingdom isn't just about following some rules and doing some rituals. We actually have to train our eyes to see the world the way God does. We can miss the Kingdom because our eyes are greedy, wanting more; or because our eyes are lustful, looking on people of the opposite sex as simply objects for our pleasure; or because our eyes are judgmental of others, like these workers in the vineyard. In other words, to fully experience life in God's Kingdom, we have to learn to see people the way God sees them.

Foundation Issues

Matthew 7:24-27

There are many of Jesus' teachings that go down like a cool drink of water on a hot day. We love them. We memorize them. We put them in calligraphy and hang them on our living room walls. But then there are the sayings of Jesus that we would rather ignore. They are the ones that don't comfort us; they challenge us. They remind us how far we are from where God wants us to be. So we don't memorize those passages; we don't put them on bumper stickers or bracelets. We prefer to see Jesus as being kind, gentle, comforting, and always approving of everything we do. But that's not realistic. The world doesn't crucify gentle, comforting, approving people. Jesus was controversial in His time. And I believe if He came today, preaching the same message, He would be equally controversial. This is one of His teachings that I believe would offend a great many people, both inside and outside the church. Think about how counter-cultural these truths are:

No matter what you do, storms are coming. Notice in the parable that both the wise man and the foolish man were hit by the terrible storm. No matter how or where they built their houses, they couldn't escape some pain. Where I live, floods happen from time to time. After a deluge, you see carpet and furniture piled up outside $300,000 homes and outside rickety old shacks. The waters don't discriminate. The floods come on the rich and the poor, the just and the unjust. We don't want to hear this. We want to believe that if we cut out carbs, invest well, and follow the rules, we can fortify ourselves against all pain. But as long as we live in a sin-tainted world, there will be suffering. The question is, are you ready for it? **All lifestyles aren't equally valid.** This is not a parable from the Jesus of our imagination, a non-judgmental hippie who winks at our indiscretions and affirms all our choices. He clearly believed there is a right way to live…and every other way is wrong. **We are only as strong as our foundation.** What is the foundation of your life? In other words, what one thing, person, or idea drives your priorities, fuels your dreams, fills you with joy and establishes your identity? Jesus had the audacity to say that if your foundation is anything other than His words, your life will not stand the test. How could He say such a thing? Well, perhaps it was true…

The Rich Fool

Luke 12:16-21

In case you missed it, Jesus called this man a fool for doing something which our culture endorses…working hard and saving up his money to make a secure, comfortable life for himself. And by the way, just in case you think this parable only applies to the wealthy, consider this: 40% of the world's population—that's 2.6 billion people--lives on less than $2 a day. 15% live on less than a dollar a day—that's 1 billion people. The average American, by contrast, lives on $105 a day. Put it another way: If you make $25,000 a year, you are richer than 90% of the people on Earth. If you make at least $50,000 a year, you are in the top 1% of richest human beings on the planet. Chances are, every person reading this has money left over after we have fed and clothed our family. We all make decisions on what to do with what's left over. There has never been a group of people who were a more perfect target of this parable than Americans in the 21st Century.

By the way, the rich fool's sin wasn't in getting rich. His sin wasn't even in building barns to store his grain. The book of Proverbs commends this sort of industriousness. His sin was in thinking that accumulating wealth was the purpose of life, that if he could make enough money to last the rest of his life, he would be successful and happy. As usual, it's important to see the context in which Jesus told the parable. Jesus has just had a young man approach Him asking for help in negotiating the terms of an inheritance with his brother. And Jesus says, "Who made me a judge between the two of you?" Essentially, Jesus is saying, "That's not my mission. I didn't come to help you get rich; I came to make you holy." Then He says, *Be on your guard against all kinds of greed; a man's life does not consist in the abundance of his possessions.* Then Jesus tells this story to prove His point: Wanting more for ourselves is spiritual suicide. Notice what God says in v. 21 (and by the way, this is the only parable where God Himself is a main character): *This is how it will be for anyone who stores up things for himself but is not rich toward God.* It's not our money and stuff, after all. It's just on loan to us.

In 2009, Americans spent over $1 billion on virtual products for online games. Imagine you have a friend who plays an online role-playing game, and spends so much time and money on his imaginary farm, his house gets repossessed. He comes to you and says, “Hey, check it out. I’ve got 2000 acres of farmland and 500 head of cattle.” You would say, “But you’re living in a cardboard box! Why are you spending money on something that’s not real, and neglecting the place you really live?” You would call this man a fool, and rightly so. Jesus is reminding us in this parable that bank accounts, possessions and retirement funds are like products you buy in a game. They’re nice to have, but they cease to exist once the game is over. The wise man spends most of his energy and resources building wealth outside the game, in the world that’s real and eternal. The fool doesn’t know the difference, and when the game ends, he’s left with nothing.

The Myth of Private Faith

Mark 4:21-23

Some of Jesus' parables are brief; they are more like metaphors than stories. Let's consider three of them. This one follows an extended parable (Mark 4:3-20) about sharing the Gospel--or good news--that Jesus brought to the world. The lamp in this parable is meant to represent the Gospel as well. It reminds me of two different stories: The first is about a church in a northern state that was off the main highway a mile or so. Their new pastor convinced them to spend a little money and buy a sign on the highway that would tell people about the church and how to get there. For the first few months the sign was up, it drew in several new visitors. Then one day, the pastor noticed one of his church members carrying the sign from his car into a storage room. He asked him why he had removed the sign from the highway, and the man said, "Well, it'll be winter soon. That sign won't last very long if we leave it up in the winter." The second story involves a friend of mine who was pastor of a large church in a city where there was a prison. He began a ministry to prisoners and law enforcement officers. He would preach in the prisons, mentor new believers behind bars, and help parolees start a new life. He saw many lives changed for good. Then his church leaders began to pressure him. They said, "You're spending all your time on these prisoners. That's not what we pay you for." Eventually, they gave him an ultimatum. Quit this ministry, or quit being our pastor. The man resigned his pastorate, and continues his ministry to prisoners and police today. He realized that, according to Jesus, God leaves the ninety-nine sheep to go search for the one who is lost. But his church was asking him to spend all his time with the ninety-nine and ignore the lost one, and he couldn't do it.

The church member in the first story was right, of course. If you kept the sign in a storage room, it would last a whole lot longer. But then, that's not the purpose of a sign, is it? Jesus invested in His disciples so that they would tell others about Him after He was gone. In the years after His departure, they would discover that His mission for their lives included far more than their fellow Jews. He wanted them to carry His message even to people who currently hated them, even to parts of the world they'd never heard of before (Acts 1:8). It wasn't easy; they had to overcome their own prejudices, travel great distances, even face persecution and possible martyrdom. Churches today, on the other hand, have to reckon with society's insistence that religious faith should be strictly a private affair. This external pressure combines with our own natural selfishness (as demonstrated by the church in the second story) to make us people who hide our lamp under a bowl. But if the story of Jesus is true, then it can't be kept under wraps. If Jesus is who He claimed to be, and did what Scripture says, we owe it to the world to share in the most authentic and engaging way possible. That will never be easy or popular; but it's our purpose.

The Final Score

Mark 4:26-29

Picture a pot full of soil. I put a dry pinto bean into it. Then I wait. Nothing happens. I get impatient. I start to think maybe this was all a mistake; perhaps there are no more beans to be had in the world. Perhaps I am doomed to a miserable, bean-less existence. So I give up on my beans, walk away and forget the whole thing. Ridiculous, right? We all understand that, below the surface, invisible to my eye, something is going on. We have to be patient, do the hard work of tending the crop, and only on the day of harvest will we get to see the results. Think for a moment about why Jesus would use this metaphor. People in Jesus' time were excited about His life and miracles and teachings. They thought He was what they'd been looking for. But nothing seemed to be changing. Rome was still in charge, which meant that their people were still under the thumb of a government of pagans. Roman culture was still the hottest thing going, with all of its materialism, militarism, and sensuality. And they—God's chosen people—were still poor, not the lords of all creation that their forefathers had been in the days of David and Solomon…days they thought were supposed to return when the Messiah showed up. So while they wanted to believe in Jesus, they were also thinking, "Why aren't we seeing some results?"

We often face a similar discouragement. Whether we are working on growing in some area of personal character, addressing an injustice in our society, trying to lead a friend closer to God, or just noting the rampant problems of our world, we often feel as if good is losing, and all our efforts to change things are fruitless. The image of a harvest is often used in Scripture to speak of Judgment Day. Joel 3:13 is a good example. So is Jeremiah 50:16 and Revelation 14:14. People who heard Jesus tell this parable would have immediately thought of the End Times when Jesus started mentioning the harvest. What He's saying is, "I know it looks bad now, but you don't know the final score. I do. And you will know it on the day I return." We look at the world today, and wonder, "If God is God, why are things in such a mess? Why does evil seem to win all the time?" The very first believers in Jesus wondered the same thing. But something very important was going on beneath the surface, where no one but God could see. And on the right day, that seed that had been buried burst forth into glorious new life.

Mustard Seed and Yeast

Matthew 13:31-33

In the first story, Jesus compares the Kingdom of God to a mustard seed. Jesus was trying to show how in nature, something very small becomes something quite large. The second story makes the same point in a slightly different way. This time, the Kingdom is like yeast. For those of you who like to bake, don't picture a little packet of yeast. Instead, picture what they called leaven back then, a little bit of fermenting dough saved from the last time you baked. This woman has nine gallons of flour and a little handful of leaven. Yet that will make enough bread to feed 150 people. Why? Because that little bit of leaven works through the entire mass of dough. The point here isn't just that God's Kingdom starts small and grows. It's that God's Kingdom has a disproportionate impact on the world around it. God's people may be in the minority in every way, numerically, economically, politically, culturally, but they can transform the community around them like that leaven transforms dough.

But there's even more going on here. From the very beginnings of Judaism, leaven was used as a symbol for sinfulness. It's not that the Jews believed yeast was bad; they used it every day. But as a metaphor, leaven was consistently used to symbolize evil. For instance, every year at Passover, they spent seven days eating unleavened bread (matzoh). One of the rituals of Passover prescribed in Scripture was that a family had to go through their house at Passover time, making sure that every trace of leaven was removed from the home. Why? Because God wanted them to understand the need to go through their lives meticulously, ridding themselves of every trace of sin. To be without leaven was a symbol for being holy.

We read on in the Old Testament Law and see that every sacrifice involving bread was to be given with unleavened bread. Jesus even used the term this way later when He said to His disciples, *Beware of the leaven of the scribes and Pharisees.* Paul also uses the term in a negative way when he writes to the Corinthians and says, "Get rid of the old leaven and become a new batch of unleavened bread." Virtually every time in Scripture where leaven is mentioned in a symbolic sense, it is used negatively, to represent sin. So for Jesus to use it here in a positive way is remarkable. It would be like a Baptist preacher in the 1920s saying to his congregation, "You're the ice cold beer of Heaven that refreshes God's Spirit." People would have said, "What is this guy up to?" I believe that's exactly what happened here. Jesus used this term for effect. He wanted people to see, "I'm the God who takes what has always seemed ruined and worthless, and I turn it into something powerful." Nine gallons of flour can feed a few families, but throw in a little leaven, and you can feed 150. God can do more with our failures than we can do with our strengths. In fact, God can take our weakness and make it a source of glory for His Kingdom. There are no more excuses. You are qualified to change the world through God.

Shameless

Luke 11:5-8

This story is a little hard for us to grasp because it has to do with hospitality and honor, two concepts that meant much more to the people Jesus was talking to than they do in our culture. To the first hearers of the story, if someone—even a stranger—came to your house, you were responsible for meeting their needs. If they were hungry, you gave them the best food you had, even if you were very poor. If they needed to rest, you gave them your bed. And if they were in some danger, you put your life at risk to protect them. Why? Well, they didn't have restaurants or police in that time. They had inns, but they were often more like brothels than a Motel 6. But even more importantly, you did this because your honor was at stake. If someone came to your door and you didn't meet their needs, it brought dishonor on you, your family, and your village. People would sooner die than be dishonored. So in the story, a man is trying to help a friend who has come to his house and is hungry. There are two problems: First, the man doesn't have any food in the house. And second, it's midnight. But he knows one of his neighbors has bread. Perhaps he saw the man's wife baking earlier that day. So he goes to his door and asks for bread. The man says, "Leave me alone. My kids are in bed with me. If I get up, that wakes up the whole family. Come back in the morning." That's how any of us would react.

The word in v. 8 that our English Bibles translate as "boldness" or "persistence" is interesting. That word (*anaideia*) literally means "shameless." It is never used as a compliment. Jesus here isn't praising this man for being bold or persistent. He's saying, "This guy was rude." He didn't have a proper sense of respect for the person he was approaching. And every person in the crowd that day would have said, "Yep, he was rude alright. But I would still get up and help him, because my honor is on the line." So He is saying: "If you would help a rude, shameless friend in the middle of the night, how much more would God help you?" Jesus is saying that God loves our audacity, our shamelessness, in coming to Him with our needs. Are there times when His answer is no? Absolutely, because He is God, and He knows giving us what we want would be irresponsible. But it's the shameless people, those who lose their sense of stuffy propriety before God, who change the world when they pray.

The Unjust Judge

Luke 18:1-8

In this story, an unrighteous judge is being hounded by a woman who needs justice. In those days, people could have their land or house seized, or even be put in jail, if they owed a debt. This might have been a widow whose late husband had owed the debt, and now his debtors were trying to rob her to get satisfaction. This kind of thing was quite illegal under the Israelite law, and God had told Moses to set up judges to prevent it from happening. But judges didn't help if they were on the take, as this one apparently was. Here we must point out that Jesus is *not* saying God is like this judge. This is a "how much more" parable, a type Jesus was known to use. In other words, if a persistent woman could get justice from even the most crooked magistrate, how much more will we get justice from a God who is absolutely righteous?

What was the woman asking for in the story? Protection from her enemies. And that is just what Jesus promises in verse 7. He is not promising that, if we nag God often enough, He'll give us a fat bank account, marital bliss and perfect abs. This promise was given to people who were oppressed by their Roman occupiers. Some had surely experienced other injustices: They had been sold into slavery to pay their debts, or been cheated in court by a richer claimant, or been stiffed on their wages by their skinflint boss. Yet Jesus told them to love their enemies. In this parable, He's telling them how such forgiveness is possible: There will be justice in God's time. The scales may seem tilted against the innocent in this world, but there is another world coming. The wait may seem long, as it surely was for the woman in this story, but God's justice is always right on time.

The Strong Man

Luke 11:21-22

The larger context of this story starts with verse 14. Jesus had been called a lot of names in His day. They called Him a drunkard and a glutton. They said He was crazy or demon-possessed. They called Him a friend of sinners, which considering Jesus' gracious view of the world was actually a compliment. But here they went over the line; they said His power was actually the power of Satan. In other words, in their view Jesus wasn't just misguided, He was evil. Jesus' defense is ingenious. You may recognize v. 17 from American history. But long before Abe Lincoln borrowed those words to argue against an America divided between slave and free states, Jesus used them to point out, logically, that the power of evil can't possibly be responsible for the destruction of evil. Instead of trying to find fault, Jesus is saying, why not rejoice that evil is being overcome, even if it isn't happening the way you want?

Then Jesus tells this strange little parable. There are three characters here. The first character is the Strong Man. In the Greek, the definite article "the" is there, so we know Jesus isn't just talking about some hypothetical strong man, He's talking about someone specific. And considering the context, it's obvious that He's speaking about Satan. In spite of what people think they know about the Devil, the picture the Bible gives of him is really pretty murky. That's intentional, by the way. We're not supposed to study him or become fascinated with him, like some Christians unfortunately do. In this passage, we see him called by three names. Satan, the one with which we're most familiar, simply means, "Enemy." Beelzebub, the name Jesus' accusers used, was originally the name of a pagan deity, Baal-zebub, one of the gods of the Philistines. It literally means "Lord of the Flies." And Jesus calls him The Strong Man.

I propose that the second character, the "someone stronger" Jesus mentions in verse 22, is Jesus Himself. And the third character, the strong man's plunder, represents humanity. You and I are characters in this story, helpless captives desperate for rescue. Certainly, that is the way Jesus' life and work are described consistently in the rest of the New Testament (more on that in other sections of this book). If that's what this story means, it casts the life of Jesus in a very different light than the way it is often presented. Jesus wasn't just a kind, wise teacher who lived out a great example for us and left us some wonderful life lessons. His life was a rescue mission against the bully who had oppressed people He loved. There are hundreds of great rescue stories in history, but one of my favorites is one you probably haven't heard. In 1868, Queen Victoria authorized a rescue mission for 53 people, including some missionaries and a British consul, who had been held captive for four years by Emperor Theodore III of Ethiopia in a remote 9,000-foot-high bastion. The invasion force included 32,000 men, heavy artillery, and 44 elephants to carry the guns. Provisions included 50,000 tons of beef and pork and 30,000 gallons of rum. Engineers built landing piers, water treatment plants, a railroad, and telegraph line to the interior, plus many bridges. In terms of the money and logistics involved, military historians say this was an undertaking on the scale of the Normandy Invasion. Surely old Theodore III thought he was safe and sound way down there in Ethiopia. He never figured Victoria would send a full-scale invasion just to rescue 53 people. Yet that's just what she did. On paper, it certainly didn't make sense for Jesus to invade this world, either. But that's just what He did. It stirs us to wonder: Just how valuable must we be to God?

The Pharisee

Luke 18:10-14

We'll look at the tax-collector in this two-character parable in our next reading. For now, let's consider the Pharisee. As I've already discussed, Pharisees were one of the sub-sects of Judaism in the time of Jesus. They were dedicated to helping the people of God obey His Word, which is a mission I can heartily endorse. And yet of all the groups within Judaism, Jesus had more arguments with the Pharisees than with all the other groups combined. Why? There are many reasons, but we see two in this story: **First, they thought they didn't need God's grace.** One of the ironies of religion is that the more religious we become, the more we tend to think we don't need God anymore. Instead of seeking God in a desperate bid for salvation, our faith becomes all about us; Look at all the good things I do, listen to these wonderful things I've learned, gaze in wonder on my righteous lifestyle. This is one of the reasons that the Pharisees resented Jesus so much; they were so proud of their meticulous observance of God's law, and yet He had the audacity to say they needed to repent, that they couldn't enter the Kingdom of Heaven unless they were born again. **Second, they looked down on other people.** Mark Twain once observed of a devout acquaintance, "She's good…in the worst sense of the word." Have you ever noticed that some of the most religious people you know are also the most unlikeable, unkind, unmerciful people around? Jesus pointed out that the Pharisees were so meticulous about religious devotion but they ignored justice, mercy and faithfulness, which are more important to God (Mt. 23:23). So when you boil it all down, here's what Jesus had against the Pharisees: They were amazingly devout and incredibly moral, but they didn't love God and they didn't love their neighbors. In other words, they totally missed what it was all about.

If we Christians are honest with ourselves, we see disturbing parallels between the attitudes Jesus condemned in the Pharisee and ourselves. I believe Jesus knew this would happen. Jesus wasn't telling this story just to condemn the toxic, tainted religion of a sub-sect of Judaism 2000 years ago; He knew that His own people would at times be tempted to follow the path of those Pharisees rather than walking in His footsteps. And just in case you don't feel the sense of urgent heartache in that truth, consider this: According to v. 14, only one of those men went home justified before God. And it wasn't the religious one. Jesus wasn't just being melodramatic when He said (Mt. 7:21-23) that at the Judgment Day, many would call Him Lord, Lord and would hear those terrifying words, "Depart from me, I never knew you."

The Tax Collector

Luke 18:10-14

Tax collectors were universally despised in Jewish society in these days. It's not hard to understand why. Think about how you feel about the IRS. Now imagine that, instead of collecting taxes to fund our own nation's government, they were funneling your money to another country entirely…a country that had invaded our nation and was making life difficult for all of us. Now imagine that, on top of all of that, this man was collecting more taxes than his foreign bosses required, and keeping the leftovers for himself. Imagine he lived down the street from you in a much nicer house, drove a much nicer car, sent his kids to exclusive private schools and took dream vacations several times a year, and you knew this wealth was acquired by stealing from you and your neighbors in the service of an evil foreign government. It's no wonder people put tax collectors in the same category as prostitutes and other "sinners." So it was very surprising to Jesus' original listeners to hear Him tell a story in which the devout, moral, salt-of-the-earth Pharisee was the zero and the despicable tax collector was the hero.

Yet that's exactly what happened here. The parable ends with Jesus saying this man was justified. When the New Testament uses the word "justified" it means "to be declared perfect by a holy God." The tax collector is like a kid who's in way over his head in school. All semester long, he misses assignments, fails tests, and then bombs the final exam. Just before grades come out, he goes to the teacher and pleads for mercy, and the teacher says, "You have a 100 average in my book!" Why would God justify this man? Because He loves brokenness. King David, after he had committed his awful sin with Bathsheba, wrote Psalm 51, the greatest essay on sin and brokenness you will ever read. V. 17 says, *The sacrifices of God are a broken spirit. A broken and contrite heart, o God, you will not despise.* Remember, both the Pharisee and the tax collector were in the temple, ostensibly for the purpose of worshipping God. But the only sacrifice God requires, the only true worship He accepts, comes from a broken and contrite heart. So the Pharisee's exemplary moral and religious record was worth nothing before God, because he came into the divine presence with an attitude of pride and self-righteousness. But look at the tax collector's prayer. He doesn't just mean "be merciful to me." The actual term that's used here is a sacrificial term. It means, "Lord, make atonement for me." He may have been a miserable, greedy tax collector, but he was still a Jew. He knew God's Word. And He knew that God couldn't just write off all of his sin. God is far too righteous and holy for that. The entire sacrificial system was set up so that the people would understand the weight of sin, that sin had consequences. So now this desperate sinful man was saying, "I understand the weight of my sin. I know what I deserve. I can't possibly do anything to counteract that. Please make the sacrifice for me, Lord." Remember Psalm 51:17? *The sacrifices of God are a broken spirit.* This man's brokenness WAS the sacrifice that pleased God. His brokenness WAS his act of worship.

You may be bothered by that idea. Why does God want us to be broken? Is He some sadistic bully who delights in holding us down on the playground and punching us in the arm until we yell "Uncle?" No, He's not. Imagine you are friends with a young woman who is madly in love with someone who is terrible for her. He has a violent past, he's controlling and cruel to her, and you just know that he's going to hurt her. He may even kill her. You try to convince her of this, but like so many young people in love, she says, "You just don't understand. He's different than you think." Eventually, she severs the friendship with you. All you can do now is pray. But then one day, there's a knock on your door. She's standing there, weeping. You hear her story of how he has left her for another woman, and how she finally sees him for what he truly is. Her heart is truly broken, and you hurt for her, but inwardly, you feel a deep sense of joy. You want to shout, "Hallelujah!" Why? Because this woman's brokenness means she is free from bondage to someone who could've destroyed her life. That is why God loves it when we come to Him with a broken heart. It means we recognize that the biggest problem we have is us. We're finally being honest about ourselves, our sin and our desperate need for Him. Now, at last, we're free. And so He rejoices.

True Worship

Luke 7:36-50

This is the story of two people: A respectable religious man and a woman with a lousy reputation, who both offered something to Jesus. But, similar to the story of the Pharisee and the tax collector, only one went away approved by Him, and it wasn't the one most people would have expected. In the middle of the story, Jesus told a very short parable (verses 41-43) to explain to the religious man why his lavish banquet was far less meaningful than the offering this woman had brought. Let's make something clear: Jesus was NOT saying that Simon's sin was less serious than the woman's sin. But He was saying that because this woman was aware of the magnitude of her sin and of her own desperate need for God, she could truly worship Him. Philip Yancey, in his book *What Good is God*, tells about being asked to speak at a conference for ministries that reach out to prostitutes. At the end of the conference Yancey had the following conversation with the women: *I had time for one more question. "Did you know that Jesus referred to your profession? Let me read you what he said: 'I tell you the truth, the tax collectors and the prostitutes are entering the kingdom of God ahead of you.' He was speaking to the religious authorities of his day. What do you think Jesus meant? Why did he single out prostitutes?" After several minutes of silence a young woman from Eastern Europe spoke up in her broken English. "Everyone, she has someone to look down on. Not us. We are at the low. Our families, they feel shame for us. No mother nowhere looks at her little girl and says, 'Honey, when you grow up I want you be good prostitute.' Most places, we are breaking the law. Believe me, we know how people feel about us...We are the bottom. And sometimes when you are at the low, you cry for help. So when Jesus comes, we respond. Maybe Jesus meant that."*

Luke doesn't tell us this woman was a prostitute. But in that culture, if a man was considered a sinner, it was usually because of his work. He was a tax collector, or someone who worked with unclean animals or had contact with Gentiles. But women couldn't be part of the business world in that culture, so if a woman was considered a sinner, it was usually because of some sexual reason. So almost certainly, this woman was an adulteress or a prostitute. Whatever her particular sin, she was, in the words of the woman in Yancey's story, "at the low." And she cried for help. It wasn't her extravagance or her emotion, it was her desperation for God that made her a true worshipper. Because she had been forgiven much, and was acutely aware of that forgiveness, her love for God was true. Simon, on the other hand, didn't feel any need of Jesus at all. He wasn't there to give Jesus anything. He was there to check Jesus out. Essentially, he wanted something from Jesus; He wanted proof that Jesus was who everyone said He was. But the woman didn't want anything. She came to Jesus with no selfish agenda; She just came to adore Him in thanksgiving for her salvation.

Bumper Crop

Matthew 13:1-23

I get the impression Jesus told this story to His disciples at a moment when they were discouraged. They were convinced Jesus was the Messiah; why wasn't all of Israel getting on board? The soil in the story represents the people who hear the Gospel (Jesus' message). The story pictures four different kinds of people. Clearly, the first type of soil (the hard ground) represents people who reject the Gospel outright. We'll look at the second and third kinds of soil (people who seem to accept the Gospel, at least outwardly) next. But first, let's look at the fruitful soil. Jesus says that sometimes the Word is sown in good soil, and it produces fruit, 100, 60 or 30 times the amount that was sown. Farmers in that day counted on a ten-fold yield, and rejoiced if they got 20 times what they sowed, so Jesus is talking here about a fantastic harvest. But what does He mean in a spiritual sense?

The Greek word for fruit is used 67 times in the New Testament, and most of the time it has nothing to do with apples and oranges. It is almost always a symbolic way of picturing the results of a life that is obedient to God. Jesus in Luke 7 was talking about how to judge whether or not a teacher is true. He said, *No good tree can bear bad fruit, and no bad tree can bear good fruit...So by their fruit you will know them.* Paul, in trying to describe what life is like when the Holy Spirit is in charge, said in Galatians 5:22, *The fruit of the Spirit is love, joy, peace, patience, kindness, goodness, faithfulness, gentleness and self-control.* Think about it: Fruit is evidence that a tree or a bush is doing well; if it doesn't produce fruit, it's either dead or dying. But a living tree bears fruit. So in a spiritual sense, fruit is the outward evidence of life; it means that the living God is in control of our lives. Here's where that truth hits home for us: We don't determine someone's spiritual state by religious activity or legalistic moralism; we look for signs of spiritual life, for fruit. And we don't judge our church's ministry by how many people we have in the pews or by how much money we have in the bank; we judge it based on the fruit our members are producing. Think about this: fruit isn't meant for the tree, it's meant to be shared with others. So our individual lives and our corporate ministry should be a blessing to many. We should be individual people who bless dozens, even hundreds, perhaps even thousands of people who know us.

Rootless

Matthew 13:20-21

In these verses, as Jesus is explaining the parable of the sower to His disciples, He refers to people who seem to joyfully turn their lives over to Christ, then later fall away. The term that is used for "fall away" is the Greek word *skandalizomai.* It also means stumble. You get the picture of people running a race together, and some just drop out. I have had the privilege of baptizing hundreds of people. I wish I could tell you that every one of those new believers grew up to be like the person Jesus described as "good soil." But the truth is that some—the last time I saw them—had left church life entirely. They now live exactly like people who never believed. Following Jesus was seemingly just a phase in their lives. Anyone who has spent any time in church life can tell stories of friends or family members who followed this same path.

Jesus knew this would happen. It was an even bigger issue in the early church than it is today. The big debate in the first centuries of Christianity was on whether someone who renounced Christ under penalty of martyrdom was lost. Should people who had saved their own lives by recanting their Christianity be welcomed back into the church? This is why the subject of endurance or perseverance is so prevalent in the New Testament. The book of 1 John discusses this problem at length. People were falling away from the faith, and the apostle wanted his fellow believers to understand why it was happening. In 1 John 2:19, it says bluntly, *They went out from us, but they did not really belong to us. For if they had belonged to us, they would have remained with us; but their going showed that none of them belonged to us.*

This whole discussion makes many of us uncomfortable. We live in a very tolerant, live-and-let-live society. The only people we think we're allowed to judge are judgmental people, which is sort of ironic when you think about it. So we internally cringe at all this talk of who is in and who is out. Let me be clear: I don't think it's fruitful, responsible or biblical for you or I to try to decide if someone else is truly saved. We waste a lot of time and unnecessarily divide people when we do that. But as part of the family of God, we should care if there is no spiritual fruit in someone's life, just like a farmer should care if one of his peach trees stops putting out peaches. We should care if suddenly one of our members stops coming, just like you and I would care if next Thanksgiving, one of our siblings didn't show up to dinner unexpectedly. We should make sure our churches are equipping people with real, biblical faith. And we should love those who fall away, just as God does.

Failure to Commit

Matthew 13:22

In the parable of the sower, the thorny soil represents people who exhibit the best of intentions to follow Jesus, but they never fully commit. The question most of us immediately jump to is, "Are these people really saved?" That's not the issue in this parable. The issue is fruitfulness. It's interesting; if you read the Gospels, Jesus doesn't say much about "Here's how to make sure your soul is ready for eternity." But He said an awful lot about, "Here's how you make sure that your life matters for eternity right now." We think that what matters is, "How many people are in the club? How many people are destined for Heaven?" But the New Testament says, "You're putting the cart before the horse. God is building a new kind of people on Earth; people who will bear fruit for Him and lead many others to faith. Join that movement and bring others in. I'll take care of eternity." Put it this way: Not too long ago, a survey reported that 76% of Americans consider themselves Christians. Far be it from me to determine the sincerity of the faith of millions of strangers; I just know that if 76% of Americans were truly following Jesus, bearing fruit for God, the state of our nation would be quite different. Where Jesus went, lives changed for the better. That should be happening around His followers, as well.

Jesus lists two things that choke out true commitment to Him: "The worries of this life" (If I commit fully to Jesus, I might have to address a few nasty habits, I might have to forgive my enemies, I might be seen as odd by my social circle) and the "deceitfulness of riches" (Scripture doesn't teach that great wealth is evil, but that it can certainly be spiritually dangerous). Jesus is not making an exhaustive list. These aren't the only things that choke out fruitful faith in the life of a believer. We know this because in Mark and Luke's retelling of this parable, Jesus listed other things. In Mark, He mentions, "the desires for other things." In Luke, He says, "worries, riches and pleasures." What does this mean? I take it to mean that Jesus told this parable at least three times, and each time, He listed some slight variations of the factors that choke out our faith and make it unfruitful. The point is that there are things that compete for the attention of believers. God is one plant among many in the soil of our hearts. The question we each need to ask is, "How thorny is my soil?"

God's Favorite People

Luke 14:15-24

Jesus has been invited to dinner at the home of a prominent Pharisee. I am sure no other unemployed, homeless self-educated rabbis got invited to feast on well-aged mutton and wine from a year well back in the BCs. You would expect Jesus to be very grateful and on His best behavior. But instead, in front of all these well-heeled guests who've come to gape and gawk at the miracle-worker from Galilee, He makes several faux pas. First of all, He sees a man who is suffering from edema. It's the Sabbath day, and to a conservative Jew, healing wasn't to be done on the Sabbath. Jesus knew this. But He heals the man anyway, and points out the foolishness of their Sabbath traditions. Then He says, "I noticed that all of you tried to sit in the seats of honor when you came in today." In that time, the closer you sat to the host of a meal, the greater the honor. "The smart move would be to sit in the worst seat in the house. Then the host will come say, 'What are you doing way back here? Come sit close to me." Being praised by the host is so much better than praising yourself."

But Jesus isn't done yet. He then says, "When you throw a party, don't invite the people you love, the people who are good to you, the people who can pay you back. Instead, invite the kind of people who never get invited, the people who could never pay you back. I'm talking about the poor, the blind, the crippled, the lame. Because their Father loves them, and when He sees how nice you've been to them, He'll pay you back better than you could ever dream." This had to be awkward. Everyone could look around and see that no poor, blind, or crippled people had been invited to this party. Jesus was insulting His host. What an ingrate! But these were polite people, so one of the guests decided to change the subject. He blurts out, "Blessed is the man who will eat at the feast at the Kingdom of God." The Jews understood that when the Day of the Lord came, and this world ended, God was going to make this world right. It was going to be like a never-ending celebration, full of joy and laughter and feasting. That's the place everyone is going to want to be. But Jesus says, "Speaking of the feast at the Kingdom…" and tells this parable. Note that in the story, the invited guests rejected the invitation, but the poor, blind and lame were able to feast. Jesus was telling the upstanding citizens around the table, "You're missing out on God's feast, but those you ignore will enjoy it." Jesus was all about overturning society's social ladders. We, as His people, should be as well.

The Answer to Relentless Evil

Luke 11:24-26

This parable--easily one of the most obscure stories Jesus ever told--is about a man who has been demon-possessed. Possession is a murky subject to modern readers. There are many who believe that biblical accounts of possession should not be taken literally, since they come from a more primitive understanding; that people in ancient times who were merely physically or mentally ill were mistakenly thought to be possessed. But this is not the case. The Bible makes a clear distinction between illness and possession. Perhaps demon possession was so common in Jesus' day because the devil knew that the kingdom of God was on the move; this was his futile way of fighting back. At any rate, possession was a terrible thing. It took away a person's self-control, leaving him prone to violence against himself or others, insanity, seizures, even blindness or deafness. In the parable, this man has been cleansed of his demon. And the demon goes away for a while "to an arid place." Then, when he needs a new home, he finds his old host cleaned up but still empty. In other words, the man has gotten rid of his problem, but hasn't put anything new into his life. And so, after the old demon brings seven of his friends into the man, he is worse off than he was before.

Jesus told this story directly to the Pharisees. They had done an excellent job of cleaning up Jewish society. Several hundred years before, the nation had been overrun by Babylon, and the people had been taken captive for 70 years; God's judgment for their immoral, idolatrous ways. But now, the idol worship of the old days was a distant memory. Everyone worshipped on the Sabbath and kept the kosher law. But the Pharisees hadn't addressed the real problem. They had taught the people to behave well, but not to love God. The proof was in how they now treated God's only Son. Jesus' point: The people don't need your dead, legalistic religion, or money, or freedom from Rome. They need me. They need the Gospel of the Kingdom, this message of a new way to God that I am bringing. And if they won't accept it, they will face a far worse judgment than they ever had before. This parable's prophecy came true, by the way. While Jesus' generation was still alive, the Romans destroyed Jerusalem and the Jewish people were scattered. There wasn't a sovereign nation of Israel for nearly 2000 years.

Jesus' message is extremely countercultural. Our efforts to clean up society, to banish poverty, eliminate the putrid effects of racism, to bring peace between nations, and to champion the cause of life are all good. But if they don't lead to reconciliation between God and humanity, our core problem has not been solved. We have simply removed the issues that remind us we have a problem. We're a man with a broken leg who deadens it with doses of Morphine and Demerol. We're worse off than we were before. Jesus stubbornly, audaciously claimed to be the one and only answer.

The Good Samaritan
Luke 10:30-37

And who is my neighbor? asks the religious leader. "Surely not those Roman soldiers over there. Or that tax collector in the crowd. Not to mention all those Samaritans. I know I am supposed to love people, but let's face it. Some people just aren't worthy of my love. Loving them would be encouraging their evil ways." It's a funny thing about us religious people. We never want to limit morality or religiousness. But we feel perfectly fine about limiting love. We love to hear sermons about how we should abstain from certain vices. An old evangelical favorite is a sermon that lists various scandalous immoralities: Pornography, alcoholism, atheism, homosexuality. We love to tell the world about our opposition to these evils. But when someone gets into the pulpit and says we need to love the pornographer, the alcoholic, the atheist and the homosexual, we get uncomfortable. We squirm in our seats. It's so much easier and more natural to judge those kinds of people rather than love them.

This parable can never have the full impact on us psychologically that it did on Jesus' first hearers. The closest we can come to understanding the hatred between Jews and Samaritans is to imagine that the story is about an Israeli soldier who gets injured by a land mine, and a Palestinian man takes him home and nurses him back to health. The irony of calling this the Parable of the Good Samaritan is that to a 1st century Jew, the only good Samaritan was a dead one. And yet in Jesus' story, this man sacrifices so much to help someone who, all things being equal, would rather spit in his face than speak to him. The Samaritan sacrifices his time. He sacrifices his clothing—no one carried spare clothes around in those days; he must have torn his own garment to make bandages. He sacrifices his transportation—now he had to walk the rest of the way. He sacrifices his money—two denarii equals two day's wages. And he sacrifices his prejudice. I know this isn't a nice thing to say, but it is somehow satisfying to look down upon a group of people. That is why racism is such a common sin. We all want to think we're superior to somebody. We all feel justified hating someone. But the Samaritan had to set all that aside and see this injured Jew as a real person. That is tough.

But that's the unique and revolutionary call Jesus was presenting to people. It means more than being moral and religious. The religious leader already had those things. It means more than handing a poor person some money to get them to leave you alone. It means putting yourself in their shoes. Often, when it comes to helping others, our basic motivation seems to be, "What is the least I have to do? If I do this, will it be enough? Can I then go back to living for myself?" But the Christ-follower says, "If I were the one in that kind of need, what would I want someone to do for me?"

Wheat and the Weeds
Matthew 13:24-30

In the world Jesus lived in, people often expressed a strong desire for justice. We see this in many of the Psalms (often called "Psalms of Complaint") in which the Psalmist asks God how long He will allow those who are cruel and selfish to victimize people with impunity. When will He bring down His righteous hand and punish the bullies? Psalm 73 is a good example. It says, *I nearly lost my foothold...when I saw the prosperity of the wicked.*

Jesus may have had this question in mind when He told the parable of the Wheat and the Weeds. In v. 29, the farmer tells His servants not to pull up the weeds yet, *lest while you are gathering up the tares, you may root up the wheat with them.* The weeds in a wheat field in Jesus' time were called darnel. In the early stages of growth, they looked a lot like heads of wheat. And their roots would intertwine with the wheat, so that if you pulled up a weed, stalks of wheat would come up with it. Only at the end of their growth cycle, when it was near harvest time, would the heads of wheat become significantly larger than the darnel. Jesus' argument here seems to be that God is allowing the evil to continue because He is not ready to judge the world just yet. He is not ready for judgment, because every day, He is turning weeds into wheat. If He roots up the weeds today, some potential wheat might be lost.

There is a stream of thought in the Church that says, "This world is too evil. Let's withdraw from it, so we don't become tainted." And so you have people calling for Christians to create their own separate society, with uniquely Christian institutions that will allow us to spend our entire lives separated from unbelievers. You have little Christian conclaves, holy huddles, where we talk to each other about how evil the world is but never go outside to face the darkness. There was a sect of Judaism in Jesus' time (the Essenes) who thought this way. They lived in caves and intermarried, never venturing out into the pagan world outside. They thought this was what God wanted them to do until He brought an end to it all. They died waiting. But Jesus wasn't commanding His people to create a legally-mandated Christian Utopia or to withdraw from secular society. His calling is to go out among the weeds and help them become wheat, because the harvest is coming.

Rich Man and Lazarus
Luke 16:19-31

People sometimes wonder if this story is really a parable. Nowhere else in Scripture did Jesus give names to the characters in His stories. It was always, "A certain farmer," or "a certain merchant." But here, He names both Abraham and Lazarus. We know Abraham was a real person; could it be Lazarus was a real man who died, and Jesus somehow knew his eternal fate, as well as that of this unnamed rich man? Other people get caught up in the details of the story: Did Jesus believe that people in Hell can see Heaven?

All of these questions are missing the point. Like any good story, this is a tale of surprises. Surprise number one: In that society, everyone assumed riches were a reward for a righteous life, while poverty and sickness were God's curse for disobedience. But the rich man dies and goes to Hell, while Lazarus goes to Heaven. Surprise number two: This man calls Abraham "Father" and Abraham calls him "son." Most Jews at that time assumed that since they were descended from Abraham, they were good to go in the afterlife. Yet here's a certified child of Abraham broiling in hellfire. But it hasn't really changed his attitude, has it? He asks him to send Lazarus to bring him a little water. He still thinks of Lazarus as his social inferior, someone who should serve him. The third surprise is Abraham's response to the rich man's request. It sounds noble for this man to say, "Save my brothers from my fate." But his implication is, "I didn't know that I was doing wrong." Abraham calls him on it. "They have the Law and the Prophets." He's talking about the Old Testament. Anyone who has access to the Scriptures, as this son of Abraham would have, can know God's will. He doesn't need a visit from beyond the grave. There are no excuses for missing out on God's grace.

The point of this story is not that wealth is evil, but that God's grace makes up for inequities in this world. In life, most of us would envy this rich man. But after reading this story, envy is far from our minds. Another way of saying this: Any Gospel that doesn't sound like good news to the poor isn't the Gospel of Jesus.

Ten Virgins
Matthew 25:1-13

Jesus went against social custom by making women the subject of His story. Men in those days were unquestioned rulers of the culture. All the rules benefited them. Women, on the other hand, were seen as someone to bear your children and cook your meals. There was rarely any concern for a woman's trials and tribulations. But Jesus, all through His ministry, was different. He went out of His way to talk to women, to address them as equals, when it wasn't socially acceptable. Here in this parable, Jesus could have used any number of male-centered images to emphasize His point about being ready for the last day. But He chooses the image of a wedding, and focuses on ten young girls chosen to be bridesmaids.

For women today, being asked to be a bridesmaid is often more a hassle than a treat. It means buying an expensive dress she'll never wear again (which, by the way, she didn't get to choose and which isn't remotely her color), giving up at least one weekend, throwing showers and standing for a good hour in uncomfortable shoes. But in the first century, being chosen as a bridesmaid was a tremendous honor; something young Jewish girls dreamed of (Jewish girls were married between 12-15 years old). Their job was to wait in the darkness on the wedding night, with their torches (or lamps) lit. When the bridegroom showed up, they were to escort him to the bride's house. Once she was picked up, the entire procession, led by the bridesmaids with their torches, would proceed through town, to the sound of music and dancing. Finally, they would return to the groom's house, where the bride would symbolically enter, never to leave again. This would be followed by 7 days of feasting. Now, if it was a young girl's dream to be a bridesmaid, it was her nightmare to do anything that might mess up the wedding. So when Jesus told a story about this, every woman in the crowd must have perked up.

This is one of several stories Jesus told in Matthew 24-25 about the return of The Son of Man. That was a Messianic title, one Jesus used to refer to Himself. Imagine the audacity of this unlettered carpenter, to say that He was not only the long-awaited Messiah, but that He would one day return to Earth to judge the living and the dead! His point in this story is the same as in all biblical prophecy: Be ready. The five foolish bridesmaids looked like they were ready for the bridal party. They had their wedding clothes on, and the torches at their sides. But when the moment came, they were shut out. There are a few chilling details in this parable. First is the sense of terror when the bridegroom arrives. Next is the shutting of the door. Jesus' message is clear. There is a final moment in history when the age of grace is over. Once The Son of Man returns, there are no second chances.

Talents
Matthews 25:14-30

Jesus told two very similar stories which we know as the Parable of the Talents and the Parable of the Minas. The differences between the two stories seem subtle, but they point to two very different messages.

In the first story, Jesus tells of a man going on a journey. He leaves his **three** servants in charge of his money, which is measured in talents. A talent was a large sum—as much as 20 years' salary for a regular working man, so the servant who had 5 talents was given an enormous responsibility. Most interpreters agree that these talents represent the resources God gives to each of us. In fact, it's because of this story that the word "talent" first began to be used in English to mean a gift or an aptitude. Poor as they were, Jesus' listeners understood that God had blessed them all with certain resources. Some of these "talents" were material things, like money, land, or possessions. Some were relational: Their family and friends. Some were their gifts, abilities, knowledge and passion. In the story, the servants are given different amounts to oversee; in the same way, some people seem to have more resources than others. But here is where the story is countercultural: According to Jesus, greater blessing equals greater responsibility. To whom much is given, much is required. In other words, the resources we have are not ours to possess. We are managers of money, possessions, relationships, talents and opportunities. In the end, our Master will want to know what we did with those resources He left in our care. In other words, the parable of the talents is about faithfulness. Are we faithful and trustworthy with the things He has given to us? Or are we like the foolish servant who buried his money in the ground so that he wouldn't have to think about his responsibility? Are we wasting our lives?

Minas
Luke 19:11-27

In the second story, a man is going away to be made king, and he leaves his **ten** servants with a mina each. A mina was a much smaller unit of money, worth around 100 days' salary. But this is still a significant responsibility. I believe the master in both stories represents Jesus. He knew He would soon be leaving the world, and leaving His Kingdom work in the hands of these men and women who followed Him. He wanted them all to know that this was a big responsibility, and that when He got back, He would hold them all accountable for the way they handled that task.

In the story of the minas, each servant is given the same amount, but they produce different results. One servant multiplies his master's investment by ten, and the master says, "Now that I'm king, you be in charge of ten cities." Another servant multiplies the same investment times five, and he is rewarded also, but with less. He gets to rule over five cities. Do you see the difference in the two stories? In the story of the talents, the faithful servants all heard, "Well done, come share in your master's happiness." But in the story of the minas, the rewards are different based on the production of the servant. So while the first story is about faithfulness, the second story is about fruitfulness. If we only pay attention to the first story, we might say to ourselves, "Jesus just expects me to do my job well." But when we read the second story, we realize Jesus expects us to expand His Kingdom. He expects our lives to make a positive difference in the world, and we will be rewarded differently in Heaven based on the difference we make down here.

There is one more difference between these two stories: a subplot in the story of the minas. The master is being named king. His new subjects try to prevent this from happening. At the end of the story, the master destroys them. Jesus may have been referring to relatively current events. When Jesus was born, the ruler of Israel was King Herod the Great, who ruled because Rome gave him authority to do so. Herod's cruelty, paranoia and megalomania are well known to anyone who studies the ancient Middle East. When he died, his son Archelaus went to Rome to ask for his father's kingdom. A delegation of Jews from Jerusalem also went to Rome to plead with Caesar NOT to let Archelaus become their king. They were joined by over 8,000 Roman Jews who also stood against Archelaus. Everyone in the crowd was familiar with these events. They would have drawn the parallel between Jesus' story and Archelaus. Why would Jesus compare Himself to the son of a cruel dictator? Jesus was saying, "I am the rightful king of this world. Some of you reject me. You treat me just like you treated Archelaus, when unlike him, I deserve your allegiance. But I am going to be king whether you like it or not. And when I become king, it will be too late to change your tune." It's not a politically correct notion these days, but Jesus taught that our status in eternity will be determined first and foremost by whether or not He is king of our lives.

Sheep and Goats
Matt 25:31-45

A young corporate hot shot was to be interviewed by one of the world's largest corporations for an executive VP position. They flew him into the city where they were headquartered, and reserved a room for him in a luxury hotel that they owned. As he walked through the automatic glass doors, he knew he was a shoe-in for the job. He had the Harvard MBA, he was wearing his Armani and his Cole-Haans, and his resume was impeccable. And although he'd never say this out loud, it didn't hurt that his dad played golf with the Secretary of the Treasury. Still, he was anxious to make a good impression. He addressed the man behind the hotel counter, an ancient little fellow with big ears, wispy gray hair and glasses three sizes too big for his face. "Hi, I'm to meet Mr. Murray for a very important meeting tonight over dinner. I'd like to go ahead and get to my room as soon as possible so I can prepare." "Right away, sir," said the old guy, ringing a little bell. When a porter didn't materialize immediately, the young guy said, "Looks like I'll need you to handle these bags for me, old timer." "Right away, sir." But as the old man walked around the counter, his elbow hit a big crystal vase, knocking it to the floor. It shattered, and sent thousands of clear glass marbles rolling all around the lobby. He apologized profusely, called someone from housekeeping to take care of the mess, and then said, "This way, sir. Mind your step."

When they got to the elevator, the old man said, "I'm sorry sir, but I seem to have forgotten your room number. Would you wait here for a moment?" The hot shot sighed loudly, then stood impatiently tapping his feet while the old man waddled painfully back to the desk, checked his computer screen, and then hobbled all the way back. As they exited the elevator on the 19th floor, the old guy stumbled a bit, dropping one of the bags. The hot shot yelled out a few choice expletives and then, "My laptop is in there! And you better pray you didn't break it!" When they finally arrived at the room, the hot shot said to the old man, "I know it's customary in this situation to give a tip. So here's a tip for you: This afternoon, Mr. Murray is going to offer me a very high position in the corporation that owns this hotel. I can tell you that my first order of business is going to be firing you. So you might want to get that resume ready." A few hours later, the young hot shot sat in front of his glass of white wine in the hotel restaurant. He was surprised to see the old man walk up and take the seat across from him. Same big ears, wispy hair, and big glasses, but now in a three-piece suit. The old man said, "I didn't introduce myself earlier. I'm Mr. Murray. Sometimes I like to spend a day working in one of my hotels. Keeps me grounded, you know. And by the way, you might want to keep YOUR resume ready."

In the Parable of the Sheep and the Goats, Jesus warns that many spiritual hot shots will be unpleasantly surprised on Judgment Day. The biggest surprise of all will be when they find out that the needy, marginalized people they ignored were actually Jesus in disguise. "For whatever you have done for one of the least of my children, you have done for me," He will say to those who enter His Kingdom. Which side will you be on?

Dishonest Manager
Luke 16:1-13

This may be the most unusual story Jesus ever told. The "hero" of the story is a crook. He's a man who oversees the financial affairs of a rich man, and he gets caught cheating. When he knows he's about to lose his job, he goes to the people who owe his boss money and says, "Take your bill and mark it down." These are huge bills, by the way. In both examples the amount he tells them to "write off" is equivalent to two years' salary for a working man. His motive is clear: He wants these people to be so grateful for their reduced debts that they will help support him after he is fired. He has put his boss in a bad position. The boss will either lose money by accepting a reduced payment, or lose face by going back on his manager's word. And then comes the surprise ending: The boss finds out about this deceit and praises him! This is such a bizarre story, some Christian interpreters try to change the meaning of it by tweaking some of the details. They'll say, "The manager was just cancelling the interest on the debt, and charging interest was illegal by Jewish law anyway," or "He was just forgoing his usual commission." But those can't be true, because Jesus Himself calls the man unrighteous or dishonest in v. 8. At the same time, Jesus praises him! What is going on here?

I think the key to understanding this story, and what Jesus wanted us to know through telling it, is found in dissecting v. 8. Jesus is saying that quite often, people who profess to follow God are not wise when it comes to life in the Kingdom. Unlike the man in the story, we don't understand our current situation. He saw that life as he knew it was going to end soon, so he moved quickly to get himself ready for the next stage. But most Christians don't live like this. Too often, all of our efforts and thoughts and prayers and dreams are focused on stuff we want in this present world, which is passing away. Some of us are good at living that way, and most of us aren't. So those who aren't good at it end up unhappy because we don't have the stuff we want in life, and we blame God for our unhappiness. Meanwhile, the people who are good at living that way spend their whole lives thinking they're successful—because they're living the dream, after all—only to find out at the end of their lives that it was all a waste.

If you want to put Jesus' wisdom into effect in your life, you could use v. 9 as your daily prayer and say something like this—"Lord, help me today to use my life to win friends for your glory, so that when it is gone, they will be welcomed into eternity." Or you can pray the prayer I learned from David Platt, author of the book *Radical*: "Lord, let me make a difference for you today that is utterly disproportionate to who I am."

Chapter 5: His miracles
Matthew 9:27-31

Most people, even those who know very little else about Jesus, know that the Bible says He performed miracles. Should we take these stories literally? After all, most of us have never seen anything like this happen in our own day—a man lays His hands on two blind men, and suddenly they can see. Contemporary preachers who claim to have such power give off an unmistakable whiff of phoniness (Why must they only "heal" people on stage, before TV cameras? Why not go to a hospital and heal whoever is sick?). Some are exposed as frauds by intrepid investigative reporters. So can stories of healing ever be believed? Clearly the apostles testified these stories were true, and the early church believed them. At least three of the four Gospels were written when many of the eyewitnesses of Jesus' life were still alive; if the Gospel writers had invented these stories, people would have called them out and the Gospels would have never caught on. So yes, I believe we can take these stories as historical fact. Based on the Four Gospels, Jesus must have performed hundreds of miracles in His three year ministry, most of which were never recorded in print (see John 21:25).

Why did Jesus perform these miracles? After all, He didn't wipe out disease entirely. Healed people—even the few people Christ raised from the dead--eventually died anyway, just like the rest of us. Also, as we will see, being known as a healer made Jesus' life increasingly difficult, as He was swamped around the clock with requests for help (which explains why He often told people, as He did in this story, to keep their healing secret—He didn't want the publicity). What I see in Scripture tells me there are two answers to this question: First, Jesus performed miracles because He wanted everyone to see that "the Kingdom of God has come." Nothing would be completely the same after this. His life was leading to something brand new, and ultimately, to a world where there was no disease, pain or death. But second, we see Jesus filled with compassion whenever He saw people hurting. He couldn't walk away from suffering without doing something about it. It simply comes down to this: Jesus performed miracles because He wanted to. It brought Him joy to help people. If Jesus was who He said He was (God in the flesh), then it should make us very glad to know that our God is so compassionate.

Demon Possession?
Matthew 9:32-33

When you read the Gospels for the first time, you may be struck by how many of Jesus' miracles involved casting demons out of possessed people. (We briefly touched on this in our earlier look at the parable in Luke 11:24-26). Modern readers often find this confusing. Some explain it away by reasoning that the Gospel writers were merely reflecting a primitive way of looking at illness. After all, they say, the "demons" in the Gospels manifested themselves in ways that sound to modern ears like blindness, muteness, epilepsy or schizophrenia. But this explanation doesn't hold up to scrutiny: The Gospel writers are careful to distinguish between people who had an illness and those who were afflicted by demons (see Mark 1:32, for example). It's also interesting to note that demon possession isn't mentioned at all in the Old Testament. The ancient Israelites didn't blame their illnesses on evil spirits; why should their New Testament-era descendants do so? In many of the Gospel accounts of Jesus' encounters with demons, He converses with them. The Gospel writers clearly saw demons as personal beings who meant serious harm to those they afflicted. Why was this phenomenon of demonic possession—which had never before been seen—so prominent in Jesus' day? The Bible doesn't give us an explanation. Perhaps it was the feeble effort of the forces of evil to counteract the presence of God's Messiah in the world. If so, the strategy backfired spectacularly.

This brief account in Matthew 9 is one of many in the Gospels. We'll look at a few of the notable ones in the readings below. But here are a few things we can learn from these accounts, when taken as a whole: 1) Jesus was stronger than the demons—and it wasn't close. Nowhere in Scripture do we see Jesus fighting a tooth-and-nail battle against an evil entity with the outcome uncertain until the very end, like we see in epic fiction (think Jedi vs. Sith in Star Wars, or Harry Potter vs Voldemort). Instead, Jesus simply commands the demons to leave, and they do. 2) The demons recognize Jesus. Often, they would cry out, "You're the Son of God!" Ironically, the forces of evil knew Jesus' true identity long before any humans did. And this is significant: They were terrified in His presence. 3) This is not something we should worry about. Whether demon possession still happens today is debated by theologians. But the letters of the New Testament (the books of the New Testament that come after the Gospels and Acts) are words of the apostles to the early church (and to us) about what it means to follow Jesus now that He is no longer here in the flesh. Demonic possession doesn't seem to have been a big concern to them, based on their instructions. Certainly, we're not commanded to act as amateur exorcists, or to ascribe the bad behavior of others to demonic possession. You may think your boss, your ex-boyfriend, or your mother-in-law is the Devil incarnate, but the advice of Scripture is to love that person in the name of Christ. Jesus wasn't afraid of evil, and neither should we be.

Water to Wine
John 2:1-11

John in v. 11 identifies this as the first of Jesus' miracles. It is an unusual one, indeed. It doesn't seem to meet an urgent need like healing a disease, feeding hungry people, or rescuing sailors from a storm. Jesus even seems a bit reluctant to perform the miracle. It's almost like He has to be talked into it by His mother. Almost.

It's hard for us today, in our "my home is my castle" world, to understand how important hospitality was to the ancients. It was such a treasured virtue, the typical Israelite would open his home to a stranger in the street, so that the honor of his village wouldn't be impugned. So the newly married couple in this story wasn't merely facing a premature end to their wedding reception when their wine ran out; they were facing potential embarrassment in their community that would dog them for years. Mary comes to Jesus with her concerns. She knows what He is capable of. Jesus' answer seems harsh. But an adult man calling His mother "woman" in First Century Israel is not as rude as it would be in our culture. He is not rebuking Mary, but He is reminding her about His true mission, His "hour" or "time." Essentially, He's saying, "I don't take orders from you, Mom. I follow my Father." Again, this wasn't meant as a rebuke, and Mary doesn't seem to have taken it that way. She tells the attendants, "Do whatever He tells you." Jesus was in charge. From there, we see some interesting details. The jars filled with water that Jesus changes into wine held between twenty and thirty gallons of wine each. Jesus has just given this couple a substantial wedding gift of up to 180 gallons of very fine wine.

The detail that makes me smile, however, is the comment of the "master of the feast." Jesus would later say that human history will close with a great wedding feast, as His Bride (all those who belong to Him) is joined with Him forever. We sometimes think of Heaven as a pious but rather dull place. The master of the wedding feast in Cana would disagree: This future Bridegroom, Jesus the Christ, knew how to make the best wine of all. If He did that for a bride He barely knew, what will He provide for us, His true Bride?

Showdown in the Synagogue
Mark 1:21-28

It's just another Sabbath day in the small seaside town of Capernaum. You hear there's a visiting rabbi who will be teaching today; Since nothing new ever seems to happen in a place like this, a little variety can't hurt. Then He begins to speak. After only a few minutes, you begin to realize your heart is beating faster. The tiny hairs on the back of your neck are standing up. The emotion inside you: Is it anger, joy, excitement, fear, or some combination of them all? This man is saying things that you've never heard before. The Torah cannot change, so surely He can't be right…yet somehow in your heart, you know He's telling the truth. Suddenly, you hear a blood-curdling scream that nearly startles you out of your seat. You turn to see Jacob, the dairyman, standing and pointing a trembling finger at the teacher. Just yesterday, you and he were joking about the tailor's daughter marrying the carpenter's lazy son. Now there is sheer terror in his eyes as he begs this man not to harm him. Only he doesn't say, "Don't destroy me," he says, "Don't destroy *us.*" Before you can puzzle these things out, the teacher's voice rings out sharply, "Shut up! Come out of him…right now!" Immediately, Jacob utters a sound you'll never forget—part animal, part something not of this world—and collapses. After a few breathless moments, he pushes himself up on his elbows. His forehead is lined with sweat, and his eyes are large, but his expression is one of relief. The teacher's face has changed again; He looks like a man surveying his own ill child. "Are you alright?" Jacob mutters a shaky, "Yes. Thank you." The teacher continues with His lesson, about how the long-promised Kingdom of God has now come into the world. Hours later, back at home, you sit and wonder. Nothing new ever happens in the little seaside town of Capernaum. But this man is definitely something new. And you're not totally sure how you feel about it.

Everyone who ever met Jesus had to confront the same questions: Is this man who He claims to be? Can I accept Him? That is still true today.

It Begins
Mark 1:29-32

The people of Capernaum must have been in an absolute uproar after the scene in the synagogue. But it was the Sabbath day; Jewish law said it was a day of rest until sundown. After the service, Jesus was invited to the home of Simon Peter, His new follower, where he healed Peter's mother-in-law, who was sick with a fever. I have been to Capernaum. I saw the ancient synagogue, unearthed by archaeologists, and a building many believe to have been Peter's home. If they're right, Peter's house was only a short walk from the synagogue, and (in the opposite direction) from the waters of the Sea of Galilee, where we can assume Peter's boat was docked. This would become home base for Jesus for the rest of His earthly ministry. Imagine three generations of one family under the roof of one small house, plus now Jesus and His constantly growing band of followers. It must have been one chaotic place.

That evening when the sun went down and the Sabbath had ended, it became wilder still, as people from all over that region brought their friends and relatives for Jesus to heal. His life up to this point had been rather quiet; growing up in a small town, doing the somewhat solitary work of a carpenter. Even the first days of His ministry were obscure: His baptism was followed immediately by His retreat into the desert for forty days of fasting and being tempted. But now, He would never know another slow, uneventful day again. Verses 35-37 tell us that after ministering to people late into the night, Jesus got up early to spend time alone in the presence of His Father (obviously, that was more important to Him than sleep). But this sweet time of refreshment was interrupted by His disciples, blurting, "Everyone is looking for you!" He was as human as we, and surely such a schedule exhausted Him. Yet He never walked away from a needy person. One day, He would say "It is finished." But not yet.

The Touch
Luke 5:12-15

Early in this book, we looked at Matthew's version of this same event. We acknowledged that Jesus didn't have to touch this man in order to heal him. Jesus more than once healed people when He wasn't even in their physical presence (see our next story). But Jesus touched this man. Perhaps it was because, due to the Jewish laws concerning his leprosy, this man hadn't been touched by another human since the day of his diagnosis, which may have been years. Jesus didn't touch him just to heal him; He touched him so he could feel human again. And this miracle story, which lacks so much of the spectacular flair of most others, is told not once, but three times in the Gospels (in Matthew, Mark and Luke). Why?

I'd like to propose a reason: I think the Gospel writers were just as impressed by Jesus' compassion as they were by his miraculous power. A righteous Jew in that era would have been obsessive about ritual cleanliness; to touch something or someone considered unclean meant that one was disqualified from public worship for a time. Yet Jesus touched a woman with a chronic hemorrhage, the casket of a dead young man, this leper, and many other people who were ritually unclean. His heart went out to them in their suffering and isolation, and that overrode any selfish concerns He might have possessed. In doing this, He was turning religion on its head. Religion should not exist to separate us from the "unclean." It should motivate us to reach out to those who are hurting. What about those of us who consider ourselves devout today? We may not have the power to heal diseases with a touch. But we can pay attention to people who no one else notices. Who do you know who needs to feel human again?

Walls Will Crumble
Matthew 8:5-13

It is difficult, if not impossible, for Americans to understand the attitude that first-century Jews held toward the Romans. This Empire had conquered and occupied their land and often intentionally offended the strict religious sensibilities of the Jews. When this centurion approached Jesus, he surely expected that He would refuse his plea for help. Perhaps that's why, according to Luke's version of the story (Luke 7:1-10), the centurion had brought along some Jewish friends to vouch for his kindness to their people. But Jesus didn't need to be convinced; He was ready to not only heal this commander's servant, but to teach His fellow Jews in the process.

The centurion somehow understood the spot He was putting Jesus in by asking a rabbi to visit the home of a Gentile (which would have rendered Jesus unclean). In his statement, He was essentially saying, "I know you have the same power over unseen things that I have over the hundred soldiers in my command." We've just seen how ritual cleanness was no barrier for Jesus when it came to helping people. But He did as the centurion asked, and then let everyone in earshot know that this Gentile had shown a greater faith in Him—Israel's true Messiah--than any Jew had done. He then predicted this man was only the first: Someday soon, race would no longer be a factor when it came to salvation in the God of Israel. "The feast of Abraham" was His way of describing the world yet to be, when this world has passed away and the Son of God rules uncontested. In that world, there will be no walls between Jew and Gentile, rich and poor, black and white. The intense racial pride felt by Jesus' fellow Jews, and the searing anti-Semitism that His people had faced for centuries would all be a distant, unpleasant memory.

Relentless Faith
Mark 2:1-12

In Mark's account, this is the first time Jesus faces the criticism of Israel's religious leaders. They accuse Him of blasphemy, a charge He will later face in the trial for His life. But there are so many other intriguing details. Note, for instance, where this miracle took place: V. 1 says it was at "home," meaning the house of Peter. One has to wonder what Peter thought when he saw the roof of his house destroyed by this man's friends.

In fact, those friends are the focus of the story. Jesus praises their faith and gives them credit for the paralyzed man's healing and the forgiveness of his sins (which, from an eternal perspective, was the greater miracle). What did He mean? Picture these four men. They hear that Jesus has returned to Capernaum. They know what they must do. After carrying their stricken friend for untold miles, they find to their utter heartbreak that the small house is so packed, they can't even get inside. But these guys are problem-solvers. They will not be denied. They climb to the roof, carrying their friend with them. They dig through the roof (houses in that time were covered in branches and sod, so this was an easier task than penetrating fiberglass shingles and wood, but still), then carefully rigged a way to lower their friend safely through the hole with ropes. They go to this herculean effort in spite of their weariness from the journey so far, and in spite of knowing they will face the ire of the homeowner for their damage to his roof. They do this because they love their friend, and believe strongly that Jesus is his only hope. Jesus praises them because He wants everyone to know: Whoever comes to Jesus--in spite of the obstacles from naysayers, in spite of their own backstory and sinfulness—will be welcomed, and will be saved. That kind of relentless faith is the stuff of greatness.

Healing on the Sabbath
Mark 3:1-6

Let's all admit it's hard for us to picture Jesus angry. For those who grew up in Sunday school, we picture Him smiling placidly, holding a small child. Even irreligious folks tend to see Him as an eternally chill proto-hippie. But Mark tells us straight out: Jesus was mad. The man with a crippled hand had a difficult life; this was a world without rights for the disabled, and precious few job opportunities for someone with only one usable hand. Likely, this man lived off the charity of his family. Meanwhile, Jesus knew the importance that His fellow Jews placed on the observance of the Sabbath day. It was one of the Ten Commandments, a tradition that went all the way back to creation (See Genesis 1). Perhaps more importantly, it was one of the key "boundary markers" that separated Jews from Gentiles. While the rest of humanity went hurriedly about their business, Jews put aside their burdens one day out of seven in reverence for, and in trust of the provision of, their God. They took this command so seriously, their rabbis had written massive tomes of instruction on what did or did not constitute "work." These regulations were so voluminous and complex, they would make our tax code seem like a Little Golden Book. They stipulated how far a Jew could travel on the Sabbath (and so Jewish towns were platted in such a way that everyone could legally walk to synagogue), how much weight one could carry, and what sorts of aid were allowable. For instance, one could not tend his ox or sheep, unless that animal had fallen and was in danger of dying (the proverbial "ox in a ditch"). Regarding humans, it was lawful to render medical aid if someone's life was in jeopardy, but not otherwise.

This day in the synagogue, Jesus was bringing new life to a man who had likely lost hope. But He was also making a very specific statement: If your religion takes the commands of God and twists them until they are a burden instead of a path to freedom; if your religion sets up arbitrary ways to make you feel superior to others; if your religion prioritizes man-made moral boundaries over the welfare of your neighbors, it is bad religion. Based on the Gospels, nothing made Jesus angrier than perverted religion. I wonder what He thinks of ours?

Crashing a Funeral
Luke 7:11-17

The funeral practices of ancient people would seem strange to us today, with our sedate memorial services. A first-century Jewish family would bury their loved one immediately, handling the body themselves (there were no morticians in their culture). They didn't share our embarrassment at expressions of grief, so people would tear their clothing, put dust on their heads, and wail aloud. To weep over someone else's loss was considered a kindness, so a large crowd had turned out for the funeral of this young man in the small town of Nain, six miles from Jesus' hometown of Nazareth. Their tears were surely genuine: The death of an only son was an especially tragic loss. The fact that his mother was widowed meant her future livelihood was in question. People of the village would do their best to care for her needs, but in a society where everyone lived on the knife's edge of poverty, her prospects were dire indeed.

Jesus met this procession with its open casket and dozens of weeping mourners on His way into the town. As Jesus touched the edge of the casket, the man sat up and began speaking. I imagine the startled pallbearers nearly dropped him! The people in attendance thought immediately of stories of Elijah and Elisha, great prophets who had also once resuscitated the dead. They were sure this meant God had come to help His people. But Jesus' main concern was the bereaved widow. Verse 13 says *His heart went out to her*. What a beautiful expression that is! I wonder if He thought of His own mother, who He had left in the care of His brothers. One day, she would stand on a dusty hill in Jerusalem, watching her own Son's agonizing death. On that day, He would do His best to comfort her. Until then, His heart would go out to all who needed it. It still does!

Who is this Guy?
Luke 8:22-25

One would think that, since the disciples had left behind jobs, homes, and families to follow Jesus, they must have been confident in who He was. Yet His words and actions consistently surprised them. The Sea of Galilee is several hundred feet below sea level, and the local topography makes it prone to sudden, violent windstorms. Several of the disciples were experienced sailors, but even they had seen nothing like this. Mark's account of this story (Mark 4:35-41) shows their panic, as they wake Jesus up with the words, "Lord, don't you care that we're about to drown?" When He does wake up and save all their lives, their response is not, "Thank God, we're not going to die!" Instead, it is *Who is this?* First of all, what kind of man is sound asleep in a boat that is being swamped? Given Jesus' breakneck schedule surrounded by clamoring crowds, it's not surprising that He was exhausted, taking advantage of a few hours of quiet to catch up on sleep. But this is more than natural weariness. Then, when He awakes, He doesn't show fear. Instead, He speaks to the storm and it stops. The term Luke uses is *He rebuked the storm.* It's from a Greek word that means "to punish." Jesus spoke to the storm as if saying "Bad dog!" to a yapping Yorkie. Who does that? And the storm didn't die down gradually. It was immediately calm. Modern-day people who think Jesus "got lucky" by waking up just as the storm was starting to dissipate weren't there; Matthew was. He testifies of something that cannot happen in nature. No wonder these men were confused. They hoped Jesus was the Messiah they'd been expecting. But events like this kept making them wonder, "Could He be even more than that?"

The Other Side
Luke 8:26-29

In v. 22, just before the storm, Jesus said, "Let's go over to the other side of the lake." That sounds innocuous enough to us. But I'm betting the disciples shot each other nervous, confused glances. He was talking about going over to enemy territory. The region on the other side of the Sea was called the Decapolis. The Jews thought of it as where the Devil himself lived. It was full of pagan temples, where all sorts of perverse sexual rituals were practiced. In Jewish thought, a pig was the most unclean of all animals, but in the Decapolis, a pig was an object of worship. There was a legion of six thousand Roman soldiers in Decapolis. Their symbol was the boar's head. For thirteen Jewish men to go to Decapolis was crazy talk.

When they got to the other side, they weren't met by the huge crowds that they were used to seeing in the Jewish areas. Instead, one man came to meet them. He was a notorious man, known to be so psychologically damaged, no one could control him. I imagine the disciples were terrified. They had just sailed through a deadly storm, but I bet they were ready to get right back on the boat. But Jesus didn't see this man as a monster. This was somebody's child. Notice that the demons called themselves Legion. I wonder if that was an attempt to intimidate Jesus. If so, it didn't work. By the way, this is one of only two times in the Gospels Jesus used His power to destroy something (the herd of pigs). Why did He do it this way? Perhaps to show the locals that their object of worship wasn't worth treating with such reverence. Perhaps to show the poor demoniac that he was truly free; he could see the evidence that the demons had left him. Why did the townspeople respond the way they did? After all, we expect them to be happy that the man they feared was now pacified. I think it was because Jesus was from the other side. If someone from the other side had this much power, they were afraid He might do to them what He had done to the pigs. I suppose no one in that time was able to understand a man who didn't see things in terms of "our side" and "their side." Jesus wanted to eliminate those kinds of distinctions.

My Little Girl
Mark 5:21-43

There are two miracle stories in this passage. We'll take them one at a time. As the father of a (grown) daughter myself, I find it moving to read the words, "My little girl is dying." The girl in question was twelve, so he was speaking in terms of affection. My daughter may be an adult now, but she'll always be my little girl. This man, Jairus, was the ruler of a synagogue. That means he was a layman in charge of organizing worship: He saw to it that there was someone to lead the prayer, read the Scriptures and teach on them each Sabbath day. It was a profound honor. Most members of the religious elite in Israel viewed Jesus with skepticism or even hostility. If Jairus was in that camp, he lost all of those convictions when his daughter's life was at stake. He didn't know where Jesus' power came from. He just knew that Jesus was His only hope.

The mourners assembled at Jairus' house were probably paid to be there. That seems strange to us, but it was customary in that society. The more mourners one had and the louder their weeping, the greater the honor for the deceased. In the ancient rabbinical writings known as the Mishnah, it says that at a burial "Even the poorest in Israel should hire two flutes and one wailing woman." This would explain why the people went from weeping loudly one moment to laughing at Jesus the next. In verse 41, Mark chooses to quote Jesus in Aramaic, which was the language He spoke, instead of the Greek that made up the New Testament. Why did he make this choice? I would guess that Mark found these words particularly meaningful. Jesus had just fought His way through a hysterical crowd and chased away a crowd of cynical paid mourners. If anyone had reason to feel stressed and cranky, it was Him. Yet His words, "Little girl, arise," and His instruction to give her something to eat sound more like the words of a loving Father than a harried case worker rushing from client to client. As for Jairus, we know nothing else of what became of him or his daughter. I suspect that, as the religious establishment became more actively (and violently) opposed to Jesus, he had tough decisions to make.

Desperation and Empowerment
Mark 5:25-34

When I was growing up, I raised animals for an annual livestock show in our community. One year, I raised chickens. I noticed that chickens are particularly cruel animals; if one chicken in a coop has a sore, the others will peck at it until the wounded chicken is dead. This is actually where we get the term "pecking order" from; dominant birds will peck at those who are weaker. Our world is not so dissimilar. This poor woman was far down the pecking order of society. Not only was she a woman in a world where women had few rights; she suffered from a medical issue (most scholars agree her bleeding was menstrual in nature) that rendered her ritually unclean under Jewish law. That meant that any pious Jew would not have physical contact with her. If she were married when this issue began, most likely her husband left her for another. The Law which God gave to protect the marginalized was used instead to make her an outcast in every sense. To make matters worse, the primitive medical system of her day had taken all her money without curing her condition.

She knew there was no way a great man like Jesus would render Himself unclean by actually touching her. But if she touched His garment without Him knowing it, He was free of responsibility, and there was a chance it could work. She pushed through the clamoring crowd, reaching desperately for the tassels on His shawl…then she felt it. With a surge of joy that made her dizzy, she felt somehow that her long nightmare was over. Then, just as quickly, her heart sank as she saw Him stop and slowly turn. The crowd suddenly grew silent. He demanded that the person who had touched Him come forth. Her life, which had just been restored, was now over. She confessed what she had done…and heard the most empowering words of her life: *Your faith has healed you; Go in peace and be freed from suffering.* The Greek word for "healed" is the same as the word for "saved." This woman was not just free from a terrible condition; she was saved forever. And Jesus had worded it in such a way that she knew her faith had brought it about. Years later, a follower of Jesus would write, *There is neither Jew nor Gentile, slave or free, male or female, for all are one in Christ Jesus.* Jesus made the pecking order obsolete.

Do You Want to Get Well?
John 5:1-18

Jesus wasn't always nice. I know that sounds heretical, but this story is evidence of that statement. Why would He say to a man who has been crippled, sitting impotently by the banks of a supposedly miraculous pool for 38 years, *Do you want to get well?* What sort of question is that? Then when He found the healed man in the temple, He threatened that if the man didn't repent of his sins, *something worse may happen.* It all sounds extremely insensitive to modern ears. Jesus was healing on the Sabbath again. But this time, He wasn't in a synagogue in Galilee; He was in Jerusalem, where the religious authorities were on constant high alert. Note that they were more intent on finding Jesus so they could scold Him for telling this man to carry his mat on a Sabbath, not so they could thank Him for healing one of their fellow citizens. The man, for his part, showed little loyalty to Jesus. He quickly informed the authorities who Jesus was, probably to avoid getting in even more trouble. Then things really escalated.

The authorities quickly realized that Jesus was guilty not only of breaking their Sabbath laws, but also of considering Himself equal to God. Jesus didn't deny their charges. He said, *You study the Scriptures diligently because you think that in them you have eternal life. These are the very Scriptures that testify about me, yet you refuse to come to me to have life* (vv. 39-40). His insensitive question to the crippled man was really a question for His people: "Do you want to get well? I'm here, God in the flesh, ready to save you. Do you really want salvation?" His warning to the man of "something worse" wasn't referring to his health. Eternal separation from God because of rejecting the One meant to save us all is indeed far worse than any physical illness. One has to wonder whether Jesus deliberately healed this man on the Sabbath just to provoke this argument. I tend to think He did. The truth isn't always nice.

Loaves and Fishes
Luke 9:10-17

The Four Gospels were written on the testimony of the eyewitnesses, the disciples themselves. So it's surprising how, throughout these books, the disciples are portrayed as being in a state of constant befuddlement. This story is a perfect example. Jesus had sent the Twelve out to preach and minister on their own for the first time. They came back, exhilarated but exhausted. Jesus took them away from the crowds for a time of rest. But this was during the height of His popularity; getting away wasn't so easy. Instead of being indignant, like a celebrity of today, Jesus welcomed the people (Mark's account of this story says *He had compassion on them, because they were like sheep without a shepherd).* After another long, full day of teaching and healing, the weary disciples must have been grasping for some reason to send the people away so they could get their promised rest. They seized on the perfect idea: Weren't all these people hungry? After all, they had walked for miles to this desolate place and stood in the sun all day listening to Jesus. We wouldn't want them to pass out on their way home, would we? Sending them away now would be the decent thing to do. Imagine the looks on their faces when Jesus said, "You're right. So give them something to eat."

Verse 14 says there were 5000 men there. That doesn't include the number of women and children; the total number of people could have been double that or more. We know at least one small boy was there, thanks to John's version of this story; he was the one who brought the five loaves (actually small rolls) and two fish (salted fish, more like sardines than tuna). I don't think Jesus was trying to embarrass His friends; He was giving them an opportunity. What would have happened if the disciples had obeyed Him? I believe they would have not only witnessed a miracle; they would have had the joy of performing one. As it was, they picked up twelve baskets full of food left over. People there that day may have noticed some things that reminded them of the story of the Exodus: The loaves and fishes were like the time God made manna fall from Heaven to feed His hungry people. The twelve baskets left over were symbolic of the twelve tribes of Israel. But the disciples, when they looked around at those twelve baskets—essentially a doggie bag for each of them—probably thought to themselves, "From now on, when He tells us to do something, we'd better do it."

I am With You
Mark 6:45-52

Matthew's version of this story (which we'll consider in chapter 7), features Peter attempting to walk to Jesus atop the waves. Yet Mark, who according to church tradition got his information directly from Peter himself, doesn't mention that detail? I suspect Peter, by the time he told his story to Mark, was sufficiently humble that he chose to keep the focus on Jesus instead of giving himself a supporting role. When we focus on Jesus in this story, two things stand out. One is His words to the terrified disciples when He arrived at the boat: *Take heart. It is I. Do not be afraid.* Think about it: These men, are in survival mode, struggling to stay afloat in the midst of a that threatens to send them to the bottom of the deep. Even the fishermen in the boat are terrified; how must a white-collar guy like Matthew have felt? Then, as their cramping muscles and frayed nerves reach the point of no return, they see a spectral figure gliding trouble-free across the waves. I'm assuming, since it was night, they could only see Him when lightning struck. Can you picture it? One of them sees Him first, a quick flash, and tries to convince himself it was a hallucination. Moments later, several more see Him. Every few seconds, as the lighting bolts flash and pop, this otherworldly being gets a few steps closer, until all Twelve stop rowing and bailing, and sit, awaiting what must be their Judgment. I am sure they only recognized Him as Jesus a few seconds before He climbed in. In light of all that, how could Jesus say "Do not be afraid"?

The answer is in the second statement that stands out: *And they were utterly astonished, for they did not understand about the loaves, but their hearts were hardened.* They had just witnessed Jesus feeding 5000 men (plus women and children, perhaps as many as 15,000 people) with five small loaves and two fish. They had seen Him do so many miracles by now, how could they possibly doubt that He would come through for them this time? They had Jesus with them; it was all they needed to know. That is why He could say, "It is I. Do not be afraid." We live today in a culture of people eager to disavow responsibility, to live free of obligation. But Jesus says, "Trust in me. I won't fail you. I will get you through the storms of this life and bring you safely to the other side."

Something Has Changed
Mark 6:53-56

Here we see what happened when Jesus and the Twelve reached the other side of the Sea. We may assume that this short passage is a simple summary of the busy schedule Jesus and His disciples faced in those days—from teaching and healing all day to feeding thousands to braving a storm; and now more crowds, more teaching, more healing. But there is something else going on here. The entire sixth chapter of Mark is about people refusing to believe in Jesus. It starts with Jesus being rejected in His own hometown of Nazareth. It says He could do only a few miracles there, and was amazed by their lack of faith (we'll look more closely at that later). It goes on to tell of Herod the King decapitating Jesus' cousin, John the Baptist. Then the disciples show their lack of faith during the feeding of the crowds and during the storm. Yet here in Gennesaret, the people are full of faith and overjoyed to see Him. Why the contrast? Here is an interesting theory: Remember the demoniac Jesus healed in Mark 5? He wanted to go with Jesus, but Jesus told him to stay and tell his story. The man did, spreading the news throughout the towns. Gennesaret was a region with a high concentration of Gentiles. Could it be that this man's enthusiasm about his own healing had stirred up excitement among non-Jews? And here's something else: You may have noticed that Jesus often told recipients of healing to keep their stories secret. But He rarely did so when Gentiles were involved. Why? Perhaps because He knew Gentiles didn't carry their false expectations of what a Messiah was supposed to be. They were ready to receive Jesus as He was. It was strange; the people who should have been most excited about Jesus were skeptical, and the people who should have been skeptical were excited. Something had definitely changed, and it would still take the disciples many years to understand and accept it all.

Crumbs to Dogs
Matthew 15:21-28

As we've already seen, Jesus wasn't always nice. But here, He seems downright rude. In fact, it's worse than you think. "Dogs" was a term Jews used to describe Gentiles; a dog in those days was seen more as a scavenger than a pet. So Jesus, in speaking to this poor woman who was begging for help for her daughter, called her a racial slur. Some read this story and see this woman convincing Jesus—against His will—to heal her child. Could it be that Jesus held the same hateful attitudes as His neighbors, only to be corrected and taught by this faithful woman? That is the way it appears. But there is another explanation which, I believe, makes more sense.

Jesus has healed Gentiles before. He has even spent time in Gentile territory. But now He is deep behind "enemy" lines in Tyre and Sidon. He withdrew there after a long, intense dispute with religious leaders in Israel over laws of ritual purity; as always, the religious elites were most interested in what kept people outside God's family, not in bringing them in. Now this woman comes to Jesus, calling Him "Son of David." Interestingly, Mark calls her a Greek (to the Jews of that time, it was an all-purpose name for Gentiles) in Mark 7:26, but Matthew calls her a "Canaanite," which was the name of Israel's ancient enemies from the time of Joshua and the Judges. He perhaps wants to highlight the oddity of a descendant from a hated pagan race using the Jewish term for Messiah. Yet Jesus treats this woman like He's never treated anyone before, Jew or Gentile. At first, He refuses even to speak to her (Whereas before, He has always healed people—of any race--immediately). Then, when she throws herself at His feet, He speaks in exactly the way a self-righteous religious purist would speak. Her answer is revealing. Just like a dog in a house benefits when the humans in that home have a big meal, so even Gentiles are blessed when God sends the Jews their promised Messiah. That was God's promise centuries before to Abraham (Genesis 12:3, *all peoples on earth will be blessed through you*), although the children of Abraham rarely acknowledged it. Rather than being corrected by this woman, Jesus was allowing this woman's amazing faith in the wideness of God's grace to correct His disciples. They likely were struggling with the idea that following Jesus meant offending the leaders of their people, and going against ideas they had been raised to believe. Jesus was showing them that if they wanted to join the Kingdom God was bringing into the world, some things had to be left behind.

The Enigma
Mark 7:31-37

There was no such thing as a boring day when one followed Jesus. Here He is back in the Decapolis, a place He was once asked to leave. Now the people bring Him a man who has lost the ability to hear or to speak clearly. Jesus once again does something new. This time He touches the man's ears and spits on His hand, touching the man's tongue. He looks up to Heaven before He speaks the healing words. Why? Mark doesn't tell us. Perhaps He wants the man to know what is about to happen to Him, and where the power comes from. I love the reaction of the crowd. Mark says they are *overwhelmed with amazement.* Scholars call this term a "hapax legomenon," which means a term that appears only this one time in Greek literature. In searching for the right term, Mark was forced to invent a new one to describe how this miracle affected the eyewitnesses. They weren't just amazed, they were overwhelmed with amazement. Think about it: Jesus didn't just fix this man's ears. That would have been miraculous enough. But He also enabled the man to immediately speak clearly. Learning to talk again should have been a process that took the man months or even years. Jesus was unpredictable. For those with desperate faith, He consistently exceeded expectations. For those who wanted to silence Him, He constantly foiled their censorious plans. And for those still trying to figure Him out, He refused to fit into any known category.

Deja Vu
Mark 8:1-10

The fact that Jesus already fed a crowd of thousands leads many to believe Matthew and Mark simply repeated the story of one event for emphasis. But there are many differences between the two accounts: the number of people fed, the number of loaves and fishes, the number of baskets full of leftovers. Even the type of basket mentioned is different; the baskets in this second story were much larger than in the first. More significantly, the first feeding took place in Jewish territory, while this one seems to have taken place in the Decapolis, yet another clue from Jesus to His disciples that He had come to redeem the entire world, not just Israel. If we still need more convincing, in Jesus' own words in Mark 8:18-21 He speaks of two separate feeding miracles.

So how do we then explain the disciples' question in v. 4? Having seen Jesus do this once before, why did they not expect Him to do it again? Perhaps this indicates that Jesus did miracles only when absolutely necessary. There were no frivolous miracles, no "miracles of convenience." I wonder how often Jesus and His disciples went hungry, when He could have easily conjured food for them. Even more, I think this story shows us something about the nature of faith. Even people who have seen God do amazing things in their lives can easily slip back into a narrow-minded mentality. Faith is like a muscle; if you don't use it often, it atrophies. In that analogy, the disciples were like life-long couch potatoes. Their long-dormant faith muscles had had quite a workout in their time with Jesus, but they were still far from being in fighting shape.

The Two-Stage Healing
Mark 8:22-26

In a class during my freshman year of college, one of the texts we read was the Gospel of Mark. This was in a state university. Many of my fellow students had no experience with the Bible at all; others had grown up in religious homes and were eager to prove they had transcended their stuffy upbringings. When we got to this story, several students in my class observed that Jesus' attempt to heal this man had failed on the first try (or only partially worked), so He needed to do it again. That's one way to look at it. Is there another possibility? First, this is yet another example of how Jesus personalized each contact. He took this man by the hand and led him away from the crowds. He spit on His eyes and laid His hands on Him; He doesn't use this precise method with anyone else in the Gospels.

So why does He have to do the same miracle twice? Perhaps the man lacked the faith he needed until he had partial sight. Or maybe Jesus was letting the blind man decide how much grace he wanted to receive: "Here's what I've done for you so far. Is that enough, or would you like me to go all the way?" It is noteworthy that this is the only recorded time Jesus ever asked someone if His healing had worked. Based on the way Jesus dealt with people, He always showed extraordinary insight. He seemed to tailor His interactions with them to the spiritual needs of the person. Even in His healing miracles, it was the person's soul, not their body, that He cared most about (remember Him forgiving the sins of the paralyzed man, then, almost as an afterthought, healing his body?). I believe Jesus knew that a two-stage healing was what would change this man's soul. Even if my classmates were right, that Jesus needed two tries to get it right, the end result is that the man was healed! To quibble over how a blind man was healed seems to me to be the ultimate example of burying the lead. By the way, Jesus' disciples were watching this. They too had been touched by Christ. They too had partial sight of who He was and what He came to do. But they needed more understanding. That would come.

Blame the Victim
John 9:1-41

There is so much to ponder in this story: Yet again, we see a religious establishment that is more concerned with their arbitrary Sabbath rules than with the salvation of a fellow human. We also see that the establishment has officially condemned Jesus, and anyone who follows Him. We see parents who would rather guard their own reputation in the community than stand by their son. And we see that son offering a beautifully simple testimony: "All I know is that I used to be blind, but now I can see." This is one of the longest miracle accounts in Scripture, and it's touching to see this man go from physical and spiritual blindness to complete transformation in both body and soul. But as we seek to know Jesus better, the very beginning of the story is what I find most significant. The disciples ask Jesus, *Who sinned, this man or his parents, that he was born blind?* Jesus quickly sets them straight. We all tend to make assumptions about people we see. We judge them for their problems: "If she had any sense, she'd leave him." "I just don't understand why he doesn't get a job." "Well, no wonder she has no friends. She's not very friendly." We do this because it makes us feel better. We feel like we have the answers; and we are at least doing better at life than these poor souls. Jesus shows His disciples—and us—that our judgmental assumptions are usually miles from the truth.

The Transfiguration
Matthew 17:1-13

This event is so important—and so confusing to modern readers—that we need to spend a little extra time on it. In the text, Jesus doesn't give a debriefing to His three friends afterward to say, "Here's what all that was about." I think that's because Peter, James and John, being devout Jews, understood certain allusions to Israelite history that we don't. That isn't to say they fully understood what was happening atop that mountain. Far from it. Mark's version of the story (Mark 9:2-10) says Peter was baffled and overwhelmed at what he was seeing. Jesus told the disciples not to tell anyone about this *until after the Son of Man is raised from the dead.* He knew that their understanding now was incomplete, and He didn't want them spreading false ideas. But these men did indeed come to understand this event later on. Peter himself wrote about it in 2 Peter 1:16-18. So, if we look at this event through their eyes, what do we see?

Moses was seen in Judaism as the man God used to bring the Law to Israel, the code by which every good Israelite lived and worshipped God. The first five books of the Bible, the Torah, are where the Law is found; these five books are commonly known as the books of Moses, and the Law is known as the Mosaic Law. **Elijah** was one of the greatest prophets. The books that modern Christians call "The Old Testament" were known to the Jews as "The Law and the Prophets." The disciples would later come to understand Moses and Elijah being there as a sign saying, "The Law and Prophets both point to this man, Jesus." In addition, Moses in Deuteronomy 18 was told by God, *Someday I will raise up a prophet like you among the people*. That was a prophecy of the coming Messiah. And the prophet Malachi had said that God would send Elijah back to Earth to prepare the way for the Messiah (Mal. 4:5). Now both Moses and Elijah were here, like a neon sign saying, "This is Him!" **The cloud** was reminiscent of the pillar of cloud that the Jews followed in the Exodus from Egypt to the Promised Land. They called it God's "shekinah" glory, which was a word that meant "to dwell." When that cloud showed up, people didn't say, "Where'd all this fog come from?" No, they knew this was the shekinah glory of God; it meant, "God is here." And those words **the voice** spoke—which sound almost exactly like the words the voice from Heaven spoke at Jesus' baptism, by the way—they contain references to three different Messianic prophecies, from Psalm 2:7 to Isaiah 42:1 to Deuteronomy 18:15. Peter, James and John would have caught all those references.

And if that was all that had happened--if Jesus had simply had a conversation with these two dead prophets and God's glory and voice had been present--Peter and the others would have concluded that it was a confirmation that Jesus was the Messiah they were looking for, and nothing more. But that wasn't all. Jesus was **transfigured**. It is impossible for us to picture this, but the best way to understand it is that, right before their eyes, Jesus became something more than human. The word that's translated "transfigured" is a Greek word metamorphoo, from which we get the word metamorphosis. That's the word we use when a caterpillar becomes a butterfly. Think about it: Moses and Elijah were there, but they just looked like men. Only Jesus looked like more than a man. Jesus' followers would come to understand that this wasn't just Jesus' way of saying, "I am greater than Moses and Elijah, greater than the Law and the Prophets." This was Jesus' way of saying, "This is who I really am. This is what I gave up to live among you."

Luke wrote about the transfiguration, too. Here's a detail he included in his account (Luke 9:31): *They* (ie, Jesus, Moses and Elijah) *spoke about his departure, which he was about to bring to fulfillment at Jerusalem.* Don't you wish you could have heard that conversation? I would really like to know what was said. After this day, Luke 9:51 says, *Jesus resolutely set out for Jerusalem.* From this point on, Jesus was headed for the city where His opposition was based; the city where He would be arrested, accused, tortured and put to death. Nothing was going to stop Him or deter Him. Were Moses and Elijah there to encourage Him in this virtual death march? Peter, James and John walked down the mountain utterly stunned. It would be a long, long time before they fully understood the implications of what they had seen and heard.

The Nature of Faith
Mark 9:14-29

Jesus and His three friends encounter a chaotic scene as they come off the mountain of Transfiguration. A man has brought his son to the nine remaining disciples, hoping they could deliver the child from a horrible existence. They have failed, and now the Teachers of the Law, eager for any reason to discredit the ministry of the rogue rabbi from Nazareth, are there accusing them. Jesus' response in v. 19 seems harsh. It's clear He was rebuking His disciples, not the man and his son. His response to them in v. 29 indicates they had surrendered to arrogant thinking, assuming they possessed power over evil spirits, and had not humbly sought God in prayer like they should. It's a glimpse into how frustrating life could be at times for Jesus. A man from Heaven, with a perfectly tuned sense of righteousness and wisdom, at times found even His closest friends difficult to live with. Internally, He longed to be back home with His Father, apart from the brokenness and ignorance of our world.

Yet He continued to love His friends, in spite of their slowness to understand and believe. His treatment of this man is touching, too. The man's description of his son's plight is heartrending, and his statement to Jesus, *I do believe, but help me overcome my unbelief,* is refreshingly honest. Jesus doesn't say, "Nice try. Come back when your faith is up to par." Instead, He delivers this boy to the relief and delight of the father. This story tells us much about how God views faith. In both His dealings with the disciples and the pleading father, Jesus never says, "Just believe. Try harder." He tells His friends to pray for the faith they need. And the father does exactly that. I've talked to unbelievers who say, "I wish I could have faith like you, but I just don't. I guess I'm not wired that way." Modern religion, in contrast, presents faith as if it were something we can conjure up through sheer willpower: "Just believe in your miracle, and you'll have it!" Jesus reveals a way different from either one. If you recognize your need for God's power in your life, but you lack the confidence in Him, ask for it. He's waiting for you to ask for faith. He won't say no.

Where Are the Other Nine?
Luke 17:11-19

Recently, I heard about a Starbucks drive-through where for 10 hours, hundreds of customers paid for the drink ordered by the person behind them in line. It was a 10 hour pay-it-forward. When I heard the story, my first thought was, "Who was the jerk who took a free drink and drove away?" The thing is, I've been that jerk. I have benefitted from the generosity of others in ways much more significant than a $5 coffee. How many of those times have I expressed true gratitude? I think about that in light of this story. Jesus healed ten lepers in one moment. Once again, this miracle is different: He doesn't touch them or speak majestic words. He just says "Go show yourselves to the priest." As they are on their way, they realize the disease is gone (don't you wish you could witness that moment?). One of them comes back to thank Jesus. Luke makes sure we know this man's ethnicity: He is a Samaritan. The hatred between Jews and Samaritans was deep-seated. Samaritans had a murky racial makeup, part Jew and part Gentile, and to the ethnically fastidious Israelites, this was reason enough to distrust them. But Samaritans also had their own site for worshipping Yahweh, the God of Israel, which they claimed was the true place He dwelled. Most respectable Jews would avoid contact with Samaritans. They would even walk the long way to a destination to avoid going through Samaritan territory. This is not the only time Jesus pointed out the righteous actions of a Samaritan in order to highlight the hypocrisy of His fellow Jews. But what of those other nine former lepers? I doubt they meant to show Jesus any disrespect. Surely they were so overjoyed at this incredible miracle, so excited about returning to the lives they had lost, so intent on being reunited with their families, they forgot to acknowledge the source of their miracle. Jesus in this story isn't trying to shame them. But He is hoping to show us what we miss when we lack gratitude. The joy of being healed eventually goes away. The typical drudgeries of life overshadow a momentary triumph. The exhilaration may last longer than a free latte, but it vanishes, just the same. Only those who acknowledge the source of their blessing get something more lasting. Wouldn't you love to meet the One who is the source of everything good you've ever received? Wouldn't you like to know what He has planned for you? That is what Jesus is asking us in this story.

Raising Lazarus
John 11:1-44

This is a famous story, and quite moving. Jesus has brought the dead back to life before, but this is different. This isn't in a private room with only His most trusted disciples in attendance, as with Jairus' daughter. It's not at a funeral in far-off Cana, either. This is in Bethany, just a short walk to Jerusalem. When word got out about this particular miracle, many people became followers of Jesus. The enemies of Jesus even considered murdering Lazarus (see John 12:9-11). V. 35 is well known as the shortest verse in the Bible. It's one of only two recorded times Jesus cried. But what, exactly, made Him weep? We get a clue from v. 33. Where it says, *He was deeply moved in spirit*, that's a translation of a Greek word that refers to anger bordering on rage. In fact, it literally means, "to snort like a horse." Jesus wasn't sad; He was angry. But angry at what? Not at the poor sisters or the other mourners. I think it's clear: He was angry at death. John in the first chapter of His Gospel asserts that Jesus was God in human flesh, the Creator living in His creation. That means He made Lazarus, Mary, Martha, and all those other people weeping there that day. And it broke His heart to see, up close and personal, the way Death, the ultimate uninvited guest, was squatting on His creation and ruining everything.

At the same time, throughout this chapter, Jesus makes it clear that He allowed Lazarus to die, then raised him up for one reason: So we would believe. Believe what? Think again about what Jesus said to Martha in v. 25: *I am the resurrection and the life.* In other words, "I am the one who has the power to overcome death." The dreaded enemy who aroused such fury and sorrow in Christ, the unspeakable destiny we try to avoid acknowledging, will be defanged. This was His promise. His question to Martha ("*do you believe this?")* hangs heavily in the air around everyone who says they believe in Him. If we believed this promise, we would no longer fear aging, clinging pathetically to our vanishing youth like a dog snarling at anyone who threatens to take his nub of a bone. Grief would be forever changed; we would still shed tears, just as Jesus did, at the death of loved ones. But we also would rejoice for them, knowing we'll see them again. Our anxieties about temporary things like money, status and success would melt away, since this life would be only a dress rehearsal for eternity. If we believed what Jesus said that day, others would be able to see it in the way we live. So…do you believe this?

Bartimaus
Mark 10:46-52

Jesus is just twenty miles from Jerusalem now. Passover week will start in a day or two. The roads are clogged with pilgrims headed into Jerusalem to celebrate. Jesus clearly has much on His mind. On Sunday, He will ride into Jerusalem on a donkey's colt to the cheers of the crowds, but He knows that within days, He will hear a very different outcry from the people of that city. The shadow of the cross, which has loomed over Jesus for years, is now blotting out nearly everything else in His mind. But He still has time to help another person.

The crowds want Bartimaus to be quiet. There are beggars everywhere in Israel, and their incessant pleading grates on the jagged edges of one's nerves. But Jesus hears him. He asks a pointed question: *What do you want me to do for you?* Just fifteen verses earlier, He asked the same question of His disciples, James and John. The brothers were seeking power; this man only seeks deliverance. Did Jesus use the exact same words as a message to His disciples ("This is the humble attitude that God seeks in us")? Is He simply giving Bartimaus the opportunity to express faith? Perhaps He has both in mind.

The bigger question, in my mind, is this: In v. 52, when it says he followed Jesus after His healing, does it merely mean he joined Jesus and the crowds walking to Jerusalem for the feast, or that he became a true disciple of Jesus from this point? Consider the fact that he cast aside his cloak and ran to Jesus. The cloak was not just a garment; it was what he had spread before him as a way to gather in the alms he collected through his begging. He had little in this world, but what he had, he left behind, just like the other disciples. The fact that Bartimaus is named is also significant. The Gospels don't typically supply the names of those Jesus healed. This fact may indicate that Bartimaus was known personally to some early Christians who read this account. Consider also that the word "healed" in Greek can also mean "saved." So Jesus in v. 52 literally said, *your faith has saved you.* If this man did become a disciple of Jesus—and I think that's the case—consider this: In about a week, he will witness with his newfound sight his Savior being arrested, beaten, rejected and crucified.

Miracle of Destruction
Mark 11:12-14, 20-25

This event represents one of only two times Jesus used His power to destroy something (the other was the herd of pigs in Gadara, see Luke 8:26-29). This is one disturbing story. Jesus getting angry at a fig tree for not producing figs—especially when it wasn't even the season for figs—is bad enough. But using His power to destroy the tree seems petulant, and honestly, a little scary. It is totally inconsistent with what we have seen of Jesus so far. Unless…

Jesus had a tendency to be unpredictable, to do shocking things to get His point across (perhaps you've noticed that). In this, He was like many of the Old Testament prophets, who did shocking things like marrying a prostitute (Hosea), wearing an ox's yoke (Jeremiah), or walking around stark naked (Isaiah) to prove a point when the people wouldn't listen to plain old preaching. Consider the event that this story is "wrapped around" (a technique Mark used several times): Jesus was on His way to Jerusalem to "cleanse" the temple. We will deal with that story in more detail in chapter 8, but what Jesus did there was a shocking action, deeply offensive to many of His fellow Jews. He was essentially declaring the Temple system obsolete. Consider also that in the Old Testament, prophets sometimes compared the nation of Israel to a fig tree, with the "fruit" being their faithfulness to their covenant with God. Jesus wasn't lashing out like a spoiled child; He was acting out a parable. He was rendering judgment on His own nation, which had yearned for a Messiah for centuries, yet rejected Him when He came. If you're wondering how a man who was so compassionate for those who were suffering could blithely declare the coming destruction of His own nation, consider this: If your doctor found cancer in your body, would you want her to hide it from you? Downplay it? I would want to know the cold, brutal truth, especially if there was something I could do to change my destiny. I believe Jesus was doing all He could to save His nation by telling them the truth they would rather not hear. That's a prophet's job.

The Untold Stories
John 20:30-31 and 21:25

John ends his Gospel in an unusual and tantalizing way. All of the incredible stories of Jesus' miracles were only a fraction of the wonderful things He actually did. This stands to reason; by most estimates, Jesus' formal ministry lasted three years, and the indications from the Gospels are that He never failed to help someone who truly needed Him. John in his Gospel has only recorded seven miracles, or "signs." His purpose is not to give us an exhaustive record, but to prove that Jesus was the Son of God. His statement in 21:25 is a great example of hyperbole, but it does tend to make the reader's heart beat a bit faster. Wouldn't you love to read some of those other stories, too?

The miracles of Jesus didn't bring about any permanent changes to this world. He made sick people well, blind people see, and lame people walk. He even brought some people back from the dead. But all of those people eventually got sick and died. Jesus didn't cure any diseases permanently. He fed people who were hungry, but He didn't wipe out world hunger. He stilled storms, but He didn't abolish natural disasters. His miracles really were signs, as John says. They were signs that this was more than a mere man. And (as we will discuss in more detail later on) they were signs that there is a very different world coming, ruled over by this shockingly humble teacher who in life always refused power. His story isn't done yet.

Chapter 6: The Sermon on the Mount
Matthew 5:1-2

Matthew 5-7 is widely regarded even by non-Christians as some of the most excellent moral teaching ever delivered. Mohandas Gandhi, although a devout Hindu, used this message as his inspiration for non-violent protest that ultimately transformed India from a British province to an independent nation. Some people see this as Jesus' improvement on the Old Testament Law. In other words, Jesus is saying, "If you want to get to Heaven, here are the rules you have to follow." But the consistent message of the New Testament is that Jesus came to free us from the Law. We are saved on the basis of God's grace, not on the basis of our own goodness. Others see this teaching as idealistic and beautiful, but not really a realistic way to live. They see Jesus as a dreamer who was trying to inspire us to long for a better world. There is a Christian version of this interpretation that says that Jesus didn't really expect anyone to live this way; He was just trying to show us that we couldn't be perfect, so that we would know we needed grace. In other words, these people think the Sermon on the Mount was Jesus' way of setting us up to fail, so that we would come back to Him for salvation. I passionately disagree with this assessment, too.

I believe even the picture we have of the Sermon on the Mount is wrong. In movies about Jesus, they picture Him on top of a high mountain, with hundreds or even thousands of people scattered along the hillside (in a spoof by Monty Python, one man standing further down the mountain looks at his friend and asks, "Did He just say blessed are the cheesemakers?"). But notice what v. 1 says: Jesus saw the crowds, then went up on the mountain and *sat down,* and *His disciples* came to Him, and then He began to teach. The crowds were the people who thronged around Jesus for most of His ministry, some of them wanting to figure out whether He was really the Messiah, others wanting to be healed, and still others just wanting to catch a glimpse of this miracle-worker everyone was talking about. The disciples were the 12 we know today, along with other men and women who had left their regular lives behind to become Jesus' followers. So I believe Jesus took this opportunity to have a period of intense training for His followers. It may have lasted several hours or several days, but these words are the ones the Spirit inspired Matthew to record for us. So the Sermon on the Mount is really Jesus telling everyone who is His follower: "Here is the ultimate goal of following me. By God's grace, and through the power I give you, you'll learn to live like this; not just the spiritual overachievers, but the ordinary believers. If you'll allow me to create this life in you, you'll change the world."

Better to Be Broken
Matthew 5:3

Jesus starts the Sermon out with eight statements that Christians have called "The Beatitudes," from the Latin word for "blessed." Eight times, Jesus describes the kinds of people who were living the blessed life. That term "blessed" has a very religious sound to it today, but it actually means something like "lucky," as in, "what a lucky guy." In other words, the blessed life is what we would call the good life; the blessed people are the people we all envy and want to emulate. So, if we were writing the Beatitudes, they might go something like this:

Blessed are those who are cocky and boastful, for they get lots of attention.

Blessed are the bodybuilders and supermodels, for they always have a date on Saturday night.

> Blessed are those who are aggressive and self-centered, for they get what they want.
> Blessed are the party animals, who throw away responsibilities and live for themselves, for they have all the fun.
> Blessed are the whiners and complainers, for they get their way in the end.
> Blessed are those who know how to lie, for they get elected.
> Blessed are the bullies, for no one messes with them.
> Blessed are the rich, for they can buy all the happiness they want.

But the good life Jesus envisions is quite different. For instance, the first statement is "blessed are the poor in spirit." Jesus wasn't talking about financial poverty, although that is often part of the condition He was describing. In The Message, a paraphrase of the Bible, Eugene Peterson puts it this way: "You're blessed when you're at the end of your rope; with less of you, there's more of God and His rule." That's hard for people to swallow, especially those who live in an affluent culture. But Jesus knew what He was talking about: We see pride as a virtue, but Scripture speaks against pride more than any other sin. People who are on top of the world can't see themselves realistically; they can easily rationalize or ignore their faults. But broken people are quick to ask for help. They've run out of excuses. Every person in Scripture who did something great for God started out broken in some way. Whereas the people most opposed to Jesus were intensely proud of their own religious attainments. It's better to be broken. Even in our best moments, it's best to remember how deeply dependent upon God we really are.

Righteous Tears
Matthew 5:4

Growing up, I was often small for my age. Elementary school can be brutal, especially for a little guy. I knew that if I was going to survive, I needed to be tough. And so I resolved to myself that I would never cry; I could not show weakness. When I was knocked to the ground during touch football, I popped back up as if it didn't hurt. When my feelings were wounded, I kept it to myself. I played two Little League games with a wrist that was so swollen and sore from a playground fall, I couldn't throw the ball from second to home plate. When our family doctor examined me and told me I had a hairline fracture, I was secretly thrilled. I felt that playing two baseball games with a broken arm validated me.

That mentality may work on the playground, but not when it comes to following Jesus. According to Him, there is something holy about our tears. The rest of the Bible bears this out. Psalm 56:8 tells us that God keeps all our tears in a bottle. He knows when we are grieving, and He remembers it forever. Many of the Psalms are characterized by scholars as "Psalms of Complaint," in which the psalmist pours out his heart before God in graphic terms. There's an entire book of Scripture called Lamentations. Twice in Revelation, it says that in heaven God will wipe away every tear from our eyes. Holy people are comfortable expressing grief. We know of two times when Jesus shed tears: Once when He stood at the tomb of a friend (John 11:33-35; note that it's the tears of others that provoke His sorrow), and once as He entered Jerusalem for the final time (Luke 19:41-44). In both cases, He wept for the pains of others, but nowhere in Scripture does it say we should hide our own sorrow. The modern Christian idea that we should wear a mask of constant happiness is not only unbiblical, it's un-Christlike. And it's a sure recipe for misery. I was well into adulthood before I became comfortable with tears, but I am the happier for it.

Strength Under Control
Matthew 5:5

"Meekness" is not a word we often use these days. Because it rhymes with "weakness," it is not seen as a virtue. Yet Jesus here says meekness leads to the good life. How? Meekness is synonymous with gentleness, which can be defined as "strength under control." One year at the Houston Stock Show, we saw a draft horse competition. Draft horses are massive animals that have been bred not for riding, but for pulling heavy loads. To me, that is the perfect picture of this Beatitude. That is strength under control. Though that draft horse towers over the man driving him, he is at his command. Just a little tap on the side with a quirt gets him moving. Just a slight pull on the reins points him in one direction or another. Because that horse is under control, he enjoys a pretty nice life—warm blankets, plenty of food and water, and he is able to accomplish useful things. Unfortunately, many of us live more like the bulls I saw at the rodeo later that night. The bull is a strong animal, too, but he uses that strength and fury to hurt people. And he gets hurt himself. Someone's always trying to conquer him. It's better to be strong and gentle than wild and self-centered. Which are you? Are you a draft horse or a bull? Do you use your strength to dominate those who are weaker than you? Do you kick people when they're down, take every opportunity to exalt yourself? Or do you use your strength for good? Do you refuse to say the words you know will break someone's heart, even if they deserve it? Do you resist striking back, even when everyone says you are justified? Jesus didn't say it was easy to be meek. But think about a life without constant ego-driven conflict. Wouldn't that be a better way to live?

Satisfaction
Matthew 5:6

My bet is that few of the people reading this have ever known true hunger or thirst. We've skipped a meal or two; we've gotten hot while doing work in the summertime. But we've never felt the kind of hunger and thirst that is relentless, that makes us willing to do anything for food and water. The people Jesus spoke to knew that kind of hunger and thirst. It was an effective way of saying, "If this is your single-minded goal, you will achieve it." In a world where The Rolling Stones' iconic lyric "I can't get no satisfaction, though I try, and I try, and I try, and I try…" is true in spite of our affluence, it would be good to know what Jesus promised here. But what is "righteousness?" There are actually two ways that word is used in the New Testament. One meaning is blamelessness before God. The word "justified" is used in this sense as well. It is a courtroom word; one pictures a judge looming over a trembling defendant, banging his gavel and saying, "Innocent of all charges. You are free to go."

But righteousness is also sometimes used synonymously with justice. Isaiah 1:17 gives a good definition of justice—*Learn to do good; seek justice, reprove the ruthless, defend the orphan, plead for the widow.* In other words, justice is helping those who are hurting, poor, and weak. In Amos 5, God essentially says to Israel, "Stop worshipping me! Your services and your offerings and sacrifices are meaningless to me because of the way you treat the poor!" He climaxes this in Amos 5:24—*But let justice roll down like waters and righteousness like an ever-flowing stream.* Micah the prophet gives us our standard for living in Micah 6:8—*What does the Lord require of you but to do justice, love kindness, and to walk humbly before your God?* In Matthew 23:23, Jesus condemns the Pharisees for their legalism without love—*Woe to you, scribes and Pharisees, hypocrites! For you tithe mint and dill and cummin, and have neglected the weightier provisions of the law: justice and mercy and faithfulness.* In other words, treating people justly is more important to God than any of our religious observances.

So which kind of righteousness did Jesus say we should yearn for? I say He meant both. We should want to live in a way that is pleasing to God. And we should also fight for the rights and needs of others. Most of us tend to lean one way or the other: We are either socially conservative, morally upright rule-followers or social-justice activists at heart. But since we're called by Jesus to both love God AND our neighbors, we need to hunger and thirst for both.

Mercy
Matthew 5:7

A very wise teacher once decided to give her students a lesson they would never forget. She brought clear plastic bags and a huge sack of potatoes to school. She told each student, "Think of every person you have a grudge against. Take a potato, write their name on it, and put it in your sack. Keep that sack with you at all times, until I tell you to give it up." The students followed their assignment. As they wrote the names on the potatoes, many of them took great satisfaction in it; it was a validation of their pain. Some even wrote angry words under each person's name: "This is for stealing my boyfriend." "Thanks a lot for being the worst dad ever." "I deserved an A. Why didn't you give me one?" "I hate bullies like you." "You ruined my life." As the days went on, some of the students encountered new offenses, and dutifully added potatoes to their sacks. Pretty soon, the sacks started getting heavy. The potatoes started to mold, sprouted eyes, and began to smell bad. It was hard to sleep at night with a bag of moldy potatoes in bed with you, and lugging that sack around wasn't good for their social lives. Finally, they asked, "When is the assignment over?" The teacher answered, "You can take each potato out only when you have truly forgiven the person whose name is written on it."

A look at our favorite action movies shows that our culture admires people who bring swift vengeance upon those who have hurt them. But Jesus would agree with the teacher's object lesson: The good life, a life of freedom, is found when we show mercy, not retribution, to those who have wronged us.

Heart Matters
Matthew 5:8

An old prophet showed up unexpectedly one day in a small town. He went to the house of a local man and asked him to present all of his sons; one of the boys was to be anointed as the future King. As he surveyed them, from oldest to youngest, he saw some impressive physical specimens, but the still, small voice of God whispered, "Don't focus on the outward appearance like humans do; I care more about the heart." In the end, the prophet had to ask the man if he had any more sons; none of these would do. The man explained there was one more, out tending the sheep. This forgotten boy was called in, and Samuel recognized young David as a man after God's own heart (1 Samuel 16). The rest, as they say, is history.

If a prophet like Samuel can be too caught up in superficial things, how much more can we? Yet the path to the good life is not the same as the quest for killer abs, flawless skin, a corner office, or a six-figure salary. These are the accoutrements we call success; but those who submit their entire selves to God, allowing Him to purge them of all dark and selfish motives, truly see Him…and experience the blessedness He brings.

Peacemakers
Matthew 5:9

In the cemetery where my grandparents are buried, there is a very interesting tombstone. Two brothers are buried there, side by side, with the same death date in the mid-1940s. There are photographs on the tombstones, a portrait of each brother. Years ago, my grandfather told me the story. These two brothers, men in their forties, were involved in a dispute over property. One had built a fence, and the other brother said it encroached on his side of the family land. So, in the midst of the dispute, one brother had gone to see the other one. Their words had gotten heated. One brother ordered the other one to leave the house. He said, "I'm going to get my gun. If you are still here when I come back, I'm going to shoot you." But he didn't leave. Instead, he got a gun ready for himself. My Grandpa was a young man at the time, and he remembered being one of the first people on the scene after the shots rang out. He drove there with trembling hands, because he didn't know what he would find. What they found was two dead brothers, killed by each other.

That's our world in microcosm. The God who made us yearns for peace among His children. So when we help two acquaintances overcome a disagreement; when we confront a husband who is on the verge of cheating on his wife; when we call out the racism we see in people of our own ethnicity; when we speak up to de-escalate rising tension in a workplace, we are doing the work of God. None of this is popular or, for that matter, safe. Imagine what could have happened if someone had tried to physically intervene between those two feuding brothers. It is uncomfortable in the extreme to be a peacemaker. But it is blessed. In our hyper-violent world, we have plenty of opportunity to put Christ's words to the test.

The Paradox of Persecution
Matthew 5:10-12

Long ago, we had an exterminator who had studied for the ministry. When he came to our door once a quarter, he would bow with a flourish and say, "Greetings! I am the angel of death for bugs!" He loved to talk theology with me as he did his work. He had jokes: "How do you make holy water? You boil the Hell out of it!" But I remember something serious he once asked me: "If Christianity were illegal, would there be enough evidence to convict me?"

Jesus, in this last Beatitude, was speaking to people for whom these words would not be theoretical. History shows that they would face imprisonment and even execution from their fellow Jews, including a certain zealous Pharisee named Saul. Those who left to take the Gospel elsewhere would face even harsher treatment; Church tradition says that eleven of the twelve Apostles suffered gruesome deaths. Those who lived in Rome in the Sixties, including that one-time persecutor Saul (now known by his Romanized name, Paul) and Peter, would experience a terrible persecution at the hands of the mad emperor Nero. Of all the Beatitudes, this one is the hardest to understand. How could these faithful martyrs be blessed because of their righteous suffering? It only makes sense if this world is not all there is. That is true of all the Beatitudes, but especially this one. Jesus fervently believed in, and boldly taught, that a better world is coming. In that world, there will be a radical re-ordering of things. As He loved to say, the first will be last and the last will be first. If that's true, the world's version of success and happiness is probably the wrong target for which to aim.

The Salt of the Earth
Matthew 5:13

It's amazing how many terms we use in modern-day English came originally from Scripture. This is an example. I will sometimes hear a basically decent person being described as "the salt of the earth." I wonder, when I hear that term used, if the person speaking knows it was originally said by Jesus. Salt was not a mere seasoning in the biblical world; it was essential. There were actual wars fought over salt. Roman soliders were often paid in salt; in fact, we get our word "salary" from the Latin word *sal,* meaning salt. Even today, if we think someone is good at what he does, we say, "He's worth his salt." Salt was valuable because it was a preservative. There was no refrigeration, so the only way to keep meat edible was to pack it in salt. For this reason, it is interesting to note God sometimes described His covenant with Israel as "a covenant of salt." He even ordered them to mix some salt with their grain offerings. He wanted them to understand that this world was full of corruption and rot, but they were to be salt. They were to be distinct in a way that preserved God's original intention for the world. That makes it especially poignant when Jesus talks about salt that has lost its saltiness. He was saying, "We Israelites have failed to be the salt that we were supposed to be. So God is raising up a new movement of people—people of all races--who will complete this task."

The Light of the World
Matthew 5:14-16

Like salt, light was also a common metaphor in God's dreams for His people. One example is Isaiah 49:6, *I will also make you a light of the nations, so that my salvation may reach to the end of the earth.* You may remember that before God even made a nation named Israel, He had told Abraham, "Through you all people will be blessed." So His dream was that His people would draw the world to Him. Unfortunately, Israel turned inward. They focused only on themselves and getting God to bless them. They built up intense prejudice against Gentiles…and admittedly, we gave them good reason to be fearful of us. Jews and Gentiles built up intense walls of hostility and distrust, fueled by countless incidences of violence and deception. The Jewish people quite understandably lived in fear of non-Jews. But a fortress mentality was not what God wanted for His people. Now Jesus says, "You will be my light to the world. You will be my Jerusalem, my shining city on a hill for all to see." And then what I believe is the key to interpreting this passage: *Let your light shine before men so that they will see your good works and glorify your Father who is in heaven.* It's not enough to be different. It's not enough to live attractive lives. No, we are called to make an impact on this world. We are called to change the world around us.

When Martin Luther King was imprisoned in Birmingham during the peak of the civil rights movement, he wrote his famous "Letter From a Birmingham Jail." In it, he had some harsh words for the Church. "There was a time when the church was very powerful—in the time when the early Christians rejoiced at being deemed worthy to suffer for what they believed. In those days the church was not merely a thermometer that recorded the ideas and principles of popular opinion; it was a thermostat that transformed the mores of society." A thermometer doesn't affect anything; it just tells you what the temperature is. A church that acts like a thermometer doesn't make a difference. You can tell what is going on in the culture, because that church will either be conforming to it or complaining about it. But a thermostat changes the temperature. At the time King wrote, he was saying the church shouldn't be conforming to racism or complaining about it; the church should be fighting it. Racism should be in trouble because the church exists. Jesus envisioned a movement of men and women who would be so compassionate, so righteous, so others-centered and God-minded that sin, violence, addiction, dysfunction and alienation from God would melt before them.

A Radical Standard
Matthew 5:17-20

Verse 20 has been called the ethical core of the Sermon on the Mount; the rest of the Sermon is essentially commentary on this passage. But Jesus said two things before He got to v. 20 that also merit some serious consideration. First, consider *I did not come to abolish them but to fulfill them.* What we call The Old Testament, Jesus and His fellow Jews called the "Law and Prophets." So Jesus came along and essentially said, "I'm changing everything: What you believe about God, how you relate to Him, and how you interpret His commands. But that doesn't mean you throw the Old Testament away. No, that book was written to prepare the way for me. Everything in it is about me." That would be a breathtakingly audacious statement for a religious leader to make today; in that hyper-religious culture, it was an invitation to be stoned to death for heresy.

Also note, *Whoever annuls one of the least of these commands...will be called least in the kingdom of heaven, but whoever keeps...them, he shall be called great in the kingdom of heaven.* Eternal life, according to Jesus, will not be the same for everyone. Even among those who enter the Kingdom of God, there will be different rewards based on how well we obeyed the Father.

And then comes the radical part: *Unless your righteousness surpasses that of the scribes and Pharisees...*I imagine that when Jesus said these words, all of His followers gasped out loud. They had devoted their lives to Him; now He seemed to be saying, "You can't satisfy me. It's impossible." The scribes were the people who physically copied the Word of God, and so they were considered experts in the Law. The Pharisees were laymen who were exceptionally devoted to the Law. They were like a highly exclusive club, except instead of wealth, their entrance requirements consisted of extreme knowledge of and obedience to the commands of God. The question that was buzzing in the minds of Jesus' first stunned listeners is the question with which we must still wrestle: How can we be more righteous than the scribes and Pharisee? The rest of the Sermon will answer that question. As you read, you see that Jesus' idea of right living goes much deeper than the superficial, legalistic morality treasured by His people. And since Jesus proclaimed Himself the fulfillment of the Law, the implication is, "You can't do this without me."

People Matter
Matthew 5:21-22

Jesus was preaching a new kind of righteousness, one more pleasing to God than that of the scribes and Pharisees. This was hard to imagine, since these men had devoted their lives to memorizing, teaching and obeying the Law of Moses. In the rest of the Sermon, Jesus shows how their understanding of God's intention behind the Law was flawed. He will continually say, "You have heard it said…but I say to you…" The audacity of this is breathtaking. Jesus is implying that He has insight into what God meant when He gave the Law in the first place. In each case, we find that Jesus is teaching a more difficult path, but also one that will lead to a much better world.

First, Jesus takes on the Sixth Commandment. He references two particular insults of that time. One is the Aramaic word "Raca." (Some modern translations say "whoever insults His brother," but the original it says "whoever says to his brother, 'Raca...") It literally means "empty head." Each language has its share of dirty words. For instance, calling someone a male goat in English is a strange insult, but in Spanish it's a good way to start a fight. The opposite is true of calling someone a female dog; in Spanish, it's no big deal, but in English, it's a terrible thing to say. No one speaks Aramaic anymore, but scholars of the language believe that "Raca" was the kind of word a TV network today would bleep. The second word mentioned here is "fool," which comes from the Greek word "moros," which also gives us the word "moron." To the Greeks—as well as us—those words refer to intellectual deficiency. But to Jews like Jesus, calling someone a fool was a moral judgment—as it says in Psalm 14:1, the fool has said in his heart, "there is no God." Jesus' reference to Hell is meant to show us how serious He is. Insulting someone is not some minor thing. It is murder in His eyes, blaspheming the divine image and counting one of God's special creations as worthless in our sight. It is a sin worthy of hellfire. That is a bracing thing to realize, since our current standard for humor and political discourse is to mock and ridicule others. Yet Jesus said that is exactly the sort of thing God despises.

I know sincere Christians who believe that this passage simply bans the use of those two insults. I think Jesus' meaning was much deeper. The point of the Sixth Commandment, He is saying, wasn't just to keep us from killing each other. It was to remind us that each human being is precious to God. We may feel rage toward our neighbor. We may see him as a worthless fool. But if so, we must answer to the God who treasures him.

Reconciliation
Matthew 5:23-26

Jesus next gives us two specific examples of valuing others in the same way God does. One involves a conflict with a fellow believer—a brother. He says that if we have offended our brother, we cannot worship unless we have made things right. God won't hear our songs of praise, He won't reward our tithes or our ministries, He won't bless us with His presence and guidance in the sermon if we refuse to make things right with our offended brother. In fact, the Lord recommends doing a radical thing—getting up right in the middle of worship and finding the one we've offended. Until then, our worship is disgusting to God. He sees it like a woman would see a bouquet of flowers from a philandering husband, "If you really love me, show me by doing what I want you to do." Jesus' words are reminiscent of something the prophet Amos said: *Away with the noise of your songs! I will not listen to the music of your harps. But let justice roll on like a river, righteousness like a never-failing stream!* Those words, which Martin Luther King used often, are a reminder that religion without justice for the downtrodden is worthless. Jesus and Amos both agree that people are more important to God than worship alone.

The second example is of an opponent in a legal proceeding. Please understand that Jesus is not here saying we should never go to court. Nor is He giving free legal advice ("always settle out of court"). He is simply saying that in a legal dispute, our primary goal should not be winning. It should be reconciliation. We should try to reason with our opponent, to concede some things, even to go further than we think is just in order to reconcile the relationship. Otherwise, says Jesus, you might stake everything on winning the case and find that you not only lose the relationship—gaining an enemy for life—but you lose the case as well, incurring added expense for yourself. Just because you belong to Jesus and you feel you have a legitimate beef, God doesn't guarantee you'll get what you want from a secular law court. So again, the guiding principle here is that people are important to God and they should be to us as well—even people we don't like. In both cases, the principle is clear: God wants us to value others in the way He does. That means we take the initiative to reconcile conflict as quickly as possible. To whom do you need to be reconciled today?

The Lust of the Eyes
Matthew 5:27-30

This is a controversial teaching these days. Organized religion has used this passage as a justification for policing the way women dress. Certainly, modesty is a valid topic. But notice that Jesus doesn't address women in this passage at all. It's the height of irony that a teaching that should result in men treating women with respect and dignity has instead been twisted into a way to scold women as vile demonic temptresses, luring men to the gaping maw of Hell itself with their miniskirts and mascara.

So the responsibility falls upon the one looking, not the one being looked at. But that leaves us with a problem: How can we control our physiological response to seeing an attractive person? I think it is important to define what lust is and is not. The way we feel when we see someone who is physically beautiful is not lust. Scripture describes several biblical characters in terms of their good looks: Sarah, Rachel, Esther, and David, just to name a few. The Song of Songs contains long stretches in which two lovers praise one another's beauty. Lust is when we take that beauty and try to own it for ourselves; it's when we use it for our gratification, reducing them from a person to an object for our own pleasure. It's the lingering stare. It's going out of your way so you can walk by her office. It's buying that magazine (or clicking on that website) because you know how you feel when you see those images.

To modern Americans, this seems a ridiculous standard. We use sex to sell everything from blue jeans to Buicks. What is the harm in what we look at or imagine? Instead of looking at that question negatively, let's flip it around: What would it be like to live in a world where all men treated all women as people of worth regardless of their physical appearance? How wonderful would it be if the gender with more physical strength never used that advantage to intimidate, harass or assault the other? Think about marriages in which each man and woman could honestly say, "I have eyes only for you. You will never be compared by me to anyone else. Your face and your body are beautiful to me, because you have given yourself exclusively to me, and I to you." Think about single men and women who treated their sexual desire the way we treat fire: As something wonderful and life-giving when used appropriately, and something destructive when it's not. Imagine a humanity in which sex is returned to its rightful place binding two people together in a lifelong commitment, not a force that rips apart families and hearts and lives.

Jesus casts that vision, and gives us the cure: In vv. 29-30, He is not advocating self-mutilation. He is saying, "Take this battle seriously. Do what is necessary to bring your thoughts into submission. Fight the good fight of purity." You and I probably can all easily identify steps we could take to make our thoughts about the opposite gender more pure and respectful. We fail, not because we don't know what to do, but because we don't want to live without the cheap gratification to which we think we're entitled.

Divorce
5:31-32

There are a variety of Scriptures concerning divorce in the Bible, including Malachi 2, Ezra 10, 1 Corinthians 7, and Matthew 19, among others. In this passage, Jesus is not trying to give us an all-purpose law regarding divorce, as much as He is talking about an issue of sexual purity. It's important to know the cultural context in which He was speaking here. In Jesus' day, one of the hottest topics for discussion was what constituted a legal divorce. One group of Jewish leaders led by a rabbi named Hillel said that a man could divorce his wife for nearly any reason. As you can imagine, that teaching was very popular with men.

In the days before Israel became a nation, a man could decide to walk out on his wife for whatever reason, leaving her with small children, and she would have no recourse. Yet years later, when the sons were all of working age, he could move back in and reclaim the family as his own. When God was creating the nation of Israel, he gave Moses a Law by which the new nation would be governed. Part of the law is what Jesus quotes here: A man had to give his wife a certificate of divorce if he left her. Essentially God was saying, "I recognize that you are sinful people and that sometimes your marriages will fail (see Matt. 19:8). But at least do it in such a way that the person you leave is taken care of." In other words, God wasn't giving men permission to divorce their wives, he was trying to protect the wives by giving them rights of their own. A wife who had been abandoned then had a certificate of divorce and could remarry and provide for herself and her kids. Unsurprisingly, self-centered men had twisted the original intent of this provision to give themselves permission to leave their wives. In The Sermon on the Mount, Jesus is saying, "Stop looking for excuses to get out of your marriage. If you are married, be faithful to your spouse, even if you see someone else out there who you think could make you happier. Marriage is supposed to be for a lifetime."

Lest you think this is a word of condemnation for those who are divorced, consider this: God Himself went through a divorce when His people turned their backs on Him (Jeremiah 3:8). He knows the pain of a failed relationship. Jesus spoke from a position of compassion mixed with righteousness, a combination we're just not used to these days.

Oaths
5:33-37

Like the rest of the Sermon, this section is usually misunderstood. People read it by the letter instead of the principle, and that is the very thing that Jesus was preaching against. For instance, some Christian groups historically have refused to take legal vows because of this teaching. As much as I admire their consistency, I don't believe that's what Jesus had in mind. Several times in Scripture, God binds Himself with an oath or a covenant. Paul often used the phrase, "God is my witness" as a vow of His truthfulness. And Jesus testified under oath at His trial before the Sanhedrin (Mt. 26:63-64). Closer to home, some of us grew up under the assumption that this teaching meant it was wrong to say, "I swear." Oddly enough, we still said things like, "I promise," and "cross my heart, hope to die."

Let's talk about the real situation Jesus was addressing. In v. 33, Jesus isn't directly quoting Scripture, but He's summarizing several different Old Testament passages that teach that when we invoke the name of God, we had better be telling the truth. In those days, it was common for men to call God as a witness of their truthfulness. Deception was so common in the culture that in really important matters, a person wasn't believed if he *didn't* take an oath. That's not so different from today, is it? After all, there is a reason why in a court of law witnesses are asked to swear "to tell the truth, the whole truth and nothing but the truth so help me God," and why laws against perjury, slander and tax evasion exist. The original Old Testament laws on oath-taking were written to say that if we take a vow and break it, we're not merely lying, we're blaspheming God in whose name we swore. In Jesus' time, the rabbis had developed an elaborate system for determining which vows referred to God and which vows didn't. The subject even had its own chapter—or tractate—in the Mishnah, the collection of rabbinic teachings. Whatever the rabbis originally intended when they came up with this system, by Jesus' time it amounted to a way to excuse lying. If you could swear in such a way that *sounded* like it was invoking God but really wasn't, you had found a loophole in the honesty code. For example, if you swore by the temple, you could lie and not be guilty. But if you swore by the gold in the temple, you were bound to the truth (see Matthew 23:16-17).

Jesus used simple logic to point out how ridiculous this system was. Here is how His logic works: God created everything and owns all things. If that is true, then whatever you swear on is really swearing in the name of God, and therefore all oaths are equally binding. Whether you swear on the name of Yahweh Himself or on your mother's grave, you need to tell the truth. Then He makes another interesting logical leap. Why make vows at all? Vows are simply a way of acknowledging that you have lied in the past. If your yes is known to be yes and your no is known to be no, you will never have to vow. So don't interpret this to be simply a banning of all vows. The real truth of this teaching is much harder to keep. Jesus is saying, "My servants should be so famously honest and forthright and transparent that no one will ever ask one of them to take a vow." In other words, we should be so radically honest no one will ever have to say, "Do you promise that's the truth?"

Turn the Other Cheek
5:38-42

This is arguably the most well-known part of the Sermon, thanks to men like Ghandi and Martin Luther King, who used the principle of non-violence to change the world. In v. 38, Jesus quotes Exodus 21:24. Scholars call this *Lex Talionis,* which in Latin means "law of retaliation." God's principle behind lex talionis is that evil must be punished, but punishment must be appropriate for the crime. The law was established to prevent vendettas. Ironically, over the years people started using lex talionis as a justification for personal vengeance. Jesus here corrects the idea, instead saying that in our relationships with others, we should be guided by the principle of love, not the principle of personal satisfaction.

Let's look at Jesus' illustrations. When He says "turn the other cheek," He is not saying we cannot defend ourselves from physical attacks. Notice that He says, "If someone strikes you on the *right* cheek." I believe He makes this distinction because He is referring to a back-handed slap. You don't slap someone backhanded if you want to injure them; you do it as an insult. Or to put it another way, backslapping someone isn't the way to win a fight, it's a way to start one. When we are insulted, we usually let the principle of personal satisfaction guide us, and we strike back even harder. That doesn't solve anything; in fact, it's the cause of untold destruction in the world. Instead, let's be guided by the principle of love.

That even applies when someone sues us, as He goes on to say in His second example. Our main concern shouldn't be winning (personal justice), it should be love for our opponent. In His third example, Jesus refers to something that was common in that culture. Roman law said that a soldier could compel any civilian to carry his luggage for up to a mile. I am sure Roman soldiers often used this law just to humiliate their Jewish neighbors. The Jews thought that the presence of the Romans in their country was bad enough. But these actions were adding insult to occupation. Jesus said we should swallow all of that. We should be willing to "go the extra mile" (this is where that cliché came from) to win over our enemies with love.

In His final example, Jesus refers to our charity. When someone comes to us wanting to borrow money, our tendency is to consider carefully how likely the person is to repay us. We are following the principle of personal satisfaction—If it opens me up to the possibility of being taken advantage of, I won't do it. But Jesus wants us instead to be guided by love. Jesus wasn't contradicting other Scriptures that encourage us be fiscally responsible, and to avoid enabling bad habits in others. But we realize going in that if we are going to be generous, we will sometimes be taken advantage of. And we choose to err on the side of love.

Love your Enemies
5:43-48

Here Jesus takes the principle of love further than anyone else would have dared. In v. 43, Jesus refers to Leviticus 19:18, which said, *Love your neighbor as yourself.* You may know that Jesus once listed that along with *Love the Lord your God with all your heart, soul, mind and strength* as the two most important commands in the Bible. *...and hate your enemy* is NOT found in Leviticus. Perhaps this is where the idea came from: We know that in that culture most people interpreted the word "neighbor" to mean their family and friends, or at most, their fellow Jews. That's why Jesus told the parable of the Good Samaritan, to challenge them to expand their responsibility to love even foreigners who were repulsive to them. Over time, with the Jewish people being so frequently invaded and persecuted, the thinking grew that "we" (the Jews) were the good guys and "they" (the Gentiles) were bad. Therefore, part of being a good Jew, part of loving one's neighbor, was having a proper view of the enemy. Again, it was ironic that a command from God intended to produce love instead produced hate.

Why did this happen? Because we are selfish by nature. Because our highest value is to ensure that everything in life turns out happily for us, no matter the cost to others. That is the unspoken motto by which we live. Yet Jesus saw that if we desire nothing more than an eye for an eye and a tooth for a tooth, we all end up blind and toothless. He envisioned a better world.

Some have said that Jesus' teaching is unrealistic at best. But I have witnessed it in the real world, and it works. When I was in seminary, one of my classmates was about twenty years older than the rest of us. One day before class, when the teacher asked if there were any prayer requests, this man raised his hand. He asked for prayer for a young man who had recently dated his daughter. The dad had forced them to break up because the boy was possessive and jealous, and the relationship wasn't healthy. But this kid didn't take the breakup well. He stalked this man's daughter at school, and often parked his car outside the house at night, just so she could see him. One night as he was doing this, the dad, full of anger, went to confront him. However, on the way out the door, he was reminded of Jesus' teaching in this passage. He ended up sitting with this boy for an hour, sharing Jesus with him, and leading him to transforming faith in Christ. The rest of us listened to the story in awe. None of us had teenaged daughters, but we were all certain we would have met the kid with a loaded shotgun or a fist to the jaw, not with love. We had never seen Christ's words so perfectly lived out. What if it happened more often?

Good Giving
Matthew 6:1-4

What do you think of when you hear the term "showing off?" Perhaps an attractive person who dresses to accentuate their favorite bodily feature: a bodybuilder's biceps; an aerobics queen's flat midriff. Perhaps you think of a wealthy person who wears only designer labels and drives a flashy sports car. Or maybe you think of the go-getter who name-drops the famous people he has met, and constantly refers to his achievements (#humblebrag). We show off when it comes to looks, money, and accomplishment because those are the things our culture values. The culture in Israel during the New Testament era was much more religious, so they showed off when it came to morality and religious devotion. The three main ways one showed off one's righteousness were acts of charity, prayer, and fasting. So those are the three areas of religious expression Jesus tackles here. Let's talk briefly about some of the ways people showed off back then, and how it's not so different today.

In vv. 1-4, Jesus addresses charitable giving. Some scholars believe Jesus was just being hyperbolic when He talked about hypocrites announcing their acts of charity with trumpets—perhaps this is where we get the expression "tooting your own horn." But the principle here is clear: If you seek recognition for a charitable gift, then the recognition you receive will be all the reward you will ever get. So if we're going to be glory hounds regarding our giving, we'd better hire an excellent publicist, because the attention we get here on earth will be the end of our reward; there won't be a single whisper about it in Heaven. It will be as if it never happened. Years ago, there was a lady who had once been very active in the church I pastored but now was homebound. One day she told us she wanted to give a substantial gift; the amount was around 50% of the church's annual receipts. This was a small church, so word quickly got around about the gift and who gave it. Someone asked me during a business meeting, "Shouldn't we do something to publicize this? After all, when her husband was still alive and they used to give big donations to charity, they always got their pictures in the paper." I said something like this: "Jesus said when we give money away, we should keep it as secret as we can. If we seek recognition, we'll forfeit our heavenly reward. She has given us a tremendous gift, and she hasn't sought any recognition at all. I don't want to do anything that might tempt her to give up her reward in heaven." So we kept it a secret. I wrote her a heartfelt thank-you note, but did not otherwise recognize the giver. We did a lot of great things with that money, and I don't regret the way I handled that. I look forward to seeing her in heaven someday, enjoying the rewards that gift brought to her eternity.

Secret Prayer
Matthew 6:5-8

Jesus next turns to the subject of prayer in vv. 5-15. His words here are sometimes misunderstood to imply that we should never pray in public, but only in private. But Jesus Himself prayed in public many times. So did Paul and other apostles. Public prayer is an important part of the life of God's church. Jesus said that if we agree on something in prayer, it has a special kind of power. So Jesus isn't condemning all public prayer. He is telling us to pay attention to our motivation when we pray in public. Are we just trying to show off, to impress others? Or are we really talking to God? As someone who prays in public often, I must confess it is hard not to think about all those people listening to what I say. It is hard to just have a conversation with God and not try to sound really profound and spiritual when I pray. But this is what God expects of us.

Simply being private in prayer isn't enough. Jesus also reveals that God hates manipulative prayer. He refers to the babbling prayer of Gentiles, who used to pray to their gods using the continual repetition of a standard formula. Imagine you were God and someone was praying to you the following, "Oh Father hear my prayer…Oh Father hear my prayer…Oh Father hear my prayer." You'd want to annihilate them just to shut them up! Jesus goes on to say, "Here's how you pray," then He gives us what we know as The Lord's Prayer. I think it's incredibly ironic that just after Jesus tells us not to pray publicly in a false or showy way, and then He has warned us not to use meaningless repetition in prayer, He gives us a prayer that millions of Christians mindlessly repeat, sometimes publicly as a way of demonstrating their own righteousness! I think what Jesus was trying to say is that we should remember when we pray that we are talking to someone real. We shouldn't try to manipulate God by thinking that if we say just the right words in just the right language, He'll be duty bound to give us what we want, as if prayer is some sort of magic spell and God is some capricious pagan deity. Instead, just talk to God. Anyone can do this. We just need to talk to God sincerely.

The Lord's Prayer
Matthew 6:9-15

In Luke 11, when Jesus' disciples asked Him to teach them to pray, He gave them this prayer. Here in the Sermon on the Mount, when Jesus is teaching what it truly means to live like a child of God, He uses this prayer to show us how to pray. Does this mean that the Lord's Prayer, as we call this passage, is the only thing we're supposed to pray? No, because in many other occasions, Jesus is shown praying many different prayers. This isn't some kind of catch-all prayer that we're supposed to pray verbatim in any situation. It is a model; a demonstration of what it means to have a balanced prayer life. In it we find the elements that we need in order to pray as Jesus prayed.

First, there must be reverence. We need time in prayer to consider who it is we are addressing, and how magnificent it is to have that privilege. "Hallowed be your name" simply means "You are wonderful in character." God is not some insecure fool who needs our affirmation; but we need to remember who He is, because it tends to cure us of thinking we and our requests are the center of the universe. Everything else flows from that: Ask Him for what's on your heart, even your most basic needs and desires ("Give us this day our daily bread"). Make sure you confess your sins regularly ("forgive us our trespasses"). And take time to forgive others, or pray for the ability to do so ("as we forgive those who trespass against us"). Mostly, make sure you spend time in prayer asking Him for things that matter to Him ("Thy Kingdom come, they will be done on Earth as it is in Heaven"). That includes praying for the hurting people all around you, for growth in your own areas of spiritual deficiency and disobedience, and for people to know God's love in a personal, transforming way. And don't forget to spend time praying about the hope we have in a better future ("for thine is the Kingdom and the power forever"). As you consider the Lord's Prayer, you may get the impression that prayer is not meant to change God, but it's meant to change us instead. I think that's exactly the point.

Fasting
Matthew 6:16-18

Finally, Jesus speaks about fasting in vv. 16-18. Fasting was a big deal in that era. God commanded the Jews to fast one day a year, the Day of Atonement or Yom Kippur. But the Pharisees fasted two days a week. And they wanted to make sure everyone knew they were fasting, so they didn't groom themselves so that they would look appropriately miserable. Their goal was to show off their righteousness. Fasting sounds awful to most of us today—food is an obsession for too many of us. But fasting is a gift from God. When we willingly do without food for a time so that we can focus on God exclusively, it has a way of centering our thoughts on the Lord that is just fantastic. When we fast, we are open to hearing His voice in a unique and powerful way. Actually, what Jesus says here can apply to anything we do to get closer to God. Whether we give up food for a while (actually these days, a TV or internet "fast" may be just as useful), or decide to read the entire Bible in a year, or set aside extra time for prayer, or help someone who is in need, we need to make sure our motives are true. We shouldn't brag about what we've done. Sometimes we might feel led to give a testimony of the ways God has changed us through a certain spiritual discipline. That can be a powerful encouragement to others. But always, always we should look into our hearts and make sure we are trying to encourage our fellow Christians and bring glory to God, not trying to impress people with our righteousness.

The principle flowing through these teachings about charity, prayer and fasting is that when we practice our faith, our motive is more important to God than the frequency of our attendance or the amount of our offering or the quality of our singing voice. We may be able to fool most of the people most of the time, but we can't fool God any of the time. He sees what's really in our hearts. Jesus was following the tradition of many Old Testament-era prophets, who said that religious rituals done with an insincere heart are offensive in the sight of God. How would He regard our worship today?

Put Your Money Where Your Heart Should Be
Matthew 6:19-24

Jesus had a lot to say about money. This may be His most comprehensive teaching on the subject. The principle here is ingenious and imminently practical: Let your money lead your heart, not the other way around. For instance, let's say my heart loves fast cars, but it also loves my family, and so I desire a good house in a good neighborhood. So here's what I decide if I listen to my heart: I can afford that house if I really stretch. And I can buy a really fast car and pay for insurance and gasoline. On my budget, I can just barely do all of that. I have to make some sacrifices in other areas, but it's my money, right? Why not spend it on the things my heart tells me I need?

Two problems: Jesus says I should be investing in stuff that lasts forever (Ie, the Kingdom of God). I can't do that, because all my money is tied up in my house and car. Problem two: The stuff my heart loves keeps getting more expensive. Gas prices go up. Insurance rates rise—especially if I drive that fast car the way I want to. That great house needs a new roof. The air conditioner goes out. The taxes are raised. All of which means I couldn't give to God even if my heart wanted to. I have to start asking for more overtime at work to pay for the stuff my heart wants. As a result, and because I'm not home much anymore either (and when I am, I'm waxing my car) my marriage and my family begin to suffer. In my unhappiness under all this stress, I become more angry, selfish and withdrawn. I am not the person my wife married, and I am certainly not the person God intended me to be. Why? I let my heart tell me where my treasure should go and it has led me into idolatry. Although I profess to believe all the right things, I am really trying to serve two masters.

Now let's say I decide to take Jesus' words literally. I choose to buy a house and car that cost substantially less than what I can afford. I am not doing this so that I can afford something else my heart wants; I'm doing it so that I can afford to give more to God. Now, instead of letting my heart lead me, I am leading my heart. I am putting my treasure where God says it should go, and my heart will join it there. I am not saying that buying a nice house or an expensive car are sinful choices…who decides whose house or car is too fancy? This is about each person asking, "What am I giving my heart to?" When we manage our resources generously, we become better people—people who experience joy and freedom, people who make a positive difference in the world. This is an amazing teaching that most people miss: We often feel guilty because we don't give more. We think, "If I were a better person, I would be more generous." Jesus says, "No, if you would be generous, you would become a better person." In other words, don't wait for your heart to change before you give generously. Be generous so your heart will change. What we do with our resources determines who we become.

The Cure for Worry
Matthew 6:25-33

Imagine a contemporary politician stands at a podium in an economically depressed state and says, "I know you're all worried about finding new jobs, feeding your children, managing not to have your homes re-possessed. I just want to tell you that worrying about that kind of stuff is for losers. Don't let it bother you. It'll all take care of itself!" That would be political suicide. But it sounds eerily similar to what Jesus says here to people who lived on the razor's edge of poverty. One bad harvest, one ill-timed frost or drought, and their children would starve. Yet Jesus has the audacity to say, "Those are the kinds of things pagans worry about. Don't be like them." How could He say such a thing?

Jesus was teaching us about true faith. If we believe in a God who loves us and knows more about life than we do, we will trust that His way is best. He wasn't saying that being concerned about our welfare is a sin. First of all, we cannot control the emotions we feel. Second, both Old and New Testaments of the Bible commend working hard and saving our money wisely to provide for our families. But He was offering us a better way to live. If our life is based on the quest for absolute physical security—a guarantee we'll always have enough money and never get sick—then we will live in constant fear, because that kind of security is impossible in a world stained by sin. No matter how many vitamins you take, how many pushups you do, our bodies will fall apart. No matter how much money you squirrel away, a little blip in the stock market can vaporize it all in a day. If, on the other hand, our focus is on higher things, we will live lives free of crippling worry. By "higher things," He means God's Kingdom and His righteousness. His Kingdom is His reign in the hearts of human beings. To seek God's Kingdom first means that, above all other things, we want people to know Jesus as their King, and so we work and pray toward that end. His righteousness is the kind of life we were created to live, conforming to His character. So to seek first His righteousness means that we constantly work and pray toward growing more Christlike in every way. We see areas in our own character that aren't like what we see in Jesus ("I'm not as compassionate as He was; I also lack patience with people who think differently than I do; I'm not very forgiving") and we ruthlessly attack them, seeking growth. The promise of Jesus is that when we seek His Kingdom and His righteousness first—loving our neighbors and our God—we'll achieve our goals, because God will be working alongside us. And we'll be amazed at how He provides for our needs as well. If you're the kind of person who feels irresponsible if you're not worried about every detail of your life, His words here might seem preposterous. But why not try them out?

Judging
Matthew 7:1-6

If there is one thing irreligious people find particularly distasteful about religious people, it's their sanctimonious, judgmental attitudes. From this passage alone, it's clear Jesus felt the same way. Verse one is so well-known, we know it as rendered in the old King James Version: *Judge not, lest ye be judged.* Does that mean that it's a sin to make a judgment on someone's character? Would Jesus have us entrust the care of our children to a potential babysitter with a history of child abuse, or hire someone at our business who has been fired (with cause) from his last four jobs? I don't believe Jesus was promoting blind naiveté; this is, after all, the same man who told His disciples to be *as shrewd as snakes and as innocent as doves* (Matthew 10:16). A few verses after this passage, He warns us to watch out for false teachers (7:15-20); surely discerning the difference between a false and a true teacher requires exercising judgment. Verse two helps us understand what He meant by verse one: We will be judged with the same severity (or mercy) with which we judge others. It's likely that Jesus was talking about the way our peers will judge us, not God. After all, notice the way we all feel when a blustering politician or a pompous evangelist is exposed in scandal; the way they've judged others leads us instinctively to see their downfall as a moment of justice, not tragedy.

Jesus next challenges religious people to stop functioning as society's moral police force, constantly pointing out the faults and failures of others. After all, we have our own dirty laundry to deal with. Humor doesn't translate well, especially across three languages (Aramaic to Greek to English) and two millennia of time, but I have no doubt that when Jesus mentioned a person with a plank of wood protruding from his eye nonetheless trying to pluck a microscopic speck from the eye of his friend, the crowd laughed. It's a hilarious image, but it cuts religious people like me to the heart; we love the feeling of power and superiority we get from trying to tell others how to live their lives. Verse 6 is baffling, until we realize two things: 1) In context, this is another hilarious statement from Jesus about being judgmental, and 2) Just as humor doesn't translate, neither does a sarcastic tone of voice. I can't prove it, but I am almost certain Jesus spoke v. 6 with a sardonic wink. After all, religious people love to think of their moral pronouncements as "pearls" of wisdom to the unwashed "dogs" and "swine" all around them. His warning is that our self-righteousness can lead to our very public downfall. Sadly, sometimes we religious folks think we're being persecuted for our beliefs, when we're actually bearing the consequences of our own rude behavior.

But how many of us see ourselves in these verses? Here's a chilling thought: If you thought of someone else when you read these words, aren't you being judgmental? Well?

Ask, Seek, and Knock
Matthew 7:7-11

These verses are often misunderstood to imply that if we pray in the right way, with the right amount of faith, with the right kind of persistence, we will always get everything we want. Yet Scripture is chock-full of examples of godly people who didn't get what they asked for in prayer, including Jesus Himself (Matthew 26:39). So what does this mean? Jesus uses the image of a good parent to promise that God will always give us "good gifts." Look at the two examples: Bread and fish were things people need to survive. No good parent would withhold food from his own child. But imagine Jesus had said, "If your child asks for the family fortune, don't you give it to him?" The answer, of course, would be no. You refuse his request, not because you don't love him but precisely because you do. A child is not wise enough to know what to do with the fortune; he would likely squander it, leaving himself and the rest of the family impoverished. Good parents don't give their kids whatever they ask for; they give them the things they need. When a child asks for something good, a good parent is quick to give it to him. So what are the "good gifts?" Jesus must have used this same saying more than once, because Luke records it this way (Luke 11:13): *If you then, being evil, know how to give good gifts to your children, how much more will your heavenly Father give the Holy Spirit to those who ask Him?*

We spend most of our time in prayer asking for things that are the spiritual equivalent of toys and candy; things that may make us happy in the short term, but don't really amount to much eternally. And God sometimes gives those little blessings to us, just as most of us earthly parents give our kids more toys and candy than they could ever need. But He is concerned with giving us the tools we need to accomplish His purpose for us in the world: tools like the Holy Spirit and all the spiritual gifts, wisdom and guidance we need in order to live out the instructions in this sermon. Remember, moreover, that He is saying this in the context of our relationships with our neighbors. The point Jesus is trying to make is that we should treat others the way God treats us. If He gives us all the things we need unconditionally, shouldn't we be that generous and giving toward others?

The Golden Rule
Matthew 7:12

Everything we've read in chapter 7 leads to the principle behind all of these teachings, the principle that should guide every relationship we have: v. 12, also known as the Golden Rule. I've read that some version of the Golden Rule exists in most major world religions. However, Bible scholars will note that Jesus' version is a little different from the others. For example, Rabbi Hillel, who lived during Jesus' lifetime, was challenged one day to teach a Gentile the entire Jewish law while standing on one foot. The Rabbi said, "What is hateful to you, do not do to anyone else. This is the whole law; all the rest is commentary." That's wonderful moral teaching, but notice that Jesus goes further: *Treat people the same way you want them to treat you.* Hillel's advice could be obeyed simply by avoiding people altogether. If I avoid human contact as much as possible, I can live so that I never do anything hurtful or offensive to anyone else. But Jesus' Golden Rule doesn't just ban negative words and actions, it commands me to always do something positive. It says that when I see someone in need, I should ask myself how I would want people to respond to my pain if I were in similar circumstances. When someone sins against me, I should put myself in their shoes and treat them with grace instead of thinking only of my own suffering. When I find someone obnoxious, I should realize that someone, somewhere probably feels the same way about me. I would want them to try harder to understand me better. So that is exactly how I should act. The Golden Rule calls on us to be proactive, making a difference in the life of every person we meet.

The Golden Rule is one of many things Jesus said that is so morally brilliant, virtually all people of all religions (and those of no religion at all) agree that the world would be a much better place if we all lived that way. Jesus didn't just teach this; all evidence indicates that He actually lived it out. Nowhere in any of the four Gospels do we see Jesus do anything out of selfish motives. When He encountered hurting people, He helped them, even if He was in a hurry, even if He was hungry or tired, even if helping them put Him at odds with religious regulations. When His followers missed the mark, He told them so. Love isn't always soft and comforting; sometimes love feels like a slap across the jawline. Jesus always did what was needed. The problem with such a philosophy of life is that it's extremely difficult to follow the Golden Rule and get what you want. Other people's needs seldom line up perfectly with our desires. Sooner or later, some tough choices have to be made. One day, Jesus would face the toughest choice of all, in seeking our need for salvation versus His desire for a safe, long, ordinary life…

Decision
Matthew 7:13-14

Jesus is wrapping up His sermon. He has cast for us a vision of a new sort of Kingdom, filled with people who change the world around them with love, forgiveness, and the joy of a right relationship with our God. But now, He wants to bring His hearers to a point of decision. In today's world, we are used to being "sold" on everything from toothpaste to presidential candidates. We know how it works. We expect to hear promises, only partially believing them. "Three easy payments." "No credit check required." "I'm Joe Politician, and I approved this message." But Jesus doesn't sell us anything. He is looking for disciples, not suckers.

There's another way to read these words, of course. When Jesus says the gate is small and the road is narrow leading to life, we could assume He is saying that only the morally outstanding will get in. That would be the message of virtually all religion, including much of what we often hear from Christians. But if that were Jesus' feeling, why would He have chosen the disciples He did? He chose the cunning, combustible sons of Zebedee (John and James, who He nicknamed "the sons of thunder"), an impulsive, faltering loudmouth (Peter), a violent Zealot (Simon), a corrupt tax collector (Matthew), and a doubter (Thomas). And we haven't even mentioned Judas Iscariot. Meanwhile, the descendants of the Hasidim, who had courageously won Israel's independence alongside the Maccabees just two centuries before, dwelt in Israel. They were the working-class heroes, passionate in their commitment to God's Word, loyal to their nation and their Lord. We know them as Pharisees, and if salvation were a prize that could be won by human effort, they would have been Jesus' best examples. Yet not one of them followed Him in His earthly ministry. Jesus wasn't saying, "Only the best get in." He was warning us that following Him would not be easy. The true followers will always be the minority. If being one of the cool kids is your goal, Jesus is not your ticket.

Wolves in Sheep's Clothing
Matthew 7:15-23

Jesus' words here are jarring today for several reasons. First, and most important, He names Himself as the one who will decide the eternal fate of each person. Is it any wonder the religious leaders of His day wanted Him dead, when He was making such statements about Himself? Second, His warning to watch out for false teachers flies in the face of our current desire to treat all truth claims as equally valid. Clearly, in Jesus' mind, some teachings aren't just wrong, they are deadly. Third, He foresees some of these false prophets pleading before Him on Judgment Day, referring to prophecies, exorcisms and miracles they have performed. This indicates that personal charisma and eloquence are not signs that the preacher is legitimate; nor is the size or success of the teacher's ministry; nor even spectacular displays of spiritual power.

So how do we know whether a teacher is leading us in the right direction? Christ's apostles would write often on this subject. Clearly, they saw that Jesus' warning was needed. Often, they said to watch out for a message other than the one Christ had passed down to believers through them (2 John 1:10, Galatians 1:8). Thankfully, we have the apostolic teachings preserved for us in the New Testament today. We can evaluate the words of any teacher against those objective truths. But Jesus warned us to watch out for more than heretical teaching; He said to judge a speaker by his fruits. "Fruit" is a biblical way of referring to the qualities of our character. A teacher who is leading us to Christ will exhibit the characteristics that were most important to Jesus, as displayed in the way He trained His followers. So spend some time around your spiritual leaders. Are they humble or self-promoting? Are they forgiving, or do they hold grudges against anyone who crosses them? Do they love their neighbors, or do they revile or ignore anyone not of their camp? In our celebrity-obsessed culture, we especially need to heed Jesus' warning. Of all the virtues He wanted His people to embrace, gullibility was not one.

His Teaching with Authority
Matthew 7:24-29

We've already looked in detail at the story of the two foundations in our chapter on the parables of Jesus. Here, we see that parable as the conclusion of the Sermon on the Mount, and we see the immediate response of the people. Although Jesus had begun the Sermon speaking to His disciples, this verse indicates that the crowds had followed to listen in. The people were amazed at His teaching because it was so different from that of their rabbis.

The rabbis taught by citing rabbinical precedent. They would memorize the teachings of respected sages and would quote them, along with the words of Scripture, to prove their points. We have a secular version of this in the way attorneys at court will cite previous legal decisions to bolster their arguments. But Jesus did not do this. He spoke truth on His own authority. He quoted Scripture, but only to offer His own commentary ("You have heard that it was said…but I say to you…"). He called Himself the fulfillment of Scripture (5:17). As we saw in our last reading, He implied that He would be the one to judge all people in the end. And He wrapped it all up by saying that the decision to ignore or accept His words was the most important decision one could ever make. Imagine an attorney who stands before the Supreme Court and refuses to cite any legal precedents, instead saying, "Your honors, this is the way you should rule, because I say so." He would be a laughingstock. This is what the crowds meant when they noted that Jesus taught with authority. They asked one another, "Who does this guy think He is?" In teaching the way He did, Jesus was hoping to provoke a different question: "Who do I believe He is?"

Chapter 7: Jesus and the People
A Friend of Sinners
Luke 7:31-35

Here's a paradoxical thing about Jesus: Religious people, by and large, didn't like Him at all. Meanwhile, the irreligious outcasts loved Him. Here, we see Him lobbing a charge against the religious establishment of the day. He is talking about how they rejected the ministry of His cousin and forerunner, John the Baptist, saying He was far too ascetic with his desert-dwelling, bug-eating, fire-and-brimstone ways. On the superficial level, Jesus' ministry couldn't have been more different from John's. But they won't accept Him either. Jesus compares them to children who are angry because the other kids in their group won't play the game they want. In His words, Jesus is implying that He and John taught the same message in different ways. The message was from God, but the religious leaders rejected it either way it was presented to them.

Then Jesus quotes their charges against Him. "He's a drunkard and a glutton." There is no indication anywhere else that Jesus was in the habit of eating or drinking too much; as a homeless teacher with no income, it would be hard to imagine Him being able to do so even if He had wanted to. So why would they charge Him with these vices? Perhaps because Jesus had more joy about Him than other religious leaders. Holy men are supposed to be dour, angry, depressed. Scribes and Pharisees were known to make their times of fasting especially pronounced, exaggerating their suffering for the Lord so that others would be impressed. Jesus, on the other hand, seemed to be enjoying life entirely too much. When is the last time religious people had that charge laid against them? But what drove them especially crazy was the company Jesus kept: "He is the friend of tax collectors and sinners." They were describing the people they had structured their religious culture to exclude. Yet Jesus seemed to prefer the company of these reprobates to that of decent men and women. How could He be the Messiah?

One of my favorite things about Jesus is that He genuinely seemed to enjoy people. That isn't something that is stereotypical of religious leaders. We can know so much about Him not just by His teachings, but by the relationships He formed and maintained. We'll look at those relationships in this section. For now, consider this question: If Jesus was who He said He was, and He enjoyed the company of people, especially morally tainted, marginalized, irreligious people, what does that say about God?

His First Disciple
John 1:43-51

There is so much in this short story. First, notice that John the Baptist, the man who all of Israel was buzzing about, intentionally redirected the attentions of his disciples to someone else. Who does that? Only a man who knows his place in God's plan. Soon, as his following evaporates and people start to flock around Jesus, John will say that's the way it should be: *He must increase; I must decrease* (John 3:30). Second, notice Andrew, one of John's disciples. He appears to be the first of what would eventually become the twelve disciples to follow Jesus, as well as the first to call Him Messiah. However, being first didn't lead to any prominence for Andrew. He is the subject of very few stories in the Gospels. He isn't included on some of the most prominent events of Jesus' life, unlike his brother. In fact, in all the stories about Andrew, he is simply seen as someone who brings others to Jesus (John 6:8. 12:22). Which, come to think of it, is a pretty great way to be remembered.

But since we are studying the life of Jesus, look at His response to these two men, Andrew and his brother Simon. To Andrew, He simply says "Come and see." To be a disciple meant to literally follow a teacher around. In never leaving the teacher's side, the disciple received more than an academic education. He learned how to live. Jesus was inviting Andrew to follow Him in this way. When we see it that way, having a group of disciples seems more like an invasion of privacy than a privilege. But that is what Jesus wanted. He was creating a new kind of humanity, starting with this small group. When Andrew brings his brother Simon to meet this new teacher, we see another aspect of Jesus' personality. He had a way of giving people new names. This was characteristic of God in the Old Testament, as well. Abram and Sarai became Abraham and Sarah. Jacob became Israel. Here, He gives Simon the name "Peter." Interestingly, Peter wasn't a proper name in any language before this. He was calling a man Rock. Only much, much later would Simon Peter live up to His name. Think about a God who has both inclination to change our identity into something greater than we can envision for ourselves, and the power and grace to make it happen.

The Open Door
John 1:43-51

There are a couple of statements of Jesus in this story that most of us will miss, but that would have stood out to first-century Jewish readers. In order for us to understand them, we need to go back a millennium and a half. Abraham's son Isaac had twin boys, Esau and Jacob. Jacob was born second, and emerged from the womb of his mother Rebekah grasping his brother's heel. In the ancient world "to grasp the heel" was a euphemism for trickery, sort of like "he was pulling my leg" is today. So the name Jacob means "heel-grabber." Jacob more than lived up to his name. With his mother's assistance, he tricked his father and his gullible brother out of the firstborn brother's birthright, and his father's blessing. When Esau swore vengeance against Jacob, Rebekah urged her favorite son to flee for safety to the home of his uncle Laban, far away. Jacob was shaken. For the first time, Jacob's deceptive ways were bringing real-world consequences. Exhausted on the journey, he stopped to sleep, with nothing to rest his head on but a stone. In his slumber, he saw a vision of a great stairway to Heaven, with angels ascending and descending upon it. When he awoke, Jacob was in awe that he had seen a vision of God. He named the place Bethel, meaning "house of God," swore that Yahweh would be his God from this time forth, and pledged to give the Lord a tenth of all he earned. Jacob does seem to be a different person after this, going from a cynical young con man to a revered patriarch. God ultimately gives him the name Israel, so he is the namesake of the nation.

It's impossible to overstate how familiar this story would have been to young Nathanael—and to every other first-century Jew. They would have heard it told, and told it themselves, over and over again, until every detail was ingrained in their memory. When Nathanael first hears from his friend Philip that they've found the Messiah, and that he is from Nazareth, his reply is scornful. Nazareth was a town so unremarkable, it's not even mentioned in the Old Testament. Based on the residents' treatment of Jesus when He returned to preach, it wasn't a hotbed of spiritual devotion, either. But Jesus changes his mind quickly. First, He says upon seeing Nathanael, "Here's a true Israelite, in whom there is no deceit." While we might hear that as an innocuous compliment, Nathanael heard the echo of Jacob's story: "You're a son of Jacob, but without our patriarch's lying tendencies." Then Jesus promises him something astounding. Jacob had his ladder, by which he saw the presence of God. Follow me, He promises, and you'll have access to God's presence all the time. This mind-blowing claim seals the deal. Nathanael is His man from that day forward.

Calling Peter
Luke 5:1-11

We saw from John's Gospel how Simon, brother of Andrew, first met Jesus through the testimony of his brother, and how Jesus gave him a new name: Peter. When Luke picks up the story, Simon is still fishing and still going by his old name. We can imagine that the two brothers had some intense conversations about Jesus; Andrew saying, "Didn't you see the miracles He did? How can you not believe He's the One?" Simon replying, "We're just fishermen, Andrew, not prophets. The rabbis will tell us when the Messiah comes. Now get back to work." This is now at least the second time Simon has seen Jesus. But notice two things that happen for the first time: One, Simon is immediately convinced of his own sinfulness. Throughout Scripture, this is a common thread whenever someone really meets God; whether it's a prophet like Daniel or Isaiah, a shepherd like Moses or Jacob, or an apostle like John in Revelation. They drop to their knees in the face of perfect holiness and are convicted of their own need to change. The second thing that happens to Simon for the first time is that now he is ready to leave his old life and follow Jesus. Surely he was impressed with Jesus before. He may even have lain awake some nights wondering, "Who is this man?" But now He knows: "My life will never be the same. Wherever this man is going, that's where I want to go." The amazing thing about this is that Simon has just experienced his greatest success as a fisherman. You never hear of an athlete who signs a multi-year deal to pay him millions and then says, "I'm done. I retire from sports as of today." Yet that's what Simon did. He had so many fish in his nets, both of his boats couldn't hold them all. And he walked away from that. So did his partners, James and John. I wonder what happened to all those fish!

Jesus said an interesting thing to Peter (and that would indeed be his name from that day on): "Don't be afraid. From now on, you'll be catching men." Jesus knew Peter's purpose. He knew this unsteady, impulsive man was destined to be the Rock. He knew that this boastful coward would one day stand before thousands and preach the Gospel, then stand before hostile religious councils and refuse to back down from the saving truth. This same man who was small-minded and parochial and had probably never spoken a kind word to a Gentile in his life would one day become the first man to take salvation to non-Jews. Jesus knew that this unschooled blue-collar man would write words that would be read by millions. Jesus knew this man would change the world. And this day at the shore of the Sea of Galilee was just the beginning.

From Scum of the Earth to Saint
Matthew 9:9-13

This short account is full of meaning. For one, Matthew was probably not this man's given name. In both Mark's and Luke's versions of the story, the tax collector was named Levi. Since that was the name of one of Israel's patriarchs, we can easily imagine this man's parents giving him such a patriotic name. We can also imagine their shame when their son chose to enrich himself by collaborating with the hated Roman government. Matthew, on the other hand, was a name that meant "gift of God." Nowhere in Scripture do we find an account of where he got that name, but my belief is that Jesus gave it to him, just as He gave Simon the name Peter. And this reformed tax collector, when it came time to write this story in his Gospel account, chose to use his new name instead of his old.

Before meeting Jesus, Matthew/Levi must have been a particularly hard-hearted character. He gathered taxes in Capernaum, the very headquarters of Jesus. He surely had heard stories about this Nazarene miracle worker who had healed a paralyzed man and many others in their own hometown. Yet there he was, still extorting his own neighbors for the benefit of their oppressors. Then Jesus showed up. Sixteenth-century painter Caravaggio depicted this scene in his immortal *The Calling of St Matthew.* Jesus stands partly in shadow, pointing at a table full of anachronistically dressed men huddled over a table full of coins. One of the men, with the sun hitting him full in the face, points uncertainly to his own chest. You can almost hear him say, "Who, me?" And that is probably what Matthew said to himself. Why would Jesus call someone like him? Because, as the Lord later explained to his Pharasaic critics, appalled that this so-called holy man would deign to dine with the scum of society, "Sick people need a doctor. I have the cure for what is ailing them. You religious elites don't think there's anything wrong with you. Why would I waste my cure on someone who doesn't think they need it?" Deep down, beneath his fancy clothes purchased with ill-gotten gains, beneath his cynical sneer, Matthew must have hated what had become of his life, the terrible bargain he had made with his own ambitions. Jesus offered something he never thought possible: Redemption.

The Twelve
Luke 6:12-16

Jesus prayed all night before selecting the Twelve. They weren't His only disciples. We know He had other followers, some of them so devoted, they stayed with Him on His darkest day, when most of the Twelve had fled. Truth be told, if you and I were to interview candidates to be the founders of history's most important movement, we would never choose these dozen men. Many were fisherman. Matthew was a tax collector (hardly the way to give your group legitimacy). Simon was a Zealot, a political group within Israel that advocated violent overthrow of the Romans (Do you think he and Matthew had some heated conversations?). There wasn't a scholar among them, nor was there anyone with political connections, material wealth, or noted entrepreneurial skills. They were all from Galilee, considered the least spiritual of Israel's provinces (it was even called "Galilee of the Gentiles," as in Isaiah 9, for example). Their performance once Jesus called them didn't exactly vindicate His choice. Peter was exposed as an impulsive braggart, whose mouth often wrote checks his body couldn't cash. John and James were volatile and ambitious; Jesus took to calling them "The Sons of Thunder." Thomas is known today as "The Doubter." Judas' name became synonymous with treason. And the rest were apparently so nondescript, we know little about them. And yet, today there are countless cities, hospitals, universities, and sons named for them. How did it happen? That's one of the best parts of the story…

Your Mission, Should You Choose to Accept It…
Matthew 10:1-42

The Twelve have been following Jesus, watching His life, hearing His teaching, and being awed by His miracles. But now He is sending them out, two by two, on unsupervised ministry of their own. Modern American Christianity can often seem like an academic course: Go to Bible studies and mass preaching events, and soak in the information that will change your life. But Jesus knew that real growth happens not simply through study, but through action. Jesus was not a professor; He was a commanding officer on the front lines, sending His troops out for a battle to liberate souls. And like a commanding officer, He didn't mince words about what His followers would face: *I am sending you out as sheep among wolves* (v. 16). *They will hand you over to the local councils and will flog you in their synagogues* (v. 17). *All men will hate you because of me* (v. 22). *Do not be afraid of those who kill the body but cannot kill the soul* (v. 28). In other words, "Don't worry, the worst they can do is kill you!" *Anyone who loves his father or mother more than me is not worthy of me. Anyone who loves his son or daughter more than me is not worthy of me. And anyone who does not take his cross and follow me is not worthy of me* (vv. 37-38). Jesus here is telling them, "Be fully prepared to be hated by those you love most, or even to die, because of your faith in me." And then there's v. 39: *Whoever finds his life will lose it, and whoever loses his life for my sake will find it.*

These are not the sort of things you say if you're trying to build a huge following. Instead, you promise blessings and benefits, and downplay the commitment level. But Jesus wasn't seeking fans; He was equipping disciples. Jesus wasn't interested in celebrity, with all the cushy perks that entails; He wanted to save the world. And as the anthropologist Margaret Mead famously said, "Never doubt that a small group of thoughtful, committed citizens can change the world. Indeed, it's the only thing that ever has." Matthew 10 should not be seen as God's eternal instructions to anyone who does evangelism work; there are many instructions here that are obviously meant only for the present mission, such as His command to go only to Jews (v. 6). But it shows that serving Christ isn't for wimps. It takes commitment. Today, Jesus has many fans, but few disciples. Which are you?

Work the Room
Luke 14:1-14

Remember the days when "network" was a noun instead of a verb? Remember when social situations were exactly that—an opportunity to spend time with other people—and not chances to impress people and advance our own ambitious agendas? Remember when the term "work the room" was unheard of? Those terms may not have existed in Jesus' day, but the same temptations did. Jesus here is in a position that is rare for Him: Having dinner in the home of a prominent Pharisee. I am sure the wine and food were better, and the company was more well-mannered and attractive than He was used to. You or I would have surely been on our best behavior; we would want to convince the well-heeled crowd that we fit in well with them. Jesus, instead, is a deliberately terrible party guest, breaking rabbinic protocol by healing a man on the Sabbath, pointing out the hypocrisy of all the diners, and even criticizing the host for his guest list.

He also pointed out the actions of the people around the table, how they preened and schemed to gain social advantage. He told them they would be much wiser to humble themselves; it's gratifying to have the host lift you up, and devastating to be told to move to a lesser position. After all, He said, *Everyone who exalts Himself will be humbled, and he who humbles himself will be exalted.* So Jesus wasn't just giving handy party advice. He was talking about eternal matters, as usual. God is the ultimate host, and we are invited to His banquet. This particular host isn't impressed with flashy clothes, flamboyant personalities, or dazzling resumes. But when He sees someone who is humble—who refuses to talk about herself, who constantly thinks of and serves others—He wants to highlight her. This idea of humility as a virtue was one of Jesus' favorite messages. He repeated it over and over again. It was revolutionary at the time; humility was seen in the ancient world as a characteristic fitting only for slaves. Jesus never used the term "work the room," but in His eyes, it would have meant "serve everyone you see. Be the love of God incarnated in their lives." As He would often say, *the last shall be first and the first shall be last.* That teaching is still revolutionary.

The Cost of Discipleship
Matthew 16:24-26

Have you ever heard someone talk about having a "cross to bear?" Perhaps with our current generation's biblical illiteracy, this expression is starting to fade from our vocabulary. But for years, people would use it to describe an annoying circumstance. A woman married to a lout, a man whose boss was a tyrant, or a parent with a lazy son might say, "I suppose this is my cross to bear." The expression comes from Jesus' statement here. But Jesus was not talking about a mere irritation. He was describing what it meant to truly follow Him. He was inviting His disciples (and us) on a suicide mission.

In 1937, a brilliant young German clergyman named Dietrich Bonhoeffer wrote a book called *Nachfolge* (which translates as "Following"). It was published in English as *The Cost of Discipleship.* The book is a meditation on the Sermon on the Mount, but it starts with a direct assault on what Bonhoeffer called "cheap grace." He saw the perversion of the Gospel that was being preached in Germany at the time, and urged his fellow believers to preach a true, costly grace that demands real repentance of sin and total surrender of the heart. As He wrote, "When Jesus calls a man, He bids him come and die." Bonhoeffer courageously resisted the Nazi regime. While many German Christians refused to defy Hitler, and many clergy went along with the Nazi changes to Christian liturgy and teaching, Bonhoeffer led an illegal underground seminary of like-minded believers. He was later arrested for participating in the Von Stauffenburg plot to assassinate Hitler, and was executed at the Flossenburg Concentration Camp just days before it was liberated. When Christ called, Bonhoeffer answered. Perhaps you and I will never have to literally give our lives for Christ. We can hope not. But every day, Christians must make a choice between a cheap, easy grace that is all about permission to live selfishly, or a costly Gospel that leads to a radical commitment to love others in His name.

Hundredfold
Mark 10:28-31

Some things are so ironic, it's hard to believe they're true. This verse is often used by "Prosperity Gospel" preachers to say, "See, Jesus promised that if you give to His work, He'll multiply it and give it back to you!" Some even cynically make it both literally mathematical and baldly self-serving, promising that if you give, say, one hundred dollars to their ministry, you will receive back $10,000…or more. Curiously, I've never heard one of them ask for believers to donate their children to the ministry, or predict that if they do so, they'll get back 100 kids! I don't want to stand in the shoes of such preachers on Judgment Day.

The truth about this passage is that it's yet another example of Peter's impulsiveness and lack of understanding, and the patience of Jesus. This comes directly after the encounter of Jesus and the rich young man, who sincerely wanted to follow Jesus…until he found out he would have to give up his wealth. Peter's question seems to be, "Lord, if we did what this rich man couldn't do (give up everything to follow you), what will be our payoff?" Peter, I assume, is speaking for all the disciples. They can't help thinking in mercenary terms. Jesus gives them the gentlest of rebukes. How can He promise His faithful followers a hundredfold return in family members who they have left behind? Because joining the Kingdom means gaining hundreds of new brothers and sisters, mothers and fathers, sons and daughters. Jesus was creating a new kind of family: The family of God. This isn't about enriching ourselves in an earthly sense. It's not a promise that following Jesus will make our dreams come true. Jesus was, as always, brutally honest about the cost of following Him (note that he mentions persecutions even while saying something comforting). But the sacrifices we make for Him will be worth it. That is the promise.

Walking on Water
Matthew 14:22-33

The first thing to know about this famous story is that Peter was exhausted, physically and mentally. The day had started with Jesus finding out that John the Baptist had been executed. John was Jesus' cousin; Andrew had been close to John, and quite possibly others of the Twelve had known him, too. Jesus said, "Let's get in the boat and get away for a while." Even Jesus needed time to grieve, and I'm sure the disciples were glad to get a break, too. But the people on the shoreline saw them in the boat, and ran to meet them. With every village they passed, the crowd got larger, running along the coast. So when they landed, Jesus stepped off the boat and went to work. The long-awaited break wasn't to be. This went on all day, with no time to stop and eat or rest. The sun was starting to go down. One of the Twelve came up with a brilliant idea to convince Jesus to send the people home; why not play on His compassion? "Lord, these people haven't eaten all day. Send them home now, so they don't collapse on the way." Jesus didn't bat an eye; "You feed them," He said. Andrew came up with the little boy who had loaves and fish, and Jesus somehow turned that into a buffet for thousands. Peter and the others had to serve that massive crowd, then pick up the leftovers. It was probably dark by this point. Jesus told the Twelve, "Get in the boat and cross the Sea. I'll meet you on the other side." He somehow convinced the hysterical crowd to disperse, then went up on a hillside to pray, alone.

So it had already been a long day when the storm hit. Peter and the others were fighting to keep the boat afloat, rowing and bailing out water with depleted muscles while the wind blasted them and wave after wave swamped them. Salt was in their eyes and mouths; it was hard to breathe. This went on for hours, until the fourth watch of the night, sometime between three and six AM. By that time, there was nothing keeping them going but sheer survival instinct. Suddenly, one of them spotted the impossible: A man walking on the water. They'd never seen a ghost, but what other explanation could there be? Worse yet, this terrifying spirit was headed straight for them. Then He came close enough that His face could be seen, only a few feet from the boat; It was Jesus! And Peter said, "Lord, if it is you, command me to come to you on the water."

What on earth was he thinking? As far as we know, Peter had no previous qualifications for water-walking; there was nothing in his past that indicated he had a gift for that sort of thing. He was a fisherman, so he had been on the water many times. He knew there was a name for people who got out of the boat in the middle of a storm on the Sea of Galilee: Fish food. If he would have asked the other eleven men in the boat, "Hey, do you think I can walk on that water?" they would have said, "You're joking right?" So what made him think he could do it? Simple: Jesus said he could. Peter was still far from understanding who Jesus really was or what He had come to do, but He was starting to catch on.

Upon this Rock
Matthew 16:13-20

One of Peter's leading characteristics seems to have been a tendency to speak before thinking. There are many of us who can identify. But here, at long last, Peter says the right thing. As surprising as that is, the response of Jesus is even more astonishing. Some scholars have called v. 18 the most controversial verse in the entire New Testament. I want to unpack four important terms, so that we all understand what Jesus is saying here.

First, there's *Upon this rock*. The name Peter, which Jesus has given to Simon, means "rock." So it's obvious He's talking about Peter himself. Next, there's the word *church*. At the point Jesus said this, there was no such thing as a church. The term Matthew uses in Greek is *ecclesia,* which means "community" or "assembly." So Jesus is saying, "Peter is going to be the starting point for the group of people I am building." The disciples thought the Messiah was going to lead Israel; it must have surprised them to hear that Jesus was building a new group of people separate from the political nation of Israel. Our Catholic brothers point to this verse as proof that Jesus named Peter as the first Pope; the infallible, unquestioned leader of the Christian movement. But the early church certainly didn't seem to see him that way. In Acts 8, we see the Church sending Peter and John on an assignment. Get that? The Church told Peter what to do, not the other way around. In Acts 11, people in the church question a decision Peter made. In Galatians 2, Paul publicly rebukes Peter. That doesn't sound like an unquestioned leader to me. So I believe what Jesus is saying is, "I am starting a new kind of people. Peter is going to be the first one in the group. I can build on this guy."

Next, He says *the gates of Hades will not prevail against it.* I always believed Jesus was saying, "Hell itself won't be able to stand up against my church." In saying that, I thought He was referring to Hell as the domain of Satan, the headquarters of evil, the way we used to talk about "the iron curtain" during the days of the Cold War. But Jesus didn't use the term *Gehenna,* which we translate "Hell." He used the term "Hades," which is another way of referring to death. So what He's actually saying is, "Death won't be able to stop my Church. My Church will last forever." Finally, let's look at that term, *keys to the Kingdom.* Based on everything else Jesus told His disciples between this time and the day He ascended into Heaven, it's obvious that He's talking about the Gospel. He's saying, "By the time I'm done here, you'll have a story to tell, and it will be the greatest story ever told. When you tell this story, people will get set free. Chains will fall off. Lives will be transformed. The people you rescue down here on Earth will be truly rescued because of the power of Heaven itself." Jesus had just brought us all in on His rescue movement, starting with this one man, Peter.

Get Thee Behind Me
Matthew 16:21-28

Jesus' words in v. 23 are part of our cultural vocabulary. They are usually used humorously. For example: A woman came home with a very expensive dress. When her husband questioned her about why she spent so much, she replied, "I think the Devil just whispered in my ear about how good it looked on me." When the husband asked her why she didn't tell the Devil to get behind her, she said, "I did, and he said, 'it looks good from back here, too."

We can be certain that there was nothing humorous about these words when Jesus spoke them. To Jesus, Satan was not a comic figure with scaly red skin, horns and a pitchfork, or a shadowy boogeyman. He was a personal figure with whom Jesus was well-acquainted. They had spent forty harrowing days dueling in the desert (Matthew 4:1-11), and if Jesus was who He said He was, they had been adversaries since before time began. For Jesus to call Peter "Satan" (a Hebrew word meaning "the enemy") was the most severe condemnation He could utter. It would be similar to a man's wife calling him by the name of her abusive ex-husband. For Him to call Peter such an awful thing just after praising him effusively is an even greater shock. But the epithet was well chosen. Recall that in Jesus' temptations in the desert, the Devil seemed intent on luring Jesus into making life easier for Himself: Turn stones into bread to fill your hunger. Prove to the world you're the Savior by doing some spectacular act like throwing yourself from the pinnacle of the temple. And, most insidious of all, bow down to me, and rule the world, no strings attached. Victory without suffering…that is a temptation all of us would find alluring. But Jesus knew His path led to suffering of the most purposeful and painful kind. Now Peter was filling that same role, hoping to keep Jesus from the cross. It was a true betrayal.

Peter seems to be thinking of Jesus' own safety, but it's clear Jesus saw a different motive in His friend. The Twelve were still hoping their years of personal sacrifice for Jesus' sake were going to pay off in terms of earthly fortune and power. Now Jesus was saying that He was going to the cross. History was clear about what happened to the followers of would-be Messiahs…they died along with their masters. That's why Jesus went on to say the difficult things we find in vv. 24-28. These words challenge us to this day. Jesus never promised us He would bring us earthly bliss; the reality for many of His followers would be quite the opposite at times.

A Mother's Request
Matthew 20:20-28

The woman who Matthew calls "the mother of Zebedee's sons" had a name, of course. Comparing Matthew 27:56, Mark 15:40 and John 19:25, it seems likely that her name was Salome, and that she was the sister of Mary. That would make her Jesus' aunt, and her sons—James and John—Jesus' first cousins! She was one of several female followers of Jesus, who turned out to be even more faithful to Him than His male disciples; Salome was at the cross where He died, and went to His tomb to anoint His body. In this story, Matthew isn't concerned with her relationship to Jesus; He wants to focus on the request she makes. It seems likely that James and John put her up to this, based on how Jesus and the other disciples focus their response on the two sons, not on Salome. Perhaps that's why Matthew doesn't name her here as he does in 27:56…perhaps he doesn't hold her responsible for this faux pas either.

Why is this such a terrible request? We love people with big ambitions. The legendary football coach Vince Lombardi famously said, "Winning isn't everything; it's the only thing." The Super Bowl trophy is named after him for a reason. Before his conversion to Christianity, political hatchet man Chuck Colson boasted he would trample his own grandmother to win an election. But Jesus said the highest of ambitions is to put others first. True success looks more like servanthood than self-promotion. We've already seen how that idea changed history; We want our successful people to at least put on a show of humility. After all, we would never elect a politician who called himself "The Great" as kings did in the ancient world. But Jesus is talking about much more than superficial modesty. He's describing a radically new way to live. He predicted His own death for the sake of others. Somehow, in His mind, that would be the ultimate victory.

Missing the Point
Luke 9:49-56

The Twelve had an exceptionally hard time with Jesus' teaching about humility. He had to repeat it several times in different forms. In this story, He has just finished giving the same lesson when John changes the subject to highlight his own loyalty to Jesus. He wanted to stop a competing preacher from rescuing a demon-possessed soul. When we next read of James and John wanting to call down fire from Heaven on the stubborn Samaritans, we begin to understand why Jesus called them Sons of Thunder. It was a way of teasing them about their type-A personalities (at least, I think it was teasing!).

I love the stories in the Gospels that show how slow-witted and cowardly Jesus' disciples were. First of all, it's a sure sign the stories are authentic. If these first eyewitnesses of Jesus had been making up fanciful tales to invent a new religion, they wouldn't have cast themselves as buffoons and backstabbers. But mostly, I love them because they show us how patient Jesus was. When I was sixteen, I acquired my first steady job, working in the butcher shop of a local grocery store. I was fired after less than a month. Granted, I deserved to be fired. I had failed to clean a meat grinder at the end of a night's work; when the boss arrived the next morning, the whole store smelled like a dead cow. But that's just the point. When I read the Gospels, I see plenty of moments when Jesus could easily have said, "Alright, you guys are out. There is no way I can entrust the most important movement in human history to you." But He didn't. He stuck with them. And, thank God, I have no doubt He'll stick with me, too.

Doubt
Matthew 11:2-19

This story is surprising in many ways. Every other thing we read about John the Baptist shows him to be a man of rock-solid faith and fiery boldness. But now, he sends messengers to ask Jesus if He truly was the Messiah after all. Isn't this the man who as a pre-born infant leapt in his mother's womb at the sound of Mary's voice? Didn't he call Jesus "the Lamb of God, who takes away the sins of the world?" Didn't he baptize Jesus, and hear the voice from Heaven proclaiming, "This is my Son…"? Yes. But He was also a devout Jew who yearned for God's justice to fall at last on Israel's enemies (we as affluent Americans cannot properly appreciate how important this idea is to any oppressed people). Jesus, instead, was saying we should love our enemies and turn the other cheek when struck. John thought when the Messiah arrived, evil would be destroyed and righteousness exalted. But here he was rotting in jail for criticizing the king's adultery, while pagan Rome still ruled and amoral collaborators like Herod still enjoyed unfettered prosperity and power. John is one of many biblical examples that show us, no matter how much evidence we have of God's presence, power and love, we all experience doubt sometimes.

The response of Jesus to John is even more surprising. He could be just as blunt as John in His own way, but His answer here is touchingly gentle. First, He sends a response that is a mash-up of Isaiah 35:5-6 and Isaiah 61:1-2. John would have recognized the words immediately as prophecy, and would also have caught implication: "You're forgetting what the Scriptures said about me, my friend. I am doing everything that God foretold." He then lavishly praises John as belonging in the top ranks of the greatest people ever to live. Considering the source of this praise, it is a high honor indeed, and we can assume these words made their way back to John's cell, cheering him and steeling him for his imminent martyrdom. He also criticizes the crowds for neither accepting John's dourness or His own cheerfulness. His words are those of an exasperated parent, saying to her incorrigible children, "I'm trying everything I can to get through to you, but you just won't let me love you." Once again, as with our last reading, we see the amazing patience of God. He doesn't even turn away from us when we doubt Him.

Brothers
John 7:1-9

If you've ever felt overshadowed by a high-achieving sibling, imagine what it would be like if your older brother was Jesus! He was the kid who always knew the right answer in Hebrew school, who never made Mom or Dad angry, who always did the right thing. There is no biblical evidence that He worked any miracles during His growing-up years, but we can assume the same magnetic, compassionate personality that one day would draw thousands to His side was there when He was young, too. Perhaps that sense of sibling rivalry at least partially explains the brothers' attitude in this story.

Whatever their reasons, it is hard for us to comprehend how it must have made Jesus feel. John the apostle must have known this, because the way he words v. 5 is so incredibly poignant: *For not even His brothers believed in him.* It reminds us of Isaiah's prophecy in Isaiah 53: 3, *He was a man of sorrows and acquainted with grief.* Yet there is no trace of bitterness in Him at any time. For most of us, rejection by our closest loved ones would be so devastating, we would never recover, yet Jesus poured out selfless love toward others consistently. Something unimaginably powerful was going on at the core of this man's character that enabled Him to rise above even the most painful personal wounds. Could He convey that same power to us? We all need it eventually.

True Family
Matthew 12:46-50

Earlier in our study, we looked at the story (recorded in Mark 3:20-21) of how Jesus' mother and brothers came to take Him home by force, thinking He had lost His mind. Matthew now tells the rest of the story. Told that His family is waiting to speak to Him, Jesus refuses to go out to them. "My family," He asserts, "Is right here." Did He know why they had come? Jesus often had supernatural insight into the thoughts of people, so that's highly possible. If so, is this a sign Jesus reacted angrily out of hurt feelings? Perhaps. But there is another explanation. Jesus knew there would be people in this world (far too many, sad to say) whose own families rejected them. His disciples, we can be certain, had already experienced this to some extent; I can imagine Zebedee, for instance, thought his wife and sons were out of their minds to leave behind a thriving fishing career to follow a penniless, unschooled teacher. Countless more people come from families shattered by things other than religious conviction: Abuse, adultery, addiction, workaholism, mental illness…the list is practically endless. Yet, as He says here, true family is still available. Accept my words, become my disciple, and you are part of my family. Jesus would teach His disciples to call God "Abba," the Hebrew word for "daddy." This was a brand-new way of seeing the Lord for them, and it should speak volumes to us, since we think of "Father God" as a commonplace idea. Jesus' family would later come around. Mary would be at the cross. James would be a prominent leader in the early Church. He and Jude would write books in the New Testament, both of which describe their brother Jesus as fully divine. But Jesus' words here are a powerful reminder that, even when the bonds of blood dissolve, the family we've found in Him remains strong to the end.

You Can't Go Home Again
Luke 4:14-30

Perhaps you've heard the expression, "You can't go home again." It's a warning that, if you try to move back to your hometown after years away, you may be disappointed. The sentimental memories you carry may be destroyed when you see beloved people and places with new eyes. Worse, those people may not accept you for the person you've become. But no one ever experienced this more disturbingly than Jesus. When He visited Nazareth, it was still early in His ministry, but already He had acquired notoriety. The homefolks must have been proud of their native son. When He was asked to read from the scroll of Isaiah that morning, He chose a passage that was known to be about the Messiah (and one He would later reference in His message to John the Baptist). The people loved hearing those thrilling words of God's coming deliverance. But then He spoke of the ongoing motif in Israel's Scriptures the people of God steadfastly ignored: God's plan to extend His salvation to non-Jews. He says, in essence, "You probably want to see me do miracles, as you've surely heard that I've done in Capernaum. But if I did, you wouldn't accept them. After all, in the previous time in history when God's miracle-working power was on display—the time of Elijah and Elisha—the people turned away from Him. His power and love ended up blessing people outside the family of Abraham. And that will happen in this case, too."

It's astonishing for us to see how infuriating this truth was in the ears of His former neighbors, people who had known Jesus when He was a boy. How angry did they have to be to grab Mary and Joseph's son and physically drag Him to the edge of a cliff, fully intending to shove Him to His death? But let us not pretend that we gently accept offensive truths. Jesus walked away safely that day. It wasn't His time to die yet, and He had sufficient power to make sure no one would take His life before He was ready to give it. We can be sure His heart was deeply wounded, and that He never went home again. He lost His home, but if His mission succeeded, He would provide a new home for millions.

The Unjust Death of a Righteous Man
Matthew 14:1-12

If you study history long enough, you see too many stories like this one, of good people dying needlessly at the whims of evil rulers. Herod Antipas was the son of Herod the Great, the man who slaughtered infants in Nazareth in an attempt to kill Jesus just after His birth. This Herod was a mere Tetrarch, a petty governor of Galilee and Perea under the auspices of Rome. He had divorced his wife to marry the wife of his brother, Philip. This decision caused not just hard feelings within the Herod family, but had political consequences as well; Herod's first wife was the princess of a neighboring nation. So when John courageously pointed out the Tetrarch's immoral behavior, he did not receive the rebuke well. Historians have estimated that Herodias' daughter (Josephus, who lived then, says her name was Salome) was between 12 and 14 years old, which just makes this story all more tawdry. One has to wonder if in future years, young Salome thought back to this event with regret; if not because of her guilt at the death of a great man, then at least for wasting an opportunity. She could asked for almost anything money could buy, but instead she listened to the hateful words of her vindictive mother, and ended up with a truly ghastly prize. It doesn't seem right that John the Baptist, who had turned the hearts of so many people back to God and had faithfully prepared the way for the Messiah, should die in such a way. Sometimes—often, in fact—this world seems to offer no real justice.

But that's because we don't know the final score. Matthew told this particular story backwards. The end of the story is really in verses 1 and 2. Sometime after Herod had taken John's life, he heard about the ministry of Jesus. Perhaps he was informed by Cuza, his household manager, whose wife Joanna was one of Jesus' followers (Luke 8:3). His instant assumption that these deeds were done by John, risen from the grave, doesn't make sense. John had never done miracles before; why would he now be able to do so? Herod was no theologian, but beyond that, his fears betray a strong sense of guilt. If the Scriptures teach us anything, we know that no one ever really "gets away with it." Even those powerful enough to commit horridly evil acts with impunity will one day pay the price. So yes, history tells many such stories. But it also tells us something else: killing a righteous man doesn't stop the Kingdom of God. John was gone. But Jesus was still here, and His impact would be far greater than that of John.

He Never Said it Would Be Easy
Matthew 8:18-22

We can learn many things from Jesus: How to build a large following is not one of them. In the Gospels, we see Jesus break just about every rule known to recruiters. Here we see Him seemingly chase away two willing followers. One is a scribe, a part of a group that was consistently opposed to Jesus. Yet instead of embracing this man, who pledges his undying loyalty, and seeking to capitalize on his social status to legitimize His ministry, Jesus tells him how hard life will be if he follows through on his promise. He doesn't tell this scribe about any of the benefits of joining the Messiah's movement; only the liabilities. His interaction with the other unnamed disciple is even more harsh, and frankly, offensive to modern readers. Some scholars speculate that the man wasn't asking for a chance to attend his father's funeral service; instead, he was saying, "Just let me wait until my father dies." In other words, perhaps what held this man back was the objections of his father. Since he didn't want to stand up to his father, he hoped to follow Jesus when that was no longer a problem. But Jesus would have none of it. He would later warn that following Him would divide fathers and sons (Matthew 10:35); we see proof of that here.

Why would Jesus treat so cruelly those who simply wanted to follow Him? Perhaps it wasn't cruelty at all. Jesus did not want them to be deceived. Dazzled by His miraculous powers and His dynamic speaking, people may have thought that chucking it all and following this amazing man would be a life full of excitement, reward and ease. After all, a man who could feed five thousand with one little boy's lunch would surely rain down prosperity on his most loyal friends, right? Jesus wanted them to see the true cost of standing up against the forces of evil. He was here to win a war, to break the power of darkness that held men and women in bondage forever. That fight would be won, but it wouldn't come without high cost. For Jesus to explain that high cost to His followers up front was an act of love.

Sheep without a Shepherd
Matthew 9:35-38

Verse 36 tells us a great deal about the character of Jesus. He saw "the crowds," those teeming masses of people, most of whom wanted something from Him, some of whom actually hated Him, and His gut-level emotion was compassion. This is remarkable enough, when we think about times when we have tried to serve a large group of people and quickly burned out. Our painted-on smile and smooth customer service is only a façade. Deep down, we wish these people would go home and leave us alone! Even more remarkable is the meaning of the word compassion. The Greek term Matthew uses here is the word for "bowels." So it really was a gut-level emotion. Jesus felt it deep inside Himself. This wasn't the sort of pity affluent people have when they see starving children on TV and simply say, "Isn't that awful?" This kind of compassion always results in action.

Jesus urged His disciples to pray for God to send workers into the harvest field. The Church has always seen that as Christ calling for us to do our part, to take His love with us wherever we go, intentionally, sacrificially, tirelessly. Of course, the Church often fails at this task. But here's a thought that should bring us all joy: If Jesus was right in claiming to be God in human flesh, aren't you glad that God feels this way?

Come to Me
Matthew 11:28-29

If I had the money, I would put these two verses on billboards in every major city in the world. If there is one thing that's true of humanity in the 21st Century, it's that we are weary and heavy-burdened. That's true even in prosperous America, where our rates of addiction, depression, and suicide seem to grow even faster than our standard of living. If only everyone could hear this compelling invitation! But what was Jesus promising? This isn't a guarantee of a trouble-free existence for all who follow Him; as we've already seen, Jesus never oversold the benefits of discipleship or denied its trials. The key word in this promise is the word "yoke." People of Jesus' time, like most people throughout history, lived off the land. They knew that a field was plowed by oxen or donkeys, and those animals were connected to the plow by a yoke, a bar that fit across the animal's shoulders. When Jesus says *take my yoke upon you and learn from me...for my yoke is easy and my burden is light,* He is implying that each of us is already pulling a yoke. No wonder we're exhausted and stressed! But instead of offering us freedom from work, He offers us a new yoke. This one, He promises, is "easy" and "light." The picture is of an animal pulling a yoke which was not intended for it. That heavy, mis-matched yoke is killing the animal, slowly, painfully. We can imagine what our mis-matched yoke looks like: Money, success, approval, revenge, power, popularity…the possibilities are endless. Each one promises the feeling we're hoping for, but none ultimately pay off. All eventually make us miserable. But Jesus' yoke fits just right. The burden is exactly what we're meant to carry. It feels like a joy to do the work.

We often think of work as a curse, but that's not the biblical idea. The book of Proverbs teaches often about the value of hard work. My favorite Scripture verse, Ephesians 2:10, says *We are God's workmanship, created in Christ Jesus for good works, which He prepared beforehand for us to do.* I think that's the yoke Jesus was talking about. God created each of us for a purpose; there are good deeds, world-changing actions we have opportunity to take every day of our lives. God created us with those deeds in mind, and custom-designed us to make the world a better place in His name through doing those good works. How do you find your yoke? There's not a seminar to attend or a book to read. Just follow Jesus' invitation: *Come to me.* Tell Him you are weary. Tell Him you're ready for a different kind of life. Follow Him, and see where He takes you.

Born Again
John 3:1-21

Jimmy Carter was elected President of the United States in 1976. During the campaign, many Americans (including, seemingly, a large portion of the news media) learned a new term: Born-again Christian. Of course, many people from the South, like Carter, had grown up hearing the term. But even among Southerners, the term was used in a curious way. I can remember, for instance, reading a quote from a local businessman: "Me and my family aren't born-again Christians or anything like that, but we are Christians." In his mind—and, it seems, in the minds of many—"Born-again" was a special category of Christian. Perhaps it was another way of saying "Holy roller" or "Jesus freak."

Jimmy Carter didn't actually invent the term, although the man who did had the same initials. When Jesus said these words to Nicodemus (in v. 3), He wasn't saying, "Only the most committed, most devoutly religious people get into Heaven." If that were the case, Nicodemus, a Pharisee and member of the Jewish ruling council, certainly would have qualified. No, Jesus was saying something much more offensive to a man like Nicodemus: "Even with all your religiosity and morality, you can't be part of God's Kingdom. You have to become someone brand new." When Nicodemus asked "How can these things be?" He was asking an appropriate question. Jesus' response is the truth: You can't do it, but the Holy Spirit can make it happen.

We tend to focus on v. 16, which is arguably the most well-known verse in the Bible. That's a good thing: John 3:16 is essentially the whole Gospel in a single verse. But v. 3 is every bit as important and transforming as v. 16. A few years later, another devout Pharisee, full of such violent religious zeal he became a terrorist, would be transformed by this power of which Jesus spoke. We know him today as the apostle Paul, a man who went from persecuting people who believed differently to the author of our most beloved texts on the free grace and forgiveness of God. He went from nationalistic pride to spending his entire life working for the reconciliation of Jew and Gentile in the name of Christ. He would write in 2 Corinthians 5:17, *Therefore if anyone is in Christ, he is a new creation; the old has gone, the new has come!* He was the number one testimony of that verse's truth. Jesus doesn't want to convert us to a new religion. He wants to change our lives. Has that happened to you?

Jesus and the Outcast
John 4:1-26, 39-42

Jesus had at least three good reasons to ignore this woman. The first is an ethnic reason: Jews and Samaritans were part of a mutual hatred relationship that went back centuries. The second was a gender-based reason: a respectable Jewish man, especially a rabbi like Jesus, would never have a conversation with a woman he was not related to. Then there was a societal reason: It's not trivial that John chooses to tell us the time of day. That is not a detail found in most biblical stories, so it is meant to tell us something. Drawing water was typically a social event for the women of a village. They would come early in the cool of the evening and draw water together. This was their chance to interact with other women, to enjoy some contact outside the home. So when this woman comes carrying her water jug all alone in the heat of the day, she might as well be wearing a big scarlet "L" (for loser) around her neck. She is an outcast even among her own people, for reasons borne out in the story. Yet Jesus chooses to engage this woman in conversation. He saw her as more than some potential seductress, more than a dirty Samaritan, and more than a social leper. He cared for her.

Notice also how patient He is with her. The woman keeps trying to draw Jesus into debate on whether Samaritan worship was more legitimate than that of the Jews, but Jesus doesn't bite, and He doesn't get frustrated and give up. He patiently explains the truth. Then the bombshell: Jesus tells her who He is. Even His own disciples had not figured that out at this point, but Jesus reveals to, of all people, a woman rejected by her own people, a people who Jesus' countrymen despised. The story ends with this woman's words leading her entire village to faith in Jesus. The unlikeliest preacher of all turns out to have been one of the most successful. We see it again and again in Scripture: God doesn't judge humans the way we do. We see a barren old couple; God sees the parents of a race that will bring salvation to the earth. We see a frustrated octogenarian with a murder rap; God sees a great deliverer, the leader of the most successful slave revolt in history. We see a forgotten shepherd boy; God sees a giant-killer and future king, a man after His own heart. We see an unmarried pregnant teenager in a backwater town; God sees the mother of the Messiah. Wouldn't you like to know how He sees you?

A Wee Little Man
Luke 19:1-10

When I was a child, we sang a song in Sunday School, "Zacchaeus was a wee little man, a wee little man was he. He climbed up in the sycamore tree, for the Lord he wanted to see…" I still remember every word of the song. It made this story seem comical, and it probably was to the people of Jericho…to a point. We've already talked about how despised tax collectors were, and why, but Zacchaeus was a *chief* tax collector. His ill-gotten wealth was no doubt far larger than what Levi had enjoyed before following Jesus, and so was the animus of the people against him. There are several details in this story that would have struck the original readers in a deeper way. For one, Zacchaeus climbing into the tree was a massive social faux pas. Not only did it spotlight his short stature, but—to put it delicately—it exposed one's undercarriage to the views of people passing by below. It was a humiliating thing to do, but that's precisely the point: Zacchaeus was so desperate to see Jesus, he was willing to un-dignify himself publicly. Then when we see him promise to donate half of his income to the poor and repay any he had cheated with four times the amount (the Jewish law only stipulated that reparations be equal to the amount stolen, plus a fifth, so Zacchaeus was going way above legal requirements). This was not a way to win Jesus' favor. Jesus, in choosing to dine in the tax collector's house, was conferring His favor upon him. Zacchaeus' generosity, instead, was a sign of true repentance. He wasn't just sorry for his previous life of fraud, deceit, and collaboration with the enemy. He was excited to embrace a brand-new life, in which he gave to others instead of stealing from them.

Jesus shocked the crowd, who must have been laughing to see their hated enemy, dressed in his impressive finery, hanging from a tree. The laughter ended when He said, "Come down. I am going to your house." When He told His disciples, "this man too is a son of Abraham," He was saying, "I am the Good Shepherd of all Israel's sheep, even this one." Some have said that v. 10 is the key verse in the entire Gospel of Luke, because it shows what Jesus' ministry was truly about. If He had been just another religious teacher, the encounter with Zacchaeus would have been the perfect opportunity to highlight His own righteousness by publicly scorching the stumpy little crook, telling him in no uncertain terms there was no room in God's Kingdom for the likes of him. Instead, He embraced this man as a long-lost child of God. Here's a humbling thought: That is how God sees the people you and I hate the most, as well.

The Man Who Had it All
Mark 10:17-27

Here is another story of Jesus' encounter with a rich man, this one much more tragic. Unlike Zacchaeus, this unnamed rich man was pious and respectable. Jesus seems to agree with his self-assessment, saying, "One thing you lack…" Like Zacchaeus, this man knew there was something missing in his life, and like Zacchaeus, he had a feeling Jesus could tell him the answer. But unlike Zacchaeus, he loved his riches in the end more than God. Bystanders may have thought at first that Jesus gave this man an impossible challenge in order to chase him away, since as a blue collar Jew, Jesus would naturally be expected to resent a wealthy person. But verse 21 is insightful: Jesus felt a love for this man, *therefore* He told him to give away his possessions. This isn't a universal command. There is no indication that the early Christians shunned private ownership. However, Jesus is giving the same command to this man that He gave to Peter and His other disciples: "Follow me." Following Jesus on His earthly mission was a huge commitment. Peter, Andrew, James and John had left behind their thriving fishing business. Levi had left behind his lucrative tax booth. Jesus must have had a supernatural insight into this man's heart, knowing that his vast holdings would keep him from following the Messianic mission. He loved the man enough to expose the one thing keeping him from what he was truly looking for. When we love something more than God—even a good thing—the Bible calls it idolatry. When God calls us to give up our idols, He does it not as an elaborate, sadistic test of our devotion. He does it out of love for us. What stands in the way of you living the life God has planned?

The Party Crasher
Luke 7:36-50

Society was very different in first-century Israel. Their tradition held that when a party was given, the poor should be allowed to come by and grab a few scraps. It was their idea of charity. So no one was surprised when a well-known "sinner"—probably a prostitute-- came into the home of Simon the Pharisee in the middle of a dinner party. But what she did next *was* a surprise. She began to weep over Jesus' feet…perhaps because she couldn't bear in her shame to look at His face. Then she wiped the tears from his feet with her hair and kissed them in unashamed adoration. Then she pulled out a bottle of expensive perfume, probably the most valuable thing she owned, and spilled it all on Jesus. This act of lavish love has inspired millions of sermons, songs and stories and lives today as an example of what true worship is meant to be. But one man didn't see it that way: Simon. In his mind, he was engaging in some seemingly airtight logic: *This man is reputed to be a prophet. Yet if he were a prophet, he would know what kind of woman this is. If he knew what kind of woman she was, he would never let her touch him. Therefore, he is no prophet.*

The great irony in this story is that Jesus not only knew what kind of woman this was, He was reading Simon's thoughts at that very moment. Jesus now had an interesting situation on his hands. His mission in life was to seek and save the lost, yet here was a man who didn't know He was lost, and had no interest in being saved. How did Jesus respond? He confronted him with grace. Jesus wanted Simon to see that it wasn't about one's past or present sins. It wasn't about religiosity or morality. It was about grace, or unmerited favor. This woman's sins were forgiven because she recognized that she was in need of forgiveness, and because she had the faith to believe that Jesus could give her a brand new life. She was confronted with grace and went away forever redeemed. Simon was confronted by that same grace and went away more convinced than ever that Jesus was a fraud who must be eliminated. Grace is a terrific spiritual litmus test: When you hear that God's forgiving, saving love is free to anyone, no matter what they've done, do you hear it as good news, or as a scandal? Do you rejoice or do you protest?

Good Things vs. The Ultimate Thing
Luke 10:38-42

We've seen these two sisters once before, in the story of the raising of their brother Lazarus from the dead (John 11). Scripture doesn't tell us how they were acquainted with Jesus, but it's obvious they were close. Perhaps they grew up with Jesus, then later moved to Bethany on the Mount of Olives, just across the Kidron Valley from Jerusalem. This is the first time they are mentioned by Luke, so he introduces them to us as new characters in the story. We learn something new about these sisters in this story: They have very different personalities. That's common in families; often a younger sibling will gravitate toward activities and interests that are the opposite of the older child. Martha, we learn, is a diligent person who highly values hospitality. We know this because, in the only other story about these two, in John 12, we find Martha serving people in her home once again. That was expected of women in the ancient Middle East. But on this day, Mary flouted those cultural norms, and Martha took her to task. She appealed to Jesus because she believed that God valued hospitality as much as she did. She was absolutely right (Isaiah 58:7, Romans 12:13, 1 Peter 4:9), but Jesus corrected her, anyway. Jesus wasn't dismissing her thoughtful way of serving her guests. He was simply saying, "Sometimes, Martha, there are more important things. This is one of those times."

Think about that for a moment. Jesus lived a hard life; always on the road, often sleeping outside, often doing without adequate food, constantly in demand from the nagging, needy crowds. Now, at long last, someone was willing to serve Him, instead of the other way around. I am sure Jesus was grateful for all that she was doing. He could have said, "Yes, Mary, after all I have done for you, get in there and help your sister serve me!" Mary's choice wasn't just unusual; it was revolutionary. Teachers in that time didn't have female disciples. To sit at the feet of a teacher was a male role. Yet Jesus wanted Mary, Martha and everyone else to see that while serving one's guest is a good thing, spending time with the Messiah is the best thing. Mary's devotion endured. In the story I referenced earlier from John 12, while Martha continues to serve, Mary does more than just sit at Jesus' feet. She follows the example of the fallen woman from Luke 7:36-50, anointing Jesus with expensive oil. That action drew the rebuke of some of the disciples, but Jesus praised her. She knew what was best. How often do you let good things in your life get in the way of you enjoying the ultimate thing?

The Women
Luke 8:1-3

As we have already seen, Jesus broke new ground by allowing women to follow Him as disciples. They may not have been included among the Twelve, but they were every bit as faithful…and in the end, some were even more faithful than any of His male followers. Luke tells us about three of those women here, including the detail that they supported Jesus and the disciples out of their own income. It was extremely difficult in that era for a woman to become independently wealthy; these women must have been remarkable characters. We know nothing else about Susanna. But Joanna is called the wife of Herod's household manager. We are left to wonder what happened when Herod inevitably found out about his manager's wife and her attachment to this strange Nazarene troublemaker. We do know that Joanna was with Jesus to the very end of His earthly life, as she is listed among the women who stood beneath the cross as Jesus died. We also know that, years later, a man named Manaen, a childhood friend of Herod's, was a Christian preacher in Antioch (Acts 13:1). Perhaps Joanna had something to do with his conversion.

Mary Magdalene is easily the most famous of the three. She is mentioned twelve times in the Gospels, more than a majority of the Twelve. Her surname indicates that she was from the Galilean town of Magdala. We don't know when or where Jesus drove seven demons out of Mary, but we have seen the catastrophic effect even a single demon could have on a person; we can only imagine the hell on earth that was Mary's life before Jesus delivered her. It's interesting how many false ideas exist about this one woman. Somehow in the Middle Ages, an idea arose that Mary was a prostitute or an adulteress, but that's not found anywhere in Scripture. Contemporary artists ranging from the filmmaker Martin Scorcese to the novelist Dan Brown have crafted scenarios in which Jesus and Mary were in a romantic relationship, but that idea has no basis in fact. It's almost as if the world itself can't accept the fact that Jesus would value this woman for who she was. But it's clear He did. The events of Resurrection Sunday show us how much He valued her (we'll get there soon). This world can't seem to get over our stereotypical roles for various categories of people; even the Church struggles with this. But Jesus delighted in bursting those stereotypes.

God Bless the Child
Mark 10:13-16

The historian OM Bakke has written a book called *When Children Became People: The Birth of Childhood in Early Christianity*. He shows that our modern notions of children as being valuable came about largely because Jesus loved children. That's not to say parents in ancient times didn't love their children; certainly most did. But there was no societal idea of childhood as being a particularly important time, or that the education and nurturing of children should be of high value to a culture. Greco-Roman culture believed that unwanted children should be "exposed," or abandoned somewhere outside. Aristotle taught that exposure was the best treatment for babies born with a deformity. Roman households would often expose baby girls, since they were seen as an economic drain. In their minds, this was not murder, since theoretically the gods could rescue the child.

Jews did not practice exposure, but like most ancient peoples, they thought children were best seen and not heard. We see this in the Twelve chasing away parents who want their children to be blessed by Jesus. This made Jesus furious. His statement, *anyone who will not receive the Kingdom of God like a little child will never enter it,* was a serious rebuke to His disciples. Essentially He was saying, "These kids know more about what it means to follow me than you do." Children know they are weak, and aren't ashamed to ask for help. They want nothing more than their parents' presence. And while children can be as willful and turbulent as adults, they are also eager to make things right when they know they've strayed too far. A child still dreams of a better world, and still believes it's possible. Jesus came to bring us that world. The improvement in the lot of children wherever the Gospel has taken root is one indication that world is on its way.

On a Mission from God
Luke 10:1-24

Jesus earlier sent out His Twelve disciples, empowering them to preach and work miracles. Now He does this with a larger group. We are not told the names of any of these disciples. We see His instructions to them, which largely parallel the instructions He gave the Twelve. We see His warnings to Israelite cities (vv. 13-15) whose reception of His message has been less warm than that of certain Gentile towns. And we see His celebration when the group returns (v. 21).

Most Americans react negatively to the words "evangelism" and "evangelist." That's increasingly true even in Christian circles. Those words conjure up images of slick-haired hucksters swindling gullible people's savings on religious television to pay for their mansions and private jets. They call to mind crazy street preachers crying out "The end is near!" or the awkward religious guy who tries to shoehorn His Christianity into every conversation. The consensus these days seems to be that evangelism is the cause of great division and harm in society. If one must be religious, then the responsible, civilized thing to do is to keep one's beliefs private, and respect the rights of others not to be confronted with new ideas.

But if the message of Jesus is true, then keeping that message private is not responsible or civilized; it's diabolical. The magician and entertainer Penn Jillette (of Penn and Teller fame) is an outspoken atheist. But several years ago, he met a Christian who offered him a Bible. Jillette was struck by this man's sincerity, and he posted a video blog in which he said a shocking thing: "I don't respect people who do not proselytize…How much do you have to hate somebody to believe that everlasting life is possible and not tell them that? I mean, if I believed beyond the shadow of a doubt that a truck was coming to hit you, and you didn't believe it, and that truck was bearing down on you, there's a certain point where I tackle you. And this is more important than that." Penn Jillette and Jesus Christ may have little in common, but they would agree on that.

Unprecedented
John 7:32-52

The Gospels tells us over and over that Jesus was a powerful speaker. Of course, people said the same thing about cult leaders like Jim Jones and David Koresh, or megalomaniacal dictators like Hitler or Mussolini. The difference is that Jesus' message called people to put others first, even their enemies. His was a message of love and forgiveness. It changed the world in ways even unbelievers can be thankful for (as we explored in Chapter 1). The story of the Temple Guard in John 7 may be the most humorous story about Jesus' oratorical power. The men in the Guard were Levites, part of the Israelite tribe that was dedicated to service in the Temple complex. They had heard rabbis teach time after time. Now they were sent to arrest this Nazarene self-styled prophet who was stirring up so much trouble, so that the Council could put a stop to His blasphemy. The job seems cut and dry. But they came back mesmerized. "No one ever spoke the way this man does." What was it about His speaking? None of the ancient witnesses indicates that He was particularly dynamic or innovative in His presentation. We know He used many parables, but He didn't invent that form of teaching. The only physical description of Jesus found in the Bible—a prophecy written seven hundred years before His birth (Isaiah 53:2)—tells us it wasn't any outward beauty that attracted people to Him. Something in His message touched people in a way that mere religion could not. Everyone who ever met Jesus went away changed in some way. Some left sad, like the rich young ruler. Others wanted to kill Him. And many wanted to worship Him, to follow Him wherever He went. No one was neutral about Him. He had the power to completely change the direction of a life, as He did for the Temple Guard that day. Has He changed yours?

Devotion
John 12:1-8

Scripture tells us we were made in the image of God, which I take to mean we were created for a relationship with the Divine that is unlike any other. If that's true, then we are at our best, and most happy, when we are rightly relating to our Creator. That means that true worship is a lifeline for us. God does not command us to worship Him because He needs our affirmation; He commands it because we need it. So what is worship? Many Christians mistakenly believe it is an organized group activity involving songs, prayers, an offering and a sermon. But worship is much more. We live in a severely worship-deprived society. We see glimpses of worship in daily life: In a mother's adoration of her infant; in a hiker who pauses to gaze, breathless, at the sun peaking over a ridge; in a lover who forgoes sleep just to spend another hour in the presence of his beloved (We might even say, "He worships the ground she walks on"); in a young athlete who, motivated by the knowledge his parents are in the stands, plays the game of his life. All of those ideas: Adoration, awe, affection and complete surrender, when they are directed at God, give us some idea of the worship relationship we were created to enjoy.

Mary of Bethany is a great example of true worship. Judas Iscariot stands as a perfect example of what stands in the way. Mary poured out a bottle of perfume so costly, it would have taken a year's wages to buy. She rubbed Jesus' feet with her hair. Think about how long that smell would have clung to Mary. She didn't do a cost-benefit analysis before this extravagant action; she didn't ask Jesus what her reward would be afterward. Judas was all about cost vs. benefit. He had followed Jesus for three years now, and that certainly involved sacrifice, but he had an eye on a future reward. Even now, according to John, he was skimming money from the ministry. His outward signs of devotion were all a sham. He had his own agenda for everything he did. Jesus' words in v. 8 have been misinterpreted by some to indicate that helping the poor is a lost cause; that flies directly in the face of His teaching (*Whatever you do for the least of my children, you've done it for me*, to give one of many examples). He was simply saying that Mary didn't want to miss the opportunity to be with Him while she could. In less than a week, Jesus would be dead; whether Mary knew that or not, she was wise to worship Him now, rather than put it off. There will never be a "convenient" time to offer full surrender to God. There will always be other things, seemingly more urgent matters, to attend to first. Will you offer the total devotion of Mary, or follow the pragmatic path of Judas?

Chapter 8: Jesus and His Enemies
John 1:1-11

Some of our most beloved stories have an unexpected twist that changes the way we see the entire narrative (For instance, "No Luke, I am your father."). That's even true of the Bible's story of God's mission to redeem the world. We saw in Chapter 2 that Israelite prophets had been predicting a coming Deliverer, the Messiah, for centuries. When He came, He would set the world right. He would rescue His people and inaugurate a golden age. In John 1, verses 10 and 11 show us the ironic twist. He created the world, but the world didn't recognize Him. He came to His own people, but His own people didn't recognize Him. Think of how many faithful Jews had prayed for and longed to see the day God's Messiah would finally arrive. Think of Simeon and Anna (Luke 2:21-38) and the joy they felt when they held the promised child after years of waiting and praying in the temple each day. If you had told them that this child—Israel's Messiah—would be rejected by the religious leaders of Israel, they would have refused to believe it. On a surface level, it doesn't make sense to us, either. Yet that twist in the narrative causes us to go back and read the ancient promises with new eyes. Jesus could not have been surprised at the fierce opposition He faced; but that probably didn't make it any less painful. Yet the way He responded to their hatred tells us so much about Him. In this chapter, we'll see how He related to them. Truth be told, it's hard to find advice or instruction on how to treat one's enemies from any other source, religious or secular. The best we can find are articles or teachings about how to defeat our opponents. Only Jesus seems to have been concerned with teaching us how to redeem our enemies.

The Teachers
Mark 7:1-23

Throughout the Gospels, there were two groups of people who consistently opposed Jesus, and who He consistently criticized: The Pharisees and the scribes (or teachers of the Law). It's important for us to know precisely who these people were, starting with the scribes. The position of scribe was incredibly important in 1st Century Israel. They were responsible for copying the words of the Law and the Prophets so that future generations would know the word of God. We owe them our thanks for preserving the Old Testament so meticulously for us. They also wrote commentaries on the Law of Moses, and taught it orally. In addition, they served a civil function, helping settle disputes when there was disagreement on a fine point of the Law, and writing legal documents. 450 years before the birth of Christ, a scribe named Ezra arrived in Jerusalem, a city newly rebuilt after the Babylonian destruction and 70 years of Jewish exile. He was a strong leader, well-versed in the Scriptures, and together with the civil leader Nehemiah, rescued the citizens of Jerusalem (and the people of Israel) from descending into anarchy and chaos. In other words, the scribes were the good guys. Why then did Jesus oppose them?

Mark 7 is one of many passages that show us the huge gap between Jesus and the scribes. Over time, in their desire to make the Law of God more precisely relevant to the daily lives of the people, they had inserted their own opinions into its interpretation. For example, the Law "You should keep the Sabbath holy" was awfully unspecific, so they wrote volumes of minute laws describing what activities were and were not allowed on the seventh day of the week. As the years went on, these "traditions of men" became equal to—or in some cases more important than—the actual words of God. By the time Jesus came along, their man-made religious structures actually kept people away from the God who loved them. They had exchanged a relationship with a saving Lord for a list of rules and rituals. Since Jesus had come to bring people home to God, this ironically made the teachers of God's Law His most significant obstacle. From the perspective of the scribes, Jesus presented a massive threat. He was outrageously popular among the people, and seemed to constantly chip away at the scribes' authority; for instance, the entire theme of the Sermon on the Mount (Matthew 5-7) was "You have heard it said…but I say to you…" In other words, "Don't believe what the scribes have told you. Here's what God really wants from us." The scribes believed that Jesus and His movement had the potential to reverse the work of Ezra, leading the people away from God's law, back into self-centered chaos. The conflict between legalistic religion and true relationship with God is still one of the major issues among Jesus' followers today.

The Morality Police
Matthew 12:1-8

Often (although not in this passage) the scribes are paired with another group: The Pharisees. Yet these were two distinct groups. Whereas the scribes were what we might today call clergy, the Pharisees were laypeople, often businessmen who were zealous for the Law of God. Their beginnings were in a glorious period in Israelite history, the Maccabean rebellion. The Maccabees were a group of rebel warriors who led Israel to a stunning victory over the Seleucid empire in 167 BC (Jews celebrate this victory at Hanukkah). The Seleucid king, Antiochus Epiphanies, had defiled the Jewish temple and was determined to forcibly impose Greek culture on the recalcitrant Jews. So when Mattathias, a priest, and his sons rebelled, it was more than a political revolution; it was a fight for the glory of God and the right of His people to worship Him according to His Word. The Hasadim ("pious ones") supported Judas and his descendants as they sat on the throne of a newly independent Jewish nation from 167 to 63 BC. But as the dynasty grew more political, and less religious in motivation, the Hasidim abandoned them. The Pharisees (from a Hebrew word meaning "separated ones") were descended from the Hasidim. They felt responsible for keeping Israel true to the Word of God and away from pagan influences. They were notably devout; most had memorized the 613 commands in the Law. They were patriotic and courageous; when Pontius Pilate, the Roman governor, decided to bring Roman standards into the temple complex, the Pharisees stood in the way of the procession, baring their necks so they could be executed. Pilate backed off.

Jesus had much more in common with the scribes and Pharisees than He did with the Romans, or with the tax collectors who collaborated with them. Yet He rarely spoke about Rome, treated tax collectors with mercy, but publicly blasted the scribes and Pharisees at every turn. These were the heroes of the common man in Israel; it was incredibly risky for Jesus to oppose them. But Jesus had two motives for doing so. First, he wanted to warn the people not to follow in their legalistic ways. But He also wanted to redeem the scribes and Pharisees, to bring them back to the God they claimed to serve. His harsh rhetoric came from a place of love; Romans and their collaborators didn't know the wrong they were guilty of, but the scribes and Pharisees had no such excuse. Jesus spoke to them the way you and I might speak to a sibling who is flagrantly hurting our parents: "How dare you treat mom and dad this way? This isn't how they raised you!" His relationship with these men was more complicated than we often think. Pharisees once warned Jesus to flee from the wrath of the King (Luke 13:31-33). They sometimes invited Him to dine with them. At least one Pharisee became a believer in Jesus during His lifetime (Nicodemus), and afterwards, more followed (Acts 15:5). Jesus' most famous follower, and the author of the largest part of the New Testament, began as a Pharisee. Jesus' relationship with the scribes and Pharisees shows us that an enemy of the Gospel must be resisted openly, no matter the cost...but there is always hope, even for the worst of foes.

The Power Brokers
Mark 12:18-27

In Jesus' time, Judaism contained several sects, but the group that rivaled the Pharisees for prominence, and the group most responsible for Christ's arrest and crucifixion, was the Sadducees. We don't have a clear idea how the Sadducees originated, or even what their name means. But we do know that their ranks included the High Priestly families and most of the ruling council, the Sanhedrin. So, even though the Pharisees had the admiration of the common man, the Sadducees had the bulk of the political power in Israel.

In Mark 12, we see the Sadducees questioning Jesus on one of their favorite topics: The resurrection of the dead. Their rivals, the Pharisees, believed that at the end of time, the dead would rise and face judgement before God, with some moving on to eternal life in His presence. The Sadducees did not believe in life after death; the scenario they present before Jesus was one of their arguments against the logic of immortality. We get the distinct impression that, having seen how Jesus had befuddled the scribes and Pharisees, they hoped He would prove to be on their side. But Jesus exposed the foolishness of their arguments. Later, they realized that He represented a threat to the temple system, which was the seat of their power. The day Jesus cleansed the temple, chasing away the moneychangers, sealed His fate in their eyes. With the power of the High Priest and the Council, they delivered Him up to the Romans to die. If Jesus had been any other man, He would likely have answered the Sadducees' questions more gently. It doesn't pay to anger power brokers. But Jesus was no ordinary man.

A Man Without a Clan
Mark 12:13-17

Any child who has ever moved to a new school can testify that there is security in joining a group. As adults, we find strength and identity through our political affiliation, our favorite athletic team, or our hobbies. Jesus had no group, other than the unreliable band of followers He had recruited. The two largest and most influential groups of His day, the Pharisees and Sadducees, rejected Him. The Essenes, who we know today mostly because they assembled the Dead Sea Scrolls, had no contact with Jesus that we know of. But their policy of withdrawing from public life would not have approved of a Messiah determined to seek and save all the lost. The Zealots were fanatically opposed to foreign rule; they promoted assassinations and riots against the Romans. They must have written Jesus off the first time they heard Him teach that God's people should love their enemies. And when they heard that He ministered to Samaritans and healed the servant of a Roman centurion, they surely declared Him a traitor to Israel. Yet one of their number, Simon the Zealot, became a disciple of Jesus. I wish we knew more of his story.

In this passage, we see the Herodians teaming up with the Pharisees to try to trick Jesus. If He answered one way, He could be accused of encouraging rebellion against Rome; if He answered the other way, He could be seen as collaborating with them. We shouldn't be surprised that Jesus outwitted His accusers once again. What is surprising is that Herodians and Pharisees would cooperate on anything at all. We've already seen that Pharisees were nationalistic and ritually pure, while the Herodians supported the secular rulers, the Herods, known for their political cunning, their courtship of the hated Romans, and for their slipshod morals. We can be certain that these two groups hated one another. But mutual hatred makes strange bedfellows. Both groups wanted Jesus out of the way. We can't help but feel sorry for Jesus. There were so many groups in Israel, and it seemed all were against Him. It takes a strong person to walk alone. But where Jesus was going, no one could ultimately follow.

The Bad Guys
Luke 13:1-5

In 1996, *Braveheart* won the Academy Award for Best Picture. Many critics and viewers noted similarities between the main character in the film (a highly fictionalized version of Scottish rebel William Wallace) and Jesus. Since the director and star, Mel Gibson, was a devout Catholic and the screenwriter, Randall Wallace, an evangelical Christian, these similarities were not surprising. Both Wallace and Jesus were charismatic leaders who led revolutionary movements against great odds. Both died in ways that were gruesome, courageous and inspiring. But there the similarities end. William Wallace in *Braveheart* fights against a cruel King and his oppressive empire. Jesus faced an exponentially more powerful empire. But He refused to fight.

The Romans were the bad guys in Jesus' world. They ruled the known planet, including Israel, which they had conquered in 63 BC after a 3 month siege of Jerusalem. They were in some ways tolerant rulers; they allowed the Jews to worship their God freely and live by their own laws; they even exempted them from the legal requirement to sacrifice to Caesar. But they broke the land up into small provinces, taking away all of the Jews' economic and political clout. Jesus grew up in Galilee, governed by the Roman puppet Herod and later, his son. Judea, the center of Jewish religious life, was governed by a Roman prefect named Pontius Pilate. In this passage, we get a hint of what sort of ruler he was. Contemporary historians tell other stories of Pilate's brutality. He was no friend of the Jews. Beyond the politics, the Roman lifestyle, with its casual approach to sex, its games and dramas and parties, and its multiplicity of gods, was disgusting to the highly moral Jews. If Jesus had wanted to lead a violent revolution against Rome, He would have had plenty of support from the Zealots and many others. Yet here we see people trying to draw Him into a discussion of Roman barbarism, and He will have nothing to do with it. Jesus never spoke out against Rome, when it would have been the easiest way to make Himself popular. Apparently, to Jesus, there were no "bad" guys and "good" guys, just people who needed redemption. Whenever I see Christians today, including many preachers, endorsing certain political leaders and condemning others, or even declaring that a natural disaster was because of the sinfulness of its victims, I wonder what they make of Jesus' relationship to Rome.

The Perfect Storm
John 6:14-15

So here's another dated movie reference: In *The Perfect Storm,* a group of professional fisherman venture unwittingly into the midst of three huge storms converging off the coast of New England. Since that movie, the term "a perfect storm" has entered our lexicon to describe any combination of unlikely factors that result in disaster. Two millennia ago, Jesus began His ministry in a time of perfect storm. Three massive forces were coming together in 1st Century Israel, and Jesus would walk straight into the midst of them. Two of them we've already examined: The Romans determined to maintain control over a vast empire, and the Jewish religious elites, willing to do whatever it took to protect the Temple and its system of sacrifices that formed the core of their identity. The third storm was the wave of Messianic expectation. Israelites had been waiting patiently for God's anointed deliverer for hundreds of years, but those expectations had been especially intense since Rome conquered Israel less than one hundred years before. Several would-be Messiahs had arisen in the time since (The Jewish historian Josephus, who lived in those days, called them "deceivers and deluders of the people"). For a man looking to found a movement of non-violent piety, there couldn't have been a worse time or place to be born. Yet here is what a later Christian writer said about this: *When the right time came, God sent His Son, born of a woman, subject to the Law* (Galatians 4:4, New Living Translation). Jesus was born at the right time. Some have noted that, since the Roman Empire had built extensive roads and had brought a huge swath of the world together under a common language, this was the first time in history that a movement like that of Jesus, spread through persuasion instead of warfare, could succeed. But I think Galatians 4:4 meant more than that. Jesus was born at just the right time because He *didn't* come to establish a movement of non-violent piety. He came to die for the sins of humanity. In the movie, *The Perfect Storm*, George Clooney and his fellow fishermen cruise into danger without knowing it. They are looking for a big haul of fish, and take one risk too many. But Jesus knew exactly what He was doing. He walked into a perfect storm with His eyes wide open.

The Evil Prince and the Sacrificial Hero
John 12:27-33

These words, which Jesus spoke when He knew His death was only a few days away, tell us something important about His thinking. Jesus didn't see Himself as simply the Messiah of the Jews; He saw Himself as the Savior of the world. His saving work would involve His death (v. 32 is a clear reference to the Cross, as John helpfully points out). But who or what was He saving us from? In v. 31, Jesus says *the prince of this world will be driven out.* Remember also the Parable of the Strong Man (Luke 11:21-22)? In both of these passages, Jesus reveals how He saw the world. In His mind, we were held captive by a cruel, oppressive force. He was on a mission of regime change. He would lay down His life to rescue us from the tyrant who enslaved us. Remember also that before Jesus started His public ministry, Satan spent forty straight days trying to stop His rescue operation before it started. One of His key temptations: "Worship me, and rule the world." Satan was proposing a bloodless coup, a Kingdom without a Cross. How tempting must that have been? A few years later, when Peter tells Jesus that all this talk of being crucified is foolishness, Jesus' response is telling: "Get behind me, Satan!" Jesus recognized in the words of His friend a familiar old temptation. It would return on a Friday atop a hill in Jerusalem, in the words of His tormentors: "If you're the Son of God, come down off that cross! Save yourself!" Jesus knew that saving Himself AND saving others were mutually exclusive. He had to make a decision. Studying Jesus' life while keeping that daily struggle in mind puts the Gospel story in a whole new light. Jesus wasn't simply wandering from place to place, healing people and sharing wise words. He was marching toward an apocalyptic battle, and every day brought Him closer to the reckoning.

Off the Treadmill
Luke 9:33-39

Jesus' critics often noted that He didn't seem religious enough. In Luke 7:34, He says they called Him a drunkard and a glutton. There is no indication either of those charges were true, so the obvious implication is that Jesus was simply too joyful to be a genuine rabbi in the eyes of the religious establishment. They measured their righteousness by austerity. They were known for what they were against. But Jesus carried on with tax collectors, prostitutes and other sinners. They fasted twice a week, even though the Law of Moses only commanded one fast a year (on the Day of Atonement). Yet Jesus and His disciples never seemed to fast. We can't be certain what the Pharisees thought of John the Baptists' ministry, but they seem to say here, "At least his disciples try to take religion seriously. What's your problem?" Jesus responds with a fantastic analogy. All of these religious gyrations are an attempt to get to God…but my disciples realize they've already found what they're looking for. It would be rude to go to a wedding feast and turn down the steak and dessert by saying, "No thanks, I'm fasting." This is a time for enjoying what you have, not for wishing you had something more. Someday, He predicts, I'll be taken away, and my disciples will need to do things that bring them closer to me. In other words, religious rituals are a necessary thing, when done for the right reasons. In all of these interactions between Jesus and His enemies, His modern followers are confronted with the question: Would He say the same things about us that He did about them?

Lord of the Sabbath
Luke 6:1-5

Keeping the Sabbath day correctly was a huge element of being Jewish. Sabbath observance was embedded in the Creation story, as God rested from His creative work on the seventh day. It was the subject of the fifth of the Ten Commandments. In addition to the Torah, or the Law, the Jews studied the Mishnah, or the rabbinic writings. Two entire volumes of the Mishnah were dedicated solely to what it meant to properly observe the Sabbath. The Gospels record three separate disputes between Jesus and His enemies regarding this issue. This one is a classic example of another of the dangers of religion: Getting caught up in the minutia of our own regulations can keep us from what is most important to God.

The Law (Deuteronomy 23:25) stated that it was permissible to pick heads of grain from your neighbors' grain field, as long as you didn't use a sickle. This was part of God's provision for the landless poor; Jesus and His disciples qualified. But when they saw the disciples rubbing the heads of grain into their hands to make them edible, they interpreted that activity as "threshing the grain," which was not permitted on the Sabbath. Jesus' response is masterful, as always. He refers to a story from 1 Samuel 16, about David and his men, on the run from the murderous King Saul, stopping and being nourished by the priests of God, who had no food other than the sacred bread which represented the presence of God. Those priests understood that a symbolic ritual was less important than human lives. The same should apply here. Jesus then made an astonishing claim: *The Son of Man is Lord of the Sabbath.* We will discuss the title "Son of Man" in chapter 12, but there can be little doubt that the Pharisees knew Jesus was referring to Himself. Any current follower of Jesus must read this story with wisdom and self-examination. Jesus wasn't saying, "Bend the rules when they are inconvenient." After all, He and His men weren't breaking God's Law, only the interpretation of the rabbis. Sadly, Jesus' modern followers are often known for making the same mistake as the Pharisees: Using our own interpretation of God's commands to justify rejecting people. Jesus came to seek and save the lost. He never settled for merely pointing out their flaws.

Healing on the Sabbath (Again)
Luke 13:10-17

Once again, Jesus is teaching in the synagogue. Once again, He sees someone there who is obviously crippled. And once again, He heals them, in flagrant violation of what He knew to be the religious traditions of His own people (Notice that the synagogue ruler chastises the people for this, not daring to confront Jesus directly). It should be obvious to us by this point that, while Jesus was obedient to the commands of the Old Testament, He made a sharp distinction between the commands of God and the religious traditions of God's people. It's also clear that in His mind, righteousness wasn't measured merely in rule-keeping, but in how we treat others. In other words, people came first. Still, couldn't He have waited until after the synagogue worship was over, then healed this woman in secret? Better yet, couldn't He have waited until sundown (the end of the Sabbath), so He would have been doing the same good deed without angering the rulers of His people? He certainly could have. And He knew this. Jesus was being deliberately provocative. Why?

There are two possible answers. Perhaps Jesus was a natural-born troublemaker, who pushed buttons because He resented anyone in a position of authority. The other possibility is that Jesus was making a point, hoping to change the minds of everyone who witnessed His actions. His words indicate this second possibility is the truth. He talks about this woman being held in bondage to Satan for eighteen years. As we've said before, that doesn't mean that Jesus believed all illnesses were caused by the Devil; most diseases that Jesus and the apostles heal in the Gospels and Acts aren't attributed to demonic activity. But He saw humanity as a species in captivity to forces of evil, cursed to live in a sin-warped, self-destructive world. His role was to bring freedom from that captivity, and He wanted devout men and women to join Him in that mission. In His actions in the synagogue, He was hoping to wake up His own people to a new reality: In this reality, a religion that builds walls between people is precisely what stops us from doing God's will. We have to step outside those walls and outside our stained-glass windows to join our God in His work.

Clean Hands and Impure Hearts
Mark 7:1-13

My wife and I are different in so many ways, but one is in the area of cleanness. To her, cleanliness really is next to godliness. The companies that make anti-bacterial hand gel should give her some sort of award for lifelong loyalty. I, on the other hand, am a firm believer in the five-second rule…I have eaten enough food dropped on the floor to feed a small nation. So I chuckle when I read this story, as it seems as if Jesus is on my side. But when I do a little research, I find it's not so. The Pharisees and scribes have sent out a group from Jerusalem to follow Jesus and the disciples, looking for flaws and infractions to use against them. Imagine if a band of religious leaders scoured your life! When they pointed out the lack of hand-washing, they weren't concerned with germs…they didn't even know about bacteria. There were ritual requirements; a devout Jew would often wash himself completely after coming home from the market, in case they had accidentally made contact with a Gentile or another source of ritual uncleanness. This idea of purity came from the Law of Moses. God created purity laws to emphasize to His people that they were holy, God's distinct people. When a Jewish man or woman refrained from certain activities in order to be ritually pure enough to attend a worship service, a sacrifice or festival, he or she was reminded that God is real and righteous, and that His claim on our lives is total.

These men who were there to find fault with Jesus suddenly found themselves the ones on trial. V. 8 is a great summary of what we've seen in the previous stories about the Sabbath: The religious leaders are more focused on their own traditions than the actual commands of Scripture. But as Jesus goes on to show, it's even worse than that. He mentions the "Corban" vow, which was a word that meant "temple treasury." The leaders of Israel and other devout people were devoting their money to God's temple. Please understand: They weren't donating the money, but simply setting it aside. So by using the Corban vow, a religious man could tell his elderly parents, "Sorry mom and dad. I know you need help to survive, but all my money is Corban. I can't give it to you, in case God later on tells me to donate it to His temple." In a headshaking irony, a religious tradition wasn't just competing with the overt command of God, it was causing that command to be broken. And, Jesus said, *you do many things like that.* Religious men and women today are vulnerable to the same thing, so we need to prayerfully ask ourselves the question: How do I use religion for my selfish benefit? How do my own religious traditions keep me from obedience to the express commands of my God?

Food for Thought
Mark 7:14-23

It's helpful to read Matthew's account (Mt. 15:10-20) of this story alongside Mark's, because both writers include a few details the other was unaware of or left out. According to Matthew, the disciples found out that the Pharisees were angry at what Jesus had said about handwashing. To the disciples, the Pharisees were heroes of righteousness. Their anger was very upsetting. So they asked Jesus to explain Himself. In Matthew's account, Jesus calls them "blind guides" (from which we get our contemporary expression, "the blind leading the blind"). He wanted His disciples to know that the Pharisees were not to be trusted or followed. Then He said something else (recorded by both Matthew and Mark) that was equally stunning: Righteousness isn't determined by the food you eat. The Jewish dietary laws listed in Leviticus 11 and Deuteronomy 14 were seen by Jews as a key part of their identity. The Kosher diet was one of the things that made them distinct as a people. That was hard to let go of; which explains why Peter was still observing Kosher years later (see Acts 10). But Jesus wasn't just giving His people permission to eat bacon (Although…hallelujah for bacon! Am I right?). His point was much larger. True righteousness is what happens on the inside of a person and cannot be measured by mere external obedience to rules.

Let's get personal here: I am a lifelong Baptist. When I was growing up, I assumed that people who refrained from drinking alcohol were more righteous than those who drank. I now realize how ridiculous that notion is; Jesus and His disciples wouldn't have qualified. But Adolph Hitler, a famous teetotaler, would have. Even an unspeakably evil person can adhere to an external moral code. What we need is not more laws; we need to be renewed from the inside. Jesus had made much the same point to Nicodemus when He said, *You must be born again.* Jesus demanded the impossible. That is cruel…unless He could also make the impossible happen.

The Tax Trap
Matthew 22:15-22

Give the Pharisees and Herodians credit: They knew how to set a clever trap. If Jesus said that God's people were exempt from paying taxes, then Jesus could be reported to the Romans for encouraging rebellion. But if He advocated paying taxes, He would sound like a collaborator, and His popularity with the people would be in jeopardy. The very coins used in paying the annual tax were considered by the Jews to be idolatrous. In Jesus' day, they featured an image of the Emperor with this inscription: "Tiberius, son of the divine Augustus." The other side said, "Pontifex Maximus" or "High Priest." Surely, this was a trap that even Jesus couldn't wriggle out of.

But His enemies had underestimated Him again. His answer means much more than "pay your taxes." It means there is a new way to understand what we owe to the State. Paul and Peter would both later write on this subject (Romans 13:1-7, 1 Peter 2:13-17). God's people should be good citizens of whatever nation we live in. We should obey the laws. We should pray for our leaders. We should be a blessing to our cities (see also Jeremiah 29:4-14 for God's earlier instruction to His people in a foreign land). But our true allegiance is to God Himself. Patriotism and discipleship are not the same thing. If our government commands us to do something that contradicts God's will, our response should be like that of the early church in Acts 5:29, *We must obey God rather than men.* They would live those words, and it would cost them everything…yet in the end, their movement outlasted even Rome.

The Greatest Commandment
Matthew 22:34-40

There are a couple different ways we can look at this Pharisees' motive in asking the question. "Which is the greatest commandment in the Law?" was a common debate topic among religious scholars. It could be that he was putting Jesus to the test by asking Him what seemed like an impossible question. On the other hand, Matthew tells us this is in response to Jesus shutting down the Sadducees, this man's enemies. So perhaps this expert in the law was probing to see if Jesus was an ally after all. It's impossible for us to know for sure. Jesus' reply is a combination of two commands from the Law: Deuteronomy 6:5 and Leviticus 19:18. Why these two? And what did He mean in v. 40 when He said, *all the Law and the Prophets hang on these two commandments*?

Some have assumed that He means love trumps law. Therefore, all previous commands are obsolete; we just need to love. But Matthew 5:17-19 shows us that Jesus had no intention of doing away with the commandments in Scripture. He did, however, want people to see those commands in a way far different from what they had been taught by their religious leaders. Under the current system, the commands were an external code, a way of measuring who was "in" and who was "out." But Jesus, in calling Deuteronomy 6:5 the greatest command, said that if we are not motivated by love for the Lord, then all of our conspicuous morality is just a cynical attempt to impress people and manipulate God. And if we don't obey Leviticus 19:18, we clearly don't love God, since our neighbor is made in His image. Reverence for the Law without love for God or neighbor accomplishes the opposite of God's will. It leads to arrogance, prejudice, and terrorism. Once again, Jesus took a penetrating question by a religious expert and used it to deftly expose the difference between mere religion and true righteousness.

Give Me a Sign
Mark 8:11-13, Matthew 12:38-42

We have no record of Jesus ever refusing to do a miracle for someone who genuinely needed it. Even though at times He was up all night, and at other times could not even stop to eat a meal, He helped everyone who came to Him. But here, when His opponents asked for objective proof of His claims, He refused. Even on the day of His trial, when He stood before a man who had the power to free Him, He would not perform a miracle when asked. Interestingly, there was a book written over a century after Jesus' life, The Infancy Gospel of Thomas, which claimed that Jesus as a child did do miracles for His own benefit. In one, He makes clay sparrows and brings them to life. In others, He strikes some griping neighbors with blindness and kills two children who offended Him in some way. The early church rightly rejected these stories as false. But they show us the dark side of spiritual power. What if Jesus, when asked to give a sign, had zapped His opponents with a lightning bolt? Surely a man who could still a storm could have done such a thing. And it certainly would have silenced His remaining critics.

I have had conversations with unbelieving friends who ask, "If God loves me and wants me to know Him, why doesn't He just prove Himself? Why not speak to me Himself instead of hiding?" I respond that it's impossible for me to know the mind of God, but I also think about these stories. There is something about demands for absolute proof that Jesus refuses to honor. That is not the relationship He wants with us. John 10:24-26 says *The Jews who were there gathered around Him, saying, "How long will you keep us in suspense? If you are the Messiah, tell us plainly." Jesus answered, "I did tell you, but you do not believe. The works I do in my Father's name testify about me, but you do not believe because you are not my sheep."* Some people are looking for a Shepherd. They are eager to believe. Others will not believe even after they have seen evidence. Perhaps God knows the heart with which a person asks for a sign, and refuses to indulge the determinedly skeptical. On this day, Jesus did promise to give His critics a sign: The sign of Jonah, who spent three days in the belly of a whale. Even Jesus' disciples didn't know what this meant until after the resurrection. That miracle would be the ultimate sign. In a later chapter, we'll talk about the evidence for the reality of Jesus' resurrection. But no matter how much evidence is presented, some see it as a miracle, and others as a fairy tale. Not much has changed in two thousand years.

The Insecurity of Religion
John 9:13-34

I once pastored a church that had experienced a significant split in the decades before. This was during the "Golden Age" of the church, when they were growing like wildfire. Their pastor was a visionary with powerful leadership gifts, and he was beloved in the congregation. He had heard about an evangelist in the city who was preaching a message this pastor thought sounded suspicious. He stood up behind his pulpit on the next Sunday and declared that any member of his church who attended a meeting led by this evangelist would no longer be welcome in the church. Many families left the church after that; not because they had attended those meetings, but because they resented the authoritarian tone their pastor assumed. There is something in religion that tends toward insecurity. Religious leaders often feel threatened by people who ask questions, who express doubts, or who seek answers their religious leaders aren't providing.

Jesus saw that insecurity up close in the religious leaders of His nation. In this story, we see that the Pharisees have moved beyond simply criticizing Jesus and trying to turn people away from Him. Now, they are forcing anyone who believes in Jesus out of their synagogue. That is far more severe than the pastor who drove families out of his church. In the first place, they chose to leave, whereas these people had no choice. In the second place, those families could easily join another church, as I'm sure most did. But people who were removed from a synagogue in 1st Century Israel had no spiritual home anymore. They were outcasts in their community. The insecurity of religion devastated their lives, and fear caused by that insecurity kept countless others from knowing their true Messiah. I want to be clear in what I am saying here: Spiritual leaders must be watchful for false teaching. The pastor I spoke of earlier was right to be concerned about what his people were hearing. But we also must allow people to think through tough issues on their own, asking difficult questions and wrestling honestly with their doubts. There is nothing to fear from those who seek the truth. All truth, after all, is God's truth.

Practice What You Preach
Matthew 23:1-4

By this point, Jesus has had more than enough of the criticisms of the scribes and Pharisees. He draws a line in the sand. Matthew 23 is known by many Bible students as the "seven woes" passage, since Jesus says "Woe to you scribes and Pharisees, hypocrites" seven times. He is saying these things in Jerusalem, the center of their power base. He has traveled behind enemy lines and is openly defying them to do something. But in His words of criticism against Israel's religious elite, we see troubling accusations that He might also lodge against modern Christians. He begins with this textbook definition of hypocrisy: *They don't practice what they preach.* This may have puzzled His hearers, since the Pharisees particularly were known for their conspicuous obedience to the Law of Moses. They didn't follow the rules; they went above and beyond. But to Jesus, this wasn't the point. Their religion consisted of nothing but rules. There was no repentance or mercy.

Chuck Colson once visited a church in Naples, Florida, and afterward told about what he saw there: *The pastor riveted his congregation with a bold confession. "My message today is on the parable of the Good Samaritan," he announced. "Let me start with an illustration. "Remember last year when the Browns came forward to join the church?" he asked. Everyone nodded; the Browns were a very influential family. "Well, the same day a young man came forward and gave his life to Christ. I could tell he needed help—and we counseled him." No one nodded; no one remembered. "We worked with the Browns, got them onto committees. They've been wonderful folks. The young man...well, we lost track. Until yesterday, that is, as I was preparing today's message on the Good Samaritan. I picked up the paper, and there was that young man's picture. He had shot and killed an elderly woman." Chins dropped throughout the congregation, mine included, as the pastor continued. "I never followed up on that young man, so I'm the priest who saw the man in trouble and crossed to the other side of the road. I am a hypocrite."* It's hard to imagine a religious leader being that openly repentant. Yet that was the righteousness Jesus was hoping to inspire in Israel's leaders. It's what He hopes to see in us.

Playing to the Wrong Audience
Matthew 23:5-12

Jesus is just beginning His "Seven Woes" against the scribes and Pharisees. But first, He identifies a key problem with mere religion in v. 5: *Everything they do is done for people to see.* True worship is directed toward God alone; but hypocritical religion is intended for a wider audience. Jesus mentions phylacteries: leather boxes that Jewish men wore strapped to their wrist or their forehead. Inside the boxes were pieces of paper with scripture verses written on them. In Deuteronomy 6, Moses had commanded Israelites to bind the word of God to their foreheads and wrists, and they took that command literally. This was standard practice in Jesus' day. The other symbol He mentions is the tassel of your garment. Moses had told the Israelites to wear gold tassels on the corners of their robes. This was meant to remind them that they were always under the law of God. The problem was not the symbols themselves; after all, we know Jesus wore tassels (in Matthew 9:20, the fringe of Jesus' cloak the woman touched is the word for the Jewish tassel) and He might have worn a phylactery, too. The problem was the way in which they used the symbols. They weren't using them as a reminder to themselves, but as a sign to others of their righteousness. They would make their phylacteries bigger and their tassels longer than everyone else's. It was as ridiculous as a modern-day Christian slapping a fish bumper sticker on the back of his car that was wider than the car itself. Imagine such a man being pulled over by a policeman, who tells him that the sticker is a traffic hazard. The man would probably protest, "But if I remove it, how will people know how righteous I am?"

I knew a mother whose teenaged daughter was doing typical teenager stuff, like asking to dye her hair strange colors, wearing odd clothes. The mom was careful not to make a big deal out of these small rebellions, but she asked, "Why are you making these choices?" The daughter said, "The girls at school are so mean. I don't want to look anything like them." The mom nodded. Then she said, "But if you really want to stand out, why not do it by being more compassionate, more kind, more courageous than them? What does it prove just to look different?" That's a hard message for a teenaged girl to grasp. I guess it's hard for us all. It's so much easier to focus on surface-level righteousness than it is to yearn for a truly changed heart. But Jesus urged us not to settle for the superficial.

Slamming the Door of Heaven
Matthew 23:13

This is the first of the seven woes. The term translated "woe" can be used in terms of sympathy or condemnation. Jesus is condemning the scribes and Pharisees here, but His purpose, like the Old Testament prophets before Him, is to inspire repentance. He is not writing off Israel's leaders; He is hoping to wake them up. Here is the great irony: For centuries, these learned men had taught the people that when the Messiah came, He would pour judgement upon Israel's enemies. Jesus came, claiming to be the Messiah, and instead poured out judgment on the teachers themselves.

The most obvious way to interpret Jesus' words here is to note that the scribes and Pharisees were trying their best to keep anyone from following Him. Since He saw Himself as the Way, the Truth and the Life, in His mind, they were keeping people out of Heaven. Yet there is a double irony in this passage for Christians today. We believe in Jesus, yet there is no one more responsible for driving people away from God than us. I don't have objective proof of that last statement, by the way. But I have met many people who want nothing to do with organized religion in general and Christianity in particular. Almost none of them reject Christianity for intellectual reasons. But they have met Christians who were arrogant, proudly ignorant and unscientific, homophobic, xenophobic, hateful, judgmental, hypocritical, or some combination of the above. They concluded, "If that's what it means to be Christian, I want nothing to do with it." Wouldn't it be tragic for you or I to learn, on our judgment day, that we were more responsible for creating atheism than for spreading God's good news? Jesus' first woe, intended to wake up religious folks two thousand years ago, ought to sound an alarm bell for each of us today.

Negative Conversion
Matthew 23:15

This second woe speaks loudly against two popular opinions today. One is the notion that, "It doesn't matter what you believe, as long as you are sincere." This idea seems like the height of enlightenment and tolerance, especially compared to the seemingly primitive concept of most religions, which asserts, "My way is the only way to God." There's a fable often used to illustrate this: Blind men encounter an elephant. One touches it's tusk and says, "Whatever this thing is, it feels like a spear." Another touches it's snout and says, "No, it's a hose." A third touches its side and says, "It feels more like a wall to me." And so it goes: a broom (its tail), a fan (its ear), a tree stump (its leg). The teller of the fable says, "This is what the world's religions are like. They are all touching the same God in different ways, and they don't even know it." Again, that sounds so very tolerant. Yet it's actually an arrogant idea. The teller of the fable assumes that she is the one with true vision, while religious people are blind. The idea that all religions lead to the same God is equally offensive to a variety of religious traditions; there is nothing tolerant about it. Jesus was not an adherent of this view. No one was more sincere in their beliefs than the scribes and Pharisees, yet Jesus called them sons of Hell.

This woe also shoots down the contemporary idea that religion is fine, but evangelism is the true evil. "It's fine to believe whatever you want," we say, "But when start you trying to convert others to your beliefs, that's when the trouble starts." Converting to Judaism in the First Century was a tall order; it didn't mean simply attending a new church and adopting a new set of doctrinal ideas. A convert to Judaism would have to give up his belief in the Greco-Roman gods, which would make him instantly suspicious in the eyes of his neighbors. He and the other males in his house would have to be circumcised, start abiding by Jewish rules of diet and observance of the Sabbath. The Pharisees and scribes must have been working awfully hard to bring about these conversions. Jesus doesn't criticize them for trying to convert others to belief in Israel's God. In fact, Jesus clearly wanted His disciples to do the same. He criticized them for leading converts down the wrong path. As politically incorrect as it may be today, Jesus believed there was only One Way. His people should always ask themselves, "Are we leading people the right way?"

The Lure of Legalism
Matthew 23:16-22

Legalism is a fitting name for the natural result of religion: 1) Replacing the rules of God with the intricate, obsessive rules of human beings. 2) Measuring our faith by our ability to stick to these rules. 3) Making those rules more important than people. Here in this third woe, we see the laughably ridiculous lengths to which legalism had taken otherwise devout people. Jesus satirized their haggling over what constituted a proper vow: "Is a vow on the temple binding? Or is it only binding if you swear by the gold in the temple?" He pointed out that they were essentially finding ways to legally lie. That is the ultimate problem with legalism: It doesn't produce righteousness. A person can train himself to keep a list of rules, but that doesn't defeat the sin in his heart. He may not cheat on his wife, but he's still cruel to her. He may not blaspheme his God, but he still drives people away from him with his arrogance and lack of compassion. No list of rules, no self-improvement plan, no religious ritual can overcome the evil in us. We need a miraculous intervention.

Case in point: In 1934, just after Hitler came to power in Germany, the Baptist World Alliance international meeting was held in Berlin. One of the American delegates to the congress gave a report to Baptists back home in America on what life was like in Germany under Hitler. He said the nation was being steered in the right direction. Pornography was now outlawed. Deviant books were being burned. German society was becoming a place where men were conservative, women were modest, and children were respectful. Yet only the most morally deviant person today would assert that Hitler's regime brought about a change for the better. On their own, rules don't work. Something more is needed.

Swallowing the Camel
Matthew 23:23-24

Anyone who thinks of Jesus as a dour, humorless figure needs to envision a diner at a café, with half a camel emerging from his mouth, while gesturing furiously to his waiter at the gnat in his soup. That bizarrely hilarious image was Jesus' metaphor for the religion of the Pharisees. Even their meticulous financial giving was offensive to God because of their lack of attention to the truly important matters of the heart: Justice, mercy and faithfulness.

Philip Yancey was raised in a very conservative home in the south. He was brought up to believe that Christians do not dance or drink, go to the movies, play cards, go bowling, or wear short pants. Every time the church doors were open, he was expected to be there, and he heard many sermons warning against the evils of worldliness, communism, liberalism, modernism, and the theory of evolution. When he grew up, he went to a Bible college, where the rules were equally strict. Men could not wear facial hair (despite the paintings of a bearded Jesus all over the campus). Women could not wear slacks, except during hayrides, when they were required to be worn under their dresses, for propriety's sake. Tobacco and alcohol were forbidden, on pain of expulsion. Dating was strictly regulated. Yancey got engaged before his senior year, but he could only see his fiancee for one hour during supper, and kissing or holding hands were taboo. Every morning, a bell rang in the dorms. Each student was required at that moment to get up, open the Bible, and have his or her daily quiet time with the Lord. If a student was caught sleeping in, they were required to write a book report on a Christian book.

Now you might assume that living under such strict rules kept Yancey out of trouble, and you would be right. But it didn't lead him to Christ. In his early twenties, he rejected organized Christianity. For several years, he drifted unhappily through life. Ultimately, through the joy of beauty and art, Yancey concluded that a God must exist. The character of Jesus kept calling to him. Today, he is an influential Christian author. However, many of his friends from his childhood and from the Bible college have never gotten to that point. Still resentful at the brand of Christianity they encountered growing up, they continue to reject Christ. I think about the parents of those people and the school administrators, some now elderly, others long dead. They had good intentions. They kept young people sheltered from evil influences. They kept most of them from decisions that are so destructive to most teenagers: wanton sex, drunkenness, and addiction. But in the process, they drove many of them away from the God they believed in. They strained at gnats, but swallowed a camel.

Superficial
Matthew 23:25-28

Samuel Tewk was a reformer in England in the 19th century who came up with a radical new way to treat mentally ill people. In those days, the mentally ill were sent to horrible asylums where they were often treated miserably. Common treatments included chaining them to the walls or beating them to change their behaviors. Tewk devised a much more compassionate therapy. His theory was that if they were trained to function normally in society, they would be treated well, and good treatment would prevent their upsetting episodes. So he taught them how to behave at tea parties and church meetings. His clinics were more like finishing schools than insane asylums. Tewk's patients learned how to dress appropriately, carry on conversation, and observe standard etiquette. In many ways, Samuel Tewk was able to train his patients to appear normal. Perhaps that made his patients feel a little better about themselves; perhaps it helped their families relax a little, too. Unfortunately, his therapy did nothing to address their real problems. It is all well and good to be able to tie a bow tie, or to drink tea with one's pinky finger extended, but such external niceties cannot cure or aleviate schizophrenia, bi-polar disorder, or psychosis.

Jesus recognized the same problem in the religion of His day. Were the scribes and Pharisees highly disciplined and morally scrupulous? Absolutely. Did they live more fruitful and productive lives as a result? Of course. But at heart, they were whitewashed tombs. They were used coffee cups whose outsides had been carefully polished. Their meticulously curated exteriors masked the rottenness on the inside. Jesus came with a mission that mere religion could not accomplish. He wanted to remake human beings, to free us from the brokenness at our hearts.

Heart of Stone
Matthew 23:29-36

For decades now, pharmaceutical companies have had some of their best researchers working on what are called transdermal medicines. Those are medicines that can be applied through the skin. Wouldn't that make life easier? Some of you take many pills every day. Wouldn't it be easier if you could just apply a patch once a month and forget it? What if we never had to take a shot again? For those of us with small children, life would be so much better if we never again had to coax a child to swallow that awful-tasting medicine, or hold her down, screaming, as the doctor poked her with needles. The researchers have tried everything. They have experimented with different creams and ointments. They have tried mild electric currents. They have tested small bandages with tiny microneedles that pierce the skin, but do not touch any nerves. They have had a few successes; the nicotine patch is one example. But overall, their efforts have been in vain. What they have found is that human skin, which looks so thin and soft, is really a very effective suit of armor. It is hard to penetrate. That is the way God made us.

The heart, which in literary terms represents the human will, is meant to be soft and welcoming. God wants to be able to speak to our hearts, to shape and mold them any way He chooses. Unfortunately, we tend to grow a shell around our hearts. Nothing can penetrate this armor, not even the love of God. That was the last thing about the Pharisees that Jesus chose to criticize in Matthew 23. He may have saved the worst for last. This is why, all through history, the people sent by God to tell us the truth have always been unpopular, even hated. Jesus talks about this in verse 35, mentioning two such people. The first one is Abel, part of the first family in human history, killed by his brother because Cain was jealous of Abel's righteousness. His story is found in Genesis, the beginning of the Hebrew Bible. The second is Zechariah, a man who was stoned to death at the command of the king of Israel, because he preached God's judgment against Israel if they didn't stop worshipping idols. His story is in 2 Chronicles, the last volume in the Jewish Scriptures. Jesus is saying, "From the beginning of God's Word to the end, from A to Z, you have rejected everything I have tried to tell you." The Pharisees knew all these stories. They tried to show that they were different. And so they would build monuments over the tombs of the prophets. It was their way of saying, "If the prophets had been alive today, we would not have killed them. We would have responded to the Word of God." But Jesus said, "You are no different than your forefathers. They killed the prophets, and you will kill my apostles, who I will send out in my name to give you the good news." History shows that Jesus' prophecy came true; 11 of the 12 apostles were martyred for preaching the Word, and the 12th, John, spent many years in exile for his preaching.

It comes to this: If the god you believe in never offends you, never challenges you, never demands change, then perhaps you have created a god in your own image, instead of the other way around. If the god you believe in hates the same people you hate, then you aren't truly worshipping a deity; you're sanctifying yourself. That is hardness of heart.

Jerusalem, Jerusalem
Matthew 23:37-39

Today, we have negative associations with spiritual judgment. We think of a repellently pious old woman with a tight bun in her hair, scowling at young people who seem to be enjoying life, or a pompous, red-faced preacher inveighing against the sins of people outside his church, ignoring or rationalizing the sins he and his church members are guilty of. Those people seem to delight in pointing out the evils of others; you get the distinct impression they are happy about the reality of Hell. As Jesus closes out the seven woes, we have heard him say some incredibly harsh things. But unlike the pious old woman and the pompous preacher of today, Jesus is speaking these judgments against the devoutly religious, not the unwashed heathens. And as His closing words indicate, He is anything but delighted about their status or their destiny.

For Jesus and His people, Jerusalem was everything. It was not only the national capitol; it was the seat of spiritual connection to God. In Jerusalem and its temple, the Jews had a resource no other people group had. For a small, often oppressed group, the emotional strength that knowledge gave them is impossible for us to overstate. They had lost it once before, in the Babylonian exile that occurred some six centuries before Jesus. The restoration of their home and temple was a miracle, and a sign God had not given up on them, after all. Yet now, Jesus was telling them Jerusalem would be laid waste once again, the temple once more leveled. His words came true some forty years later, when the Romans sacked the city. There has never been a temple in Jerusalem since. Jesus, in speaking of these things, compares Himself to a mother hen. God is often depicted in Scripture in masculine terms, but it's important to remember that this is just a metaphor. God Himself is neither male nor female. And Jesus, who claimed to be God in the form of a man, sees nothing wrong with pointing out typically feminine characteristics in the Godhead. As He thinks of Jerusalem's coming devastation, He doesn't feel satisfaction; instead, He feels like a mother desperate to gather her wayward children.

I once read about a mom who woke late one night when she heard her teenaged son stagger into the house. Her husband rose from bed a few minutes later and found her kneeling beside her son's bed. He lay there, still in his clothes, reeking of alcohol, practically comatose. His mother was gently stroking his hair. "What are you doing?" asked the father. "This is the only time he'll let me love him," was the mother's reply. The metaphor of a mother's love is apt for Jesus. He had endured three years of solid abuse, slander, even murder plots on the part of the religious leaders. He stood in the midst of a city that would within days cry out "Crucify Him!" Yet He felt the love of a mother for her rebellious son. If Jesus was God indeed (and I believe He was) then we should be very glad that He feels that way about us when we're at our worst.

The Conspiracy
John 11:45-53

John is able to pinpoint the exact moment the plot against Jesus was settled. Up to now, the scribes and Pharisees had seen Him as a threat, with His attacks on their authority and His motley band of undesirables. But the high priest and his fellow Sadduccees had been mostly unconcerned about this rogue teacher way off in backward Galilee. Now, however, the news filtered out about Lazarus. Yes, Jesus had raised a widow's son from the dead in Nain, and a synagogue ruler's daughter as well. But those two people had expired the same day Jesus raised them; they both could be dismissed as near-death experiences. Lazarus, on the other hand, had been in the ground for four days. And this miracle was in Bethany, just a short walk from the temple in Jerusalem. Things were getting out of hand. The scribes worried that this Jesus movement would become so large, the Romans would see it as a threat to their rule. If they sent the legions to stop this uprising—as they surely would; standard Roman operating procedure was to use a sledgehammer to kill a spider—there would be widespread bloodshed. For over a century, the Jews had lived in relative peace with their Roman overlords, able to continue worshipping their own God and ruling on matters of religious significance without pagan interference. It would take little provocation for the Romans to overturn that status, destroying the temple and abolishing the Sanhedrin. Soon, Jews would be forced to worship the Roman gods or die, like most other people.

This is the first time we've discussed the High Priest, Caiaphas, so a word about him is in order. Caiaphas was the son-in-law of Annas, who had previously served as High Priest. When God created the sacrificial system in Exodus, He stipulated that a descendant of Aaron was to serve as High Priest, to stand between God and the people, especially on the Day of Atonement (Yom Kippur). The position was to last for a lifetime. But in the First Century, the Romans installed and deposed High Priests at will, so the position was as much political as it was spiritual. And Caiaphas was a master politician. He held onto his High-Priestly power longer than anyone else in that era, serving eighteen years. His prophecy here is incredibly accurate, as John is careful to note…only not in the way Caiaphas anticipated. He thought that Jesus' death would bring political stability to his regime. That death would indeed save the people, and bring in scattered souls from other nations, but they were not all the people Caiaphas intended. Proverbs 21:1 says *The king's heart is a stream of water in the hands of the Lord; He turns it wherever He will.* God is not threatened by the machinations of politicians; When He so desires, He uses them to accomplish His purposes. Here, the darkest of plots would be repurposed to accomplish the salvation of millions.

The Conquering Hero
Luke 19:28-44

This is a famous moment. We know it today as The Triumphal Entry. In churches like mine, we celebrate it on Palm Sunday, the week before Easter. Children carry palm branches down the church aisle and chant, "Hosanna!" But what was it all about? Specifically, what was Jesus up to? This was a symbolic action. It was an action that was supposed to signify something important. We still have symbolic actions. When you see people do certain things, you understand a message is being sent, even if they don't say anything. For example, when you see a young man get down on one knee in front of a woman, you're pretty sure you know what he's doing…and it's not checking her for stray nose hair. In the Old Testament, prophets often did symbolic actions. Jeremiah made a yoke and wore it around his shoulders like an ox, to show Israel they would soon become slaves of Babylon. Hosea married a woman he knew would be unfaithful to him, to show God's people how their unfaithfulness made God feel. Isaiah walked around naked for three years, to warn Israel they would be carried off in shame for their sins (I personally think Jeremiah got off easy). Jesus' action symbolized two things: **I am the Messiah**, and **I'm not the kind of Messiah you expected**.

His actions were a way of claiming Messiahship, because Zechariah 9:9 said the promised deliverer would ride in on the colt of a donkey. Everyone there knew exactly what Jesus was indicating by this action, and it made the crowds, so hungry for a hero, very excited. But His actions also indicated that He would not be the Messiah they expected. Jesus' actions would have reminded the people of a Roman triumph, the huge parade held for a military hero after a big victory. The closest analogy in our culture would be the ticker-tape parades we throw for sports champions. Jesus didn't act triumphant; instead, He began to weep. This is one of two times we know that Jesus shed tears. He predicted the destruction of the great city of Jerusalem. Why did He do this? For the same reason a parent will say to his child, "If you don't straighten up your act, you're headed for trouble." The same reason a teacher will say to a student, "If you don't study harder, you won't pass this class." The same reason a doctor will say to a patient, "If you don't change your ways, you'll be dead in five years." They are hoping to see repentance, a turnaround toward something better. Jesus knew what the future held for His city. He wanted everyone to have the opportunity to be saved. His was not a mission of military conquest (at least, not the way we conceive of that idea). It was a rescue mission.

The Final Straw
Mark 11:12-21

We've already seen that the Sanhedrin had decided to put Jesus to death. But if there was any doubt about the wisdom of their plan, it vaporized on this day. This event sealed Jesus' fate. And make no mistake about it, this was a violent event. I know we prefer a Jesus who is gentle and dignified, but the evidence says otherwise in this case. John's account (John 2:13) says Jesus made a whip out of cords. I'm willing to bet some people went running out of the temple with whip marks on their cheeks and bloody noses. Mark says He drove the sellers out, and "would not allow anyone to carry merchandise through the temple courts." Think about that. He was disrupting their commerce. Do you realize how hard that is to do? Imagine going into the food court in a mall and trying to scare the manager of one of those fast-food joints into abandoning his shop (and all the money inside). Think about how unhinged you would have to be to scare one businessman that badly. Now, how scary would you have to be to clear the entire food court? Jesus cleared out an area much larger than that. He was livid...and terrifying to behold.

But why? The temple was not simply a religious building, like one of our modern church facilities. It was a bridge between humanity and God, the one place on Earth where humans could come to God to make their relationship right. The temple was composed of various sections. There was the sanctuary, the Holy of Holies, and various sections extending out from there. Jesus actually cleared out one of the outermost sections, called the Court of the Gentiles. This was the furthest any non-Jew was allowed to go into the temple complex. The intention was that Gentiles would worship God there; but they couldn't, because it had become a place of commerce. This is why He quoted from Isaiah, referring to God's temple as "a house of prayer for all nations." This is why Jesus cursed the fig tree and cleared out the temple on the same day. He was saying a shocking thing: Israel is no longer the vessel God uses to lead the nations to Himself, and the temple is no longer the place you go to meet with God. God made a bridge so men and women could get to Him. Then established religion turned that bridge into a roadblock. Jesus was mad. But fortunately, He didn't just throw a fit. His anger was real, but in confirming the Sanhedrin's decision to kill Him, it led directly to a solution.

Chapter 9: His death
Matthew 20:17-19

Our look at the life of Jesus hasn't been strictly linear. We just got done reading about His entry into Jerusalem and the cleansing of the temple, which steeled the determination of His enemies to put Him to death. Now we bounce back to the weeks before Jerusalem. I hope that's not too confusing to the reader. But now we need to focus on His death. Jesus' life is unique in many ways, but one is the importance of His death. In most biographies of famous people, the death of the subject may occupy a chapter. But in the four official versions of Jesus' life, it takes up as much as one-third of the story. Here we see that He knew all along that His mission was not to be a teacher, a miracle worker, a political leader or a prophet. His job was to die an atoning death. As He said at other times, He came to be a ransom for many. So far, we've looked at many aspects of Jesus' amazing life, but we cannot truly know the Man unless we examine His death. Why did He die? Why did He die by crucifixion? What does it all mean? That's what we'll explore in this chapter. But first, a quote from Fleming Rutledge's outstanding book, *The Crucifixion: Understanding the Death of Jesus Christ.*

"There have been many famous deaths in world history; we might think of John F. Kennedy, or Marie Antoinette, or Cleopatra, but we do not refer to "the assassination," "the guillotining," or "the poisoning." Such references would be incomprehensible. The use of the term "the crucifixion" for the execution of Jesus shows that it still retains a privileged status. When we speak of "the crucifixion," even in this secular age, many people will know what is meant. There is something in the strange death of the man identified as Son of God that continues to command special attention. This death, this execution, above and beyond all others, continues to have universal reverberations. Of no other death in human history can this be said. The cross of Jesus stands alone in this regard; it is **SUI GENERIS**…"

The Plot Thickens
Matthew 26:14-16

The Sanhedrin knew that they had to put Jesus to death; with only a couple of exceptions, every one of the seventy members of the council seems to have been on board with that plan. But how to do it? This was Passover week; the city of Jerusalem was swollen with pilgrims, many of whom were chattering excitedly about this Galilean rabbi. If they arrested Jesus in the street while He was teaching or stoned Him to death as a blasphemer, their actions would probably provoke a riot. And a disturbance of the peace is exactly what would bring the steel-gauntleted hand of Rome down upon them. The key was to arrest Him at night, get Him before the Roman governor early in the morning, and have Him crucified by Rome before the crowds realized what was happening. But in order to do this, they needed to know where Jesus was at night. Suddenly, they got the break they needed. One of Jesus' own disciples had turned on Him. He could lead them right to the man Himself under cover of darkness.

The name "Judas" is today a synonym for treachery. It arises in surprising ways: Bob Dylan was called "Judas" by music fans for switching from acoustic guitar to electric. In English Premier League soccer, if a player switches to a rival team, it's called a "Judas transfer." In recent decades, many have sought to paint Judas in a more sympathetic light, including the musical *Jesus Christ Superstar* and the book and film *The Last Temptation of Christ*. The Bible doesn't tell us his motives for betraying Jesus. We're told he was stealing money from the ministry (John 12:6), so perhaps three years of financial deprivation got the better of a man who clearly valued wealth. On the other hand, some point to the fact that all the Gospel accounts say Judas' betrayal was part of the Divine plan. Jesus knew about it ahead of time, and did not attempt to stop him. So some see Judas as merely a pawn in a larger drama. But the verdict of Jesus Himself tells a different story: *Woe to that man who betrays the Son of Man! It would be better for him if he had not been born* (Matthew 26:24). Somehow, although Judas' actions were his own choice, they were also key to the salvation story. This should encourage us when we experience tragedies and injustices in our own lives. God can and does weave even the worst acts into His redemptive plan.

Getting Ready for Dinner
Luke 22:7-13

This seems like a rather mundane story, yet three of the four Gospels record it. Clearly, there was a deeper meaning here. Peter and John were sent to prepare the Passover meal. The elements of that ancient observance were very specifically laid out in the book of Exodus, and all of them had distinct meanings. The centerpiece was a whole, unblemished lamb, slaughtered in such a way that none of its bones were broken. The lamb, of course, reminded Jews of the lambs whose blood had saved their ancestors' lives on the night of the first Passover. Peter and John would need to purchase the lamb and either pay someone to roast it or roast it themselves. They would also procure the unleavened bread that symbolized the haste with which their ancestors left Egypt, bitter herbs that represented the hardship of their years in slavery, and charoset, a sort of relish made of nuts, fruit and honey. There may have been other Middle-Eastern staples, such as olives, beans, chickpeas (maybe even hummus) and parched grain. These were poor men, so it was certainly not a lavish feast. But we definitely know there was wine to drink.

Peter and John not only had to gather and prepare the meal, they also had to find the room for it to be eaten. Luke describes an almost cloak-and-dagger plan for them to arrive at the pre-arranged place for their Passover. They were to see a man carrying a water jar; since carrying water was considered woman's work, that would have been conspicuous. They were to wordlessly follow him until he entered a house, then approach the owner of that house and ask him for the room "The Teacher" requires. Why so much secrecy? Jesus clearly knew He was being hunted. The owner of the house must have been on His side, but He could not chance anyone else knowing where He would be. So to answer the question implied in our first two sentences: Why do the Gospel writers tell us this story? I believe it shows us how important this supper was to Jesus. He took a chance in making it happen. Verse 15 affirms that notion. We have a tendency to look for big things from God, obvious signs that prove His activity. But this story is one of many that show God is interested also in the small, seemingly mundane details: Following mysterious directions, baking unleavened bread, cleaning out an upper room for dinner. In God's economy, there are no small obediences. Everything matters.

The Last Supper
Luke 22:14-23

Even those who reject the divinity of Jesus must admit that this simple Passover Seder was the most important meal of all time. Think of how it affected history. Although Christians have often disagreed—sometimes vehemently—about the precise meaning of the observance, the fact remains that millions of people reenact this supper every week (in obedience to His command in v. 19, to *do this in remembrance of me*). There's DaVinci's painting, one of the most famous and oft-imitated in history (I saw an internet meme recently that depicted someone pouring a bucket of crawfish in front of Jesus and the Twelve. I must admit it made me laugh). But for the disciples, the experience must have been baffling. Passover was an important ritual in Judaism; there was a specific order to the meal. Yet Jesus flipped the script. He spoke of eating and drinking again with them in the kingdom of God. He broke a fragile piece of matzoh and compared it to His own body. He told them the wine represented the new covenant, sealed in His blood. Then He predicted that one of them would betray Him…that very night.

None of this made any sense to the disciples when it was happening. It was only later, as they looked back in light of subsequent events, that they understood. Within hours of that meal, they would watch in horror as one of their own led the mob to arrest Him. His body would be broken and His blood spilled in a terrifying outburst of violence and rage against a peaceful man. Yet, looking back, they would also recognize the stubborn hope in Jesus' words. When He spoke of eating and drinking in the Kingdom, He was predicting a time of feasting and celebration, when this world is complete. When He spoke of a new covenant, He was harkening back to Jeremiah 31:31-34, a promise that God would make a way for salvation that transcended dry religion, that made people righteous and brought them into a personal relationship with Him. All that, Jesus was saying, will be accomplished through my blood. So forget the painting (it's anachronistic anyway). Forget the inter-denominational squabbles over church rituals. Read this story for what it really is: A man preparing His friends for the worst day they would ever experience, and giving them hope to hold onto.

Prelude to a Fall
Luke 22:24-34

If there was one lesson Jesus kept trying to pound into His disciples during their three years together, it was the idea that humility—self-forgetfulness—is the way to greatness. Here on the eve of His death, He was still preaching that same message. "Be like me," He said, "I have given up everything to serve others. Don't be like the famous and powerful people of this world, who promote themselves." No one seems to have found this lesson harder than Peter. For all of his earnestness, he desperately wanted to separate himself from the other disciples. He always spoke first, took the initiative, wanted to prove he was more devoted to Jesus than anyone else. Even on this somber night, as the Twelve were reeling from the news that their Master's death was only hours away, Peter wanted Jesus to know that, even if all the other disciples abandoned Him, Peter never would (see Matthew 26:33). *I will go with you to prison and to death,* He swore. In a printed work like the Bible, there is no way to convey body language and tone, but I imagine that Jesus' face was a mask of sorrow and His voice quivered with grief as He told Peter the awful failure that lay ahead for him before sunrise.

The lesson for each of us: Beware, friend, the temptation to find validation in comparing yourself to others. We can always find someone who is more socially awkward, more intellectually challenged, more morally compromised, less skilled, less attractive, or less spiritually mature than ourselves. But God doesn't judge us on such standards. On the other hand, there is another kind of comparison game that is just as harmful. To look at others and say, "I wish I were as happy, handsome, healthy or holy as him or her" is self-defeating as well. There is nothing humble about that mentality; there is nothing in that attitude that pleases God. Jesus didn't preach a message of low self-esteem. He called His followers to put others first so consistently, they simply didn't have time to judge others or themselves in an unhealthy way. Someday, Peter would learn that lesson. But it wouldn't be on this night.

He Loved Them to the End
John 13:1-17

John's account of Jesus' last night is much longer than that of the other three evangelists, and includes details the others don't. We'll look at some of these extra details in the next few readings, beginning with the story of Jesus washing His disciples' feet. It might be awkward if a party host offered to wash your feet today, but in the ancient world, with its combination of open-toed shoes and unpaved roads, Jesus' act was profoundly thoughtful. It was also shocking; footwashing was considered such a demeaning task, most people would not have asked a slave to do it. Yet here was their Messiah, stripped to the waist, cleaning the muck and grime off their feet. That's not the half of it, however. John makes it clear this episode happened before the meal, before Judas left to put his conspiracy into motion. That means that on the night before His death, Jesus knowingly washed the feet of His betrayer. The man who taught His followers to love their enemies practiced what He preached. John says in v. 1, *Having loved His own who were in the world, He loved them to the end.* His love wasn't merely the kind act of cleaning their dirty feet; it was in the words He said to them afterward. He was setting for them (and us) a pattern of life that leads to blessing. We are never more fully alive than when we are putting others ahead of ourselves.

Do it Quickly
John 13:18-30

As we've already discussed, the men who ate that last supper with Jesus must have found the occasion surreal and confusing. It was certainly like no other Passover Seder they had experienced. Jesus had shocked them all by washing their feet, talking frankly about His impending arrest and execution, changing the meaning of Passover itself, and telling Peter he would fail spectacularly within hours. Then, to make matters even more strange, He predicted that one of them would betray Him. In the middle of that discussion, Judas suddenly left the room and didn't return. It's easy for us to think the disciples were slow-witted in not understanding. Didn't Jesus say, "The man I give this piece of bread is the one who will betray me"? On the other hand, their confusion was nothing new. Jesus constantly confounded the expectations of everyone who observed Him, believer and critic alike. It was only after Jesus was gone (and the Holy Spirit arrived, as promised—see Acts 2) that the eleven remaining disciples looked back on their time with Jesus and fully understood the things He had done and said. What this story shows us is that, on the worst night of His life, Jesus was fully in command. Judas was exercising his own free will in betraying Jesus, and the authorities who arrested Him within hours were doing so as well, but Jesus could have stopped it. He could have urged the eleven to apprehend Judas. He could have run away. Based on the miracle-working power He had already displayed, He could have turned Judas and the arresting mob into dung beetles, if He had so desired. But any desire He felt to escape death and defeat His enemies was overruled by a greater passion. He gave Himself over to His enemies for a reason.

The Advocate
John 14:15-18, 15:26-27, 16:7-15

"So…you're telling me that God is like a lawyer?" That was the question from one of my church members after we had studied John 14. Jesus refers to the Holy Spirit by a Greek word, *paracletos*, which literally means "one who comes alongside." English Bibles render that word in various ways, such as "Helper," "Comforter," "Counselor," or "Advocate." The word in ancient times was often used for someone who would represent the accused at a trial--a defense attorney, as it were. My friend didn't like the sound of that; He had heard too many lawyer jokes. I said, "If you were on trial for your life, you'd want someone full of wisdom, skill and integrity by your side, wouldn't you?" And so would all of us. Jesus, the night before He died, promised us exactly that. His disciples had heard of the Holy Spirit. In Israel's history, there were many stories of moments when the Spirit of God "came upon" men or women, enabling them to do things they were not capable of on their own. But now Jesus was promising His followers something new: Constant contact with God in Spirit form. That would be a game-changer. Since this is a study of Jesus, we won't take the time to explore all that Scripture teaches about the Holy Spirit (more's the pity…I do recommend you do such a study as soon as possible).

Instead, I want to focus on one curious thing Jesus said about the Spirit on this eventful night. In 16:7, He said *it is for your good that I am going away. Unless I go away, the Advocate will not come to you; but if I go, I will send him to you.* Wait…what? Did Jesus really say it was better for the disciples if He left? Yes. That means that modern-day followers of Jesus, who have access to the Holy Spirit He promised, are spiritually better off than the disciples who saw Him face to face. How can that be true? It's simple, really. Jesus, amazing and magnetic and life-changing as He was—was encased in a human body. Therefore, He was limited to one place at a time. In order to be with Him, His followers had to leave everything else behind, and even then, had to jostle and compete with one another to be as near Him as possible. But the Holy Spirit is not bound by such fleshly limitations. He can be with you wherever you are, whenever you need Him. Jesus was promising to be with us forever in a way even the Twelve hadn't experienced.

What Was on His Mind?
John 17

The hour is late, and the disciples must be in a state of shock. Jesus has taken the most important night of the year for any observant Jew and given it a radical new meaning. He has shared with them in the clearest possible way that He is leaving them within hours, and that their lives will never be the same. Now, just before leaving the upper room, He looks heavenward and voices the longest prayer recorded in the four Gospels. The contents of our prayers are extremely revealing. They expose our priorities and anxieties in a way little else can. So what was most on Jesus' mind in this moment?

We can divide His requests into three categories: First, He prays that His Father will "glorify" Him, so that He in turn can fully glorify the Father. He knew that soon, He would be abused and abased in public view. No one watching those events would believe that this condemned carpenter was sent by God. Yet He hoped and prayed that God would vindicate Him, so that His plan of salvation would be complete. Second, He prays for His disciples. Given how clueless the Twelve often were, and how frustrated Jesus sometimes seemed with them, His words here are touchingly affectionate. He prays for their protection. Then, He prays for us. *I pray also for those who will believe in me through their message.* If you follow Jesus as Savior and Lord, He is praying for you in that moment. And what does He pray for us? *That all of them may be one, Father, just as you are in me and I am in you.* One of my favorite sounds in the world is the sound of my children laughing. Even if they are laughing at me (which is not infrequent), it is still a sweet sound. But the sound of them arguing, accusing, screaming at each other is on the other end of the emotional spectrum for me. When I see how often Jesus and the other writers of the New Testament spoke about love among fellow believers, I think God feels the same way about His children. If you are at odds with a brother or sister, get over your foolish pride and make things right. It was important enough for Jesus to pray about it in the most stressful hours of His life…it's important enough for you to take action.

Agony
Matthew 26:36-46

Jesus has just entered the crucible. The emotion on display in this story is breathtaking. A man who has never asked His friends for anything now pleads for Peter, James and John to "keep watch" with Him. Suffering is such an intensely lonely experience; we all want someone to be with us through it, and Jesus is no different. He falls on His face in prayer. Luke (who was a doctor by trade) records that Jesus begins to sweat blood (Luke 22:44). This is a condition known as hematidrosis, in which the capillaries that feed the sweat glands burst, causing blood to seep from the pores. It is an indication of extreme emotional or physical stress. Jesus prays over and over again, *My father, if it is possible, may this cup be taken away from me.* The image of a cup is used often in Scripture to represent God's wrath against sin. Jesus saw before Him a foaming cup of liquid judgment, and like a child begging not to take medicine, asked to be excused.

We all know of stories of people who faced execution bravely, even stoically. Socrates, for instance, comforted his friends and asked the women around him to stop weeping before he drank his glass of hemlock. Why would Jesus, who has never shown fear before (even in the face of countless conspiracies and attempts on His life), lose His composure at this moment? The answer is hard for us to comprehend: He was facing something far worse than mere physical torment and death. In 2004, Mel Gibson's *The Passion of the Christ* shocked filmgoers with its graphic depiction of Christ's scourging and crucifixion. But based on the evidence we see here (and the words Jesus spoke while on the cross—more on that soon), the gore that Gibson depicted wasn't nearly the worst of what Jesus suffered. He knew what He was facing, and honestly asked for the Father to find another way. Yet the most amazing words in that prayer are, *Yet not as I will, but as you will.* Courage isn't a lack of fear; it's facing fear and doing what needs to be done. In the Garden of Gethsemane, Jesus showed us the supreme example of courage.

Betrayal
Matthew 26:47-56

Suddenly, the peaceful olive grove is lit with countless torches. The drowsy disciples are jolted awake. To their shock and horror, one of their own emerges from the angry mob, approaches Jesus, and kisses Him, calling Him "Rabbi" in false magnanimity. The thugs grab Jesus, who does not resist. And now, each of the Twelve runs, terrified, into the darkness, running from death with all he is worth. But first, there is one brief spasm of violence. John tells us that it's Peter who draws a sword and attacks a man in the crowd (John also tells us the man's name was Malchus—John 18:10). Luke, the doctor, tells us that Jesus picks up the severed ear and reattaches it (Luke 22:51), the only case of a healed amputation that we know of. That moment is Jesus' life and message in microcosm. He healed a man who was only there to do Him harm. He gave Himself up, so His friends could go free. Don't you wish we knew what happened to Malchus after that? He was the servant of the High Priest, the man most responsible for the conspiracy to have Jesus executed. Did he follow his boss to the hill where Jesus would hang, dying, and watch as Caiaphas mocked Him? Did he continue to serve his employer in the days ahead, as Caiaphas justified what he had done, talking about how the people were better off with the Nazarene dead? Or did Malchus walk away that night, refusing to serve the man who would kill the one who healed him? The Scriptures don't mention him again, so we can't possibly know in this life. If the Gospel is true, then each of us faces the same question: How will we respond to such amazing grace?

Trial
Matthew 26:57-68

When the position of High Priest was created approximately 1400 years before Christ, it was intended to be a mediator between God and humans, someone who could stand before the Lord on our behalf, making things right between us. The High Priest was to be a person uniquely devoted to God's righteousness and the spiritual welfare of people (see Exodus 29). But the High Priest had been a political appointee for years by the time of Jesus, and the tawdry spectacle of this trial is evidence of how far the position had fallen. Sadly, people have used this incident as reason for violent anti-Semitism for centuries, which is absurd: First of all, Jesus Himself was a Jew. Second, this trial was in violation of Jewish laws and the will of the population. There was no reason for the trial to take place at night, except to keep greater Jerusalem from knowing about the miscarriage of justice until it was already done. This was a conspiracy on the part of a small group of people against a man they considered a threat. The actions of the High Priest contradicted the Law of Moses he was sworn to uphold (for instance, the High Priest was never to tear his garments—see Leviticus 21:10). Matthew's statement in v. 59 sums up the event well: It was a sham, a show-trial designed for a pre-determined outcome. Yet even so, it took all night to get their intended verdict. And Jesus was the one who sealed His own fate.

Speaking of Jesus, note His behavior during the trial. He kept silent as people spoke slanderous falsehoods about Him, or took His words out of context (Compare v. 61 to John 2:18-22). Just as the prophet had foretold in Isaiah 53:7, *He was oppressed and afflicted, yet He did not open His mouth; He was led like a lamb to slaughter, and as a sheep before its shearers is silent, so He did not open His mouth.* But then, at the moment when keeping silent might have saved His life, He spoke the words He knew would condemn Him. "Today you judge me," He was saying, "But a day will come when I will judge you." Those defiant words were clearly blasphemous…unless they were true. The fear Jesus showed in Gethsemane was gone. Jesus weathered the hatred of powerful men and did not falter; He dove headfirst into the maelstrom. When we read stories of soldiers leaping from a foxhole to rescue a fallen buddy, or first responders running into a burning building, it should remind us of a heroic Messiah who faced even greater danger and charged ahead anyway.

Denial
Luke 22:54-62

I distinctly remember the first time I saw the movie *Titanic*. It was the first time my wife and I had ever left our baby daughter with someone else. As much as we needed a pleasant night at the movies, we were both on edge. The movie didn't help matters. I felt such a sense of tragic inevitability. I knew the ship would hit that iceberg; I knew there wouldn't be enough lifeboats on board; I knew 1500 people would die…yet I kept hoping that, somehow, it would turn out differently. That's how I feel whenever I read this story. Just as the words of Titanic's captain (or shipbuilder, or a crewman, depending on which story you read), "Not even God Himself could sink this ship," Peter's boastful words, *Even if all fall away, I will not* (Mark 14:29) and *Lord, I am ready to go with you to prison and to death* sounded ironic and hollow in the aftermath of failure. If you haven't yet decided whether or not this story is true, ask yourself the question: Why would the first-century church make up details like this one? How embarrassing is it that the leader of the early church was a coward in the moment of truth? It must have happened as it was told. And if that detail is true, why would the others not be also?

Speaking of details, only Luke tells us that at the moment the rooster crowed, Jesus looked directly at Peter. I wonder what expression was on His face? Was it disappointment? Sorrow? Forgiveness? Was He already so battered from abuse at the hands of the mob and the council that Peter couldn't tell? The disciple who seemed most devoted to Jesus; the one who always wanted to prove His commitment to the cause—who was first to try walking on water, first to proclaim Jesus as Messiah—had just failed spectacularly. Now, by all accounts, he would never see Jesus again, would never have the chance to make it up to Him. If this were any other story, Peter would disappear from history, never to be heard from again. But this isn't any other story…

Pontius Pilate
Luke 23:1-7

Ironically, the fate of the Son of God winds up in the hands of one man, the Roman prefect Pontius Pilate. We know very little about this man—where he came from, or what happened to him after he left Jerusalem for good in 37 AD. The first-century historian Josephus wrote that, whereas most Roman prefects were tolerant in allowing their Jewish subjects to practice their faith, Pilate often intentionally offended the Jews' religious convictions, and punished them cruelly when they protested. Philo, a philosopher who lived at the same time, wrote of Pilate's "vindictiveness and furious temper," his "corruption…cruelty…continual murders…and most grievous inhumanity." Luke 13:1 relates a story in which Pilate's soldiers murdered some Galileans while they were offering their sacrifices in the temple. All evidence indicates this was a pitiless man who had no affection for the people he governed.

It's interesting to read all four Gospels' account of the dance between Pilate and the Jewish leaders. He prefers to let them handle matters of local criminal justice. However, they lack the legal authority to order an execution. If they had simply stoned Jesus to death, Pilate would probably have looked the other way. But they want the crowds to see the hated Romans at fault in His execution, since Jesus is so popular. So they need to manipulate a man who loathes and distrusts them. They had charged Jesus with blasphemy at their own trial, but that charge won't be compelling to a pagan like Pilate. So they accuse Jesus of refusing to pay taxes (perhaps because one-time tax collectors like Matthew and Zacchaeus are among His followers) and declaring Himself a king; both are capital charges. Pilate sees exactly what they are up to, and does his best to avoid becoming a pawn in their scheme. Meanwhile, the Man at the center of this controversy seems to be utterly without power. Just as at His trial before the Sanhedrin, He does not try to defend Himself, speaking only when spoken to. To a master politician like Pilate, it must have been baffling to see a man who refused to play the game…even with His life at stake.

Before Herod
Luke 23:8-11

Pilate's first attempt to recuse to himself from the Jesus case was to send Him to Herod. Pilate governed Judea, where Jerusalem was located. But Herod ruled Galilee, where Jesus did most of His ministry. This wasn't Herod the Great, who had tried to kill baby Jesus; this was his son, Herod Antipas. This Herod had originally been given the Kingdom of his father, but was later demoted by his Roman overlords to the title "tetrarch" instead of "King" and given only Galilee and Perea to govern. Antipas built a city he called Tiberias in order to flatter the Roman emperor, but later found that the city was built on a graveyard, and no observant Jew would live there. Antipas also stole his brother's wife, Herodias. This brought two very different negative consequences: The father of the wife he abandoned for his sister-in-law, who happened to be an Arab king, declared war on Antipas, and defeated him. And John the Baptist publicly denounced Antipas for his adultery, which ultimately led to John's beheading. Later, when Antipas heard about Jesus' ministry, he was convinced that John had risen from the dead (perhaps he had inherited a touch of his old man's paranoia). In Luke 13, we read that when Jesus found out Antipas was trying to kill Him, He said, *Go tell that fox that I will keep on driving out demons and healing people today and tomorrow, and the third day I will reach my goal.* Hebrew scholars tell us that to Jews like Jesus, a fox was considered a lesser animal, the very opposite of a lion. Jesus was essentially saying, "I've got too much work to do to worry about the threats of an insignificant runt like Antipas."

Now this man sees Jesus for the first time. His response is consistent with what we already know of his character. In all the world at that time, there may not have been two men more dissimilar than Herod Antipas and Jesus. One was born into privilege and power, and spent his entire life grasping for more. The other left His privilege behind for poverty, and spent His entire life serving others. Yet the shallow, self-seeking man on this day mocked and ridiculed the righteous man, refusing to rescue Him from false charges. It's one of the frustrating things about our world: The bad guys often seem to win. But, in this story at least, we know the truth. The victory of the dark side is short-lived and illusory. Perhaps it always is.

The Verdict
John 18:28-19:16

John's account of Pilate's conversation with Jesus is much longer. He omits the detail about Jesus before Herod, preferring to focus on the back and forth between the prefect and the accused. I must confess: Even though I know Pilate was not a very likable man, I feel sorry for him when I read this story. You can sense the pressure this man was under. He has governed for nearly a decade a nation of people who utterly despise him—and the feeling is mutual. Now the leaders of those people drag before Him a man they say is a threat to national security. Since Jesus was obviously a poor man, had been up all night, and had been repeatedly beaten already, I doubt He looked imposing. Pilate knew he was being manipulated. And his wife added to his feelings when (see Matthew 27:19) she urged her husband not to render judgment on "that righteous man" because of a dream she had. On the other hand, Caesar wanted peaceful provinces. Pilate had antagonized the Jews enough; one more riot or rebellion might mean exile or even death for him. And these Jewish leaders were cunning enough to start a riot if they didn't get what they wanted. It's easy for us to say, "If I had been in Pilate's shoes, I would have set Jesus free." But he had never heard of this man before. He had every reason to try not to render judgment at all.

That's exactly what he tried. Pilate offered the crowd a choice: Would you rather me release to you a violent murderer in Barabbas, or this peaceful teacher, Jesus? To his shock, the crowd chose Barabbas. So he had Jesus scourged, a terrible punishment that would have reduced Jesus to a mass of bleeding flesh. But even this didn't slake the crowd's bloodlust. "Crucify! Crucify!" they called. According to Matthew, he even took a basin of water and publicly washed his hands, renouncing responsibility for the man's death. But the crowd was willing to take responsibility upon themselves. In between all these tactics, Pilate came back, again and again, to the man in question. There is much we cannot know about their conversation without having been there: For instance, tone of voice and body language might tell us what Pilate meant when he asked Jesus, "What is truth?" But it is obvious that he had never met anyone like this man before, and found him incredibly puzzling. Why wouldn't this peasant grovel for his life, like every other man? Jesus gave him the answer: *You would have no power over me if it had not been given to you from above.* In Jesus' mind, Judas, the priests, even this Roman governor were all part of God's plan of redemption. He had settled His fear several hours before in Gethsemane. Now He was ready for the worst.

Scourging
John 19:1-3

I realize we just read this short story as part of the last reading. But I wanted us to focus on two questions: What does it mean that Jesus was scourged (or flogged or whipped, depending on which English translation you're using)? And why was this done? The Roman practice of scourging was very different from the Jewish lash. Jews followed the Law of Moses, which said a condemned man was not to be beaten more than 40 lashes. The Romans had no such restrictions. Their instrument of torture was far more destructive than the simple leather whip of the Jews. It had several straps, with pieces of metal and bone embedded in them. The purpose was not just to scar the skin, but to remove it. Scholars tell us a man who had been scourged was often at the brink of death itself. Some men, in fact, died of shock or blood loss from their beating.

Why was this done to Jesus? As we have just seen, John indicates that Pilate hoped it would be a sufficient punishment to satisfy the crowd. But he also tells us of the sadism of the Roman guards, mocking Jesus with a crown of thorns and a purple robe (which, of course, would have clung to his wounds, leading to still more blood loss), and beating Him with their fists. Why would they do this? The obvious answer is that these were pitiless men who probably had grown to hate the Jews. This man, considered by some "The King of the Jews," made an easy target for their frustrations. But there is a deeper, unwritten reason that I suspect. Satan knew what Jesus was hoping to accomplish. Just like in the wilderness, when he had tempted Jesus for forty days, he hoped to stop the Son of God from accomplishing his mission. It must have seemed a tantalizing prospect: Now the Deity he despised was encased in frail human flesh; now He had surrendered Himself to the pagan authorities; now the Enemy could unleash his full fury on Him. Jesus may have been Divine, but He was also a man…surely if He were beaten and mocked enough, He would rise in righteous indignation, destroy his tormentors, and walk away from the cross forever. Surely that's what any of us would have done, in His shoes. But He didn't. To what must have been the immeasurable frustration of the Devil, Jesus was driven by something greater than pride or self-preservation, and so He absorbed every blow.

Barabbas
Luke 23:13-25

At some point in the history of Rome's occupation of Israel, they had started an unusual tradition: During the Passover festival, Judaism's most significant holiday, they would release one person from jail. I suppose it was a way for prefects like Pilate to say, "See, folks: We Romans aren't so bad. Straighten up your act, and you'll see the softer side of Roman rule more often." My theory is that typically, non-violent prisoners and beloved figures would be released. But this time, Pilate deliberately chose a despicable man, a murderer and revolutionary—exactly the kind of man the stately Sanhedrin would want dead—so that they would be forced to choose Jesus. If so, he underestimated their determination.

Luke and the other Gospel writers don't tell us Pilate's motive. They don't tell us much at all about Barabbas, either. Even his name ("son of Abbas" or more literally, "son of the father") gives us no clues. They have another reason for telling us this story. Notice that in this short passage, Luke tells us four times that Jesus was innocent (verses 14, 15, 20 and 22), but he describes Barabbas as a man guilty of two capital crimes: insurrection and murder. So the man deserving of death goes free, while the man deserving of life is killed. The tables of justice were turned. It would be an unspeakable miscarriage, a perversion of the way things ought to be, the worst example of the injustices of this world...unless this was the plan all along.

Via Dolorosa
Mark 15:21-23, Luke 23:26-32

Via Dolorosa means "Way of Sorrow." It's the traditional name for the winding, 2000 foot path from the Antonia Fortress (where Jesus was tried by Pilate) to the Church of the Holy Sepulchre, the traditional site of the crucifixion. Jesus walked that road, long ago. Death awaited Him at the end. Roman Catholic Christians remember that walk by meditating on The Twelve Stations of the Cross. But as you can see, the eyewitnesses give us a sparse record. We assume Jesus was too weary from loss of blood to carry His own crossbeam (although I'm certain the soldiers made Him try). Simon of Cyrene was forced to carry the cross; there is no indication that he knew Jesus before this day. But the fact that Mark names his sons Alexander and Rufus leads many readers to assume that they became Jesus-followers later; Mark seems to assume Christian readers will recognize their names. Only Luke tells us of Jesus' words to the women weeping as He walked. I suppose by now, we shouldn't be surprised that Jesus was thinking of others, even at a moment of profound crisis,

Mark tells us that Jesus refused the wine mixed with myrrh that He was offered. A tradition says this was an act of mercy done by the women of Jerusalem, mixing a sedative (interestingly, one of the gifts of the Magi from His infancy) with the wine to dull the pain. Why would Jesus refuse this? I can think of only one reason. Jesus knew that for the next several hours until His death, He would have one last audience. His enemies would be watching Him carefully for signs of weakness, anything they could repeat to His followers as evidence that He wasn't truly the Messiah. Jesus had no intention of giving them anything of the sort. Instead, as we will see, He had things He wanted to say. He endured the full extent of the pain, but He did so with His senses sharp.

Crucifixion
Mark 15:24-25

Notice that Mark and the other Gospel writers don't give us the details of crucifixion, instead simply saying, *And they crucified Him.* First-century readers wouldn't have needed a description of the act; they had seen it often enough for themselves. Many books and articles have been written detailing what a crucifixion was like, and what effects it produced on the body. You can find that information easily online, so I will not dwell on that. After all, the physical pain of the cross was not the main point of Jesus' death, as we will soon see. Still, the method of Jesus' death was significant.

Crucifixion was not invented by the Romans—the Persians get that dubious honor—but Rome perfected the practice. When we consider the pain that the victim must have endured, the hours or even days it took the victim to die, and the way crucifixion stripped away the victim's human dignity along with his clothes, we are left to conclude that this idea came from the darkest, most sadistic region of the human mind. Little wonder that Roman citizens were not allowed to be crucified, no matter how severe their crime. The cross was a powerful tool for controlling the population. To slaves, it said, "Stay in your place." To prospective rebels, it said, "Don't mess with Rome." To the followers of troublesome would-be revolutionaries, it said, "The man dying before you is no hero. He's not even a man. Forget him forever." To the Jews, the cross was a terrible scandal; the Law of Moses declared that any man hung on a tree was cursed by God (Deuteronomy 21:23). The enemies of Jesus must have been overjoyed at how well their plans had come together. Not only had the mighty Roman Empire declared Jesus an enemy of the state (and therefore, anyone who followed Him shared the same status), but God had now cursed Him as well. Surely now the movement of this infuriating Nazarene teacher was over. Surely.

Mockery
Mark 15:26-32

When our kids are small, we tell them old proverbs like, "Sticks and stones may break my bones, but words will never hurt me." We don't really believe that. Words do hurt. Any one of us, if we thought hard enough, could conjure up a memory of terrible words hurled our way. Some of those wounds never seem to heal. Jesus faced that, too. He had dealt with criticism, false accusation, and name-calling since His ministry began. But now, as He hung exposed on the cross, His life ebbing from Him, the abuse grew more intense. It started with Pilate: It was standard practice to post the charges against a crucified man. "King of the Jews" was probably a barb aimed at the Jewish leaders, but it also mocked Jesus (see also John 19:19-22).

Crucifixions usually took place by a main thoroughfare, to serve as a warning to the people. The people shuttling in and out of Jerusalem that day took time to revile Jesus. This is ironic; less than a week before, the crowds had cheered His arrival. We love to acclaim new heroes, but we also love to tear them down. Even the two thieves crucified on either side of Him muttered words of slander. And then, of course, there were the priests and scribes, those who had hounded Jesus for nearly His entire ministry. They had to be there to witness His final defeat, to remind the crowds how right they had been all along. One of the worst things about religion (when it is divorced from God's grace) is how it leads us to arrogantly assume God loves us more than our enemies and how it makes us delight in the downfall of those with whom we disagree. However, they were absolutely correct in one thing they said: *He saved others. He cannot save Himself.* Jesus' followers only realized it later, as (under the Holy Spirit's guidance) they saw that awful day through new eyes: Jesus couldn't save both Himself and others. By refusing to save Himself, He was indeed saving many, many others. Hallelujah.

Tragic Remorse
Matthew 27:3-10

We should feel nothing but sorrow for Judas Iscariot. We've made him out to be the worst of villains for two thousand years now. Yes, he did a terrible thing. Who among us has not done things we wish we could reverse? We don't know Judas' motive in betraying Jesus. Whatever it was, it melted away quickly. Judas, in hanging himself, showed the most tragic remorse of all. I say "tragic" remorse for this reason: Judas had been there the day Jesus taught the disciples to forgive others "seventy times seven" (Matthew 18:21-22). In other words, our forgiveness must be limitless. Judas should have trusted Jesus to practice what He preached. Had He ever failed to do so? Yes, to be clear, I think Judas still could have been forgiven for betraying Jesus. That is how vast and unstoppable the mercy of God is. Somehow, after three years spent constantly in Jesus' presence, Judas missed that. Remorse without repentance is tragic. But remorse that leads to repentance is the path to reconciliation and life.

Father, Forgive Them
Luke 23:33-34

Experts say that most crucified people died of asphyxiation. Hanging from one's wrists would collapse the lungs, making it difficult to breathe. To take a breath, the victim would need to push up against the nails in his feet, while the bones in the wrist would rotate against the nails that had penetrated them, and the wounds on his back would be scraped once again by the rough wood. All of this would bring excruciating pain. Eventually, the victim would stop making this effort, and would die from lack of oxygen. The four Gospels record four times Jesus spoke while on the cross. The effort it would take to draw in enough oxygen to speak means that these words must have been exceptionally important to Him, and therefore, important to study for those who want to understand Him. Consider, then, that one of those seven statements was Him praying for His enemies to be forgiven. Why would He do this? Jesus taught His disciples to love their enemies and pray for those who hated them. That is the requirement of God, and Jesus, as the righteous Son of God, would have sinned if He had not obeyed it.

Yes, I do believe that. Forgiving one's enemies isn't an "extra credit" option for God's people; it is a command. Jesus was fulfilling His role as a perfect sacrifice for sins. But He was also giving His followers an example to emulate. So if you consider yourself a Christian, think about what this moment means in light of the people who have hurt you. Remember, forgiving someone doesn't mean you have forgotten the pain (you can't control how you feel, after all). It also doesn't mean that you trust them and put yourself in harm's way (for instance, an abused child can forgive his father, but that doesn't mean he has to go back home and subject himself to more abuse). It simply means that you don't wish them evil, but hope for their best. You surrender your longing for vengeance.

Notice some things about Jesus' forgiveness here. Notice how He forgave: verbally. He didn't keep it a secret. He let them know in words they could understand that He forgave them. Notice when He forgave: before they were sorry for their actions. He didn't wait for them to apologize. He forgave first. And notice why He forgave: Because they didn't know what they were doing. He understood that they were just human, only sinners. They were not His enemies; they were the ones for whom He was dying. Ask the Savior to teach you to see people through His eyes, including the one who has hurt you. He is not your enemy; he is a lost and hurting soul who Jesus desperately wants to save. Look at him with pity, not resentment, and say, "there but for the grace of God go I." Your forgiveness may be the catalyst for his conversion. And then you have defeated your enemy by making him your friend.

Today You Will be With Me
Luke 23:39-43

We know very little about this man. We don't know his name, how old he was, or what his specific crime was. Luke says he and the other man crucified with Jesus were "criminals." The actual Greek word Luke uses means "evil-doers." This man was no mere petty thief. The Romans did not inflict their cruelest punishment on shoplifters. It can be assumed that he was the worst kind of individual. He had selfishly taken what wasn't his from those who were weaker than he, using violence to do so. He may even have been the leader of a band of thieves. Sooner or later, he picked the wrong target, and was caught. Now this sorry, unrepentant soul faced hard justice, Roman style. Both Matthew and Mark record that both criminals mocked and ridiculed Jesus. Even at the cross, this man was spewing hatred. But somewhere during those six hours, this one criminal had a change of heart. It's easy to see why. Death was approaching, and surely he knew his destiny was dark. He may have started the day a skeptic about Jesus, but after seeing Him face death with courage, forgiving His enemies, this man began to see that Jesus was more than a man. Listen to his words: "We deserve our sentence." He admitted his guilt; always the first step to salvation. "Lord, remember me when you come into your Kingdom." He proclaimed Jesus as Lord. This man would never contribute one thing to God's Kingdom. He would never join a church. He would never be baptized. He would never give a tithe or share the Gospel. Yet Jesus, with one of His precious final breaths, declared Him redeemed. That, my friends, is grace.

Two more words need to be noted: Jesus said "Today." He wasn't promising a future moment of hope. This very day, Jesus said, this man would be with Him. The second word is "paradise." That was actually a Persian word that had entered the language of Israel from their time in exile in Persia. It originally referred to the private gardens enjoyed by the elite Persian nobles. Jesus was telling this dying man of a much better place that awaited Him, within a few brief moments. For all Christ-followers, this is a story of incredible hope. If this man, who only turned to Jesus in his final moments, had paradise in his destiny, we surely have something to look forward to as well.

Behold your Mother
John 19:25-27

There are so many questions I want to ask you, Mary. What were you doing in Jerusalem that day? Were you just there to celebrate the Passover, like so many devout Jews? Or had you joined His band of followers? Either way, we know you were there. We know what you saw. How did it make you feel to watch your first-born son, your little Yeshua, go through so much pain? You saw His body ripped to shreds. You heard the crowds scream their profanities, their hateful ridicule. Did you understand that He was willingly undergoing this? Did you plead with Him, "Isn't this enough, Yeshua? Make it stop!" Or was His death just as shocking to you as it was to His disciples? We don't know. We can only imagine how you felt; it must have been like having your own heart ripped out. It must have felt like a sword piercing your soul (Luke 2:35). We know who was there with you, too. We know Mary Magdalene was there, that woman even more faithful than the Twelve. We know Mary, the wife of Clopas was there. We also know your sister was there, and Matthew mentions the mother of the sons of Zebedee. Is this the same woman? If so, and we think it is, then James and John were Jesus' cousins. That explains the last person on our list: John. He identifies himself only as, "the one whom Jesus loved." That was His identity.

As far as we know, Jesus only said one thing to you on that day. He said, "Woman, behold your son." Did you think He was talking about Himself at first? Clearly He wasn't, because He then looked at John and said, "Son, behold your mother." Even there, at the cross, He was providing for your needs. He was obeying the fifth commandment, "Honor your father and mother." He was performing the basic responsibility of a child of God. As His apostle Paul would later say in 1 Timothy 5:8, *If anyone does not provide for his own, and especially for those of his household, he has denied the faith and is worse than an unbeliever.* Oh, how can we contemporary believers call ourselves people of God if we don't take care of our aged parents? No matter how much "religious" stuff we do, it is like filthy rags in the sight of God if we, having been brought into adulthood by our mother and father, now ignore them. It is worship that is pleasing in the sight of God to take care of our parents as best we can, to be there for them, to continue to show them love. One more question: Why didn't Jesus entrust you to one of His brothers? Perhaps none of them were believers. Ah, but that would change.

I am Thirsty
John 19:28-29

Before His crucifixion, Jesus had refused to drink wine mixed with myrhh, which would have dulled His senses along with the pain. Now, He asks for a drink. He is given wine vinegar, the beverage of poor men. It's not surprising that Jesus was thirsty. The hours of exposure on a Spring day, along with the blood loss, would inevitably lead to a raging thirst. Jesus is worshipped as divine by billions of people today, but He was also fully human. His body was subject to the same frailties as the rest of us. However, John makes sure we know that Jesus' request wasn't just a result of bodily shortages, but was intended to fulfill scriptural prophecy. John doesn't stipulate which prophecy Jesus was fulfilling, but Psalm 69:21 seems to fit. The entire Psalm is the cry of someone who has experienced unjust suffering, but v. 21 says *They put gall in my food and gave me vinegar for my thirst.* Even the instrument the soldiers use to offer Jesus His last drink, a branch of hyssop, is significant. On the first Passover night, the Jews used hyssop to mark their doors with the blood of lamb, to protect their homes from the death angel. Now Jesus, the once and final Passover Lamb, is shedding His blood to save untold millions.

The theologian AW Pink wrote, "How completely self-possessed the Savior was! He had hung on that cross for six hours and had passed through unparalleled suffering, yet His mind is clear and His memory unimpaired. He had before Him, with perfect distinctness, the whole truth of God. He reviewed the entire scope of Messianic prediction. He remembers there is one prophetic scripture unaccomplished. He overlooked nothing. What a proof is this that He was divinely superior to all circumstances!"

My God, my God
Matthew 27:45-49

Theologians call this "the cry of dereliction." It is a deeply troubling and mysterious utterance. I cannot claim to fully understand it. But here is my attempt to convey what I do understand: There are two main theories of why Jesus said these words. One says that Jesus was describing exactly what He felt in that moment. He had absorbed the guilt of all human sin, and therefore the righteous Father poured out His justified wrath on Him. This is impossible for us to comprehend, since it requires understanding of two difficult doctrines: The idea of the Trinity, and substitutionary atonement. The Trinity is the idea that God is one, but is made up of three distinct persons: Father, Son and Holy Spirit. There has been a joyful relationship of love within the Godhead for all eternity…but it was shattered in that moment. Notably, this is the only time we know of that Jesus didn't refer to God as "Father." Substitutionary atonement means that Jesus took the punishment we deserved for our rebellion against God. Though some see this as cruelty on God's part, or "cosmic child abuse," those objections melt away when we consider that Jesus and God the Father are one. In Jesus, God Himself was standing in our place. In the body of Jesus of Nazareth, He had lived the life we should have lived and now was dying the death we deserved to die. These two difficult concepts are unquestionably biblical, and so perhaps the cry of dereliction was Jesus offering us a small taste of what He was experiencing as our substitute. If Hell is separation from God and His love, then Jesus was suffering the Hell that billions of people (including me) rightly deserve.

The other theory says that Jesus, in quoting the first line of Psalm 22, was signaling victory. After all, if you read that entire Psalm (which we did in the chapter on Messianic prophecy), you see that the second half of the Psalm promises that future generations will know the Lord because of this suffering One. I recently read a list of the "100 Most Epic Opening Lyrics That Will Make You Want to Burst into Song." Some of the songs I knew, and indeed, reading the opening line did bring the entire song to my remembrance. That wasn't true at all for the songs I didn't know, however. For the Jews standing at the foot of the cross, both enemies and friends of Jesus, the songbook they knew was the Psalms. Once they understood what He was saying (apparently some mistook His words for a call for Elijah to rescue Him), they would have remembered the rest of the Psalm. Which theory do I believe? Both, actually. I think Jesus really was experiencing Hell on Earth. I also believe He knew the victory His sacrifice would bring, and referencing Psalm 22 was a way of signaling that victory to all who heard.

On the evening of November 22, 1963, a British audience was watching a satirical play by David Lodge. On stage, an actor portrayed a worker doing his job while listening to a transistor radio. Suddenly, a voice came over the radio with a live news bulletin: "Today, the American president John F. Kennedy was assassinated..." The audience gasped and the actor quickly switched off the radio, but too late. In one sentence, the reality of the outside world had shattered the artificial reality of the play. People were awakened to what was real, and the theatrical production no longer seemed relevant. When we hear these words, "My God, my God…" it wakes us up to the reality that the stuff we think about every day—bills, hobbies, careers, petty conflicts in our relationships—these things are just smoke and mirrors. The true reality is that God exists in perfect righteousness. And He wants us to exist there with Him in a state of righteous bliss. And that hope, that dream was so important to Him that He paid a price we will never fully understand until that moment when we see Him face to face with spiritual eyes. Once we dwell on the cry of dereliction, we never really see the world the same way again.

It Is Finished
John 19:30

When Jesus said, *It is finished,* some assume He simply meant, "My work here on earth is done. Now I can go on to my reward." Certainly, Jesus did everything God sent Him here to do. Certainly, it must have been a relief for Him to die after six hours on that cross, and a night's worth of ridicule and torture before that, and most of all, experiencing the wrath of Almighty God on our behalf. But this was not some murmur of resignation, "Finally, I'm through!" In Greek, it is a single word, *tetelestai.* That word is in the perfect tense. In case you slept through English class in High School, that means He was saying, "It is finished once and for all." In addition, Mark 15:37 says that Jesus uttered a loud cry just before He died, although Mark doesn't say what this cry was expressing. Each of the four Gospel writers tell us different things Jesus said on the cross, so it's hard for us modern readers to know what Jesus' final words were: Was it *Father, into your hands I commit my spirit,* which we are going to look at next? Or was it *It is finished?* We can't know for certain, but here is my theory: The loud cry that Mark records was *It is finished,* then He bowed His head and said *Father, into your hands...* as He breathed His last breath. After all, Mark probably wasn't at the cross, but John was. John was in a better position to hear that last cry and know what He said. So His cry of *tetelestai* was not a sigh of relief, but a shout of victory. I think of the iconic image of Muhammed Ali (then known as Cassius Clay) standing over Sonny Liston, the heavy weight champion who Clay has just knocked out, challenging him to get up if he dared.

There is another meaning to *tetelestai.* In the ancient world, when a customer paid a debt, the merchant would write *tetelestai* across the top of the bill. It was synonymous with "paid in full." I believe that both meanings are in play here. Jesus, as He died, was shouting in triumph over His enemy, while at the same time asserting that a debt had been fully paid. What enemy had He defeated? Whose debt had He paid? Those are very good questions, and we will take them up eventually. But this is what I want us to focus on. Considering the difficulty of speaking while being crucified, everything Jesus said as He died must have been incredibly important to Him. But this statement was so important, He not only spoke it, He shouted it.

Into Your Hands
Luke 23:44-46

Years ago, a woman in my church was dying. She was a devout Christian woman who believed in heaven and had no doubts about her salvation. Yet as death approached, she became very fearful. She lingered for a good two weeks longer than the doctors thought she would, and every moment of those two weeks was agony for her and for her family. She would cry out, over and over again, "Give me life! Give me breath, Jesus!" We asked her if she was uncertain about where she would go when she died. We asked if she felt that there was unfinished business here on earth. To both questions, she answered no. This really distressed her granddaughter, who was a member of my church. She said, "If Granny is a believer, shouldn't she be excited about death? Why is she clinging to life?" The only answer I could give is that while her Granny wasn't afraid of death itself, it was the process of dying she was scared of. After all, she had never experienced that before. Neither had I, and so I couldn't tell her what that would feel like. All I could do was pray for them, and for myself, that someday when I die, I would be able to face death in a way that comforted my loved ones.

As Jesus died, He spoke these words, which must have brought His friends and loved ones a great deal of comfort. Instead of fighting death like my friend, He embraced it. Moreover, He quoted Scripture with His last words: Psalm 31:5. Take a moment to read that Psalm, or at least the first five verses. These are the words of a suffering soul who is calling on God for rescue. Jesus, in His dying breath, expressed confidence that God would rescue Him. Those gathered around the cross didn't know what happens after death. They had seen Jesus raise people from the dead, so they must have figured He knew more about death than they did. They must have wondered how Jesus expected His Father to rescue Him from death, and why He could face it with such calm. They would soon find out.

Strange Day
Matthew 27:45-56

Jerusalem was a major city, so the majority of the populace wasn't at the hill called Golgotha as Jesus died. Chances are, most Jerusalemites didn't even know it was happening. But according to this account by Matthew, who was in Jerusalem that day, eventually everyone in the city must have known something very unusual was going on. First, there was the darkness, lasting from noon until 3:00. Then the earthquake struck. The tearing of the curtain in the temple would have made big news in the city; it was the veil that separated the main temple court from the Holy of Holies, where God's presence dwelt. The raising of *many holy people who had died* is the most mysterious item in this account, and one of the strangest statements in all of Scripture. It is not mentioned anywhere else. Who precisely was raised? To whom did they appear? What happened to them afterward—did they ascend to Heaven or promptly die again? Regardless, this event, monumental as it was, seems to have been overshadowed by the other bizarre happenings of that day.

The most surprising thing of all in this account is the statement of the centurion in v. 54. The term "Son of God" was hardly the terminology a Roman would use. Perhaps He had picked it up in the mocking words of Jesus" enemies (vv. 40 and 43). Moreover, this was a man of violence. He had surely put many men to death. He had also overseen the flogging of Jesus, his cruel treatment at the hands of the soldiers, and the dividing up of His clothing. Why now was he suddenly convinced this man was something more than a common criminal; more, in fact, than a man? Was it only because of the darkness and the earthquake? Or was it the courage and compassion He saw in a man willing to forgive His enemies as He died? Did this man even understand the words he was saying? Was this a true conversion, or simply a rough customer forced to admit, "There was something different about that fella"? Again, as with our questions about the saints who were raised, we can't know these answers fully. What we can say is that, once again, a person far from God comprehended things about Jesus in a way the religious elite missed.

Chapter 10: His Resurrection
1 Corinthians 15:1-8

Paul writes that there are certain things that are "of first importance." These are the things I learned when Jesus came into my life. These are the things that have brought us from death to life. They are the gospel (a word that means "good news" in Greek), the message that can save the world. And what is this message? Jesus died for our sins and was raised on the third day. This is one of many things that sets Christianity apart from all other world religions. Christianity isn't based on one man's revelation and teachings about God; it's about what one man (who claimed to be God) did. In other words, a seeker's decision about Islam comes down to whether she believes Muhammed was telling the truth about his vision of Allah. Her decision about Buddhism depends on whether she believes the teachings of Buddha really do lead to enlightenment. In her mind, Mormonism stands or falls based on whether she believes that Joseph Smith actually heard from God. But with Christianity, it all depends on one event: If Jesus rose from the grave, He was who He said He was. If He stayed dead, then nothing about His life—not His teachings, His alleged miracles, or His courageous death—matters to us. This is why Paul writes later in this same chapter: *If Christ is not raised, our preaching is worthless and so is your faith* (v. 14). For the Christian, the resurrection of Jesus is the most important event in the history of the world.

According to the Internet Movie Database (imdb.com), the most popular movie of all time is *The Shawshank Redemption*. Numerous articles have been written about why a movie about a prison in Maine in the 1940s, a movie that is at times very brutal in content, a film that wasn't commercially successful when it was released, is so beloved today. The general consensus is that it's because *The Shawshank Redemption* is a movie about hope, and that is what the world is looking for. There's a running dialogue in the film between the narrator, Red, and the main character, Andy Dufresne, about hope. Red has been in prison most of his life, and he tells Andy there's no room for hope in prison. Hope can break your heart, drive you insane. Far better to just accept your fate in this lonely, cruel, miserable world. But Andy says hope is the one thing the world can't take from you. In one of the movie's most famous quotes, he tells Red, "Hope is a good thing, maybe the best of things, and no good thing ever dies." We live in a world full of people just like Red. They're longing for something to hope in, but have given up. If the resurrection is true, the gospel is what they need to hear. If the resurrection is true, hope is indeed the best of things…for no good thing really dies.

The Tomb
John 19:38-42

We've already met Nicodemus, the man who visited Jesus at night (John 3) and went away undecided. But Joseph is new to us. Mark tells us that Joseph was a respected member of the Council (ie, the Sanhedrin). Luke tells us that he had not consented to their decision to condemn Jesus to death. And Matthew informs us that the tomb in which they buried Jesus was Joseph's own tomb (perhaps this is what Isaiah was prophesying when he wrote that the Messiah would be *with a rich man in His death*—Isaiah 53:9). So Joseph provided the burial place and claimed the body, and Nicodemus brought the burial spices. He brought 75 pounds worth, which is an exorbitant amount. This was a burial fit for a king. Yet it was given to a man condemned by the most respected men in Judaism and executed by the Roman Empire in a matter befitting the worst of criminals. We cannot begin to understand the courage it took these two men to do what they did. We don't know what happened to them afterward, but we can assume they knew they would be forfeiting their vaunted positions on the Council, as well as their reputations in the community. Family members and friends who had once venerated them would now shun them. Their businesses would suffer. Perhaps they would even lose their homes. And all to declare their allegiance to a dead man. They probably thought to themselves, "I wish I had stood up for Him sooner. Now it's too late."

The Guard is Set
Matthew 27:62-66

After the resurrection, a rumor arose that the disciples of Jesus had stolen His body (see Matthew 28:11-15). Matthew includes this detail so we can know the rumor was not true. The disciples weren't even considering such a daring caper; they were cowering behind locked doors (John 20:19). Whether you believe the account of Matthew of the story spread by the priests, we know the tomb was empty. How do know? Because why else would Matthew mention this story? If Matthew were trying to invent a story about Jesus rising from the dead, he wouldn't make up a plausible explanation for why the tomb was empty. He mentions this story because the tomb WAS empty, and he wanted to dispense with the popular explanation for why that was so. It should be noted that none of Jesus' followers expected Him to rise from the dead. Certainly, He had predicted His resurrection on several occasions, but His disciples were famously unable to understand what Jesus was saying, even when His meaning seems crystal clear to us. First-Century Judaism had no teachings about a resurrected Messiah, either. God's plan in this case seems to have caught everyone by surprise. But then again, so did Christ's birth, His teachings, His life and His death. Sooner or later, people who believe in God need to start realizing that His ways are higher than ours. We cannot predict what He will do next. All we can do is trust that His plan is better than anything we can dream.

Contradictions in the Easter Story?
Mark 16:1-7

Since, as we have already discussed, our decision about Jesus stands or falls on the veracity of his resurrection, many people have noted the apparent discrepancies in the four accounts of the event. True, if you read all four accounts in succession, you quickly notice differences. John says the women went to the tomb while it was still dark, while Mark says it was just after sunrise. Matthew and Mark say that one angel addressed the women when they arrived at the tomb, while Luke and John say there were actually two angels. Some sincere believers find this deeply troubling. Some skeptics think it's proof that the entire story is false. But I say it actually adds to the story's reliability.

First of all, none of these differences represent irreconcilable contradictions. The women were probably staying in Bethany, two miles away from Jerusalem (after all, that's where Jesus and the disciples had spent the previous week). If they left their house in Bethany while it was still dark, it's possible the sun rose while they were on their way to the tomb. So both accounts could be true. Regarding the number of angels, Matthew and Mark do not explicitly say there was only one angel at the tomb. Their focus is on the words that the women heard, not the number of angelic messengers. Saying one angel spoke does not prove that there weren't two angels present. Besides, imagine that all four Gospel accounts of this event were identical. If that were the case, most people would assume collusion on the part of the Gospel writers. As it is now, the four accounts read exactly the way we would expect if four people who weren't present at the events simply shared the parts of the story they could confirm.

To put it another way, imagine a mother has four children. The oldest runs into the house and says, "Mom! The dog was just bitten by a snake! It bit her close to her nose!" The second child enters, and says, "The dog was just bitten by a snake! It was long and dark brown, and it bit her near her ear!" The third child comes in just then and says, "A medium-sized, blackish snake just bit our dog on the side of the face!" Then the fourth comes in and says, "I heard the dog yelp, and I checked her out and she has fang marks near her mouth!" The mom wouldn't know where precisely her dog was bitten, or what precisely the snake looked like who bit the dog. But she would certainly know the dog had been bitten by a snake. Even if you think the differences in the resurrection accounts are irreconcilably different (that is, if you disagree with the previous paragraph), this much is sure: All four writers, recording independently an event that occurred in their lifetimes, believed that Jesus rose from the dead. That is what matters.

A Rolling Stone
Matthew 28:1-4

It's not my purpose here to prove to you that the resurrection happened. That I'll attempt to do in Appendix 2. Here I am focusing on the account of the eyewitnesses. Notice that neither Mark nor Matthew tells us what the actual resurrection was like. I'll save you the trouble of looking it up; neither do Luke or John. All four writers tell us how the resurrection was discovered, but not how it happened. That's because no human was there to see it. Matthew tells us that, in the midst of a great earthquake, an angel from Heaven rolled away the stone that covered the tomb of Jesus, then sat on it. What an odd little detail, don't you agree? Every scholar I have read who has an opinion on this detail agrees that sitting on the rock was the angel's way of signifying triumph. It was as if he was saying, "Well, that stone was no match for me! Now my work here is done." It gives us an idea of the mindset that existed in Heaven on that day. Think about it: The angels had known Jesus for as long as they had existed. They had worshipped Him since time before time. For the past thirty-odd years, however, they had watched, probably in confusion and agony, as He endured poverty, skepticism, criticism, and persecution. Then, most horrifying of all, they saw Him destroyed by His own ungrateful creation. Think of how happy it made the angels to set Him free from that tomb! Think about how joyful they were to see death defeated once and for all! So the angel rolled away the stone so all the world could see that the tomb was empty, and Jesus was alive. Then he sat triumphantly on that rock, swinging his legs, watching in bemusement as the soldiers fainted...and waited for the women to arrive.

Nonsense
John 20:1-2, Luke 24:1-11

Here is another example of the same story told in two very different ways. John reports that Mary Magdalene went to the tomb, saw the stone rolled away, and ran back to the disciples, telling them she didn't know where Jesus was. In Luke's account, Mary and several other women met two angels at the tomb, who reminded them Jesus had predicted He would rise. As I said before, these two accounts aren't necessarily in conflict with each other. John focused on Mary, since (as we shall soon see) she turned out to be a very important figure in this story. The fact that he doesn't mention the other women doesn't mean they weren't there. And the differences in their reports are not irreconcilable, either. Perhaps the women reported everything just as they experienced it (as Luke recorded), but they doubted their own senses, and wondered if perhaps someone had simply stolen Jesus' body (as John indicated). What we know for certain is that women were the first at the tomb. This fact was highly inconvenient for the Jesus followers who wanted to convince the world their Lord had risen. The ancient world was extremely patriarchal, and so the testimony of women was not well regarded. We see this in Luke's account of the disciples' reaction: *But they did not believe the women, because their words seemed to them like nonsense.* If the women themselves were a little shaky on the reality of what they had experienced that morning, the dismissive attitudes of their male colleagues would not have helped. How often are we too arrogant to accept the truth, when it comes to us from a messenger we don't adequately respect?

The Race to the Tomb
John 20:2-10, Luke 24:12

One thing we know about Peter: He liked to be first. First to walk on water. First to identify Jesus as Son of God. First to say, "Even if I have to die for you, I will never leave you." Therefore, it must have gotten under his skin that the other disciple outraced him to the tomb. I wonder if he made an excuse: "I had a rock in my sandal. I tweaked my hammy." And who is this "other disciple?" Scholars are nearly unanimous in agreement that it represents John himself. In the ancient world, it was considered bad form to include oneself in a narrative. John in his gospel refers to himself as "the other disciple," or more often "the disciple whom Jesus loved." In giving himself this title, he isn't implying, "I'm the only one Jesus loved," or "Jesus loved me more than the others." Rather, this is a sign of humility: "I won't include my name, because I'm not important. I'm just someone Jesus loved. That's what gives me significance."

True to fashion, Peter barges straight into the empty tomb. He sees the linen wrappings and—according to Luke—is puzzled. If someone were going to steal the body, why would they unwrap it first? John says of himself that he "saw and believed." Yet in the very next verse, he admits they didn't understand that a resurrection was the plan all along. So what did John believe, precisely? He doesn't tell us. Think about these poor disciples. They had given up everything to follow Jesus. Then, in less than 24 hours, they had seen their master arrested, condemned by His own people, and crucified by the State. They had just spent what was surely the longest, most miserable Sabbath day of their lives trembling and weeping behind a locked door. Then, at the crack of dawn, they encounter their frantic female friends, talking about angels and an empty tomb. When they go to investigate, they find mysterious clues, but no real answers. But the answers were coming…

Mary Magdalene sees Jesus
John 20:11-18

Why didn't Mary recognize Jesus at first? It's important to note that when it says Mary was crying, it refers to the noisy lamentation that is typical in the Middle-Eastern world, not the reserved public mourning of Westerners. Also notice it says in v. 16, "she turned toward Him." So Mary is standing there, weeping violently, stunned by the appearance of two angels and trying to process their message, when someone comes up behind her and asks why she's crying. She sees this person out of the corner of her eye, but doesn't look up at Him until she hears Him call her name. Why does John leave Mary's reply in its original Aramaic instead of translating it into Greek? Because despite what our English translations say, Rabboni doesn't just mean teacher. That would be "rabbi." Rabboni is like saying, "My beloved teacher." Finally, what did Jesus mean by saying, "Don't hold onto me?" He asks her this because soon He will be ascending to be with His Father. So most scholars think what He's saying is, "I know you're excited to see me again, and you should be. But things aren't exactly going to be like they were before. I'm going to the right hand of my Father. So don't cling to my physical form. My Spirit will be with you instead, and that's even better."

But for me, here is the key point about John's version of the story: All four Gospels agree that Jesus rose from the dead that day (vv. 3-10). But only John tells us that both he and Peter were at the tomb, and so was Jesus, but He didn't make Himself known to them. No, He waited until those two had gone, and then He stepped out of the shadows and called Mary. And there was Mary Magdalene, who no one else would have chosen for such an honor. She's a woman, and so her testimony won't be trusted, even by the apostles (see Luke 24:11). She's someone who spent a long time seriously disabled, probably both physically and mentally, and so most of society sees her as damaged goods (see Luke 8:2). She's a woman following a male teacher around, and that just wasn't done. But Jesus says, "I could choose anyone, but I choose Mary." He chose her, not a male disciple, not a religious scholar or a statesman, to be the first eyewitness of His resurrection. In a world where the scales of success are tilted toward a certain privileged few, our God consistently chooses people who most of us would otherwise ignore.

Road to Emmaus
Luke 24:13-21

It's the first Easter (although these people wouldn't have called it that). It's late afternoon (we know this because it's evening when they get to Emmaus, and it would take about two hours to walk there from Jerusalem). Two followers of Jesus are walking to Emmaus, which may be their hometown. The text is about to tell us one of them was named Cleopas. Some believe the other was his wife, but we don't know. We can assume they were in Jerusalem for Passover, and to be near Jesus. After He was crucified on Good Friday, they may have stayed with the other disciples in the upper room. That morning, they had heard the wild stories from Mary Magdalene and some of the other women who said Jesus was alive again, and then Peter and John had run to the tomb and found it empty. They didn't know what to make of this new information. A resurrection was impossible of course, but something weird had happened. Now they were leaving, going home. And suddenly, a stranger comes walking beside them…

Picture these two when Jesus asks them what they were talking about. They stop walking. They stare at Him for a while. They fumble for words, choke back the emotion. Then they tell Him the story of Jesus from their perspective. Note those words: "We hoped He was going to be the one." They had it all mapped out. Jesus was going to be the Messiah they had hoped for, prayed for, dreamed of for generations. They were going to witness the destruction of Israel's enemies and the liberation of her people. And since they were some of the first to believe in Him, surely there would be rewards for them, too. Sure, life was tough now, but soon all the sacrifice would pay off. That's what they had thought just four days ago. Now it was all over. Not only was Jesus dead; He had been crucified. That only happened to the worst criminals. Scripture said *Cursed is anyone who hangs on a tree,* so not only had their own leaders rejected Jesus, so had God, as far as they could tell. Yet their view of reality wasn't even close to the truth—as they were soon to find out, to their immense joy. As they learned that day, only God knows the final score. When it seems most obvious evil is winning, He has a redemptive plan that we can't possibly imagine. And so we need never get discouraged.

Reframing the Story
Luke 24:22-27

In 1972, singer Carly Simon wrote and recorded, "You're So Vain," a scathing indictment of a former boyfriend. For decades, music fans speculated about the identity of the song's subject. In 2003, Simon actually revealed the truth to the highest bidder in a charity auction. For $50,000, one person heard from Simon herself who the song was about; with the condition that he could not reveal the answer to anyone else. Why pay so much? There was only one sure way to know the answer to a question that had been debated for forty years: Talk to the author.

On this day, these two travelers had that same opportunity with the author of the greatest story ever told. Don't you wish you had been there to hear this? We don't know exactly what Jesus said, but I imagine he reminded them of Genesis 3, and how God told the serpent, *You will strike his heel, but he will crush your head,* and then said something like, "Jesus in dying crushed the Devil's power over us forever." I imagine He told the story of Abraham going to sacrifice little Isaac on Mt Moriah, and how the old man told his boy, "God will provide a lamb for the sacrifice," and sure enough God did. I picture Him saying, "Jesus was that lamb! He died so the sons and daughters of men wouldn't have to." I imagine He reminded them of Joshua leading the Israelites into the Promised Land, and then said, "Jesus has opened the door for you to enter into a new kind of life, life more abundant." I imagine he reminded them of Isaiah's prophecies about the suffering servant, who would be bruised for our transgressions and crushed for our iniquities, and by His stripes we would be healed. I imagine He reminded them of Jeremiah's prophecy about God creating a New Covenant with humanity, so that one day, people would be able to know God personally. They wouldn't need to offer sacrifices or go to a priest or worry about whether they were good enough. God would be among them and would be their God. All this time, He's talking, they're walking and drinking it all in. Stories they've heard their whole lives are suddenly opening up to them, and they're seeing all of reality in a brand new way. As they would say later, "Our hearts were burning within us." That is what happens when we learn the truth that sets people free.

Their Eyes Were Opened
Luke 24:28-35

These two people would never be the same again. They had seen Jesus as Israel's Messiah. Then those dreams were crushed. Now they realized that Jesus was so much more than they had even dared to hope. He was the fulfillment of the entire Old Testament. All the Scriptures and stories they had learned and memorized led up to this one man who was God in human flesh. And He was alive! Death had not defeated Him! Their hearts were burning within them because suddenly they knew their world had changed forever…for the better.

Have you ever met a famous person? I've met a few. Once you get beyond that whole feeling of "Wow!" you realize that they are just people. Your life doesn't change when you meet a celebrity. But Scripture tells several stories of people meeting God personally, and they all have this much in common: Whenever anyone comes into contact with God, they are changed forever. When you meet Jesus, you have met God. And if you meet Jesus, really come to know Him, your life is changed forever. You don't just get new information about life. It's not that you are inspired to try harder, either. You literally become a new person. Others who know you say, "What happened to you? You're not the same person you used to be." That's what Jesus came to do. He came to change your life.

The Shock of their Lives
Luke 24:36-44

I think it's entertaining to picture the scene here: Ten of the eleven remaining disciples are there in the upper room after a long, strange day. It started with some of the female disciples telling them the tomb was empty. Then Mary Magdalene claimed to have seen Jesus. Now, near day's end, these two disciples have come racing back from Emmaus to tell the story of their encounter with the risen Christ. As they huddle, puzzling over these bizarre happenings, suddenly Jesus says, "Peace be with you." Ironically, such a soothing greeting startles everyone in the room, as you can imagine; He might as well have said, "BOO!" I doubt the disciples found it as amusing as I do (although I imagine they laughed about it later).

Two things to notice: First, Jesus looked like Himself (nail scars and all), but He had some new abilities. He was now able to appear and disappear at will. That's how He ended up crashing this locked-door party. Second, notice that the disciples themselves doubted. This seems surprising to many, but they weren't expecting Jesus to rise. Some elements within Judaism believed in a general resurrection of the dead at the end of time, but no one in Jesus' day believed a man could cheat death on His own. Even though, as Jesus told them in v. 44, the Word of God had foretold this; even though He had Himself predicted it several times, His followers didn't have any idea it would happen. He went to great lengths to make sure they believed. It was important that they knew He was really back. For those men, it had to be the greatest surprise they had ever experienced.

Doubting Thomas
John 20:24-25

For centuries, this disciple has been known as "doubting Thomas." I don't think that's fair. We don't know much about Thomas, but we do know he was a realist. Back in chapter 11, when the disciples heard that their friend Lazarus had died, they tried to convince Jesus not to go see him in Bethany. They said, "Teacher, didn't they try to stone you the last time you went there?" But Jesus was determined to go. So Thomas spoke up: *Let us also go, that we may die with Him.* Think about His logic. Those men had given up everything to follow Jesus, believing that He was the Messiah, believing that soon, all their hardship and sacrifice was going to pay off. But if He was going to die, then they might as well die too. If He wasn't the Messiah they wanted, it would be better to just be done with life, rather than try to re-build everything they had lost. In chapter 14, we see Jesus talking to His disciples the night before He went to the cross. He tells them, *I am going there to prepare a place for you...I will come back to take you to be with me that you may be where I am. And you know the way to the place where I am going.* Thomas, Mr. Practical, spoke up and said, *Lord, we don't know where you're going. How can we know the way?* And that's when Jesus said, *I am the Way, the Truth and the Life. No one can come to the Father except through me.* Thomas was a detail man. He wanted things spelled out for him. But Jesus said, "You don't need the details Thomas. You just need to know me. I'll take care of the details."

A few days later, when Thomas heard from the ten remaining disciples that they had seen Jesus risen from the dead, he knew what was going on. These poor men were in an extreme state of denial. But Thomas was different. He was a realist. He was practical. It was time to move on and face the hard, cold truth. So Thomas, to make his point more emphatic—and simply for the good of these dear friends of his—said, "I won't believe it unless I shove my finger into those nail scars in His hands and feet. Not until I shove my hand into that gaping spear wound in His side. Now get over this foolishness!" Then, when a full week passed with no sign of Jesus, Thomas' realistic, practical viewpoint was validated. But then came the next Sunday…

My Lord and My God
John 20:26-31

Once again, the Eleven are behind the locked doors of that upper room. It has been a week since ten of them saw Jesus with their own eyes, touched Him with their hands. I wonder if they were starting to doubt that experience, wondering if they had dreamed it all. Yet they were still here in Jerusalem, instead of home in Galilee. Even Thomas was still there. All were hoping for a miracle. Suddenly, they hear a voice: *Peace be with you*, just like before. But this time, He walks right up to Thomas, whose eyes must be like saucers at this point, and He takes Thomas by the index finger and says, "Do you feel that? That's where the nail pierced me." And He lifts His tunic and pushes Thomas's hand into the spear wound at His rib cage. And He says, *Stop doubting and believe.* I don't think Jesus was rebuking Thomas for His slowness to believe the report of the other disciples. No, Jesus was saying, "It's time to start believing in me." You may wonder about this. Thomas had, after all, given up everything to follow Jesus. But that was when he thought Jesus was the Messiah he wanted, as all the other disciples did. He had a plan for His life, and for the nation of Israel. When he met Jesus, he thought to himself, "God has heard my prayers. He is going to make my plans succeed. I just have to bide my time, put up with a few sacrifices for now, and then it will all be great."

Tim Keller was a young man in Sunday School when he heard something that changed his life forever. His teacher said, "Let's assume the distance between the earth and the sun (92 million miles) was reduced to the thickness of this sheet of paper. If that is the case, then the distance between the earth and the nearest star would be a stack of papers 70 feet high. And the diameter of the galaxy would be a stack of papers 310 miles high." Then Keller's teacher added, "The galaxy is just a speck of dust in the universe, yet Jesus holds the universe together by the word of his power." Finally, the teacher asked her students, "Now, is this the kind of person you ask into your life to be your assistant?" Keller realized that his belief in God was invalid. He believed in God as a very powerful assistant, almost like a genie in a bottle who granted your wishes if you rubbed His lamp the right way. But if God is this powerful and you actually met Him, you wouldn't dare try to get Him to do what you wanted. You would instead say, "What can I do for you?" That's what happened to Thomas the Sunday after Easter. He fell on His face and cried out, *My Lord and my God.* Now he didn't just believe in the resurrection, he believed in Jesus. He didn't believe Jesus was the Jewish Messiah, the answer to his dreams…He now knew Jesus was God, and worth devoting his entire life to. Christian tradition tells us that after Jesus ascended into Heaven, this very practical man named Thomas did a very impractical thing. He started telling people about Jesus, and made it all the way to modern-day India. To this day, there are Christian churches in India who claim Thomas as their founder.

Peter is Restored
John 21:1-19

Think of how Peter felt. This was the man who needed to be first. He had boasted that he would never turn his back on Jesus, yet he had denied Him three times. Now the other disciples must have looked at Him differently. Even after Jesus rose again that third day, Peter must have wondered, "Do I still have a place here?" Judas had killed himself; Perhaps Peter thought, "If I had any honor, I'd do the same thing." Jesus had appeared to the disciples twice: Once on Easter Sunday, when He appeared in the middle of a locked room. Then suddenly, He was gone. A week later, He came back to show Himself to Thomas. Then He vanished again. Peter had no time to ask Him where he stood.

Eventually, the disciples left the city and made the long trek back to Galilee. They had to feed themselves and their families, so Peter suggested they go fishing. But after a long night on the water, they came up with nothing. Then they saw Jesus by the water's edge, and Peter dove into the sea in his hurry to get there. Think about it: When Judas realized the enormity of what he had done to Jesus, he ran away. He took his own life. But Peter was the opposite. When he realized what he had done, he just wanted to see Jesus again, just wanted to make things right. So he threw himself into the water, like Forrest Gump swimming to Lieutenant Dan in Bayou Le Batre. And when he got there, what did he find? Another charcoal fire. Another question put to him three times in a row. It had to have reminded him of the courtyard of the High Priest.

I have absolutely no doubt this was engineered by Jesus for Peter's benefit. Why did he specifically ask, "Do you love me more than these?" This was the man who had to be number one. Jesus was asking, "Do you really love me more than anyone else?" But Peter has changed. He doesn't rise to the challenge. He just says, "You know I love you." And why did He ask the question three times, around yet another fire? It was the Lord's way of saying to Peter, "You're still mine. I forgive you. Not only that, you're still the Rock. I still want you to tend my sheep." Peter was never the same after this day. He preached at Pentecost, healed a crippled man, stood boldly before the Sanhedrin, overcame racial obstacles in Caesarea, escaped miraculously from jail twice, wrote Scripture, and ultimately died the courageous death of a martyr. But none of it would have happened if he hadn't come to Jesus when he was broken.

Appearances
1 Corinthians 15:1-6

After His resurrection, Jesus appeared to other people not recorded in the Gospels. Paul wrote 1 Corinthians in the mid-50s AD, probably before any of the Gospels were written, and he tells of Jesus appearing to five hundred believers at the same time. Who were these people? Where did it happen? What did He say to them? Unfortunately, this is the only account we have of this event, so we don't know any of those answers. But Paul does include one important detail: *...most of whom are still living.* His point is, "If you ever doubt that Jesus really rose from the dead, check with one of these people. They're still alive, and they will tell you." Keep in mind also that speaking about the resurrection of Jesus was a high-risk activity. It was likely to get you booted from your synagogue and ostracized by your neighbors at best. At times, it could result in more violent persecution against the growing Jesus movement. Yet there were still hundreds of people who claimed to have seen Jesus risen from the dead. As Paul goes on to say in that chapter, without His resurrection, the entire Christian enterprise would be a farce. Actually, he puts it better: *If Christ has not been raised, our preaching is useless and so is your faith...If Christ is not raised, your faith is futile; you are still in your sins* (v. 14, 17). Why is this so? Because the Jesus movement wasn't a new religion; it was good news. This good news said that our God had come to this world, faced death for us, and conquered it forever. Sadly, in the centuries since then His movement has often presented the world with a message that seems like anything BUT good news. We need to return to the spirit of those five hundred eyewitnesses: "I don't know all the answers. I'm nowhere near perfect. All I know is that our Savior is alive."

My Brother the Messiah
1 Corinthians 15:7-8

We have already talked about the tension that existed in Jesus' own family. His brothers didn't believe in Him and mocked His claims (John 7:1-5). They even, along with Mary, tried to interrupt His ministry and take Him home by force (Mark 3:20-35). I wonder if there was any sibling resentment involved in their feelings. I can't imagine how many times James must have heard, "Why can't you be more like Jesus?" from neighbors, teachers, even his own parents. Keep in mind also that the oldest son was expected to provide for a widowed mother, but Jesus was instead traveling the country as a penniless, homeless teacher. When the criticism and rumors began ("He consorts with sinners," "He's possessed by a demon," "All the leaders of our people are opposed to Him"), they were probably filled with rage toward Him. Nowhere in the Gospels do we see any indication that any of His brothers had come around, either. It gives an added poignancy to what John wrote in John 1:11, *He came to His own, but His own did not receive Him.*

Yet when we read Acts 1:14, we see His brothers there with the men and women who believed in Jesus, including Mary. Keep in mind, they joined the Jesus movement just when things were getting really tough. This little band would face hardship and persecution on a level we can't possibly imagine. Many would be martyred. James would go on to be the leader of the Jerusalem church and would write a book of the New Testament. Jude would write a book in the New Testament as well. Why would His brothers change their minds? Paul tells us why: They (or at least, James) saw Jesus risen. I have one brother. I love him and am very proud of him. But I am also well aware of his humanity and flaws. What would it take for me to decide my brother was divine? He would have to rise from the dead. The faith of Jesus' own brothers is a wonderful confirmation that Christ really did rise.

The Great Commission
Matthew 28:16-20

Christians know this passage as "The Great Commission." Many can quote all or at least part of it from memory. Mission agencies and churches have these words inscribed on plaques or etched into walls. Countless sermons have been preached on this text. These are our marching orders as followers of Christ. Yet scholars tell us that there are actually several "Great Commissions." Jesus delivered very similar messages in Luke 24:44-49 (which we'll look at next), John 20:21-23, and Acts 1:8. When you study these passages side-by-side, you can see that these are not recordings of one moment told four different ways; the language of each is unique. That means that, on at least four occasions during the forty days Jesus spent on Earth after His resurrection, He told them to focus on taking His message to others. Many times, I have heard irreligious people complain about the attempts of Christians to convert them. "Keep your religious beliefs to yourself. I hate it when people try to force their beliefs on me." "The world would be better off if religious people wouldn't try to convert others." The problem with such sentiments is that a Christian who doesn't talk about her faith is not being faithful to her Savior. In fact, she's directly disobeying a command so important, He repeated it over and over again in His final days. Do Christians ever do a poor job of communicating the Gospel truth? Absolutely. Does God want us to be obnoxious, judgmental, arrogant or accusatory? Of course not. But one gets the distinct impression that the greatest thing we can ever do for Him is to tell others about His saving love.

Power from on High
Luke 24:44-49

If you had been a bookie in first-century Jerusalem, what odds would you have given that the Jesus movement would survive once he was gone? Keep in mind, His disciples had shown almost zero aptitude for leadership. They were spiritually obtuse, cowardly, uneducated, and prone to fighting amongst themselves. If someone came to you and said, "I'll bet my life savings that these Jesus people will be bigger than the Roman Empire someday," you'd take that bet in a heartbeat. Yet within a couple decades, people were calling the Jesus followers, "These people who have turned the world upside down." As one historian said, "Today, we name our children after Peter, John, Matthew, and Mary. We name our dogs after the Roman Emperors." How did that happen? Jesus' words came true: His followers waited in Jerusalem until they were clothed with power from on high. The story is in Acts 2. The Holy Spirit comes to live inside ordinary men and women on that day, and two thousand new believers are added to the Jesus movement before the sun sets. That was just the beginning. This power included the ability to (at times) heal the sick or even to raise the dead. But those were scattered instances. Mostly, the power meant they loved their enemies. They sold their possessions to help the poor. They lived such joyful lives, people started wanting what they had. They told people the story of Jesus, His death and resurrection wherever they went. They even—eventually—started crossing racial boundaries, led by a man who was once an uber-nationalist, Gentile-hating super-Jew named Saul of Tarsus.

The book of Acts records the story of the first few decades of the Jesus movement (it didn't become known as Christianity until much later). When we read Acts, it's heartbreaking to notice how different the Church's behavior and impact on society is today than in those early days. What happened? Certainly God hasn't changed. His love for the world is still the same. His power is still available. The conclusion I reach is this: Those of us who call ourselves by His name should be praying daily—with all our hearts—for that power from on high to change us as well.

Ascension
Acts 1:6-12

Luke wrote the book of Acts, which means that he actually recorded this same story twice. His other version is at the very end of his Gospel, Luke 24:50-53. From that account, we know two details: First, the ascension took place on the Mount of Olives, a hill just two miles from Jerusalem, near the village of Bethany where their friends Lazarus, Mary and Martha lived, and near the Garden of Gethsemane. Second, the disciples returned to Jerusalem filled with joy after they saw Jesus go into the clouds. That detail still surprises me. One would think that their emotions would be a combination of shock and terror. "No, Lord! We just got you back from the dead. Now you're leaving? You've told us we have to take this message around the world. How are we supposed to do that without you?" At least, that's how I imagine I would feel. Even in the moments just before Jesus ascends to the sky, they are asking Him, "When does the Kingdom start?" In other words, they still don't understand the plan. They still think Jesus is here to bring an earthly Kingdom in this age. So how did they go from confusion to joy? For one thing, they must have been happy for Him. He was their Hero, their Savior, and now, like a valiant soldier after the end of a war, He was going home. But they also must have been joyful for themselves. They now knew, like never before, that Jesus was absolutely right about Himself. He was God come down to Earth. And that meant that God was with them, would enable them to fulfill all that He had commanded them to do, and would keep all of His promises.

In his outstanding book *The Jesus I Never Knew,* Philip Yancey admits he views this story with a very different emotion. He finds himself wishing Jesus had not ascended. After all, He left the movement in the hands of frail, foolish creatures like us. Centuries later, we look back at the Crusades, the Inquisition, the slave trade, clergy sex scandals, and a multitude of other ecclesial atrocities, and wonder, "What was He thinking?" Yancey concludes with three observations that have helped him with the idea of the ascension. First, the Church has brought much more light to this world than darkness. If you doubt that assertion, re-read the first chapter of this book. Second, Jesus knew full well how fallible His people were. Yet He loved them anyway. Look at how He treated Peter, especially after Good Friday. And third, as he puts it: "How can an unholy assortment of men and women be the Body of Christ? I answer with a different question: How can one sinful man, myself, be accepted as a child of God? One miracle makes possible the other."

Chapter 11: The promise of His return
Acts 1:11

William Miller was a farmer in upstate New York, a veteran of the War of 1812, and a devout Baptist. He became convinced that one could use Daniel 8:14 as a key to anticipate the day Christ would return and this present world would end. Eventually, friends persuaded him to publicize his theory. Soon, as many as a half million people in multiple countries and across multiple Christian denominations had become swept up in "Millerism." As the day approached, many sold houses and farms and began to gather in churches, awaiting the trumpet call of God. When Miller's date passed with no Second Coming, he recalculated and set another, then another. The failure of his third date is known today among his latter day followers as "The Great Disappointment."

I wish I could tell you that was the only time Christians had embarrassed themselves—and their cause—by claiming to know when, where and how Christ was returning. Sadly, there are too many of these stories to name. And it certainly didn't end with William Miller. It seems that every year, there's another wild-eyed preacher or would-be prophet who gains brief notoriety (or enters the bestseller list) with the latest End-Times prediction. Unfortunately, today many Christ-followers make the opposite error: They avoid thinking, studying or talking about His return. Many seem to think, "It's impossible to understand this stuff, anyway. Whatever is going to happen will happen." His first followers certainly didn't think that way. His return was a subject they thought about constantly. It motivated the way they lived. In this chapter, we'll take a look at the things Jesus and the apostles said about His Second Advent.

Jesus the Judge
Matthew 16:24-27

There's a common perception of Jesus that many Christians find too comforting to abandon. Some call it "Gentle Jesus, meek and mild." We hear it in some of our favorite old hymns ("In The Garden" comes to mind). We see it in religious art: Jesus holding a baby lamb; Jesus stooping to look a small child in the eye. In these depictions, Jesus is frail, handsome and therapeutic, like a long-haired Mister Rogers. He certainly doesn't look or sound like a Palestinian carpenter. Nor does He seem like the sort of man who would cast out demons, flip tables, or call the religious elites "whitewashed tombs" to their faces. It's impossible to reconcile that image of Jesus with what He says here. Yet, if you are a Christian, you must come to grips with the hard sayings of Jesus, too. This is the One who died for your sins. Your Savior is not just a gentle, loving shepherd (although He is certainly that); He is also a righteous Judge who will hold each of us accountable.

Keep Calm
Matthew 24:1-8

Matthew 24 contains Jesus' longest single teaching about His return. It's often called The Olivet Discourse, since it happened on the Mount of Olives, where Jesus and the disciples were spending nights the week of Passover (Jesus would be crucified that Friday). It began when Jesus prophesied that the Temple would be destroyed. For proud Jews like the Twelve, this was a terrifying statement. The Temple was a symbol of national pride; with the Romans in charge, the Temple was all they had left. If Israel had possessed its own currency, it's quite possible the Temple would have been on one side of the coins. But even more, the Temple was thought by Jews to be the place where God dwelled. It had been destroyed once before, by the invading armies of Babylon. Judah's prophets at that time—Jeremiah and Ezekiel—had made it clear that God was allowing this to happen. For the Twelve, hearing that the Temple would be destroyed again was tantamount to hearing that God was leaving Israel. Jesus' prophecy came true, by the way. The Romans under Titus destroyed the Temple in 70 AD. Most of those who heard the Olivet Discourse were probably still alive when it happened. It has never been rebuilt.

The Twelve couldn't imagine such an event occurring unless the end of the world was upon them. So in v. 3, they think they are asking one question, when in actuality, they are asking two: "When will these things happen?" and "What will be the sign of your coming and of the end of the age?" Jesus will answer both questions here. Interestingly, He begins by urging us not to jump to conclusions. Wars, rumors of wars, false Messiahs, natural disasters…these are all just the beginning of birth pains. When my wife was pregnant with my son, the pastor of my home church put this message in the church bulletin: "Pray for Jeff and Carrie Berger—baby imminent." A lady in the church called her daughter-in-law, a nurse, concerned because she thought "imminent" meant the baby had some dread disease. We had a good laugh when we heard that story. But it's appropriate that Jesus uses the image of labor pains here. When a woman feels a contraction, it doesn't mean the birth is happening in the next few minutes. But it is a reminder that a baby is coming. Jesus wants us to look at earthly turmoil the same way. Don't lose your mind and start predicting the End…but remember that this world is giving way to something far better someday.

Then the End will Come
Matthew 24:9-14

Biblical prophecy is notoriously difficult to interpret. And, as I have said, Jesus was prophesying about two future events here, not one: The destruction of the Temple and His return at the end of earthly history. So there are plenty of times when one must wonder which event He is talking about. My theory is that in these verses, He is describing for His disciples what life will be like for them in the coming years before His return. Everything He foretells in these six verses indeed happened in the first decades of the Church: Disciples were handed over to hostile powers, who tortured and killed them (Church tradition says eleven of the twelve were martyred). Under threat of persecution, some Christians did renounce their faith, while others boldly braved the flames, the sword, and the ravenous beasts in the arena. False prophets did arise; there is a long list of heretical movements that arose in those early days. And the Gospel did begin to spread throughout the world. That last prophecy must have surprised His disciples, who thought of Jesus as exclusively a Messiah of the Jews. It would take them and their followers quite a while to embrace the idea of a worldwide Jesus movement, but it happened…just as He said. It is still ongoing to this day. So when life seems difficult for us as Jesus followers, we need to remember: He said it would be this way.

Dark Days
Matthew 24:15-28

In 70 AD, Titus, the son of the newly christened Emperor Vespasian, laid siege to Jerusalem. Three months later, the city fell. Of this event, D.A. Carson has written, "There have been greater numbers of deaths—six million in the Nazi death camps, mostly Jews, and an estimated twenty million under Stalin—but never so high a percentage of a great city's population so thoroughly and painfully exterminated and enslaved as during the Fall of Jerusalem." Jesus knew many of the people listening to Him on the Mount of Olives this day would live to see these events. He wanted to spare them as much pain as possible. Picture Him, perhaps with tears rimming his eyes, as He helps them foresee one of the darkest moments in human history.

He speaks of "the abomination that causes desolation," a term used several times in the book of Daniel (9:27, 11:31, 12:11). Most scholars think Daniel was referring to the Syrian King Antiochus Epiphanies, who erected an altar to Zeus in the temple and sacrificed a pig on it. But that event happened hundreds of years before Jesus. So here, He must be talking about the Roman armies, with their pagan standards, invading and desecrating the holy city. His warnings are practical: Run from roof to roof to get out of the city; don't take the time to go downstairs and pack your belongings. They are also compassionate: It is hard to imagine any other first-century male expressing concern for pregnant women and nursing mothers. But most of all, He wants His followers to avoid being deceived. In times of great stress, charlatans and lunatics can often accumulate their own cults. We have seen it many times in our own nation's history. Jesus' words in vv. 27-28 seem mysterious to us, but His point was straightforward: "When I come back, everyone will know it. Until then, don't be deceived by those claiming to be me."

Be Ready
Matthew 24:29-44

As I said when we started our look at Matthew 24, it's hard to get a handle on biblical prophecy, especially the prophecies regarding the End. That shouldn't surprise us; in spite of the abundance of prophecies that described Jesus' first coming—including His place and manner of birth, His life, miracles, personality, rejection by His people, humiliating death and rise from the grave—none of God's people predicted it would happen in the way it did. Their vision of those prophecies' fulfillment turned out to be miles from God's actual plan. What makes us think we're going to do better the second time around? So here, as Jesus turns His prophecy from the events of 70 AD to "the end of the age" (at least, that's how I interpret this passage), we need to approach His words with great humility. Here is my opinion on a couple of key questions: First, when Jesus says in v. 29, "immediately after the distress of those days," He is not prophesying His return immediately after the Fall of Jerusalem. Remember, up to this point He has been describing life on Earth before His return. All of "the distress of these days" will lead up to a climactic end to this era of world history. Also, when He says in v. 34 that *this generation will certainly not pass away until all these things have happened*, He is not predicting His return will happen while the current generation is still alive. After all, in the very next thought (v. 36), He says no one knows when that will happen, *not the angels, nor even the Son* (a remarkable statement in itself), *but only the Father*. He must be talking about the events of this era, the "distress" of these days, including the fall of Jerusalem. People listening to Him that day would experience all those things.

Sadly, people have taken these words of Jesus, intended to keep us from becoming hysterical, and misused them to promote end-times hysteria. They have taken the teachings of a Savior so humble He disavowed complete knowledge of the time and place, and used them to read their own opinions into current events, authoring bestsellers and garnering donations from people whose devotion is sadly far greater than their discernment. In the end, there are two things we know for sure from Jesus' teachings on the End: 1) He is coming back. 2) We'd better be ready. If we focus on those two truths, we cannot fail.

A Comforting Promise
John 14:1-3

This passage is often read at Christian funerals. Often, the reader (or preacher) reads from the King James Version, in which v. 2 reads as follows: *In my Father's house are many mansions: if it were not so, I would have told you. I go to prepare a place for you.* The preacher will often say something like, "Jesus was a carpenter. And he has been working on a mansion for our friend for over 2000 years now. Can you even imagine how beautiful her mansion is now?" That is a comforting thought. But it's not what Jesus meant when He spoke those words. First of all, when the King James Bible was translated (in 1611), the word "mansion" didn't mean a huge, elaborate home. It meant a room. This should be obvious from the context; how could the Father's "house" contain many "mansions"? This is why most modern translations render it differently. The point is that there is plenty of room for us to be with God. When Jesus says "I am going to prepare a place," He is not talking about building a literal structure, but about the work that He is about to do. He is speaking these words during the Last Supper; in mere hours, He will be arrested. By the next sundown, He will be dead. That is how He is "preparing a place for us." He is doing what it takes to make sure we can be in His Father's house (in other words, with Him) forever.

Finally, note v. 3. This isn't about where we go when we die. The focus is on Jesus' return. "I will come back and take you to be with me." Many of us yearn for information about the world to come. Many of the answers we're seeking are in the Bible, but here, we are left only with the knowledge that we will be with Jesus for eternity. If you grew up in church, you might find this new look at a familiar passage disconcerting. You've probably heard a lot of "mansion" imagery in sermons and hymns. Might I make a suggestion? You could consider the possibility that the God who owns all things, possesses all power, and loves you beyond measure has a better plan for your eternity than living in some celestial version of a gated community. Somehow, I think you and I won't be at all disappointed.

The Coming Feast
Matthew 26:27-29

Growing up, Christmas was always my favorite holiday. Now that I am an adult, I prefer Thanksgiving. I'm not talking about the deeper meaning of the day; in that case, my answer would be Easter. I'm talking about how we observe the holiday. I enjoy Thanksgiving more than Christmas because there is no pressure to find the perfect gift, no forced deadlines or indebtedness. It's just food, family and football, all day. And those are three of my favorite things (though not necessarily in that order, of course). On the night before He died, Jesus said something else that gets us excited about His return; He gave a hint of what will one day be by far my favorite holiday.

When He predicted He wouldn't drink from the fruit of the vine until He drinks it anew in His Father's Kingdom, that was a significant statement. Wine was a drink of celebration in His culture. Remember, His first miracle was providing wine for a wedding feast. Jesus spoke several times about a great wedding supper at the end of this age (Matthew 22:1-14, 25:1-3, John 3:29). This idea was embraced by the early church (Revelation 19:6-9, 21:1-17). Did Jesus mean that His return would set off the greatest celebration in history? I think so. Doesn't it comfort you to know that when Jesus was trying to picture for us what would happen when He returned, He didn't compare that event to a somber service in the synagogue? He said the closest thing we have on Earth to which to compare that day is a party. That is such good news!

Restoration Time
Acts 3:11-21

The context here is that Peter and John have healed a man outside the Temple in Jerusalem. This, naturally, draws a crowd of onlookers, and the two apostles don't waste the opportunity. Note how bold Peter is. He lays the blame for Jesus' death on the people of Jerusalem without reservation (*You killed the Author of life...*), yet He also extends to them a beautiful offer of grace: *Repent...so that your sins may be wiped out, and times of refreshing may come from the Lord.* The appeal worked; many—perhaps thousands—became believers that day. They felt the weight of Peter's words. They knew they were responsible for the death of an innocent man—not just any man, but the Author of Life Himself. Yet in the same breath, they heard that there was total forgiveness and new life available. Is it any wonder the message of the Church was called the Gospel (Good News)?

But notice what Peter says in v. 21: *Heaven must receive Him until the time comes for God to restore everything, as He promised long ago through His holy prophets.* Jesus isn't just a present Savior. He's coming again. And when He does, everything will be restored. What did God promise through His holy prophets? Isaiah and Ezekiel both speak of a New Earth. As you read their descriptions (Isaiah 11 and 60-66, Ezekiel 40-48), it sounds in some ways like the present world: Physical, familiar. But some things will be radically different. Wolves will lie with lambs. Death will be abolished. Cities will be places of beauty, not blight. Every molecule that exists will point perfectly to its creator. And there will be peace among men and women. That became the hope of every Christ follower. It still is.

The Transformation of Our Bodies
Philippians 3:20-21

Paul is writing about something that is promised to us many times in Scripture, that was the hope of Christians for most of history, but few people today seem to know about it: We will be resurrected. That means that eternity is not going to be like what you see in movies or comic strips, with clouds and harps and haloes. It's not even going to be like what you sometimes hear fellow Christians say: "Well, God needed another angel, so He took her home." No, God didn't need anything. And she's not an angel. She is very much herself, waiting in paradise for the day Christ returns, when she will receive a brand-new body. Notice it says our bodies will be like Christ's glorious body. That means a body that will never get sick, never get hurt, never die (There's a more detailed look at the resurrection—and our new bodies—in 1 Corinthians 15). That means my friend who contracted polio as a little girl and has been in a wheelchair ever since, will run and jump and dance. That means my family members who have faded away from us with Alzheimer's will have clear, diamond-sharp minds. That means we'll never go the hospital again, or the nursing home, or the funeral home. But it means something even better than those things.

The word "glorious" refers to the glory of God. We were created by God to display His glory. But ever since the first sin, these bodies of ours have gotten in the way. Our mouths say hateful stuff. Our minds are full of anger, lust, greed and fear. Our hearts want the wrong things, and we make terrible decisions that hurt other people and leave us miserable. I don't know about you, but this is my testimony: I am a lot better than I once was, and that's exciting. But I am still tired of failing. I wish I could hard-wire my body to always want the right things, to always say what benefits others, to always think pure thoughts. The good news is that is our future. At the beginning of Philippians (1:6), Paul wrote, *He who began a good work in you will bring it to completion on the day of Christ Jesus.* In other words, this massive renovation project that God begins in your life on the day you come into His family will finally be complete. God will unveil His masterpiece, and it will be you. You will be redeemed and glorious from your head to your toe, and you will never, ever have any cause for shame or guilt again.

Creation Groans
Romans 8:18-25

In one of C. S. Lewis' *Narnia* books, *The Silver Chair,* the three young heroes are captured by the Queen of the Underworld. She tries to convince them that Narnia, the world they know, is just a child's fairy tale. Only the underworld is real. There is no sun, no grass, no trees, no wonderful talking lion named Aslan. At first, her spell works. Then one of the three heroes breaks the spell by saying, "Suppose we *have* only dreamed, or made up, all these things…Suppose we have. Then all I can say is that the made-up things seem a good deal more important than the real ones. Suppose this black pit of a kingdom of yours is the only world. Well, it strikes me as a pretty poor one. And that's a funny thing, when you come to think of it. We're just babies making up a game, if you're right. But three babies playing a game can make a play-world which licks your real world hollow." The three soon escape the underworld and return to Narnia, where they see once and for all that the things they dreamed of and desired were real after all.

According to Romans 8, the entire universe feels like Lewis' heroes. Now, obviously, the universe itself doesn't have feelings. Paul is using an anthropomorphism to say that all of the things that seem wrong about this world, from the cruelty we see in the animal kingdom to the chaos created by natural disasters to the violence in human civilization, testifies to the fact that things aren't the way they are supposed to be. As v. 20 indicates, this world is under a curse. Our sin brought a curse upon us and upon the world around us. So as we follow Christ, He begins His process of redeeming us. And as we follow Christ and do the things He leads us to do, we're redeeming the world—stamping out hate and loneliness and violence and poverty and sickness and emptiness through the love of Christ. Someday, that redemption will be complete. We will be fully redeemed as we enter new, imperishable, powerful, sinless bodies. And this world will be redeemed as God strips away the last vestiges of sin's curse. Creation is yearning for us—the sons of God—to be revealed, because that's the day Creation gets its redemption, too.

What Success will Look Like
1 Thess. 2:19-20

We have a weird way of defining success in our times. For instance, we think fame is an indicator of success, yet celebrities often appear to be the unhappiest people on earth. We value wealth, which seems more practical, until you consider that money is fleeting. One bobble in the stock market, one foolish investment, one encounter with a huckster, and our whole house of cards comes tumbling down. We treasure power, but when you're on top, there is always someone out to unseat you. In the words of Shakespeare, "Uneasy lies the head that wears a crown."

Paul sought a different kind of success. He knew that on the day Jesus returned, money, fame and power would be irrelevant. The only thing that lasts forever is people. He looks forward to the day when he will "glory" in his friends the Thessalonian believers in the presence of Jesus. That word "glory" means, "take pride in." I picture the old apostle introducing his friends to Christ the way a grandfather would show a friend pictures of his grandkids. Only, instead of bragging about their accomplishments in academics, athletics or music, or even about their good looks, Paul would boast in the way his friends had been formed into the image of Christ. He even calls them his crown. That is not a royal crown, but the wreath a champion would receive in the Olympic games. Paul says to the Thessalonians, "You are my trophy, my gold medal. You are my life's work. The most significant thing I will ever do is invest myself in your spiritual growth." People matter to God. Jesus believed that so profoundly, He died for them. That's what He calls His followers to devote their lives to.

We will Rise
1 Thess. 4:13-5:4

What do you say to someone who is grieving a loss? In my experience in ministry, it is often best to say as little as possible. Our words can't take away their grief. In fact, they can compound it. So don't try to explain why this happened, defend God, or show them the alleged silver lining of their current cloud. Just be there for them. That is what they need.

There are exceptions, of course. Paul the apostle spoke words of comfort to his friends who were upset about members of their church who had died. Apparently, they were under the impression that Jesus would return during their lifetimes. They worried that their friends who had died would miss out on the glory of His coming. Notice what Paul doesn't say here: "Don't worry. They're with Jesus now. All their problems are over. And we'll go there too someday." That is, in fact, what Paul believed happened to a Christ-follower at death (see 2 Corinthians 5:1-10), but it wasn't what comforted him. Instead, He tells of the resurrection at the end of this age. For most of Christian history, that has been the hope of God's people. Older tombstones often bear slogans such as "I will rise." It is only in the past hundred years or so that Christians have begun to focus on a disembodied existence outside this world. But Jesus isn't planning an evacuation for His children; instead, He is ready to complete this world's redemption.

Payback for the Persecuted
2 Thessalonians 1:5-10

We Americans are inconsistent when it comes to the idea of vengeance. We seem to love movies about a wronged hero who exacts bloody justice on his/her persecutors (*Death Wish, Braveheart, Gladiator, Taken,* and *John Wick* are just a few examples of blockbusters with this theme). I suspect their popularity is because we enjoy watching bad guys get what's coming to them. We can vicariously feel that we, too, are getting some measure of justice for the wrongs done to us. At the same time, passages like this one are rarely preached in American churches. Believers would rather not contemplate a vengeful Jesus. And the irreligious find the concept repulsive.

But deep down inside, we know there is evil in this world that must be set right. The popularity of the revenge action movie is proof that, in our hearts, we want to see justice done. For yet more proof, think about how we feel when a rapist goes uncaptured, or a murderer walks away scot-free on a legal technicality, or a corrupt executive receives a slap on the wrist while thousands lose their savings because of his malfeasance, or a cruel dictator rules in luxury for decades. To take the argument even further, remember Jesus' command to love our enemies, and to pay back evil with good. If He gave us this command without also promising to defend us, He would be unspeakably cruel. As it is, we can obey Him knowing that there will be justice in the end, one way or another. The Thessalonians, facing persecution for nothing more than their faith, could avoid descending into either hatred or despair through knowing that right would triumph in the end. And finally, God's mercy is present even in these words. When Paul writes in v. 8 that He will punish those *who do not know God and do not obey the Gospel*, think about what that means. The Gospel isn't a list of rules to be obeyed; it is good news. Even the rapist, the murderer, the crook, the despot…even they can be redeemed through the shed blood of Christ for their sins. The one who, in the end, is *shut out from the presence of the Lord* has chosen that destiny for himself by rejecting Christ's sacrifice on their behalf. God's justice is complete.

The Finish Line
2 Timothy 4:6-8

To me, 2 Timothy is Paul's most emotionally resonant letter, and these words are the high point. The apostle is old here, locked in a Roman jail once again. This time, he knows he will never again taste earthly freedom. He is cold, tired, and—aside from his faithful friend Luke—all alone. He writes to his young protégé Timothy, hoping to see him before winter. The executioner's ax is waiting; a bitter end to a life full of courage, eloquence and tireless communication of God's grace. Yet he writes defiantly of rewards that neither Rome nor his enemies can take away. He pictures his life as a race, and the finish line is approaching. He knows that he has done what he was put here to do. He has stayed faithful to one who changed his life on the road to Damascus (see Acts 9). Now he knows a "crown of righteousness" awaits him. We might read Paul's words as arrogance, similar to an athlete who guarantees victory before the game begins. But when you read Paul's writings, you see a man who often called himself "the chief of sinners," who frequently reminded people that he had once persecuted the Lord's Church, who said his greatest strength came when he was at his weakest, and who is responsible, more than any other human, for our understanding of salvation by grace alone (See Ephesians 2:8-9 for one of many examples). He is looking forward to seeing Jesus face to face, not because he feels worthy, but because he knows that the Christ who died for his many sins will not turn him away. He knows that on that day, he will not receive what he deserves, but what Jesus purchased for him at the atonement. That is how a person can face certain death with joy and hope.

The Blessed Hope
Titus 2:11-14, 1 Peter 1:13

Randy Alcorn has written a book, simply titled *Heaven,* which does a fantastic job of compiling all the Biblical information about the world to come, and helping the reader think through it, even visualizing it. Near the beginning, he tells the story of Florence Chadwick, a young woman who, in 1952, attempted to become the first woman to swim from Catalina Island to mainland California. She braved frigid, shark-infested waters and pea-soup fog for fifteen hours. A boat lingered nearby, with her mother and others onboard to assist her if needed. At last, she begged to be taken out of the water. It was only then that she found out she was less than half a mile from her goal. She said later that the fog was what discouraged her the most: "I think if I could have seen the shore, I would have made it."

What she was speaking of was hope: The certainty that something better is coming, which keeps us going when life gets hard. We can't exist without hope…at least, not for long. Both Peter and Paul, the twin pillars of the early Church, believed in hope. It enabled them to do incredibly courageous things. But as Red says in The Shawshank Redemption, "Hope can be a dangerous thing. Hope can drive you insane." He's right. Unless…unless the thing you hope in is foolproof. Peter, Paul and the other early Christians weren't hoping in romance, wealth, success, freedom or any human being when they willingly offered their bodies up for martyrdom. They were looking for "the blessed hope." They were waiting for the return of Jesus, when all wrongs will be made right, and all tears will be wiped away. Why were they so certain? Because they had seen Him risen. They knew He would not fail.

Skeptics will Come
2 Peter 3:3-10

Two things are remarkable about this passage. First, it shows that even in the first century, Peter was predicting that Christ's return would take a while. It would take so long, in fact, that people would begin to doubt it. Some would publicly scoff at the very idea. It has been two millennia since Christ walked the Earth, and we have seen more than our share of skepticism at those promises in that time. The second remarkable thing is the attitude of God toward those skeptics. *He is patient with you, not wanting anyone to perish, but all to come to repentance.* It reminds us of a passage written hundreds of years before Peter's time, Ezekiel 18:23: *Do I take any pleasure in the death of the wicked? declares the Sovereign LORD. Rather, am I not pleased when they turn from their ways and live?* The irony is that when we scoff at the idea of a physical return of Jesus Christ, and a final judgment, it's because of us that He delays. He is giving us time to change our minds, to seek Him and find Him before it's too late. For all the squeamishness modern people feel about the idea of Judgment Day, realize that God the Father desires for everyone to be saved. It is not intolerance to tell people about the Second Coming. It is mercy of the most profound kind.

We will be Like Him
1 John 3:2-3

When American Christians think about the world to come, we often think in terms of our earthly concerns: "Will I be able to play golf (or some other favorite activity)?" "Will my favorite pets be there?" "What will my resurrected body be like?" "Will I recognize my loved ones?" These questions are not inconsequential. Books like Alcorn's *Heaven* are helpful in working through questions like these with the information we have in Scripture. But John indicates that the best part about our new existence is that we will be like Jesus. That doesn't mean we'll be divine; that would contradict the clear teaching of Scripture. It means that the work the Holy Spirit begins in us at our conversion, painstakingly rebuilding our character until it matches that of Christ, will be complete. Imagine never again feeling shame or guilt, never again seeing the wounded look of a loved one you have hurt. Imagine being constantly filled with joy, peace and selfless love for everyone. Imagine seeing every other person through the eyes of a God who loved them enough to die for them. That is our future.

So why does John say we should purify ourselves if we have this hope? Once we know how wonderful our future will be, we naturally want our future to start as soon as possible. We want to experience as much of it as we can right now. We're like residents of a slum who know that someday, at some unknown time, we will move into a community of pristine, white-picket-fence homes. Instead of continuing to live in squalor until that day arrives, we want to clean up what we have. That helps us keep hope alive. And it tells our fellow slum-dwellers, "There's something better coming. This is the best I can do for now, but someday soon, I'll have something far better…and you can too!"

He is Coming
Revelation 1

According to Church tradition, the apostle John was the last living apostle, exiled to the Greek island of Patmos, when he wrote the book of Revelation. It is easily the most controversial book in the Bible. Its imagery is well-known even in our increasingly secular world: 666, the Antichrist, the Four Horsemen of the Apocalypse, Armageddon, and the Day of Judgment are all terms that frequently appear in popular culture. Its meaning is so obscure, some Christians are able to read into it their hopes and fears about current events, while many others find the book so baffling, they avoid it altogether.

I believe Revelation was not written to give us a coded guide to uncover secrets about the End Times, although the return of Christ is certainly a major theme. I think it was written for two reasons: First, to make us aware of unseen realities. The book of Revelation is a reminder that, while we are obsessed over earthly events, there is another dimension of reality we can't even see, and that unseen world affects our lives. Revelation peels back the curtain and gives us a glimpse of what is going on in the world beyond this one. We get peeks at the throne room of Heaven, as well as the unseen armies of darkness. In a way, we're like Frodo at the beginning of The Lord of the Rings; we're just living our lives, eating and drinking and wasting our time, when all along there's a war for the soul of our world that we're totally unaware of. Then one day someone shows us this war, and we have to stand up for good. Life is never the same again. Second, it was written to encourage us. Those first readers of Revelation felt like the darkness was winning. Their children and grandchildren would live in a world in which the Roman Empire would suddenly see Christianity as a threat, and would tell them, "Worship the emperor or be thrown to the lions." They would be the most hated people in the Empire. Do you think these words became meaningful to them? Do you think they took comfort in knowing that someday, Christ would triumph, evil would be destroyed, and this world would be redeemed? I think this is what gave them the courage to face those lions and not back down. I think that's why, in spite of the persecution, over the next two centuries, the Church would spread like wildfire

He is worthy
Revelation 4-5

John gives us a glimpse into the throne room of Heaven. He uses symbolic language, fitting for the apocalyptic style of writing that was often used in that time. I believe the scroll in these chapters represents the plan of God for setting this world right. John weeps when no one steps forward to open the scroll, because he fears this world will never be fixed. Then up steps the Lamb…

He is worthy. That means our world is in good hands. I have a friend who woke up once during surgery. He lifted his head and saw his own body cut open, and saw the blood, and saw the surgeon working on something that he had never seen before, but which was protruding from his body. Fortunately, he was so doped up, he didn't panic. It all seemed like a dream…A dream in which some masked stranger was playing with his innards. The surgeon, in a very calm voice, explained what he was in the process of doing. After a few seconds, my friend fell back asleep. Here's my point: Sometimes our world is so messed up, it seems like we're in the middle of surgery, and we're wide awake for the whole thing. That would be terrifying, unless we know the one doing the surgery, and we trust Him to fix things just right.

Just Wait a Little Longer
Revelation 6

The language that John uses is steeped in Old Testament imagery, and is probably not meant to be taken literally. The sky rolling up like a scroll, the moon turning blood red, and the sun being blotted out...these were ancient ways of saying awful things are going to happen. We do the same thing: If someone says, "All hell broke loose," you and I don't assume they mean that the realm of the unredeemed dead suddenly manifested itself on Earth. At any rate, these are frightening images. But what do they mean? This is part of a theme in Revelation; after the seven seals, there will be seven trumpets, and after that, seven bowls full of God's wrath. There is a lot of speculation about what all these things mean. Some say they describe a time of Great Tribulation just before the End. Others say they describe the pain and hardships of life on Earth until Christ comes back. Remember, in Matthew 24 Jesus said when we see wars and rumors of wars, natural disasters and famines, *don't be alarmed; these are just the beginning of birth pains*. This much is clear: The seals, trumpets and bowls describe an ever-increasing intensity of judgment. In other words, the trumpets are worse than the seals, and the bowls are worse than the trumpets. What does this tell us? At the very least, it means that life on this Earth will get worse before it gets better. Some may say, "No, we are making progress." Yes, we create technologies that enable us to live longer, more comfortable lives. And yes, we write laws that create more freedom and equality. But the heart of man gets darker and darker. We use technology to destroy more lives than before. We stamp out one sinister force, and another, far greater evil rises to take its place.

But look back at **vv. 9-11**. This is a powerful segment, and it tells us several things. **First**, it reminds us of fellow believers through the centuries who have died for their faith. Right now in places like Iraq, Syria and Sudan, it's still happening. God sees and knows. **Second**, it shows us that those who die in the Lord go to be with the Lord. These martyrs are in the presence of Christ, not asleep in the ground waiting for the last trumpet. It's comforting to know that if you know Jesus, you'll see Him as soon as this life ends. Therefore, we don't have any reason to fear death. But **third**, notice that these martyrs, even though they're in the presence of Jesus, are looking forward to something else. They want justice. They want evil to be destroyed, and it hasn't happened yet. They may be in the presence of Jesus, but they still care about what's going on down here on Earth.

The Best Party Ever
Revelation 7

John has just heard that God is going to seal the servants of God, to protect them for something. He then hears a number of those who will be sealed: It's 12,000 people from each of the twelve tribes of Israel. Except the list of the tribes doesn't match any list in the Old Testament: Judah's listed first here. More importantly, the tribe of Dan is missing, replaced by Manasseh, who was one of the sons of Joseph. There is no explanation for this. Then John looks, expecting to see 144,000 Jews, and instead sees a massive congregation, too many to count, from every ethnic group that has ever existed. There is not universal agreement on this, but let me tell you what I think this represents. I think this is the great worship service at the End of this era, when as Philippians 2 says, *every knee will bow and every tongue confess that Jesus Christ is Lord.* If I am right about that, and if what John is describing is God moving Him thousands of years ahead in time so that he could be an eyewitness to that great event…are you ready for this? If that's true, and if you're a follower of Jesus, then <u>you are in this crowd that John is describing</u>. Picture that. A crowd too large to count; every color and language group and nationality represented, joined by the angels in praising God in one voice. No more hunger, poverty, sickness, pain or death. Jesus will be with us in the flesh, and we will rejoice with Him. Can you imagine laughing with Jesus? That is our destiny; that joy is what "living waters" represents, a fountain of life that never runs dry. And God will be so intimately involved in our lives, He will wipe the tears from our eyes. There is a lot more detail about that day at the end of this book, but for now, that ought to whet our appetites.

The War of the Ages
Revelation 12

Some of the symbolic images in Revelation are virtually impossible for us to interpret with any real certainty. But chapter 12 tells a story with three main characters, and I think I have a handle on who they are. The Dragon obviously represents Satan. The child is Jesus. Some have referred to this chapter as "the other Christmas story," since it's about Christ's birth. That may lead us to believe the woman represents Mary, but I don't think so. The rest of the chapter tells us details that don't correspond to anything in Mary's life. Some believe she represents Israel. The crown of twelve stars would represent the twelve tribes, and certainly Israel has been one step from extinction many times. But I don't think the woman is Israel only. When it says the dragon wants to kill the woman "and her offspring," I think it's talking about all who follow Christ. It identifies her offspring as those who hold to the testimony of Jesus, so it couldn't represent Israel alone. So yes, I think the woman in the story is…believe it or not…you and me, and everyone who has ever accepted Jesus as Savior. John is telling them, and us, the backstory of why the forces of evil are against us; why life down here sometimes seems so tough. He is peeling back the curtain on an unseen war that has been raging against the followers of Christ since the day the Church began.

The Beast Rises
Revelation 13

I'd love to have a dollar for every page that has been written about chapter 13. In Daniel 7, Daniel talks about four beasts, one that looks like a bear, one that looks like a lion, one that looks like a leopard, and then a fourth one more terrifying than the other three. That seems to be talking about nations that would arise and persecute God's people, and this beast in Revelation seems to combine the attributes of all four of those. So some interpreters have thought it represented some powerful, hostile nation. In ancient times, people saw the Roman Empire. In medieval days, it was the Islamic empire that captured the Middle East and parts of Europe. In the Twentieth Century, it was the Soviet Union.

Others have seen the two beasts in chapter 13 as representing people who will arise toward the end of this age. That is definitely the dominant view today. In this view, the beast out of the sea would correspond to the "Abomination that causes desolation" that both Daniel and Jesus talked about, and the "man of lawlessness" that Paul mentions in 2 Thessalonians 2. This person is commonly called the Antichrist. Most see him as a future political leader who will gain worldwide power and use that power to stamp out the church. In this view, the second beast is a religious movement or leader who convinces the world that the Antichrist is actually a divine figure who needs to be worshipped. In later chapters, this second beast is referred to as the False Prophet, so that might be the right interpretation. In this view, the Dragon, the Antichrist, and the False Prophet serve as a sort of false Trinity, a counterfeit version of the Father, Son and Holy Spirit. But note that there is no command to try to identify this Antichrist, or to try to stop him. The sense I get is that, if you and I are following Christ, we won't be deceived. And evil loses in the end. Remember the words of Rev. 12:11, *They overcame him by the blood of the Lamb and by the word of their testimony; they did not love their lives so much as to shrink from death.* Romans 12:21 says, *Do not be overcome by evil; overcome evil with good.* We do not fight the way others do. We owe it to our Lord to treat everyone else with love we've received.

Downfall of the Dark Side
Revelation 17-18

So who is this woman? The people who first read Revelation most likely would have understood her to represent Rome. Babylon was a term they used back then to refer to the Roman Empire. It was not a compliment. It referred to godless power, immorality, and persecution of God's people. Also, the city of Rome sat on seven hills, as it says the woman does in 17:9. So this could be the Lord's way of telling these early believers, "Right now Rome has all the power and makes your life miserable, but someday they will fall." Certainly that happened. But most interpreters think this refers to something that will happen in the future, not something from our past. One idea is that the woman represents a revived Roman empire which will dominate the world in the End Times, ruled by the Antichrist (which is why the woman rides the beast) and persecuting the people of God.

There's another interpretation, and this is the one I lean toward. Babylon does not represent Rome or any other real city. Think about the way this woman is presented. She is beautiful and seductive. She controls financial markets and governments. I think she represents the world system that is opposed to the things of God. She represents "the way things are." Think about the values our world believes in: What matters is money, so the rich get richer while the poor fight for the scraps, and everyone measures happiness by how big your house is, how nice your clothes are, how attractive you look…even though it kills us to try to maintain that lifestyle. What matters is power, so kings, presidents and dictators plunge into wars with little if any pretext, slaughtering people by the hundreds of thousands, and nothing lasting is ever gained. What matters is individual happiness, so we ignore moral truth if it gets in the way of us doing what we want. That's the way things are. Scripture talks about this at length, including 1 John 2:16, *For everything in the world--the lust of the flesh, the lust of the eyes, and the pride of life--comes not from the Father but from the world.* We know that God made everything that exists. But He didn't make things the way they are; human sin did that. And people who oppose that state of things are often ridiculed, jailed, or even killed. You could see the entire book of Revelation as a tale of two cities. Babylon is the city this world is building, where this world's values reign, and chaos, violence, injustice and death are the result. But God is building a new kind of city, the New Jerusalem. We'll see it in chapter 21. Babylon has to be destroyed to make way for the New Jerusalem. That's what I think this section of Revelation is saying. But however you interpret the figure of the prostitute, Babylon, the bigger point is clear: Evil will be destroyed.

The Triumph of the Lamb
Revelation 19

This is it, the Second Coming of Jesus Christ. All of history has been pointing to this singular moment. We could dwell for hours just on the terms John uses here to describe Jesus. Many of them are dripping in Old Testament imagery. But let me just point out two things. First, it's quite clear from these verses that the second coming of Jesus will be very different from the first. The first time, Jesus came in obscurity; no one but a group of shepherds knew who He was. The second time He will come in majesty. Back in Revelation 1, John told us that when He comes, every eye will see Him. The first time, Jesus came in poverty and humility, a tiny, helpless baby born to poor parents. The second time, He will come in glory and power that will dazzle and awe everyone who sees it. The first time, He came to give His life away for the sake of sinners. The second time, He will come to destroy evil and claim this world. The second thing I want to point out is this army of Heaven referenced in v. 14. Ordinarily, I would assume this refers to angels. But look at Rev. 17:14, *They will make war against the Lamb, but the Lamb will overcome them because he is Lord of lords and King of kings—and with him will be his called, chosen and faithful followers.* So, along with angels, you and I might be part of that heavenly army, unless we're still here when this happens.

Armies have been waiting at a spot called Armageddon since chapter 16. It's amazing how anticlimactic the battle actually is, aside from some pretty gruesome details. This may actually not refer to a literal battle. It says the armies were killed with the sword that proceeds from the mouth of Jesus. Surely at least that detail is not literal; so what actually happens here? One explanation is that Jesus speaks a word and the enemy armies are destroyed. Another is that the entire Armageddon story is a figurative way of saying that every force opposed to Christ will be defeated on the day He returns. Either way, this much is sure: It is not a fair fight between Jesus Christ and the forces of evil. Notice that the armies of Heaven don't do any actual fighting in this story. Jesus wipes out evil, and casts the beast and the false prophet into Hell. In so many of our contemporary myths, from The Lord of the Rings to Star Wars to Harry Potter, there is this idea of an epic clash between good and evil with the fate of the universe at stake. That makes for a very dramatic story. But it's not the case here. Jesus is King, and evil is just trying to hold on as long as it can before the inevitable happens.

Judgment
Revelation 20

There is intense disagreement among interpreters about how to understand the thousand years described at the start of this chapter. Is it a literal thousand-year reign between the present age and the age to come? Is it symbolic of the current age of human history, where the Lord's Church has authority to vanquish the Devil through the preaching of the Gospel? Is it a future golden age that will be brought about by the evangelism and social ministry of His people? You can find eloquent advocates of all three views. The focus of the chapter, however, is the Day of Judgment. Notice that every person stands judgment before the Lord to have their deeds read before Him (Although many believe—and I agree—that Scripture indicates that the followers of Jesus will be exempt from this Judgment). Think about how awful it would be to stand before the ultimate righteousness of Almighty God and hear the deeds of your life read aloud. But what matters is another book, called the Book of Life. Moses talked about this book. So did David in the Psalms and Malachi the prophet. Jesus told His disciples that their greatest treasure was having their names written down in Heaven. Those whose names aren't found there will spend eternity apart from God. We don't know if "lake of fire" is a literal description of Hell; I tend to think not. The Bible has many images to describe Hell, and they don't all jive. V. 14 says that Death and Hades will be thrown into the Lake of Fire; since they aren't human beings, that leads me to believe the lake of fire is symbolic. But Scripture is clear that Hell means eternal separation from God. Since God is the source of all love and goodness, we can do the math. It's not somewhere we want to go.

Is there a way to guarantee that our name is written in that book? Is there a way to avoid having our sins read aloud by a holy God, and to avoid Hell? Absolutely. Here are the words of Jesus from John 6:40, *For my Father's will is that everyone who looks to the Son and believes in him shall have eternal life, and I will raise him up at the last day.* Jesus came and died and rose again so that you could have your name written in His book. Once you are in His book, your sins are forgiven. That isn't just a temporary forgiveness; He isn't just putting off your punishment until His return. In both Jeremiah 31 and Hebrews 8, there is this promise: *For I will forgive their wickedness and will remember their sins no more.* Micah speaks of God throwing our sins into the depths of the sea. So if you trust in the blood of Jesus to forgive your sins and make you a new person, you will not have to have your sins read from the book. I believe that in God's book, the record of your life and mine has been replaced by the record of His Son…and it says "righteous." That offer is available to everyone.

All Things New
Revelation 21

The language in this chapter is exquisite. Countless songs have been written using these words, for good reason. But interpreters disagree on what the New Jerusalem represents. Some believe it's a literal city, a description of the place believers go when they die. According to this view, once Jesus returns and evil is destroyed, that place will come down here and become the capitol city of the New Earth. Others point out that Revelation is written in an apocalyptic style, where descriptions aren't supposed to be taken strictly literally. Some of the descriptions in these chapters 21 and 22, taken literally, would certainly describe a city unlike any this world has ever seen. They point out that chapters 17-18 describe Babylon, a city that God will destroy, which represents the evil of this present world. Babylon corresponds to the New Jerusalem; evil is destroyed so that God can bring in His new way of life. You may notice also that the New Jerusalem is called *the bride, the wife of the Lamb* in v. 9. Everywhere else in the New Testament, the bride of Christ is a reference to the church—not a building or an institution, but the people of God. So I think the New Jerusalem here represents us; the glory we will possess when we are complete in Him. Still, when I read other passages about the New Earth in other Scriptural books, passages NOT written in apocalyptic form, I know the New Earth will be a real, physical place. As 1 Corinthians 15 tells us, we will inhabit real resurrection bodies. And whether you take these verses to be completely literal or figurative, they tell us some very exciting things about what life on the New Earth will be like. Let's read the next section, and sum up those details.

Home
Revelation 22

Based on Revelation 21-22, and many other Scriptural passages about the New Earth, in both the Old and New Testaments, here are some things we know about the world God has planned for us:

We will have unhindered access to God. At long last, with us finally redeemed, we will be able to fully enjoy the relationship we were created for, a love with our true soul mate. If you've ever wished you could've been there to walk with Jesus and hear Him teach, you'll have that chance. If you've ever wanted to feel the tangible presence of the Holy Spirit all the time, not just in special moments, that will be reality. If you've ever longed to ask God questions, to have Him erase your doubts, to express your love to Him face to face, then Heaven is the place to be. We'll be in awe at the presence of the perfect One, and that will never get old.

Sin and its effects will not be there. Isaiah 65:25 says, *The wolf and the lamb will feed together, and the lion will eat straw like the ox...They will neither harm nor destroy on all my holy mountain, says the Lord.* It will be a peaceful world in every sense of the word. There will be excitement without stress, joy without fear, achievement without arrogance, abundance without jealousy.

There will be worship. Rev. 21:22 says there is no temple in the New Jerusalem. But we're told many times that we will worship God in eternity. Will we sing? Absolutely, and I believe it will be like no singing ever heard. But we will also worship when we play, when we celebrate, and when we work. Perhaps when you were a kid, you had the experience of performing in a school play, a concert, or a sports event, and seeing your parents in the stands, smiling proudly. On the New Earth, I believe everything we do will be done to make our Father proud. So everything we do will be worship.

There will be celebration, reward and rest. The coming of Heaven to Earth is described by John as a wedding feast. Remember, that was the most exciting event of the year for a rural Jew. I think it's noteworthy that the religious leaders who hated Jesus accused Him of being a drunkard and a glutton. It's not because He overate and drank too much...we know He was without sin. I think they called Him that because they didn't think someone who was truly holy could have so much fun in life. Jesus often speaks of feasting in Heaven. He also speaks, over and over again, of rewards. The work we do for the Lord now will not be in vain. And there will be rest. One of my favorite Scriptural promises is, *Come to me, all who are weary and heavy laden, and I will give you rest.* That verse will find its ultimate fulfillment in Heaven.

What else will be there? Colossians 3:1-4 tells us to set our minds on Heaven. In other words, we are commanded to daydream about the world to come. Imagine yourself there. Imagine doing the things you love the most, and doing them in a way that draws you closer to the God who loves you. If what we imagine about that world is incorrect, it is only because our imaginations are too small. If, for instance, some favorite activity of mine doesn't exist there, it is only because God has something planned for me that is so much better, I won't miss this world at all. That is our future. That is our blessed hope.

Chapter 12: "Who do you say that I am?" Matthew 16:13-16

We have looked at this passage several times already. But this time, I want to focus on Jesus' question in v. 15. The men who first heard this question had proven their loyalty. They had left behind homes, jobs, and security to follow this penniless rabbi. Yet He wanted more. He wanted to know what they believed about Him. Did they see Him as simply an inspiring teacher? A miracle worker? One of a succession of Israelite prophets? Did they think He was the long-awaited Messiah, the answer to all their nationalistic hopes and expectations? Or was He something far greater than any of those things? Peter, as we've seen by now, was always quick to speak. But this time, his answer was just right. "Not only are you the Messiah," He said, "You are the Son of God Himself." Scholars agree that Peter didn't yet understand completely Jesus' relationship to the divine. But he could tell that his Master was more than just any other man.

The point for us is this: It's not enough to think highly of Jesus. It's not enough to do good deeds in His name, or to profess Christianity as your faith preference. Jesus wants you to know Him as He truly is. To be sure, we can accept a biblically correct idea of Jesus' identity and still miss out. Faith in Christ is more than an intellectual assent. But the new life Jesus came, died, and rose again to bring us begins with a question: Who do you say that He is? We'll explore that question in this final chapter as we look at the things He said about Himself, and in what His followers said in the first few decades after He ascended.

The Eternal Word
John 1:1-18

An entire book could be written on these eighteen verses alone. This extraordinary passage is so lyrical that many scholars believe it is an ancient hymn. John chose to begin His Gospel with these words, using a title for Jesus that is unique to this passage: The Word. Think about this for a moment: Mark started his Gospel with the teaching of John the Baptist, preparing the way for the Messiah. Luke began His with the story of Christ's birth. Matthew went back even further, with a genealogy that reaches to the beginning of the human race. But John was not satisfied. He chose to reach into the chasm of eternity itself, where only God dwells. Scholars debate why he selected this term "the Word." In the Greek worldview that dominated the planet at the time, *Logos* (Greek for "word") was a supernatural force that was thought to undergird the entire universe. For Jews like John, "the word of the Lord" was powerful enough to part seas, establish new nations, and punish evil. I certainly don't know how much of those two concepts John had in mind when He called Jesus "the Word." I do believe two things, however: First, that he had come to understand that his friend and beloved teacher, gone from the world decades by the time he wrote these words, was somehow God Himself. He was the Creator of all things. The thought that John had spent three years in close proximity to the Almighty must have given him chills every time he thought of it. Second, John had seen His glory. He and his friends had been first hand witnesses of what God is truly like, in the form of this Nazarene carpenter. And they were never the same again.

Call Him Jesus
Matthew 1:18-21

When I was a little boy, I went to a rural school. One day, a new student joined our class. He had brown skin, whereas I and all my classmates were white. He had a funny name, too: It was pronounced "Hay-soose." But he quickly found a place in my little class. Until, that is, the day he wrote his name on the chalkboard. No adults were present when this happened, so when he wrote the name "Jesus" on the board, there was no one to stop us from collectively insisting that he was wrong. There was only one person with that name, we said, and it wasn't him. Jesus, or Jessie, as we came to call him, seemed remarkably untroubled by our stubborn insistence that he didn't know his own name. Much later, I would realize that the name Jesus is a common one in nations south of my own.

In a similar way, modern-day followers of Jesus are sometimes surprised and a little disappointed to learn that the name Mary and Joseph gave to their firstborn child was a common one in their time as well. In Aramaic, the language they spoke, it would have been pronounced "Yeshua." Jesus was born in a time when patriotic names were popular. We see this in the names of some of His apostles: Simon, or Simeon, was one of the twelve patriarchs of Israel. James is a Greek version of Jacob, the father of those twelve patriarchs. John is Jonah, one of Israel's prophets. In the same way, there were plenty of little boys being named Yeshua in first-century Israel, since Joshua was one of the nation's greatest heroes. Yet His name was selected by God Himself, as we see in this text. We can be certain God isn't concerned with the latest trends in baby names. He chose this name for its meaning: "Yahweh saves." Names in the ancient Middle East were more meaningful than in our culture. They represented the parents' hopes for their child. In naming His only begotten Son Jesus, the Lord was telling the world this child's ultimate destiny…and His own plan for our salvation.

Savior
Luke 2:11

We all need heroes. These days, our most popular movies are based on exploits of superheroes, men and women with special powers who swoop in to save the world. The people of first-century Israel, dominated by an oppressive occupying force, needed heroes even more than we do. If they had made movies in those times, they would have been about heroes like Gideon, who led 300 ragged farmers to victory over an army so large, it couldn't be counted; or Deborah, who inspired a military upset over an enemy with iron chariots; or Samson, the original superhero, whose strength and courage struck fear into the hearts of even the warlike Philistines. They were known in Israelite history as "saviors," people God raised up to rescue His children when they were in danger of being destroyed. Roman emperors took that title for themselves: "Caesar Augustus, the Savior of Rome." So when the angel told the shepherds on that first Christmas night that a Savior had been born, one has to wonder what the shepherds pictured in their minds.

At first glance, Jesus didn't have much in common with military leaders like Gideon, Deborah or Samson. And He certainly didn't resemble the Caesars. But the people of the Samaritan village called Sychar, where Jesus had His famous dialogue with the woman at the well, proclaimed Him "the Savior of the world" (John 4:42). The early Christians adopted that title for their Lord as well. Paul alone used it twelve times to describe Jesus in His letters. Unlike modern superheroes, or the Israelite deliverers, Jesus saved people not by pummeling their enemies, but by laying down His own life. Today, most of us accept the idea of a sacrificial hero; we celebrate it when we hear of a soldier throwing himself on an enemy grenade to spare his friends, or a first-responder charging heedless into a burning building, or a single mom working two jobs to afford a better life for her kids. But we have a difficult time seeing ourselves as those in need of salvation. We want to be the heroes of our own stories. The paradox of Christianity is that it's in seeing our own weakness that we find salvation. We have to surrender to win.

The Lamb of God
John 1:29-34

All Israelite children knew the story. Each Spring, they would help their mothers rid the house of any trace of leaven—or yeast. It was their way of preparing for the most important night of the year. Meanwhile, their father would take a lamb that had been carefully chosen and nurtured for that very night, and carefully slaughter it without breaking any of its bones. The lamb would be roasted, and unleavened bread would be served with bitter herbs, wine and other delicacies. The head of the house would take his seat and would tell the familiar saga of their people, enslaved in Egypt for four centuries, without hope or heroes. Then suddenly, God showed up unexpectedly, pouring out His wrath upon their cruel masters, devastating the Egyptian economy for the stubbornness of Pharaoh. Finally, on the crucial night, in accordance with the word of God through Moses, the Jews killed lambs and marked their doors with the blood. The angel of death descended upon the region of the upper Nile that night, but the people of God—all who were covered by the blood of the lamb—were spared.

We can imagine how an Israelite child might hear that story, year after year. Did they think about the eerie quiet that must have covered the land that night, punctured by the cries of the bereaved Egyptians? Did they imagine being their forefathers, rejoicing when they realized they were finally, miraculously free? They all knew the story well. So when John the Baptist pointed to Jesus of Nazareth and said, "There's the Lamb of God, who takes away the sin of the world," those listening recognized the term. But they couldn't have possibly known what it meant. In Genesis 22 is the painful, difficult story of the binding of Isaac. God commands Abraham to offer his son, "your only son, whom you love" in sacrifice. Abraham, trusting that God has a plan to fulfill His promises in spite of this paradoxical command, prepares to obey. When the boy asks, "Father, where is the lamb for the sacrifice?" on the long walk to Moriah, Abraham swallows hard and says, "God will provide a lamb, my son." At the last instant, God stops Abraham from killing his son, and the old man sees a ram with its horns caught in a thicket nearby. Abraham was right: God provided a lamb. And now, God has done what He wouldn't allow us to do: He has given us His Son, His only Son, whom He loved. He is the Lamb who takes away the sin of the world. Hallelujah.

Son of Man
Matthew 26:62-68, Daniel 7:13

First-time readers of the Gospels are often surprised to find how often Jesus refers to Himself as the Son of Man, a title rarely heard in sermons or songs today. There are at least 78 references to the term in the Gospels, all of them spoken by Jesus. It was clearly His favorite way to refer to Himself. On the night of His trial before the Sanhedrin, He used the term in the statement that virtually handed His enemies the "evidence" they needed to condemn Him. Considering all the magisterial names that Jesus is called in Scripture, why did He favor such a pedestrian-sounding title? It's important to know that Daniel foresaw one who he described as "like a son of man" handed everlasting authority over this world by God Almighty. The Jews knew this prophecy, but few (if any) ascribed it to the expected Messiah. Remember, Jesus often had to speak in code. If He had boldly proclaimed Himself the Savior of the World, sent by God, the people, hungry for a hero, might have started a revolution to make this miracle-worker their king. So He called Himself the Son of Man. For those who weren't open to God's plan, it sounded prosaic, like a man today calling himself "guy" or "dude." But for those with ears to hear, those who were seeking God's deliverance, it reminded them of that vision from Daniel, and it filled them with hope. Could it be that this ordinary-looking, unschooled carpenter trailed by a ragged crowd of riff raff could be more than just the flavor of the month? Could He really be sent by God to set things right? Most weren't willing to believe that. Are you?

Son of God
John 3:16-18

Though most Christians—and those familiar with Christianity—are familiar with this title, many misunderstand it. Scripture very definitely does not teach that God the Father sired a son by sleeping with a human woman, like Zeus or other pagan deities. Or as I like to tell people, "Jesus wasn't the bouncing baby boy of Mr. and Mrs. God." Yet Scripture does teach that Jesus is, aside from Adam and Eve, the only human being to have no human father. Jesus was twice called "my Son" by the voice of God from the sky, heard by many witnesses. He talked about God as His Father, teaching His followers to call God by that name as well. And He would often get away by Himself to spend time alone with the Father. Yet the first Christians understood that He was not separate from God, but was God in human form (See Philippians 2:6, Colossians 2:9, and Hebrews 1:2-3, among many others). He was fully and completely God, and also absolutely human.

Are you confused yet? There is no way to understand this stuff in human terms. As a preacher, I am utterly helpless to explain it. But two things help me to accept it: First, it doesn't have to be explainable to be true. I have no idea how air travel works from a technical standpoint, but when I have opportunity, I eagerly board a plane to take me to faraway destinations. I choose to trust those who do understand the process. Besides, if He is God, it stands to reason that there are things about His character that are beyond our understanding. Second, this proves our God is a God of love. Think about it for a moment: God existed for eternity by Himself. There were no humans, animals or angels until He created them. If He was content to be alone, then He isn't really a relational God. But if, during all that eternity, He was enjoying a relationship of perfect, fulfilling love within the godhead (As Jesus so plainly indicates in John 17:5, 24), and His creation and redemption of us is His way of saying, "I have something wonderful I just have to share. Join with us in this family of love…" then we have a God who is truly "good news." I know, that's a lot to wrap one's mind around. It's also very exciting to ponder!

Ransom
Mark 10:42-45

In Jesus' time, the word "ransom" meant approximately what it does today: The price it costs to buy someone's freedom. Jesus is showing His apostles what a truly great life looks like. It's not found in acquiring power, but in giving oneself away. Jesus is the supreme example, and we are ones who've been set free. When I was a child, I learned a song that expressed this well:

He paid a debt He did not owe;
I owed a debt I could not pay
I needed someone to wash my sins away.
And now I sing a brand new song;
Amazing grace, all day long.
Christ Jesus paid a debt that I could never pay.

Any loving parent who has ever watched his child suffer has thought, "I wish I could trade places with her. I wish I could suffer instead of her." In Jesus, God thought the same thing…and did it.

Bread of Life
John 6:35

John recorded seven "I am" statements of Jesus, and we'll look at them next. When He spoke this one, He had just performed His miraculous feeding of the 5000, conjuring up bread and fish out of thin air. In that culture, bread was the main source of sustenance. Meat was for special occasions (as in "killing the fatted calf"), but bread was what kept you alive. If Jesus were speaking today, He might say, "I'm the meat and potatoes." So He's really saying two important things to us through this short verse: First, He's saying, "Don't worship me because you think I'm going to give you something. I am the 'something.' Don't miss that." Sometimes we religious types act like selfish teenagers, only approaching our daddy when we need the car keys. Later in life, when dad is gone, we have a deep sense of regret that we didn't take the time to know him, to listen to his wisdom and share life with him. In the same way, we often treat God as nothing more than a big blessing machine in the sky. But the stuff God chooses to give us isn't the point. The real blessing is knowing Him, experiencing the personal transformation that only comes to us when we get to know Him in His righteousness, justice and love.

The other thing Jesus is saying is, "There's lots of good-tasting stuff in this world. Most of it is fine in small portions. Some of it, quite frankly, is poison. But out of all of it, only I am the meat and potatoes. Only I can truly feed you. So enjoy the wide array of desserts and snacks that I give you, but feed on me." Did you notice the promise there? *He who comes to me will never be hungry, and He who believes in me will never be thirsty.* It doesn't mean that we'll always have everything we want. It just means that we'll never feel like we don't have enough. We'll be satisfied. David said something similar in Psalm 23, *The Lord is my shepherd, I shall not want.* Because He's in charge of my life, I don't need a thing. Is that the story of your life? Or are you constantly seeking the perfect "something" to make your life complete? Jesus has made it clear: Only He is the Bread of Life.

Light of the World
John 8:12

December of 1952 was especially cold in London. As Londoners heaped extra coal on their fires to heat their homes, the black smoke of the coal mingled with the famous London fog, creating a toxic smog that rendered one of the great cities of the world blind and barely able to breathe for several days. Visibility was so bad, people couldn't see their own feet when standing up. Public transportation came to a halt, aside from the Underground. Ambulances couldn't run, because of the low visibility and also the stranded vehicles littering the streets. If you needed medical help, you had to walk to a hospital. Walking meant shuffling one's feet, to keep from running into obstacles. Meanwhile, children, the elderly and those with respiratory issues struggled to stay alive. But since the smog made things even colder, people kept burning more coal, and the problem grew worse. In the end, the Great London Smog may have killed as many as 12,000 people.

That's similar to how the Bible describes our world. It's a great place, but there is a toxic blend of voices (consumerism, racism, selfish ambition, violent tendencies, to name a few) that blind us to the reality of our lives and choke out the joy we were created to find in our Father. Like those unwitting Londoners, we add to the darkness every time we do what comes most naturally to us: Seek happiness and relief on our own terms. Into this dark and poisonous world stepped Jesus, saying, "I am the Light." People could see it in Him the first time they heard Him speak: He had something the rest of us needed. Thousands flocked to Him. Some gave up all to follow. True to our nature, we extinguished the light by nailing Him to a cross. But God's light is resilient; three days later, He arose. His promise still stands: Follow me, and leave the darkness behind. Breathe free…at last.

The Door
John 10:7-10

In 2004, the Ukraine held a presidential election. As in many of the new Eastern European Republics in those heady early days of post-Soviet democracy, the election was controversial. The opposition candidate, Viktor Yushchenko, barely survived an assassination attempt by poisoning in the days leading up to the vote. The sitting government's candidate was declared the winner on election night, but this result was so profoundly doubted, thousands took the streets of Kiev in protest. Eventually, a new election was ordered. This vote, more closely supervised, went the way of the underdog, Yushchenko. These events, known as the Orange Revolution for the color associated with the winning party, are a cautionary tale for despots around the world. According to some accounts, the protests began with an unlikely source. On the night of the first election, a government spokesman appeared on state-sponsored television, announcing the sound defeat of the upstart Yushchenko. But the woman who was translating this announcement into sign language told a different story. She signed to the hearing impaired that the government spokesman was lying, and urged them to tell their hearing friends to join them in protest. One obscure person challenged the party line and started a revolution.

Jesus was also an obscure person in a forgotten backwater of the world. Like that sign-language interpreter, He had the audacity to challenge the party line of this world. He showed us that the values this world treasures—wealth at all costs, power through violent means, tribalism, self-centeredness, pleasure-seeking—are toxic. He offered a better way to live. He used a metaphor from the sheep-field: I am the gate that offers freedom for the sheep. Go through me, and find salvation and abundant life. Unlike the Orange Revolution, which was short-lived (Yushchenko's government, riddled with charges of corruption, suffered a massive defeat in the next election), the movement begun by this Galilean woodworker has changed the world. Two thousand years after He left this world, people are still walking through the door He offered, experiencing a brand-new life.

The Good Shepherd
John 10:11-18

We've seen how God in Scripture redeemed the image of shepherds, members of a disrespected profession in ancient times, by choosing working shepherds to be some of His greatest leaders (Jacob, Rachel, Moses, David, and Amos, for instance), by inviting a group of shepherds (and no one else) to the birth of the Messiah, and by using shepherding metaphors often in both Testaments. Perhaps the most famous example of this is Psalm 23, which begins with the words, *The Lord is my shepherd, I shall not want.* In a wonderful little book, *A Shepherd Looks at Psalm 23,* W. Philip Keller gives insight into the life of a shepherd in the Middle East, and what we can learn about God from this image. Shepherding, based on Keller's experience, is an incredibly hands-on profession. For instance, he talks about the phenomenon of the "cast" sheep. This occurs when a sheep has fallen and can't get up, either because it is stuck in mud or a hole, or because it has become too wooly. When a shepherd realizes a sheep is missing, he has to hurry to find it. A cast sheep will quickly become so bloated, its intestines could rupture. If the shepherd finds the sheep, he goes through an intricate process of righting it. First, he rolls the animal onto its side, allowing its intestinal gasses to settle. Then he stands the animal on its hooves, carefully bracing it between his legs so the sheep doesn't fall. He gently massages the sheep's legs to restore blood flow. Finally, he releases it, but he watches it carefully. It might very well fall again, in which case the process must start over.

Reading Keller's book, I kept thinking to myself, "I'd be a terrible shepherd. I don't have the patience to care for such stupid, helpless animals." Then, of course, I remember that in Scripture, God compares us to sheep. Jesus is not only patient with us, seeking us when we're lost and setting us back on our feet. He goes further than any human shepherd would. He lays down His life for the sheep. Why would He do such a thing? Because we aren't a job for Him. We are His joy. We are His family. The Good Shepherd motif reminds us of how much it cost God to love us, and how faithfully He loves us still.

Resurrection and the Life
John 11:25

Jesus spoke these words to his friend Martha of Bethany, whose brother Lazarus had died four days before. We've looked at this story already, but here I want to note what an emotional day this was. Both Martha and her sister said the same thing when they first saw Jesus, "If you had been here, my brother would not have died." We don't know if the sisters meant this as an accusation ("Where were you when we needed you") or not, but their profound grief is clear. Consider also that this chapter is one of two times that depict Jesus weeping. The specific Greek term John used to describe Jesus' emotion is more one of anger than of sorrow. I think I understand why. I have done a great many funerals in my life, and sometimes, I just get mad about losing good people. I get angry when I see a woman forced to say goodbye to her husband of many years, or a group of children who've lost their mother, or most of all, when parents have to bury a child. I'm glad to be of service to these people, but there's a part of me that knows: It shouldn't be this way. It's just not right. Jesus created this world. And it broke His heart to see, up close and personal, the way Death, the ultimate uninvited guest, was squatting on His creation and ruining everything.

So when he said these words to Martha, He was declaring war on Death, once and for all. Raising Lazarus was just the beginning, a shot across Death's bow, as it were. The true victory was sealed when life came back into a crucified body. A massive stone rolled away from a tomb. And the nail-scarred Savior walked out, triumphant over humanity's most implacable foe. Now, whenever a new believer is added to His family, it's signified by baptism. In other words, every follower of Jesus re-enacts His resurrection. When we do this, we're thumbing our nose at Death. We can't defeat that evil force on our own—disease, violence, and aging continue to claim victims in spite of all our technology and enlightenment. But we trust that someday, we'll each have our own personal Easter…because He lives.

The Way, The Truth, and The Life
John 14:6

In his classic work, *Mere Christianity*, CS Lewis wrote, "I am trying here to prevent anyone saying the really foolish thing that people often say about Him: I'm ready to accept Jesus as a great moral teacher, but I don't accept his claim to be God. That is the one thing we must not say. A man who was merely a man and said the sort of things Jesus said would not be a great moral teacher. He would either be a lunatic — on the level with the man who says he is a poached egg — or else he would be the Devil of Hell. You must make your choice. Either this man was, and is, the Son of God, or else a madman or something worse. You can shut him up for a fool, you can spit at him and kill him as a demon or you can fall at his feet and call him Lord and God, but let us not come with any patronizing nonsense about his being a great human teacher. He has not left that open to us. He did not intend to."

Lewis wrote those words over a half-century ago, but they still resonate today. Many people still insist on categorizing Jesus as a great moral sage, a compassionate healer, or a courageous freedom fighter…anything but divine. But Lewis is right: Anyone who says things like John 14:6 cannot be any of those things. He belongs either with the cult leaders and con artists of history, like Jim Jones or David Koresh, or He is to be pitied as delusional. But what if He was telling the truth? What if He is indeed the Way, the Truth and the Life?

True Vine
John 15:1-5

Of all the "I am" statements in John, this one may be the most uncomfortable for American Christians to comprehend. We value independence, ambition and initiative. However, since some of us realize we're incapable of preparing our souls for eternity, we'll outsource that task. We're willing to make a transaction with God: We offer our acknowledgment and some measure of obedience in return for everlasting salvation. Sadly, that is how some (many?) of us seem to view our faith. But Jesus will have none of that. He demands a relationship as intimate as that of a vine to its branches. Jesus is not being possessive. He knows that two things are true…two things we independent Americans find it hard to accept: **First**, that there is no real life apart from Him. Just as a branch cut off from its vine soon withers and dies, so will we if we try to live on our own terms. Of course, we can all think of many vibrant people who don't believe in Jesus. Then again, a bouquet of fresh flowers is quite vibrant, too. But since it's cut off from its life source, that vibrancy is only temporary.

Second, Jesus says there is no real success apart from Him. When Jesus talks of "bearing fruit," He is talking about success. Again, we can easily think of unbelievers who experience success in all its earthly forms. But I am reminded of the old saying, "Don't fear failure; fear succeeding at something that doesn't matter." In the scheme of eternity, how much of what we call "success" really matters? These two truths are highly offensive to our American sensibilities, but then again, so is this: Jesus describes us as simply plants in a garden, with God as the gardener. This life isn't even ours; we are ultimately accountable to Him. But here's the good news: This also means that we aren't stuck in our current state. God is a gardener who won't quit improving us. That means the longer we know Him, the better we become. Ruth Bell Graham, whose husband Billy was much better known, was herself an amazingly insightful speaker and writer. She passed away in 2007. On her tombstone are the words she herself chose: "End of construction. Thank you for your patience."

The Man Who Would Be King
Matt 26:47-54, Mark 14:60-62, John 18:33-36

I chose these three different accounts to illustrate a key truth. We think of Jesus as being exceptionally humble, and we are right to do so. Yet three times in the last hours of His earthly life, He displayed an incredible personal confidence: In the presence of a mob sent to arrest Him; before the religious leaders of His own people, who were accusing Him of heresy; in conversation with the Roman official who had the power to have Him executed. In each instance, Jesus didn't behave like a man in fear. He acted like a King. He made it clear, "You have no real authority over me. I am allowing this to happen because it suits my purposes." This helps us clarify what humility really is: It's not a denial of our own strengths. In other words, if you are a genius mathematician and someone compliments your intelligence, humility doesn't require you to say, "Me? No, actually I'm as dumb as a box of rocks." Humility, instead, is knowing oneself truly, but choosing to think of others first. The math genius knows she is great with numbers, but she doesn't feel the need to prove that to you and me. Instead, she is eager to talk about us, our problems, hopes, dreams, and fears. And if her math skills can help us in some way, she happily uses them for our good, with no expectation of praise or repayment.

So, back to Jesus. Although He apparently looked nothing like royalty, that is exactly what He was. Scripture is clear that He was greater in power than any earthly ruler who has ever lived; He literally created the universe. Scripture also makes clear that Jesus is destined to rule over this world for all eternity (Philippians 2:10). Jesus knew this about Himself. Yet He chose to live among the poorest, sharing their hardships. He kept His true identity secret, knowing that a celebrity following would get in the way of His life's purpose, the redemption of sinners through an atoning death. In the final 24 hours before that death, He had ample opportunity to pull rank, to insist on being treated like a King. Yet He chose the path of humility for our sake. He thought of us first.

The First Christian Sermon
Acts 2:32-41

So far, we've looked at some of the things Jesus said about Himself. After He was gone, His small band of followers wanted to tell others about Him. They did this so effectively, within only three centuries their faith became the dominant religion in the massive Roman Empire. What did the people who knew Jesus personally say about who He truly was? We will now turn our attention to that question.

We begin with the very first Christian sermon. This is a remarkable story. On the Jewish holiday Pentecost, just weeks after the crucifixion, the tiny group of believers experienced a supernatural transformation, as the Holy Spirit came upon them (see Acts 2:1-13). They each began speaking the good news about Jesus in languages they had never learned. Since it was a religious holiday, the streets of Jerusalem were clogged with pilgrims from all over the Middle East, many of whom had grown up speaking languages other than Hebrew. Hearing their own languages being spoken, these pilgrims formed a curious crowd around the believers. Peter, always the first to speak, stepped forward and delivered a Gospel presentation. Think of the irony: Peter was always impulsive, always putting his foot in his mouth; yet here, his words are perfect. He was the blustering would-be hero who denied Jesus when things got dangerous. Yet here, he boldly tells the crowd that they are responsible for the death of God's Son. He had no time to prepare this message, yet he skillfully draws upon Old Testament Scripture to prove that Jesus was the promised Messiah. His message was so powerful, three thousand people that very day declared their allegiance to a crucified man. Jesus is unlike anyone else who has ever lived. Studying a historical figure or getting to know a new friend can both be rewarding. But when we realize who Jesus was, it changes us forever.

Power in His name
Acts 3:1-20

Here's what's so amazing about this miracle: This man wasn't just disabled; He had been disabled since birth. So God didn't just fix his legs; He taught him to walk, instantaneously. And this guy didn't just walk, he leaped. People in Jerusalem knew this guy. They passed him every day on their way to pray in the temple. And now, they see him leaping and bounding around like a dog unleashed in a meadow. And I have to think that people standing there in the temple courts, who knew the word of God, immediately thought of Isaiah 35.6, where it says that in the time of the Messiah, the lame will leap like a deer. This was more than a miraculous healing; this was a sign that God was up to something.

Peter wasn't going to let a moment like this go to waste; he's the new Peter, after all, the Simon Peter who is now full of the Spirit of God. He sees the people gathered to see this amazing miracle and he doesn't want them to misunderstand, to think that he had done this by his own power. So he tells them essentially three things: One, this man was healed in the name of Jesus. That's significant. There are a lot of great men and women in history, but I don't know anyone, ever, who has been healed in the name of Ghandi, or Thomas Jefferson, or Eleanor Roosevelt. Peter is saying, "This Jesus, who you all saw in this very city a few weeks ago, was more than a man." Second, he says, "You people killed Him." He is identifying their core problem: They have sinned against God by murdering His Messiah. Third, he says, "There is still hope for you. If you'll repent, turn away from your present life and accept a new course of life in God, He'll change you and save you forever." In the next chapter (Acts 4:4) we see that Peter's message persuaded a huge number of onlookers to follow Jesus. There is power in His name! Please understand; that doesn't mean that saying the name "Jesus" gives you power to do whatever you want. Some would-be exorcists found that out the hard way (Acts 19:13-16). But it does mean that when we put our trust and hopes in this historical person, Jesus the Messiah, our lives are changed in ways that cannot be explained apart from the existence of a gracious God.

No other Name
Acts 4:1-22

This is the sequel to the last story. Again, we see the remarkable change in Peter. Just weeks before, he was so afraid of the High Priest and the other religious leaders, he had denied three times that he even knew Jesus. Now, he defies the highest authorities of his people to kill him if they must; he won't stop talking about Jesus no matter what. But what stands out to most of us post-moderns is verse 12. To say that Jesus is the only hope for humanity is incredibly narrow-minded and intolerant…unless it's true, of course.

Recently, I was conversing via direct message with a friend I know only through social media. He was raised in Christianity, but walked away as a young adult. He told me he couldn't believe in a God who would reject billions of people simply for believing the wrong religion. He said, "That seems to me a pretty poor metric to decide someone's eternity." Since this was an online conversation, I had time to think about my reply. Here's what I said: "I agree with you. But I don't think that's the message of Christ at all. Instead, I think it's more like this: We live in a crumbling, dying world. God has a rescue plan, and it cost Him everything, but He did it anyway. And now He's trying to get as many as possible to safety." My friend admitted that sounded way different from what he had heard in church growing up. If I'm right, then Peter's statement that Jesus is the only way is not intolerance; It's a plea for people to come running to the One who can rescue them.

Watershed Moment
Acts 9:1-20

It had to have been surprising, even to the disciples themselves, that their movement was still alive, much less thriving, after their Messiah had been crucified. Then along came a zealous young Pharisee named Saul of Tarsus. The idea that an unschooled self-styled rabbi from Galilee, who consorted with sinners and prostitutes, would be considered the Savior of the world was deeply offensive to Saul. Hadn't the religious authorities condemned Him? Hadn't the Romans crucified Him as an enemy to the state? Didn't God's own Word say that a man who was hung on a tree was cursed? How could anyone worship as divine a man God Himself had cursed? When Stephen, a leader in the early church, was executed by an angry mob, Saul was there. That moment of violence lit a spark in the tinder-box of his heart that exploded into a homicidal passion. Saul became the leader of a relentless persecution of the fledgling church. The believers scattered, leaving Jerusalem for the sake of their lives. But (in what must have infuriated the fervent young zealot) the persecution had an unintended consequence. As Jesus-followers fled Jerusalem, they took their message with them. New Jesus communities began to surface all across the Middle East. Saul was on his way to Damascus to continue his quest for doctrinal purity at any cost.

It's impossible to overstate how unexpected the events of Acts 9 were. Imagine today if the leader of a terrorist cell or the spokesman of a white supremacist group converted to Christianity and renounced their previous words and actions. Saul's conversion was so surprising, the disciples in Jerusalem at first couldn't believe it. It took a while for them to trust their former persecutor. And Saul's former colleagues tried to kill him when they heard he was preaching the message of Jesus. It's also impossible to overstate the impact this one man's conversion made on history. Years later, Saul's home church in Antioch would commission him and his friend Barnabas to take the Gospel to places it had never been. Suddenly, the message of the Jewish Messiah crossed over into the Gentile world. The churches he planted on his three missionary journeys would ultimately lead to the spread of Christianity into Europe. Saul, now known by his Roman name Paul, would go on to write over a quarter of the New Testament. His eloquent writing would help us clarify the meaning of Christ's life, death and resurrection. We'll look at some of those insights next. This one man's change of heart changed history.

Redeemer
Galatians 4:4-5

Many scholars believe that Paul's letter to the churches in Galatia (a region in modern-day Turkey) was one of the earliest books of our present New Testament to be written, sometime around the year 50 AD. Here, around two decades after Jesus walked the earth, Paul recognized that God had picked the perfect time to send His Son into the world. For the first time, a huge swath of humanity was united under one language, with the Roman roads making travel relatively easy and the Pax Romana making it safe. As NT Wright points out in his book *Surprised by Hope*, Jesus was also born into a perfect storm: The fervent Messianic expectations of the Jews in the First Century combined with the merciless nature of Roman justice to guarantee that a popular teacher like Jesus would get Himself into trouble. But since His crucifixion was part of God's saving plan, He really did come at just the right time.

Paul uses the word "redeem" to define Jesus' mission. That was a business term in Old Testament times; it usually referred to the transaction of buying freedom for a slave, or providing for a penniless widow by marrying her, as in the case of Ruth and Boaz. But there are also times in the Old Testament when the term was used in a different way. Job was a righteous man of ancient times who lost everything he had: His considerable wealth, his physical health, even his children. A group of friends comes to "comfort" him and instead puts him on trial, asking him to confess the sins he must have committed to earn this terrible judgment from God. Most of the book of Job consists of this debate between Job's friends and Job himself, who insists he has tried his best to live a righteous life. In Job 19:25, his words, poignant and yet filled with faith, are: *I know that my redeemer lives, and that in the end he will stand on the earth.* In the next verse, Job reveals who he expects this redeemer to be: *And after my skin has been destroyed, yet in my flesh I will see God.* Would God come to earth to redeem us, to buy us back from our enslavement, to be our rescuer? Somehow Job knew He would. Centuries later, Paul confirmed that he was right.

Atonement
Romans 3:21-26

Romans is considered by most scholars and preachers to be Paul's masterwork. Writing to Roman Christians, most of whom he has never met, Paul sketches out the good news in words that have changed history. Here in this brief, memorable paragraph, he shows us the genius of God's salvation plan. The problem God confronted was that humanity had created a seemingly irreparable breach between them and their Creator. *For all have sinned and fall short of the glory of God.* God could not simply pardon our sins and still be a just God. This is a difficult concept for modern people to accept, but think of it this way: How would we feel about a judge who, at the end of the trial of a child molester caught in the act, said, "Let's just forget this ever happened"? If sin is the force that has enslaved humanity and warped creation, it cannot simply be overlooked. It must be destroyed. But destroying sin would mean destroying us, and God loves us too much to do that. How could God's righteous mission to rid the world of sin and His loving desire to bring us back home be reconciled? Would He have to choose between the two?

In calling Jesus a "sacrifice of atonement" (some English versions use the obscure but accurate word "propitiation"), Paul was using the language of Old Testament sacrifice. In the same way an animal died to bring its owner reconciliation with God, so Jesus died to make us right before Him. In Genesis 22, God provided a lamb for Abraham so that he would not have to sacrifice his son Isaac; but God offered His own Son for us. Some have found this doctrine revolting, calling it "divine child abuse." But they forget that Jesus said He was God in human flesh. *If you've seen me, you've seen the Father,* He said in John 14:9. In another letter, 2 Corinthians 5:21, Paul put it this way: *God made Him who had no sin to become sin for us, that we might become the righteousness of God.* At the cross, Jesus took all the sin in world history, even sin that had yet to be committed, and personified it. Then His righteous judgment was poured out upon Himself, making us free, but killing Him in the process. That sin is forevermore dead, but Jesus is not. Like I said, God's plan is genius.

Dying for Enemies
Romans 5:6-11

A long time ago, I was watching Saturday Night Live. Tom Hanks was the guest host, and in his opening monologue, he mentioned that it was his fifth time hosting. That was the beginning of a sketch in which Hanks was whisked away from the audience to a private club for "Five Timers," where he was offered a drink, given an official jacket, and met fellow Five Timers like Steve Martin, Elliot Gould and Paul Simon (like I said, it was a long time ago). We're all familiar with the idea they were parodying; in life, being accomplished or well-born can lead to opportunities for special privileges. There are executive washrooms, country clubs, first class seating on airplanes. A recent series of car commercials pictures all the winners of college football's most prestigious individual award living together as a fraternity in a "Heisman House." To some, that is what the Church claims to be: A group of people set apart by holiness. Sinners need not apply.

The biblical truth is far different. Jesus doesn't court the favor of the self-made, self-important, or the self-righteous. Instead, He welcomes the ungodly. He doesn't have entrance requirements; in fact, He paid the dues Himself on the cross. He died for us while we were still opposed to Him, so we know His love is genuine. John Newton was a slave trader, in his own words "an infidel and a libertine." Then he met Jesus. He went on to write perhaps the most beloved hymn of all: Amazing Grace. He never got over the fact that Christ could save "a wretch" like him. Near the time of his death at age 82, he said to a friend, "My memory is nearly gone, but I remember two things: That I am a great sinner, and Christ is a great Savior." Amen.

World Changing Grace
Ephesians 2:8-9

These two verses, perhaps the most well-known in all of Paul's writing, are beloved by many. But they are also controversial. They say that when we come to Jesus, we are spiritually bankrupt, morally penniless. By grace, He pays all our debts, and sets up a new account in our name. It's a limitless account, more blessing than we could ever spend in a million lifetimes. But from that point on, we can't make either deposits or withdrawals. We can't make withdrawals because God has forgiven all of our sin, past, present and future. Nothing we can say or do will ever cause Him to stop loving us. And we can't make deposits because He doesn't need anything from us. As I've heard it said before, "Grace means that there is nothing you can ever do to make God love you any less than He does now, and there is nothing you can ever do to make Him love you more."

Some people don't like the sound of that. They'll say, "But I've lived a good life. I've done good things. Surely I didn't require as much grace as…that guy over there. Surely some of my salvation is because of me." That's why Paul says *not as a result of works, so that no one can boast.* People who have been carried from a burning building don't argue among themselves which of them deserved it more; they are just thankful to the first responders who rescued them. Others think this radical doctrine of grace gives a Christian license to commit any sin, knowing God will forgive them. That is a perversion of the doctrine of grace, one that goes all the way back to the beginning of Christianity—Paul talked about it in his letters. Anyone who believes that has never really tasted grace. Tim Keller planted a church in Manhattan. Most of his members came from very irreligious backgrounds, but he had a woman who joined his church from a very strict, fundamentalist upbringing. She had never really understood grace until she came to Redeemer Presbyterian. In his book, *The Reason for God,* he writes, "She had always heard that God accepts us only if we are good enough. She said that the new message was scary. I asked why it was scary and she replied: If I was saved by my good works then there would be a limit to what God could ask of me or put me through. I would be like a taxpayer with "rights"—I would have done my duty and now I would deserve a certain quality of life. But if I am a sinner saved by grace—then there's nothing he cannot ask of me."

God is not a landlord, demanding payment or He'll evict us. He's a liberator, who has set us free from a lifetime of slavery. But if you've truly been set free, then there's nothing you won't do to show your gratitude to your liberator. If there's not a desire in your heart to know God better, and to live for Him, then there's a pretty good chance you've never actually been liberated.

Master Artist
Ephesians 2:10

The good news in this verse is staggering. It says you are God's *poiema* (that's the word translated "workmanship" or "handiwork," depending on your English translation). Notice that it looks like "poem," and there's a reason for that. It literally means "work of art." God is a master artist, and you are His magnum opus, His masterpiece. This isn't a reference to your looks, by the way. Psalm 139:13 and 16 says, *You created my inmost being. You knit me together in my mother's womb...all the days ordained for me were written in your book before one of them came to be.* He created you for good works that He had in mind before you were born. When in Ephesians 2:10 it says you were created *in Christ Jesus,* that is a reference to your rebirth when you met Him. From that point on, His Spirit works inside you, shaping you to accomplish His purpose in your life. The genius of His creation is that you were custom-designed for the specific good works He had planned for you to do. You are here for an eternally significant purpose.

Some respond to this with misplaced excitement. They hear about life's purpose, and immediately think of success, money and happiness. None of those things are bad, of course But the verse says we were made for good works; that is not a promise of earthly accomplishment or relational bliss. Others doubt that this promise could be true. Whatever dreams they've had for life have been pummeled out of them by the steel-toed boots of reality. But the plans of God are true because of His work in your life; and that cannot be stopped by any mistakes of your past, shortcomings of your present, the opinions of others or even your own lack of self-worth. You are His masterpiece whether you feel like one or not. Still others read this truth with fear. They want to live life on their terms, and they're afraid that if they seek God's purpose, it's going to mean becoming a missionary or a preacher. Certainly God's Kingdom needs men and women in missions and vocational ministry. But it also needs called men and women in every walk of life. Think about this for a moment: Jesus loves you enough to die for you. Knowing that, why would you assume He'd create you for a purpose you're going to hate? I think it's far more likely, based on what we know of God, that whatever your purpose is, it will be something you'll love. After all, whatever He designed you to do, it is literally what you were made for.

Re-Creator
2 Corinthians 5:17

It was the deciding game of the 1912 World Series. The New York Giants led by one run. Glory was within their grasp. A White Sox hitter lifted an easy fly ball to centerfield, occupied by the Giants' outstanding centerfielder, Fred Snodgrass. Inexplicably, Snodgrass dropped the ball, and the runner reached second. Later in the inning, the Sox scored two runs to win the game and the series. Snodgrass, only 25 at the time, would play three more seasons of big-league baseball. He then retired and moved to California, where he and his wife raised two daughters. He built a successful career in banking, and served as a respected mayor of his adopted hometown, Oxnard. Yet when he died in 1974 at the age of 86, the headline of his obituary in the New York Times read, "Fred Snodgrass, 86, Dead. Ballplayer Muffed 1912 Fly." This world quickly forgets our achievements and contributions, but eternally remembers our mistakes.

Jesus is different. He doesn't simply *overlook* our past mistakes (which, considering His own moral excellence, is wonderful enough). He makes us new people. This is a rather complex subject, and the New Testament has so much to say about how it happens; it's not as though we awaken the day after our conversion with the ability to do right, like a spiritual version of Peter Parker after his spider bite. But, true to what He told Nicodemus in John 3, there is a new birth when we begin to believe. That new birth is just the beginning; from that day on, our character takes on a drastically new trajectory. Every day we walk with Him, we grow more like Him and less like the person we would have otherwise become. Let's face it: We've all failed in some ways that are so shameful, we would give anything to erase them from history. Jesus does something even better than delete the memory of our bad acts: He makes us the kinds of people who don't fail in those ways ever again. And in doing so, He shows everyone who knows us that His redemptive power can make something beautiful from the very worst parts of us.

Head of the Church
Ephesians 1:22-23 1 Peter 2:4-6

In the Middle Ages, a young man wandered into the Church at San Damiano one day and knelt to pray. The little chapel was falling apart. The priest there didn't even have oil for his lamp, much less the ability to fix things up. As he prayed, the young man heard the audible voice of God for the first time in his life. God said, "Francesco, go and repair my house, which as you can see, is being destroyed." The boy took the words literally. He sold some of his belongings, bought bricks, mortar and trowels and started working to repair that little church. We know that young man today as St Francis of Assisi. He lived in a time of darkness, when wars and plagues devastated the countryside, when organized religion was corrupt and lifeless. He eventually led a great revival. But he started by repairing the little church in front of him.

Today, it's common for people to distrust organized religion. Even many professing Christians have little or no loyalty to a local church. In many ways, the Church has earned that disdain: Each week, it seems there is another prominent clergyman embroiled in a scandal. Religious talking heads appear on political TV shout-fests, exhibiting behavior that hardly seems to square with the teachings of Christ. Too often, we seem more angry than gracious, more arrogant than humble. Yet God's Word is clear that Jesus considers us His Body. Just as He made the world a better place when He lived here in the flesh, now each local congregation is a manifestation of His body on earth, doing His will, spreading His love. The image of the Church as the Body of Christ (seen in the Ephesians passage) was one Paul used often in His letters. Peter chose a different metaphor: We are part of a temple Jesus is building. We are His "living stones," formed together into a tower that draws people to His salvation. We may give up on the Church, but He never will. It is His great project, His labor of love. So, whenever you and I are tempted to walk away from our own local church, we should remember the words St Francis heard: Repair my church. We can't fix everything. But we can start by working to improve the church in front of us.

Everlasting Love
Romans 8:31-39

I grew up in a rural area. From my house, I could see the home of my great uncle Welton (we called him Buddy), and the huge spreading oak that covered their house. Buddy and his wife Christa (we called her Chris) would often host dinners under that big tree. Chris was a wonderful cook and a gracious host; Buddy had a sly wit and told great stories. Chris passed away first, then years later, Buddy moved far away to be near one of his daughters. One day, I came home to visit my parents, who told me that oak tree had suddenly split down the middle one day, with one half crashing onto the house. No one lived there anymore, but it made me incredibly sad. Something so beautiful, so seemingly indestructible, was gone. Nothing in this world lasts forever.

Actually, there is something that does. The love of Jesus does not wax or wane. It is constant and unchanging. This is a relationship with demands, to be sure. But these demands are based on love for us, combined with the perfect knowledge of what is best. It is hard for us to wrap our minds around this kind of love. We are used to relationships built upon much shakier criteria: Someone falls in love with us because they find us sexually attractive; but as our appearance changes (or they meet a newer, shinier model), their love starts to dwindle. We make friends based on common interests, or because we enjoy them socially. But if we hurt their feelings or betray their expectations in some way, those friendships can end painfully. Even our family relationships can be tenuous. But Jesus' love isn't based on the way we look, how we make Him feel, any potential we have to advance His cause, or even blood kinship. He loves us because He loves us. His death on the cross has brought us into His family, and that cannot be revoked. Therefore, He will never love us any less, or any more, than He does right now, no matter what we do. What freedom there is in knowing that!

Great High Priest
Hebrews 4:14-16

We have no idea today who wrote the book of Hebrews. But we can tell he (or she) was writing to Jewish Christians in the late First Century. I do not envy them. They were ostracized by their fellow Jews for embracing a crucified Messiah. But the wider Gentile world did not accept them, either. It had to be tempting to return to the comforting, familiar traditions of Judaism. The author of Hebrews argues that they could not go back. They no longer needed a temple, sacrifices, priests; Jesus takes the place of the temple as the place where humans can connect with God. Jesus was our once-and-for-all sacrifice. Jesus is the ultimate High Priest: He has lived in our shoes, experienced temptation of all kinds, yet He is sinless enough to rescue us.

This can all seem rather abstract to first-century people like us, who have never even witnessed an animal sacrifice, much less desired one. What does this mean to us? We are used to thinking of religion in terms of quid pro quo: I obey so that God will bless. We believe this because that's the way the rest of the world works. But with Jesus as our High Priest, we come to understand two jarring truths: First, the fact that Jesus—God in human flesh—had to die for our sins indicates that we really are irredeemably evil, no matter how much religion we practice. Second, the fact that He was willing to die for us shows that we are infinitely important to Him. So, as the passage says, we can boldly approach the throne of grace. We can come to Him as often as we want, with whatever is on our hearts. As CS Lewis put it, "God is not offended that we want so much (from Him), but that we want so little." At the same time, we recognize that we have not earned this privilege. We don't come to Him like shareholders demanding better dividends from a CEO or workers asking a boss for an advance on our salary, but as grateful recipients of amazing grace.

Champion
Colossians 2:13-15

Paul uses beautifully picturesque language here to show us just how much Jesus has done for us in His work at the cross. The first image, of the charge of our legal indebtedness being nailed to the cross, fills us with an amazing sense of liberation. Jesus paid the debt that I could never pay. We've already talked about that idea. But what is going on in verse 15? Paul is referring to an event that ancient people would have recognized: The Roman triumph. When a general won a significant victory, the empire would sometimes throw them a triumph. In many ways, it was like a city throwing a victory parade when its team wins a Super Bowl. The adoring crowds would line the streets, cheering for their victorious legions. The triumphant general would ride at the head of the column, basking in his glory. Last of all would come the captured enemy. Stripped of their weapons, armor, and dignity, they would shuffle in humiliation behind their conquerors. This is what Paul was referring to when he spoke of making "a public spectacle" of "the powers and authorities."

But who are these powers? If Jesus was a triumphant warrior at the cross, who did He defeat? That term "powers and authorities" is used in Scripture to refer to demonic forces. Remember that when Jesus was alive, the demons trembled in His presence and fled when He commanded. Somehow, His death defeated them once and for all. But many theologians believe the victory at the cross was even greater than that. Throughout the New Testament, and especially in Paul's writing, sin is personified. It is seen not just as a list of bad things you or I do, but a force that dominates our world, enslaving humanity and drawing us farther and farther away from God's redemptive love. Jesus became sin for us (2 Corinthians 5:21), so when He died, sin's stranglehold was broken. He won the fight we could not have won ourselves. He is our champion.

Mediator
1 Timothy 2:5

Sometimes we have to be careful in how we interpret imagery in Scripture. For example, Jesus once told a story (Luke 18:1-8) about a widow pleading her case before a corrupt judge. The judge flatly admits he doesn't care about what is right, but he gives the widow justice so she'll stop bothering him. Jesus then said, *And will not God bring about justice for his chosen ones, who cry out to him day and night? Will he keep putting them off?* In the parable, the judge is obviously supposed to represent God. But Jesus clearly didn't believe God was cold, crooked and cynical like that judge. He was simply emphasizing the power of prayer. In the same way, this idea of Jesus as our Mediator can be taken the wrong way if we're not careful. The term refers to someone who stands between two parties that are at odds, making peace between them. 1 John 2:1 calls Jesus our *Advocate before the Father*. That's a similar idea. Both leave us with the image of a hostile Father, with Jesus playing the part of defense attorney, persuading God to let us off the hook. But that's clearly not what either Paul or John meant. After all, in the two verses before Paul calls Christ our Mediator (1 Timothy 2:3-4) he says that God wants all people to be saved. And John was the same one who told us in John 3:16 that God loves the whole world enough to give His only Son.

The point of terms like "Mediator" and "Advocate" is to remind us that we cannot come to God on our own initiative. No matter how hard we try to keep His commands (Romans 3:20) or how many good deeds we do (Isaiah 64:6), we cannot qualify for His family. One way to think about it is this: Would you show up at the White House, expecting to have a personal conversation with the President? Of course not. But if you were a friend of his daughter, she could invite you inside. Jesus is our way to the Father. But even that image isn't perfect, since Jesus IS God. So God became a man because He knew we needed a Mediator. He came to us, since we could never have come to Him.

Shepherd and Overseer of Our Souls
1 Peter 2:21-25

I had just turned eighteen when I moved from rural South Texas to Houston for college. Little in my life up to that point had prepared me for the challenges of navigating such a huge, sprawling city. Once, that first semester, I got lost late at night. I drove around, my heart pounding, feeling like I would never find my way back to the dorm. Occasionally, I would find a freeway, but I never could find an entrance ramp. At one point, I considered stopping at a pay phone, but there was no one I could think to call. If only I had brought along with me someone who knew the city well, so much anguish would have been avoided.

In the image of Jesus as Shepherd and Overseer of our souls, we see that Jesus wasn't done saving us after His death on the cross. He continues to desire an active part in our lives. The image of a shepherd is familiar enough to us by now. But what about an overseer? The Greek word that Peter uses here is episkopos. In the Roman world, it referred to a high-ranking military officer who would carefully inspect the troops, making sure they were ready for battle. When the Church was formed, they borrowed that term to refer to spiritual leaders, who oversaw a church. The King James Version translates it "bishop," leading to the novelty of Jesus being called the "Bishop of our souls." Both the terms shepherd and overseer refer to Jesus as a pastor to us, guiding us into good decisions, protecting us from our baser instincts, examining our hearts to prepare us for battle. Like me in the Houston darkness long ago, we are lost on our own in this world. We need someone who knows this world well, who can spare us from the anguish of bad decisions and can lead us into the plans He has for us. Some people might bristle at this idea. They can accept the fact that they need a Savior, but not an Overseer. They want forgiveness, but not guidance. My advice to them is to trust the One who knows more than you could ever learn, and loves you more than you can ever earn. There is such peace in having Him as the Shepherd and Overseer of our souls.

Author and Finisher of our faith
Hebrews 12:1-2

As I type this, I am facing a wall in my office that is three different shades of blue. Several months ago, I asked my wife to help me decorate the office. She painted one wall in different shades so I could decide which color suited my tastes. Then the holidays hit, and other priorities arose. Now, whenever someone comes to my office, they ask, "What's up with that wall?" Jesus told a story (in Luke 14:28-29) about a man who started to build a tower, but underestimated its cost. It sat unfinished, and the man looked ridiculous. Looking at my multi-hued wall, I feel like He was talking about me.

It's easy for us to understand how Jesus is the Author of our faith, since everything we believe as Christians is centered on His life, death and resurrection. But what does it mean that He is the "Finisher" (or "perfecter" as some versions translate it)? We just saw that He serves as our Shepherd and Overseer, guiding, protecting, sometimes even confronting us with ways we need to change. His role as Finisher means that He won't stop until His project in our lives is complete. As Paul wrotes in Philippians 1:6, *He who began a good work in you will carry it on to completion until the day of Christ Jesus.* Or as John put it (1 John 3:2), *We know that when Christ appears, we will be like Him, for we will see Him as He is.* Make no mistake, you are His life's work, His labor of love. He will not leave you half-finished. Your character will someday be complete; you will possess all of His courage, compassion, wisdom, righteousness, and selfless love.

Image of the Invisible God
Colossians 1:13-20

There was a time, not so long before he wrote these words, that Paul would have cut the throat of anyone who suggested that Jesus of Nazareth was the Jewish Messiah. But now, he is convinced that Jesus was so much more than that. Theologians call this passage Paul's "Great Christological Hymn." It is beautiful and staggering in its claims. It really speaks for itself. But I do need to clarify one thing: When in v. 15 he calls Jesus *the firstborn of all creation*, he is not implying that there was a time when Jesus was not. Jesus was born in Bethlehem 2000 years ago, but He has always existed, just as John says in John 1:1-3, and Jesus Himself asserted in John 8:56-58. We know Paul believed this too, because He calls Jesus *the image of the invisible God*, and says *He is before all things, and in Him all things hold together*. Paul's use of "firstborn" simply means "pre-eminent." He is over all of Creation.

But how could Jesus be fully God, yet at the same time have a relationship with God the Father? How can our God be One, yet in three persons? We've talked a bit about the doctrine of the Trinity, but we haven't explained it. That's because it is beyond explanation. We know these things are true. We just can't wrap our minds around them. Some Christians say, "Since I can't understand it, I just won't think about it." That, in my opinion, is a mistake. God's three-in-oneness is a beautiful aspect of who He is. Here's why: If God were not three-in-one, that means He existed in eternity before Creation with no one to whom to relate. He was all by Himself, yet was apparently content to be so. If that were the case, He would not be a God of love. We cannot be loving if we don't have someone to love, after all. Instead, we know that there has always been a deep, fulfilling love between the members of the Godhead (see John 17:5, 20-23). Tim Keller describes it as a cosmic dance. Jesus came to Earth to invite us into this dance. He enjoyed a glory, a love with His Father that was simply too good not to share. Now, we can enjoy it as well.

First Fruits
1 Corinthians 15:20-28

This is a term we don't use today, so it takes some explaining. In the ancient world, where most people made their living agriculturally, the offering they brought to God was from their field. The first fruits were a portion of the first crops harvested. The Israelites were commanded by God to bring Him the first fruits of their grain and other crops, fruit, olive oil, wine, honey, and even sheep's wool. Think about that. It would have been much more pragmatic for a farmer to say, "Lord, after I have filled my barns and silos with all the food and resources I will need to provide for my family for the next year, then I will know how much I can give to you." But God instead said, "Trust me with your first fruits, and I will take care of you." Giving the first fruits was an exercise in faith. The farmer was saying, "Here's the best I have. I trust that there will be much more coming after this."

So when Paul calls Jesus *the first fruits of those who have fallen asleep*, He's putting an interesting twist on the concept. Now, instead of us bringing an offering to God, He offers us something: His risen Son. That offering is a guarantee to us that our resurrection is coming. God is saying, "Here's the best I have. But there's much more to come."

King of Kings
Revelation 19:11-16

We've been looking at the life of Jesus for quite a while now. We've seen Him to be a man of deep humility, gentleness and compassion, who never insisted on His own way, and joyfully died for the sake of others. This description of Him, near the end of the story, forces us to reassess the way we picture Him. This is part of the vision John, His last surviving apostle, received while in exile on the Greek island of Patmos. In John's vision, He sounds more like an action hero than the Jesus we envision. But John's description is not unique; Paul in Philippians 2:9-11 predicted that someday, every living creature would bow before Jesus, confessing Him as Lord. The prophet Daniel, six centuries before Jesus, saw a vision of one "like a Son of Man" who would be given by God authority over the whole world, and a Kingdom that would never end (Daniel 7:13). Jesus, you recall, referred to Himself as "the Son of Man" more than any other title. In Matthew 19:28, He told the Twelve they would one day rule with Him over the Twelve Tribes of Israel. Mark 14:62 records the breathtaking statement Jesus made to Caiaphas, Israel's High Priest, during His trial. In essence, Jesus told him, "You're judging me now, but someday you'll see me standing at God's right hand ready to judge you." John 18:33-38 records the subsequent conversation between Jesus and His Roman inquisitor, Pilate. When asked if He was King of the Jews, Jesus said He was indeed a King, but that His Kingdom was "not of this world."

All this talk of Kingship can seem troubling to modern people like us. It sounds awfully intolerant for Christians to insist that their Savior will one day rule the world. Besides that, history has proven that when political power is concentrated in the hands of one all-powerful person, horrible abuses inevitably result. That's why we Americans revere the democratic political system. But…think back on all that we have learned about Jesus so far. This is a man who had supernatural power at His fingertips, yet never used it for selfish or vengeful purposes. This is a man who was passionate about justice for the poorest and most vulnerable, and never favored the wealthy and powerful. Furthermore, this is a man who created you and me, has a purpose for our lives, and died for the sake of our redemption. If someone exactly like Jesus were elected King of the Universe, would you honestly want checks and balances to keep Him from executing His plans? Wouldn't you be more likely to say, "Let's get out of the way and let Him rule?" I can't think of a better system of government. Every time I get discouraged with the state of my own nation's leadership, I take solace in knowing that someday, we will see the ultimate King. *And He shall reign forever and ever…*

I Shall Know Him!
1 Corinthians 13

It's hard to know how to end this quest to know Jesus better. For me, the most fitting way is to think of the day—the very sweetest of days—when our search is at last at an end, and we see with our own eyes the One we have fallen in love with; the One who first loved us. The 13th chapter of 1 Corinthians is often read at weddings, even though the love Paul is writing about here is specifically the love that should exist in a community of believers. But notice the soul-stirring hint of our future in v. 12. Someday, we will see Him face to face. Someday, we will know Him like He has always known us. Consider that, in His lifetime, this was a man whose presence was so captivating, men and women walked for miles in order to stand all day in the sun and listen to Him speak. This was a man so inspiring, people left their homes and livelihoods to follow Him into an uncertain future. This was a man so influential, everyone who ever met Him was indelibly changed as a result. Someday, we will see Him. We will know Him.

Fanny Crosby, blinded during a disease in infancy, wrote over 8000 hymns in her remarkable life. In nearly every one, she mentions watching, vision, or sight. Her songs are part of the spiritual soundtrack of millions of Jesus-followers. I want to leave you with one of her lyrics that expresses joyfully and eloquently the reason we can feel so excited about our eternity in Him:

When my lifework is ended, and I cross the swelling tide,
When the bright and glorious morning I shall see;
I shall know my Redeemer when I reach the other side,
And His smile will be the first to welcome me.

Oh, the soul-thrilling rapture when I view His blessed face,
And the luster of His kindly beaming eye;
How my full heart will praise Him for the mercy, love and grace,
That prepare for me a mansion in the sky.

Oh, the dear ones in glory, how they beckon me to come,
And our parting at the river I recall;
To the sweet vales of Eden they will sing my welcome home;
But I long to meet my Savior first of all.

Through the gates to the city in a robe of spotless white,
He will lead me where no tears will ever fall;
In the glad song of ages I shall mingle with delight;
But I long to meet my Savior first of all.

I shall know Him, I shall know Him,
And redeemed by His side I shall stand,
I shall know Him, I shall know Him,
By the print of the nails in His hand.

Epilogue: What now?

Thank you so much for seeking Jesus along with me. I hope you've enjoyed this journey as much as I have. But I also hope this is just the beginning for you; either the beginning of a personal relationship with the Savior of the world, or (if you were already a believer before you started this book), a springboard to a more vibrant, authentic and life-changing walk with Christ than you've ever enjoyed before. What you do next is of utmost importance. I hope you will continue getting to know Jesus better. There have been countless wonderful, insightful books written about Him; Here are a few of my personal favorites: All of Philip Yancey's books challenge me to see Jesus as He really is, but I especially love *The Jesus I Never Knew* and *What's So Amazing About Grace*. John Ortberg's *Who Is This Man?* does a great job of highlighting the lasting impact of Christ's life. If you have doubts about the biblical story of Jesus, Lee Strobel's *The Case for Christ* is easy to read and persuasive, and Tim Keller's *The Reason for God* is an honest look at some of the philosophical reasons modern people struggle with the Gospel. Randy Alcorn's *Heaven* is a breathtakingly vivid look at the vast amount of biblical information we have about the eternal reign of Jesus over the New Earth. Finally, I cannot recommend highly enough Fleming Rutledge's *The Crucifixion*. It's a big, intellectually challenging book, but it covers the atoning death of Jesus better than anything else I've ever read, outside of Scripture. Speaking of which, when it comes to knowing Jesus, no book can take the place of the Bible. I hope that you will become a lifelong student of that book.

But it's important to remember the invitation Jesus consistently gave: He didn't say, "Come, read these books," or "Come, believe these doctrines and perform these rituals," or "Come and try really hard to follow my rules and be a good person." He said, "Come, follow me." That is still His invitation to us. But how do we follow someone who we cannot see? That journey starts with a commitment. Simon Peter dropped his fishing nets to follow Jesus, Matthew left behind his tax collectors' booth, and Mary of Bethany walked away from her socially-prescribed role of serving visitors to sit at Jesus' feet. As the old Chinese proverb goes, a journey of a thousand miles begins with a single step. If you haven't done so already, take that step today. In prayer, tell Jesus that you are ready to follow Him. That simple prayer will change your life! But what comes after that commitment? In the two millennia since Jesus walked this Earth, there have been three essentials to following Him.

Communion with other believers. We were not meant to navigate this world alone. Recent studies have shown that people who enjoy close relationships are happier, healthier and live longer. More importantly, we were created by God to enjoy communion with other believers. Paul in both 1 Corinthians 12 and Ephesians 4 writes of how the local church is the Body of Christ on Earth, and we were made to serve a function in that body. I realize that if you have never attended church, it can be intimidating to walk into a building full of strangers. If you know any churchgoing Christians, it might be best to ask if you could try their church with them. And remember, when you walk into a church, you aren't entering a club full of spiritual achievers; you are in a hospital full of rehabilitating sinners. I realize also that you may have a painful history in church. I do not mean to diminish your suffering. But no one would tell a person who came from a dysfunctional family that they should avoid starting a family of their own. In the same way, it is worth the effort to find a church where the people are healthy, humble, accepting, and focused on seeking Jesus. I assure you, those churches are out there.

Personal spiritual disciplines. We wouldn't consider eating once a week to be advisable for a child's physical growth. In the same way, a follower of Jesus can't grow into His image and character by only feeding her soul on Sundays. There are dozens of practices, often called spiritual disciplines, that believers have used for centuries to draw near to God. Two of the more well-known disciplines are Scripture meditation and prayer. Scripture meditation is very different from the meditation practiced by Eastern religions. And it differs also from merely reading the Bible. In Scripture meditation, we find a truth, story, command or promise in the Bible and dwell on it for an extended period of time, asking questions like, "What did this mean to its first readers?" "How could I apply this to my life?" "How would my life be different if I did?" Prayer is simply communication with God. It starts with asking Him for whatever is on your heart. But it doesn't stay there. Think about how a young child communicates with his parent. In the early days of toddlerhood, he asks for things. But as he grows up, he learns how to listen and truly commune with his mother and father. Prayer may seem awkward at first, but over the course of a lifetime, it becomes a rich experience that transforms us. There are many great books on building our personal relationship with God: Richard Foster's *The Celebration of Discipline* is a practical guide to twelve of these practices. Henry Blackaby's *Experiencing God* is a twelve-week study on how to hear God's voice and know Him better. It changed my life, and I highly recommend it to you.

But the best way to learn personal spiritual disciplines is by observing them in the lives of other believers. As you navigate life alongside others in a local church, worshipping, praying, studying Scripture and serving God, you see practices in men and women who are further along than you are. It is inspiring. Do what it takes to form those close bonds; it can help you establish habits that will nurture and transform you for a lifetime.

Serving people in His name. Jesus lived His life for others. So following Jesus means loving others as He did. In my opinion, too many of us view Christianity as if it were an academic course. We attend worship services, listen to podcasted sermons, and participate in Bible studies. But none of those actions are ends in themselves. They are all intended to equip us to represent Jesus in the world. Remember, He said, *A city built on a hill cannot be hidden…in the same way, let your light shine before others, that they may see your good deeds and glorify your Father in Heaven* (Matthew 5:14, 16). That means meeting the physical and emotional needs of our neighbors, as we have the opportunity. It also means being involved in "social justice," standing up for the oppressed and marginalized. But most of all, it means sharing the story of Jesus, and the message of His saving grace. There are countless ways to do this: Telling your own story of faith is hard to beat. If this book has helped you know Jesus better, consider giving it to a friend who doesn't know Him. Either way, seek opportunities to share His story. It's the best news that has ever been heard!

God bless you as you continue following our Savior. Like those first disciples, you'll find that it won't be easy. But it also will never be boring! You will experience the joy of personal growth and the exhilaration of working on eternally significant things. And better still, you'll dwell in a constant state of living hope, knowing that in Him, the best is always yet to come. Someday (and I hope it's soon!) you and I will stand together in the glory He purchased for us with His blood, sharing stories, laughter and tears as we marvel in His presence, at last seeing face to face the One we've grown to love. Until then, may *the God of our Lord Jesus Christ, the glorious Father…give you the Spirit of wisdom and revelation, so that you may know Him better. I pray that the eyes of your heart may be enlightened in order that you may know the hope to which He has called you, the riches of His glorious inheritance in his holy people, and His incomparably great power for us who believe* (Ephesians 1:17-19). Amen.

Made in the USA
Lexington, KY
03 December 2019

58063335R00282